GODS OF
EDEN

Also by Andrew Collins

FROM THE ASHES OF ANGELS: THE FORBIDDEN LEGACY OF A FALLEN RACE

WHAT THE EXPERTS HAVE TO SAY ABOUT FROM THE ASHES OF ANGELS

'In his exciting and original intellectual quest, Andrew Collins has put important new facts before the public concerning the mysterious origins of human civilisation.'

Graham Hancock, author of *Fingerprints of the Gods* and co-author of *Keeper of Genesis*

'. . . a fascinating piece of research which does much to bring the biblical world of Eden back into the historical spotlight. Only time and further study will confirm Andrew Collins' hypothesis of an advanced culture of prehistoric date existing in the mountains of eastern Turkey. If he is right, then this book will have staked its claim as a major contributor to the study of the genesis of civilisation.'

David Rohl, Egyptologist, broadcaster and author of *A Test of Time*

'In a very persuasive manner, Andrew Collins argues his compelling new theories of the origins of western civilisation. An important literary contribution – his well researched ideas of Kurdish and Near Eastern history should keep us thinking for many years to come.'

Mehrdad Izady, Professor of History in Near Eastern studies, University of New York, and author of *The Kurds – A Concise Handbook*

'*From the Ashes of Angels* is meticulously researched and written in no-nonsense terms. It covers a wide range and a long time span, and makes a fascinating case which gains weight from not being over-stated.

'Andrew Collins' detailed research gives this book a rare

authority; his style and reasoning make it a compelling read.'

John Sassoon, authority on Mesopotamian
studies and author of
From Sumer to Jerusalem

'Andrew Collins has uncovered an astonishing revelation of the unknown vistas of prehistory, a veritable "forgotten world" holding profound implications for our understanding of human origins and the mysterious roots of civilisation . . . a magnificently researched work; its startling conclusions will undoubtedly reverberate over the coming decades.'

Nigel Jackson, authority on
comparative mythologies and
author of books such as
Lords of Misrule and *The Horned Piper*

ANDREW COLLINS

GODS OF EDEN

Egypt's Lost Legacy
and the Genesis of Civilisation

HEADLINE

First published in 1998
by HEADLINE BOOK PUBLISHING

10 9 8 7 6 5 4 3 2 1

British Library Cataloguing in Publication Data

Collins, Andrew, 1957-
    The gods of Eden: Egypt's lost legacy
    and the genesis of civilisation
    1.Pyramids of Giza (Egypt) - History
    2.Egypt - Civilization - To 332 B.C.
    I.Title
    932'.01
    ISBN 0 7472 2108 1 (hardback)
    ISBN 0 7472 7504 1 (softback)

Typeset by
Letterpart Limited, Reigate, Surrey

Printed and bound in Great Britain by
Mackays of Chatham PLC, Chatham, Kent

HEADLINE BOOK PUBLISHING
A division of Hodder Headline PLC
338 Euston Road
London NW1 3BH

This book is dedicated to

THE PEOPLE OF TIBET

for keeping alive the flame of ancient wisdom
until it was so rudely extinguished in the 1950s.
May your unique world one day rise again,
like a phoenix from the ashes.

CONTENTS

ACKNOWLEDGEMENTS

My sincere thanks go out to the following people who have helped in the creation of this book. They include Bernard, for inspiring me to investigate Giza's hidden chambers back in 1985; Nigel Appleby and friends, for confirming my findings in respect to Giza's Chambers of Creation; Debbie Benstead, for making the link between Egypt's Elder culture and the Near East back in 1990; Mark Burkinshaw, for leading me to Nevali Çori; Storm Constantine, for her invaluable help and continued friendship.

My thanks also go out to Lorraine Evans, for her research in connection with the Amun priesthood; Rodney Hale, for his constant help and dedication to my ongoing projects; Robert Hale, for his mathematical calculations regarding the Great Pyramid; Catherine Hale, for her German translations; Graham Hancock, Carrie Kirkpatrick, Lisa Munday and Matthew Adams, for their continued support and friendship; Mehrdad Izady, for his help in respect to Kurdish history; Nigel Jackson and John Sassoon, for their valued testimonials; Amber McCauley, for her French translations; Gareth Medway, for his assistance as a researcher and for checking my facts; Oren Patrick Purcell, for his contributions; David Rohl, for his advice, help and enthusiasm; Colin and Cathy Stallard, for the use of their photographs; Oliver and Danielle Stummer, for their thoughts and correspondence on sound technology; Jackie Pegg, for checking the manuscript and providing me with obscure articles on Egyptology; Graham Phillips, for understanding what I go through when writing a book and for his almost daily contact by telephone; Iben Lund Jørgensen and Dave Gladman, for the translation of Henry Kjellson's book; Peter Whitehead, for the use of his slide of the hawk-headed Horus statue in the Louvre, Paris; Wayne Frostick, Mark McCann, Steve Wilson and Caroline Wise, for reading the manuscript, and Matthew Goulding, Angela Reeve, Charles Topham,

Johnny Merron and Boyd Lees, for their constant support.

I would also like to thank Lindsay Symons and Heather Holden-Brown at Headline and Simon Trewin, Luigi Bonomi, Laura Susijn and Emma Gibb at Sheil Land Associates for their part in the publication of *Gods of Eden*.

Lastly, I would like to say a special thanks to Simon Cox, David Southwell and Richard Ward for their invaluable research assistance. Without them this book would have looked a whole lot different.

Andrew Collins, 1998

Picture credits: Bernard G., pls. 39, 40, pp. 191, 209; Ufuk Esin, pl. 29; Harald Hauptmann, pls. 30-1, 33-5, 38, pp. 240; Harald Hauptmann & Rodney Hale, p. 270; Max Hirmer, pls, 1, 3; Kestner Museum, pl. 23; Theya Molleson & Stuart Campbell, p. 264; Mehmet Ozdogan, pl. 32; Petrie Museum, pls. 11, 12; Royal Geographic Society, pl. 27; Alan Sorrell, p. 252; Colin Stallard, pl. 7-8, 21; Billie Walker-John, pl. 22, p. 266.

Every effort has been made to trace and contact all copyright holders. The author will be glad to rectify any omissions at the earliest opportunity.

CHAPTER ONE

ECHOES OF ELDER GODS

It is five o'clock in the morning and the clear indigo sky glistens with an archway of stars. On the distant horizon the pre-dawn light eats away at the night and heralds the return of the sun on the day of the spring equinox – a time of equal light and darkness and the midway point between the winter and summer solstices.

Towards the north-west is the diffuse yellow glow thrown up by the lights of modern-day Cairo – its daily hustle and bustle and street chaos not yet begun – but before us, on the edge of the Giza plateau, is arguably the most enigmatic carved monument in the world. It is a graceful leonine form with the face of a Pharaoh, a body of stone and a battered tail that curls around its hunched-up hind legs. Its extended fore legs reach out towards the eastern horizon as if to emphasise its integral relationship with the coming equinoctial sunrise. The world knows this monument as the Great Sphinx. It wears the same *nemes* head-dress as the dynastic kings that ruled the peoples of Egypt for over 3000 years.

Those academics who dedicate their lives and careers to studying the world behind such monuments tell us that the Sphinx was carved from an outcrop of bedrock by a school of dedicated stone sculptors during Old Kingdom times, the epoch of the pyramid builders. This great act had necessitated the hollowing out of a huge wedge-like enclosure, after which the fashioning of the enormous recumbent lion had taken place. A stone crown was then placed on its head, a beard was inserted into its chin and the face was chiselled into the likeness of a king named Khafre, who took the throne of Egypt in around 2550 BC.[1]

Yet those Egyptologists who have made such strong assertions concerning the origins of the Sphinx are almost certainly wrong. As we move around the edge of its sunken enclosure, the ground-lights silhouette deep undulating grooves running around the monument's badly eroded body. They are curved and smooth and seem to have been caused by severe weathering over an enormously long period of time, even though the Sphinx is known to have been buried up to its neck in sand for at least 3300 years of its official 4500-year history.[2] Here and there the deep horizontal scars are broken by sharp vertical fissures – they are plainly visible all around the Sphinx and are also present on the interior walls of the Sphinx enclosure.

The Egyptologists tell us that these weathering effects were caused by the harsh desert winds that blow in from the south and engulf the leonine form in an elemental maelstrom. It is what they have always believed, and probably always will. Yet these people are not geologists; they do not study the composition and erosion of rocks. This is a pity, for geologists say something completely different about the poor condition of the Sphinx and its surrounding enclosure. They say that the deep horizontal scars and sharp vertical fissures were caused not by the desert sands but by water precipitation – in other words, rain. Lots of it, over a very, very long period of time. One geologist, Dr Robert Schoch, an Associate Professor of Science at Boston University,[3] has argued in favour of this proposition again and again in more radical periodicals and journals, such as *KMT*, America's prestigious news-stand magazine on speculative Egyptology.[4] Repeatedly, Schoch and his colleagues have demolished any criticism raised against their water precipitation theory, so much so that the Egyptologists are going to have to come up with something pretty convincing before any open-minded individual is going to take their argument seriously any more.

So the weathering on the Sphinx and the walls of its surrounding enclosure was caused by exposure to rain over an extremely long period of time, but just how long? Egypt has seen very little rain since the age of the Pharaohs began over 5000 years ago. Indeed, to find a time in climatological history when rain of this order fell on Egypt we must go back to the 3500-year stretch between 8000 and 4500 BC, when the Eastern Sahara was a green savannah periodically drenched by perpetual downpours of the sort familiar to more tropical climates.

Torrents of water running down the Sphinx's carved limestone body and surrounding enclosure walls over a period of many thousands of years would have resulted in the deep horizontal scars and vertical fissures seen today. Yet no Pharaohs lived between 8000 and 4500 BC, and from what we know of archaeology in Egypt there doesn't appear to have been much happening at all at around this time. The only signs of life are primitive farming communities, either in what became the eastern Sahara or on the banks of the Nile, where they could take advantage of the abundance of fresh fish. Yet these early, so-called neolithic communities did not possess a structured society and are not known to have carved colossal stone monuments such as the Great Sphinx. What's more, they did not have the technology or the impetus to engage themselves in such massive engineering projects, even if we could find a suitable reason why they should have wanted to fashion themselves a colossal lion in stone.

So if these early farming communities did not carve the Sphinx, then who did?

Perhaps we are looking at the wrong time-frame altogether, and the Sphinx was carved during an entirely different age. If so, when?

IN THE AGE OF THE LION

On the eastern horizon the dull red light of the equinoctial sunrise reaches higher into the dark firmament. As star after star gives way to the light, others seem defiant, their flickering glow watched carefully by the eyes of the Sphinx. Picked out clearly on the eastern horizon are the uppermost stars of the constellation known to the Western world as Pisces. Above, and a little to its right, is the constellation of Aquarius. Like its celestial neighbour, Aquarius is one of the twelve signs of the zodiac – the chain of constellations through which the sun is seen to pass on its yearly course across the starry firmament. Each month the sign in which the sun rises changes, defining the yearly zodiac originally used in astrology to cast horoscopes.

There is, however, another zodiacal cycle that takes not a single year to complete its cycle but a mammoth 25,920 years.[5] Known as precession, or backwards motion, it is caused by the slow wobble of the earth – which if dramatically speeded up and viewed from the moon would look like the gentle sway of a child's spinning top. Its progress can be measured by the gradual shift of the starry canopy in relation to the distant horizon at a rate of one degree every seventy-two years.

The precessional cycle was equated by the Ancients with the so-called Great Year, as well as the supposed ages of man defined by classical writers such as Hesiod (*fl.* 850 BC). In astronomical terms its steady progress at a snail's pace is registered by noting the zodiac constellation that appears in the path of the sun just before sunrise on the spring equinox. Every 2160 years or so the sign changes, and when it does a new astrological age is born.

Today we are poised on the brink of the Age of Aquarius as the stars of Pisces, a symbol of Christianity for the past 2000 years, set below the equinoctial horizon for the final time; this will occur gradually over the next 200 or so years.[6] Yet before the advent of the Age of Pisces, the world was ruled by the Age of Aries, the ram, the symbol of the faith of Abraham and the cult of Amun in Ancient Egypt, which both rose to prominence some time after the commencement of this epoch, *c.* 2200 BC.[7] As the ruler of the precessional year, the ram had itself replaced the previous Age of Taurus, whose bull cult had dominated the Mediterranean and still lingers today in the barbaric bullfights acted out in the great stadiums of Spain.

Had the Great Sphinx been carved when the Egyptologists insist in around 2550 BC, i.e. during the Age of Taurus, then surely it would make better sense for it to have been modelled into the statue of an enormous bull. Each year before dawn on the spring equinox it could have gazed out at its celestial counterpart in the starry sky. Ancient cultures of the Middle East are known to have venerated, and even depicted in religious art, the equinoctial rising of Taurus during this precessional age.[8] Moreover, the bull was worshipped in Egypt's chief city of Memphis during this distant epoch under the name of Apis. Ancient paintings depict it with the solar disc between its horns, confirming its allegiance to the sun and making it an ideal equinoctial time-marker during the much-celebrated Taurean age.

Yet as we can clearly see, the Sphinx is not a bull at all but a lion, and the lion is the symbol of Leo. So when might the last Age of Leo have taken place? Computer software allows us to punch coordinates and dates into a keyboard and then watch as the sky in an age witnessed only by our most distant ancestors is displayed on a monitor screen. It makes calculations easy, and tells us that before the Age of Taurus there had been an Age of Gemini, an Age of Cancer and, prior to that, an Age of Leo, which occurred during the 2160-year period between *c.* 11,380 and 9220 BC (see Chapter Three).

Only in this distant epoch would the construction of a lion as an equinoctial marker have made complete sense, for only during this distant epoch would it have gazed out at its starry counterpart before sunrise on the spring equinox. If so, then originally the Sphinx may well have borne not the face of a Pharaoh but the head of a lion. Then, at a much later date, plausibly during the rein of Khafre in around 2550 BC, its head was remodelled into the likeness of a king bearing the more familiar *nemes* head-dress.

Such hasty assumptions might at first seem nonsensical if not a little rash. Yet there is ample evidence that the Ancient Egyptians not only understood the slow process of precession[9] but that they were also obsessed by great cycles of time stretching back over tens of thousands of years. For instance, the fragmented Royal Canon of Turin, dating to the Nineteenth Dynasty, *c.* 1300 BC, contains a list of kings that includes a long period when a succession of 10 *netjeru* (or *ntrw*), a word meaning 'divinities' or 'gods', ruled the world. Their reigns are followed by a further period of 13,420 years when divine beings known as *Shemsu-hor*, interpreted as the 'Companions' or 'Followers of Horus', are said to have governed the country prior to the unification of Upper and Lower Egypt in around 3100 BC.[10] In addition to this, Manetho, a priest of the city of Heliopolis who lived *c.* 320 BC, spoke of a period of 24,925 years before the ascent of Menes, the first dynastic king,[11] while Herodotus, a Greek historian of the fifth century BC, observed in his Canon of the Kings that 11,340 years had passed since the rule of the first Pharaoh.[12]

The Ancient Egyptians also spoke of a mythical epoch known as *sep tepi*, the First Time, seen as a kind of golden age when their land was ruled by the *netjeru*, such as Osiris and his son Horus. It was looked on by them as a time of 'absolute perfection – "before rage or clamour or strife or uproar had come about". No death, disease or disaster occurred in this blissful age, variously described as "the time of Re", "the time of Osiris", or "the time of Horus".[13]

That the Sphinx acted as a time-marker for the Age of Leo is becoming more widely accepted as the world enters the new millennium. A date of construction some time around 10,500 BC has been discussed openly in the pages of many best-selling books written by forward-thinking authors who are challenging orthodoxy head-on. Individuals such as construction engineer Robert Bauval and speculative writer Graham Hancock argue admirably that a mirror image of the starry heavens, as they might have appeared to a person on the ground during the Age of Leo, is reflected in the positioning and orientation of the monuments found on the Giza plateau.[14]

These people are now at loggerheads with the academics, who not only say their theories are new-age nonsense but claim that in the time-frame suggested, the eleventh and tenth millennia BC, the Eastern Sahara was inhabited only by 'bands of people who lived in small huts or shelters and sustained themselves by hunting and gathering'.[15] They also state that these early Nilotic (i.e. those living by the Nile) communities 'erected no large stone structures of any kind' and had not 'taken even the first steps towards the domestication of plants and animals'.[16]

This is simply not true. There is much evidence of prehistoric man along the Nile during this very age, and it clearly shows that between *c.* 12,500 and 9500 BC certain communities not only possessed an advanced tool-making technology but also domesticated animals and developed the earliest agriculture anywhere in the world[17] (see Chapter Fifteen). Moreover, just 483 kilometres (300 miles) away from Giza in what is today Jericho, its inhabitants of *c.* 8000 BC were constructing enormous fortification walls, gouging out vast trenches in the hard bedrock and erecting a gigantic stone tower in defence against an unknown enemy.[18] Engineering projects on this scale would have required a high level of social structure and coordinated operations.

This much is known; there is almost certainly more. No one can say that humanity in this distant age did not have the ability to carve the image of a 73-metre-long recumbent lion, and yet accepting this hypothesis brings with it an even greater mystery.

TEMPLES OF THE GODS

The pre-dawn light increases, allowing the eye to pick out the dark shapes of architectural ruins in varying degrees of preservation and decay. Beyond the eastern exit of the sunken Sphinx enclosure are the remains of a quite extraordinary structure known as the Valley

Temple of Khafre, which, like the Sphinx itself, is orientated east towards the equinoctial sunrise. It is constructed of enormous limestone blocks – many up to 100 tonnes in weight, some as heavy as 200 tonnes – on a square ground-plan close to the edge of the 40-metre-high Giza plateau. Each side is 45 metres in length, while its unusual foundation on a gradual slope means that the height of its walls varies considerably. Its eastern wall soars to over 13 metres, while its western counterpart rises to just 6 metres. Enormous limestone facing-blocks once lined its exterior walls, while inside ashlars of dark red granite and a paved floor of pure alabaster are to be found. The interior of the temple is shaped like a letter T, defined by a rigid network of rectangular pillars, or monoliths, 5.5 metres high, each capped with granite beams laid horizontally on them. Nowhere will you find any inscribed hieroglyphs or stone reliefs, and yet the effect is still one of great perfection and immense magnitude.

Egyptologists assert that the Valley Temple was built at the time

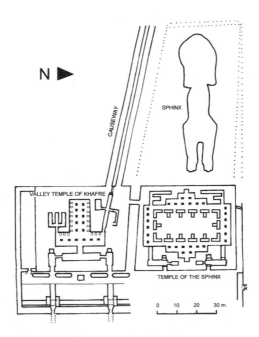

Plan of the Sphinx monument, the Temple of the Sphinx and the Valley Temple of Khafre.

of Khafre, *c.* 2550–2525 BC. Certainly, it is linked via a stone causeway to another ancient temple on the eastern side of the Second Pyramid, the middle one of the three at Giza, which is also accredited to Khafre. Further evidence of this conclusion, they say, is the Valley Temple's similarity in design to other temples on the Giza plateau, as well as its proximity to the Great Sphinx and the fact that statues of Khafre – one depicting him in the form of a reclining sphinx and another in diorite showing him seated – were found abandoned in a well located beneath its floor.[19]

Pretty strong evidence, you may think, in favour of Khafre's association with Giza's curious cyclopean or megalithic (i.e. great stone) structure. Yet there the connections cease, for it is known that the colossal limestone blocks used in the construction of both the Valley Temple and the adjacent Temple of the Sphinx, of which only the foundations remain today, were extracted from the Sphinx enclosure, which began its life as a quarry.[20] This is a slightly disconcerting prospect, for if the Sphinx really was constructed prior to the end of the Age of Leo, *c.* 9220 BC, then it implies that the nearby temples must also date back to this same distant epoch.

Confirmation that the Valley Temple predates Pharaonic times is easy, for the same weathering effects found both on the body of the Sphinx and on the surrounding enclosure are also clearly visible on its core walls. More important, the worst of these smooth, undulating scars caused, we can only assume, by water precipitation over the period between *c.* 8000 and 5000 BC were shaved away during Old Kingdom times, *c.* 2700–2137 BC – plausibly during the reign of Khafre – to allow the granite ashlars to sit flush against the rough limestone walls. If this really is what happened, then it is damning evidence against the orthodox view that ascribes the weather-worn limestone shell of the Valley Temple to the age of the Pharaohs.

Not unnaturally, the Egyptological community would never entertain the idea that the Valley Temple might be older than Old Kingdom times. Yet when the Temple of the Sphinx, or the Granite Temple as it was formally known, was uncovered for the first time by French Egyptologist Auguste Mariette (1821–81) in 1853, scholars were more than happy to admit that its cyclopean masonry and complete lack of hieroglyphic inscriptions confirmed its immense antiquity. Mariette even believed it to be the oldest structure ever uncovered in Egypt.[21]

Such a colossal style of building is not unique to the Valley Temple. As previously mentioned, the nearby Sphinx Temple also contains huge cyclopean stones, while the ruins of the so-called Upper Temple, situated east of the Second Pyramid and linked to the Valley Temple by a stone causeway, are made up of similarly sized blocks, one of which is estimated to be an unbelievable 468 tonnes in weight.[22] Furthermore, 434 kilometres (270 miles) south of Giza at the predynastic cult centre of Abydos is another megalithic temple of unknown origin. Known as the Osireion, it contains enormous granite posts capped with huge stone lintels. Set within its interior walls is a series of 17 cells, or cubicles, plausibly used for some kind of sacred function. Below this more-or-less subterranean structure is a well that floods to surround a purposely built plateau of cut stone slabs, creating the impression of an island surrounded by water. Although the building is attached through orientation and locality to a nearby temple built during the reign of King Seti I (1307–1291 BC), no one has ever been able accurately to date the Osireion.

Professor Edouard Naville of the Egypt Exploration Fund, who worked extensively on the Osireion between 1912 and 1914, compared the structure's unique architecture with the Valley Temple, showing it to be 'of the same epoch when building was made with enormous stones without any ornament'.[23] Such observations led him to conclude that the Osireion, 'being of a similar composition, but of much larger materials, is of a still more archaic character, and I would not be surprised if this were the most ancient architectural structure in Egypt'.[24]

The Egyptological community dismissed Edouard Naville's earlier findings, following the discovery by Henry Frankfurt – who excavated at the site between 1925 and 1930 – of a cartouche bearing Seti I on a granite dovetail by the main entrance into the central hall, as well as one or two other simple finds that linked the

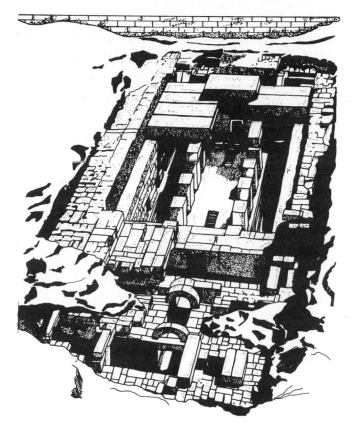

View of the Osireion at Abydos.

Pharaoh's reign to the building.[25] As a consequence, the building was henceforth seen as contemporary to Seti's reign.

That the enlightened King Seti might have constructed his own temple complex at Abydos to comply with the existing orientation and ground-plan of the Osireion, which was already of immense antiquity even in his own age, is never considered by the Egyptological community. Yet in the opinion of myself and many others working in this field today, it is far more likely that the Osireion, like the Valley Temple and many of the other cyclopean structures of Giza, is a surviving example of megalithic architecture dating to a much earlier epoch altogether.

A LEGACY FOR FUTURE TIMES

As the pale light of the equinoctial sunrise steadily increases, it lifts the veil of darkness covering the elevated plateau. It picks out the presence of Giza's most awesome legacies of the past – the three great pyramids that tower skywards like immortal sentinels marking the achievements of an unknown age we can only just begin to comprehend.

Two and a half million blocks, ranging in size from two to seventy tonnes apiece, were used in the construction of the Great Pyramid, the largest and perhaps the most enigmatic of the three matching structures. It covers an area of five hectares and weighs an incredible six million tonnes,[26] and until the construction of the Eiffel Tower it was the tallest structure in the world. There is more stone in the Great Pyramid than in all the churches, chapels and cathedrals built in England since the time of Christ.[27] Yet this great wonder of the past is more than simply an architectural curiosity, for it embodies a level of sophistication far superior to anything the world has produced in any epoch since. Over the past 200 years many hundreds of books have been written about the mysteries of the Great Pyramid, most of them more fantasy than fact. Yet shining through all of them is a hard core of evidence which really does show that the pyramid builders were privy to universal knowledge far beyond that accredited to the Ancient Egyptians by scholars today. It would be laborious to detail each and every one of the amazing facts attributed to this monument in stone, but I feel it is essential to convey just a little of the extraordinarily advanced minds behind this architectural wonder.

To begin with, its four sides, which average 230.36 metres in length,[28] are aligned to the four cardinal points with such precision that engineers today would find difficulty in matching such accuracy.

More remarkable is our knowledge concerning the perimeter of the Great Pyramid. It is said to be 921.453 metres, which, according to modern calculations by noted metrologist Livio Stecchini, is exactly equal to a half a minute of latitude at the equator, or 1/43,200 of the earth's circumference.[29] A revelation such as this might seem fantastic, and yet it is a fact that the Ancient Greeks were dimly aware of the pyramid's apparent relationship to the earth's latitude in their own day and age, which is why Napoleon's *savants* were ordered to survey the monument when the French army entered Egypt in 1798.[30] Most people believe that the concept of latitude and longitude as the geographical basis for mapping out the earth is a relatively modern invention, but if such information *is* encoded in the design of the Great Pyramid then the world is going to have to think again. Indeed, Stecchini has ably demonstrated that the Ancient Egyptians had already defined the extent of their country in relationship to the earth's latitude and longitude when the first Pharaoh took the throne in around 3100 BC.[31]

Another similar mind-boggling fact concerns the height of the Great Pyramid. The ancient mysteries writer, William Fix, calculated that from the base of its 54.6-centimetre-thick foundation platform to the tip of its apex is just over 147.14 metres. This, when multiplied by 43,200 – the same number used in achieving a half a minute of latitude in respect to the structure's perimeter – produces a figure just 120 metres short of the polar radius of the earth, or the distance from the centre of the earth to the North Pole.[32]

Look up now at the pyramid's distant apex – which is closer to heaven than the roof of a 40-storey building. Its actual height, from the lowest to the highest course, is 146.59 metres, and if you divide the perimeter by twice the height you achieve a figure that corresponds to the true value of *pi*, 3.1416.[33] The Great Pyramid therefore embodies within its geodesic form an exact model of the earth's northern hemisphere on a scale of 1:43,200.[34]

And the data continues. The Great Pyramid stands at the precise centre of the earth's largest landmass, while its north-western and north-eastern diagonals seem to define the triangular shape of the Nile tributaries that make up the Nile Delta.[35] If these waterways trace the same courses as they did in the pyramid age, then this suggests some kind of symbolic relationship between the orientation of the Great Pyramid and the actual landscape of Lower (or northern) Egypt.

Egyptologists do not deny such facts; they see them simply as pure coincidence and nothing more. In their minds the Ancient Egyptians were certainly *not* aware of the earth's diameter, so they could not possibly have encoded such information into the design of any man-made construction. Such statements are wholly unacceptable and just seem to show the utter stubbornness adopted by many academics. Are we simply to accept their opinion of the past, which more or less implies that ancient man was not capable of understanding such advanced scientific principles?

The Great Pyramid is undoubtedly a highly unique artefact of history, but it is not just its exterior design that preserves remarkable geometric precision. The King's Chamber, the bare, granite-lined room placed high in the pyramid, is seen by Egyptologists as the burial chamber of a Pharaoh because it contains a lidless box in dark granite, described variously as a coffer or sarcophagus. Yet looking closely at the measurements of this chamber, we find that its dimensions embody geometry that preserves both the $2:\sqrt{5}:3$ and $3:4:5$ triangles supposedly devised by Pythagoras, the famous Greek mathematician of the sixth century BC.[36] These observations were made originally not by some loose-minded pyramidologist but by the much-respected Egyptologist Sir William Matthew Flinders

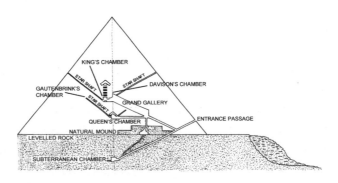

Cross section of the Great Pyramid.

Petrie (1853–1942), who conducted an exhaustive survey of the pyramids and temples of Giza in 1881 (see Chapter Four).

Could Egypt have been the birthplace of geometry, as the ancient writers such as Diodorus Siculus, Herodotus and Plato would appear to have believed?[37] And from geometry we go to metrology, the science of weights and measures. It is a fact that the internal volume of the King's Chamber coffer, calculated at 1166.4 litres, is precisely *half* the volume defined by its exterior measurements, which gives a figure of 2332.8 litres.[38]

I could go on. The list of strange facts concerning the Great Pyramid is endless. None of this is likely to be coincidence, as the academics would have us believe. It seems more credible to suggest that the pyramid builders purposely created a legacy for future times. Through the universal languages of science, mathematics and engineering, they were attempting to put on record their vastly superior knowledge and wisdom of geodesy, geometry, metrology and harmonic proportions.

We can only marvel at these people's achievements, for they beg the question of exactly where this universal knowledge and wisdom came from, or, indeed, just who *did* build the Great Pyramid. Egyptologists tell us it was constructed as the tomb of a Pharaoh. With the flimsiest of evidence they tell us it was commissioned by a king named Khufu (the Greek Cheops) early in the Fourth Dynasty, *c.* 2596–2573 BC.[39] They also tell us that the Second Pyramid was made for a king named Khafre (or Chephren), *c.* 2550–2525 BC, while the Third Pyramid was constructed for Khafre's successor, Menkaure (or Mycerinos), who ruled *c.* 2512–2484 BC.

In the absence of hardcore evidence to suggest otherwise, no one can say that Khufu, Khafre and Menkaure were not in some manner *connected* with the construction of the three pyramids. There is too much evidence to show that the Giza necropolis owes its existence to this dynasty, which is placed in the era of Egyptian history known as the Old Kingdom, *c.* 2700–2137 BC. What *can* be doubted is how exactly the designers of the Great Pyramid obtained their vast

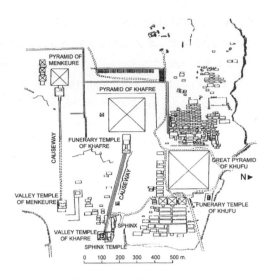

Plan of the Giza plateau.

technological capabilities in the 500 or so years from the ascent of the first Pharaoh of a unified Upper and Lower Egypt in around 3100 BC.

The presence alone of the Great Pyramid tells us that the Ancient Egyptians were no fools. Nothing seems to have been left to coincidence or chance. This monument was built to tell us a story of their past, and that past indicates strongly that they were the inheritors of a universal knowledge and wisdom that was the culmination of many thousands of years of evolution and progress in understanding the ways of this world.

If this is true, then the Great Pyramid's proximity to the Sphinx and its accompanying megalithic temples is also no coincidence. There is a clear message here, and if it could be put into plain language then it would probably read as follows:

*What we have embodied in stone and you have now understood
is an expression, a celebration, of that which was handed down
to us by those who established the sanctity of this elevated
plateau during the First Time, the age of the gods. Let this be
a monument to their memory.*

16

Mere fiction? To many it might seem so, but ancient sources speak openly of the great knowledge and wisdom preserved in the design of the Great Pyramid. For instance, the so-called *Akbar Ezzeman* manuscript, attributed to the tenth-century Arab traveller named al-Mas'ūdi and based on a now-lost Coptic historical work (see Chapter Three), says it contains:

> ... the wisdom and acquirements in the different arts and sciences ... [as well as] the sciences of arithmetic and geometry, that they might remain as records for the benefit of those who could afterwards comprehend them ... [it also preserves] the positions of the stars and their cycles; together with the history and chronicle of time past [and] of that which is to come.[40]

In my opinion there is compelling evidence to suggest that the Ancient Egyptians inherited their great wisdom from a much earlier Elder culture which was able to pass on the flame of knowledge before its own apparent demise. As we will see, all the indications are that the Elder gods inhabited Egypt some time between *c.* 12,500 and 9500 BC. They built the Sphinx and the earliest megalithic temples of Giza, and they achieved a high level of sophistication later encapsulated in the design of the Great Pyramid. Of this we can be fairly sure, but what else might they have left to the world?

SECRETS UNDERGROUND

As we enter the next millennium, many great discoveries are being made on the Giza plateau. None of these can be more extraordinary than the detection beneath the Sphinx's wedge-shaped enclosure of a series of nine concealed chambers of unnatural origin. These were first detected by seismic soundings of the hard bedrock during two tentative search programmes, one led by seismologist Thomas

Dobecki in 1991 and the other coordinated in 1996 by the University of Florida in association with the Schor Foundation[41] (see Chapter Twelve).

Myths and legends that date back to Pharaonic times speak of a subterranean world lying beneath the Giza plateau. Modern-day psychics, occult societies and new-age mystics all firmly believe in the existence of an underground complex of concealed corridors and unknown chambers. They refer to this chthonic, or underworld, domain as the 'Hall of Records', or the 'Chambers of Initiation', and say it contains the arcane wisdom and knowledge hidden from the world by Egypt's Elder culture.

Once again, ancient sources appear to support such bold assertions. For example, the Roman historian Ammianus Marcellinus (*fl.* AD 360–90) spoke of the pyramids of Egypt before adding that

> There are also [in their vicinity] subterranean fissures and winding passages called syringes, which, it is said, those acquainted with the ancient rites, since they had foreknowledge that a deluge was coming, and feared that the memory of the ceremonies might be destroyed, dug in the earth in many places with great labour . . .[42]

What exactly were these 'ancient rites' that needed to be preserved from being lost in 'a deluge'? What on earth lay beneath the Great Sphinx? Might the revelations contained in these mysterious 'syringes' be connected with the previously unknown chambers found by sensitive scanning equipment during the 1990s? Have the geophysicists working on these projects really registered the echoes of Elder gods whose collective memory still lies slumbering beneath the limestone bedrock of the Giza plateau?

With the weathered eyes of the Sphinx fixed on the orange solar orb that now rests like a ball of liquid fire on the eastern horizon, a sense of great expectancy overwhelms me. As the world moves imperceptibly towards the precessional Age of Aquarius, it is as well to remember that, since the fall of the Age of Leo, the background canopy of stars has shifted almost 180 degrees against the distant horizon, or exactly one half of a precessional cycle. For the first time since this forgotten epoch of mankind, the stellar background will be a mirror reflection of how it might have appeared to those who built the Great Sphinx.[43]

Sensing its approach is like waiting for the alarm to sound on some imaginary celestial clock. What therefore is it timed to release? Is it the secrets concealed in darkness within the chambers beneath the Sphinx? If so, then it is important that we learn everything there is to know about the almost alien world of those who might have constructed them. We need to establish their identity, their effect on humanity, their ultimate fate and the extent of their technological achievements, for only then will we stand a chance of comprehending the Elder gods' greatest legacy to mankind.

CHAPTER TWO

APING THE ANCIENTS

The Great Pyramid is arguably the most accomplished engineering feat of the ancient world. Yet exactly how it came to be built is still one of the most perplexing enigmas of modern science. Few would deny it is the culmination of nearly 150 years of constructional experimentation, begun with the building early in the Third Dynasty, *c.* 2678 BC, of King Djoser's famous step pyramid at nearby Saqqara. Despite this realisation, there are clear signs that the Great Pyramid and its two neighbours – the pyramids of Khafre and Menkaure – incorporate elements of engineering, mathematics and technology vastly superior to those of their assorted predecessors. Where did this additional knowledge come from? Did it really derive from centuries of trial and error or might it have had a quite separate source of origin – a secret mystery school, perhaps, who had held true to the ways of the Elder gods?

American Egyptologist Mark Lehner was asked to build a scale model of a true pyramid on the edge of the Giza plateau as part of a television series for the BBC and NOVA/WGBH-Boston entitled 'Secrets of Lost Empires'. Using only primitive tools and ancient techniques to move, lift and manoeuvre the stone blocks into position, he was given just three weeks to complete this mammoth task. Lehner and his team were allowed to use modern technology to cut and transport the stones to the site provided, but after that they were to attempt to re-create the method by which the original pyramid builders had erected their own masterpieces in stone.

After quarrying and cutting 186 limestone blocks weighing on average between 750 and 3000 kilograms apiece, the Egyptian-led workforce manoeuvred them into position using strong ropes and sheer manpower. With the aid of a wooden sled and rollers, the great blocks were then hauled up a gradient constructed of *tafla* – a tan-coloured desert clay mixed with limestone chips and gypsum. Wooden planks provided a firm base while water obtained from the Nile acted as an efficient lubricant. In this way Lehner and his team found that '12 to 20 men could pull a 2-tonne block'.[1]

On the upper courses, where the manoeuvring became difficult, the workforce used levers and coordinated brute force to tease the cumbersome blocks around right-angled corners. Once this procedure had been completed, the stepped pyramid was covered with shaped facing-blocks – defining its unique 52-degree angle of ascent – and then capped with an appropriate limestone pyramidion. A true north–south orientation was also achieved using calculations based on the sun's daily course across the sky (even though the Ancient Egyptians probably used the rotation of stars around the celestial pole to attain the same result).

The whole operation was completed in the allotted three-week period, and the finished result looked impressive. Mark Lehner and his team were understandably jubilant at their success, having in their estimate equalled the engineering feats of their Old Kingdom predecessors. In Lehner's words, 'this limited experiment made it abundantly clear that the pyramids are very human monuments, created through long experience and tremendous skill, but without any kind of secret sophistication',[2] a dig at those pyramidologists who advocate some kind of lost science behind the construction of the Great Pyramid.

The miniature pyramid built by Lehner and his jubilant team was 'a tiny fraction' of the enormity expressed in the other Giza pyramids; indeed, it would sit pretty on the level platform at the *top* of the Great Pyramid! In spite of this admission, the viewer was expected to believe that the technological might of the Ancient Egyptians had finally been harnessed, and given enough time, money and expertise anyone with a little common sense could match anything achieved by our most distant ancestors.

Or could they?

To any open-minded viewer who enthusiastically followed this highly entertaining television series when it was first screened in 1996, there was a sense of being short-changed in respect of the claimed accomplishments of the experts involved in each of the programmes. Whether it be erecting a Stonehenge trilithon, replacing the polygonal walls of Incan Peru, raising an Egyptian obelisk or constructing a pyramid, one was left with the overwhelming feeling that these replicas paled into insignificance in comparison with the real thing. It was as if these well-meaning and obviously highly qualified teams of experts were simply aping the Ancients in an almost irreverent manner. Admittedly, they were given just three weeks in which to put their plans into practice, and yet the bold assertions of these academics seemed to belittle, even mock, the achievements of the ancient world.

What exactly were these people missing? What was it that the ancient engineers appeared to possess that we now only dream of mastering? What is it that makes wonders such as the Great Pyramid appeal to us not so much as heaps of hewn rock stacked on top of each other but as sanctified places that enliven the emotional character, or spirit, within us all?

Understanding the mysterious mentality of the Old Kingdom pyramid builders seemed difficult enough. Yet attempting to comprehend their superior capabilities in the knowledge that at least some of Giza's most ancient structures were several thousand years older than their sentinel-like neighbours simply plunges us into an unknown quagmire of uncertainty and speculation.

BUILT BY GIANTS

Take, for instance, the Valley Temple. Its core walls are constructed of literally hundreds of immense stone blocks regularly weighing as much as 100 and occasionally even 200 tonnes apiece.[3] Their sizes are simply stupendous: many are as much as 5.5 metres in length, 3.6 metres in width and 2.4 metres in height; some are an incredible 9 metres in length, 3.6 metres in width and 3.6 metres in height.[4] It might almost be suggested that this structure was built not by human hands but by giants.

Several of the stones used in the Valley Temple are larger than a freight container and heavier than a diesel locomotive, yet despite their enormous size and weight its builders were able to cut them free of the bedrock around the Sphinx and transport them for a distance of anything up to 75 metres to their current position. The sheer extravagance of this feat, let alone the insurmountable engineering problems it would surely have presented to the builders, is almost beyond belief.

Even more curious is that prior to the pyramid age, the Pharaonic Egyptians are not considered to have used large stone blocks for building construction. In what is referred to by scholars as the Archaic Period, the first two dynasties of Pharaonic Egypt, *c.* 3100–2700 BC, temples were built almost exclusively of mud bricks measuring 24 centimetres in length, 10 centimetres in width and between 5 and 7 centimetres in height.[5] We are thus expected to believe that in the course of just 120 years the Ancient Egyptians switched from using simple mud bricks to blocks of stone between 100 and 468 tonnes in weight and up to 9 metres in length. Such a view seems totally absurd, especially if one considers that pyramid designers of the Fifth Dynasty, *c.* 2480–2340 BC, reverted to using much smaller stone blocks, and by the Twelfth Dynasty, *c.* 1991–1786 BC, the Egyptians were once again using mud bricks to construct their pyramid tombs.

Interior view of the Valley Temple of Khafre.

Why the builders of the Valley Temple – or indeed any of the other megalithic structures of Egypt – should have needed, or wanted, to use such ridiculously large stone blocks in its construction is a question that seems to have bypassed the Egyptologists, their official view being that cyclopean masonry was the standard style of Old Kingdom times. To them the kings of the pyramid age were simply megalomaniacs who thought big all the time, not just in the choice of tombs but even when it came to the design of their funerary temples.

Such flippant assertions miss the point altogether, for they fail to explain why any architect should have needed to build a temple using 100-, 200- or even 400-tonne blocks when it would have been much easier to have used stones 100 times smaller. Stone blocks with an average weight of just two tonnes, like those that make up the walls of the Great Pyramid, would have had the same desired result – a monument suitable as both a regal tribute and a house of the gods. All this implies that there was a more specific reason for employing the use of such building-blocks. So what possible reason could this have been?

Were buildings made of cyclopean masonry *easier* to build, like the prefabricated concrete buildings of the modern age, or was there some other, more profound reason behind such mammoth constructions?

More immediately important was attempting to discover how the engineers involved in the construction of the Valley Temple were able to transport, manoeuvre and position 100- and 200-tonne stones into place. Even today the transportation of building-blocks of this weight is extremely difficult. Until the 1970s the largest weight a crane could raise was just 100 tonnes. Since then a number of lifting devices have been designed to take weights of up to 250 tonnes, although this is achieved only by using huge counterweights. In more recent times enormous mobile cranes have been developed to lift payloads as large as 1000 tonnes,[6] matching the weight of the largest building-blocks ever known to have been used in building construction.[7] Yet this does not explain how the builders of the Valley Temple were able so easily to build cyclopean walls up to 12 metres in height.

Egyptologists with an understanding of ancient building techniques have suggested that structures such as the Great Pyramid and the Valley Temple were erected using so-called 'bury and re-excavate' techniques. This is where an inclined ramp of compacted earth, probably lined with planks of wood, would be built in stages to match the ever-increasing height of the building under construction. The blocks would be placed on sleds or rollers and pulled upwards by haulage gangs located on the other side of the structure until each one reached its required height and position. A similar process is thought to have been used in the construction of the Great Pyramid[8] and in the raising and positioning of the sarsen lintels at Stonehenge.[9] Yet as the height of a wall increases, so the length of the ramp must be extended to retain the same optimum angle of incline. In confined working environments this would become impracticable, so ramps are thought to have been increased in length, while at the same time retaining their existing angle of incline, by being wrapped around the building under construction, like a gigantic winding staircase.

This same process was employed by Lehner and his team to build their mini-pyramid at Giza. They found that '20 men could pull a 1-tonne block up the incline',[10] meaning that similar methods could easily have been used in the construction of the Great Pyramid. Yet Lehner's statement is itself revealing, for when his figures are applied to moving a 200-tonne block along a similar incline, it implies that pulley-gangs of anything up to 4000 individuals would have been required to build the walls of the Valley Temple.[11] Surely an operation on this scale would have created unbelievable problems in coordination and control. An even greater problem is that, because the stones were transported south-eastwards from the Sphinx enclosure to the location of the Valley Temple, any inclined ramp constructed for this purpose would have had to follow this same line of passage. If so, then to raise the blocks into the air, the 4000-strong pulley-gangs would have needed to be positioned beyond the south-eastern or eastern limits of the temple, in other words on the plateau's sloping bank. The acute angles created by such a situation would have made it virtually impossible to have hauled a 200-tonne block along an ascending ramp to its final resting-place on top of an existing wall anything up to 9 metres in height, and yet somehow the impossible *was* achieved.

And how were the great stone blocks lifted from the sleds or

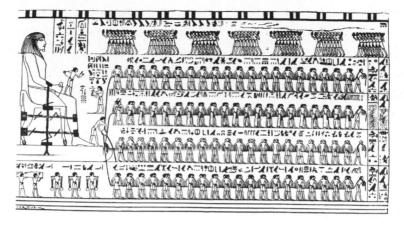

Egyptian workers using a sled, rollers and ropes to transport a large stone statue.

rollers and manoeuvred into position? Scholars might propose the employment of scaffoldings, ramps or even windlasses (i.e. capstans) like those utilised by the Italian Renaissance artist Domenico Fontana to erect a 327-tonne Egyptian obelisk in front of St Peter's Basilica, Rome, in 1586. To achieve the amount of lift necessary, he used an incredible 40 windlasses, which necessitated a combined force of 800 men and 140 horses.[12] Such ideas are, however, pure speculation, while those engineers working alongside the Egyptological community seem completely oblivious to these apparent dilemmas. And if such feats of engineering are difficult to conceive, even in our own age, knowledge that the Valley Temple is conceivably the product of a culture that thrived as much as 8000 years before the pyramid age is mind-boggling in the extreme.

The extraordinary engineering capabilities of these ancient peoples cannot be denied. Yet even this does not explain how they were able to build structures such as the Valley Temple with such ease, or why they should have needed to use 200-tonne blocks in the first place. There was almost an irrationality in their actions that went way beyond our current understanding of building construction. The Valley Temple seems almost alien in our own technological environment. Whoever built it thought differently from us. They would seem to have had different priorities in life. We do not think as they did, and so can only guess at the reasoning behind their use of strange cyclopean masonry.

Although we must assume that this ancient race used conventional forms of building construction, which did indeed include the employment of workforces up to 4000 strong, there are grounds to suggest that they also had at their disposal other, more unorthodox forms of technology no longer available to the world. Certain archaic traditions handed down generation after generation by the Coptic Christians, the lineal descendants of the Ancient Egyptians, speak openly of these unknown practices, yet to proceed with this line of enquiry will now require us to enter into the world of the illogical.

CHAPTER THREE

THE OLD COPT'S TALE

Squeezed between the claustrophobic, run-down streets of Old Cairo are a handful of insignificant-looking churches used for the last 1500 or so years by the city's ancient Coptic community. Some are in a state of disrepair and neglect; others have become the targets of ghoulish thieves who desecrate their abandoned graveyards looking for anything that might bring a price on the black market. Yet despite their dismal appearances and bleak reputations, these archaic houses of God exude an air of concealed mystery kept alive by their priestly guardians, some of whom may well be direct descendants of those who built the pyramids at nearby Giza.

The dictionary tells us that the word 'Copt' is derived from the Greek *Aiguptios*, an adjective taken from the noun *Aiguptos*.[1] It was used to determine the original inhabitants of Egypt as opposed to the many Greek immigrants who flooded into the country in the wake of Alexander the Great's celebrated entry in 332 BC. Coptic Christianity traces its lineage back to St Mark the Evangelist, the writer of one of the four Gospels, who is said to have preached the words of Jesus to the Egyptians in around AD 50.[2] In actuality the Coptic faith derives much of its inspiration from the different religious cults that thrived across Egypt in the years prior to the birth of Christianity. These included the cult of the goddess Kore in Alexandria and the widespread veneration of Serapis, a hybrid god made up of an amalgam of religious traditions concerning the god Osiris and the sacred Apis bull of Memphis.[3] In addition to these influences, the Copts' rich religious art bears all the hallmarks of their dynastic predecessors, while their spoken and written languages are simply bastardised forms of those in common use during Pharaonic times.[4]

Despite the foreign nature of the Coptic faith to the Islamic world, many early Arab travellers believed that its priestly elders preserved age-old traditions that shed light on the wisdom of the Ancient Egyptians, whose undeciphered stone inscriptions and carved reliefs invoked a world of mystery and imagination. Many of these roving historians made a special point of visiting Old Cairo in the hope that the elderly Coptic priests might be persuaded to reveal the ultimate secrets regarding the construction of the three pyramids of Giza.

IN THE WORDS OF AL-MAS'ŪDI

One such person was a tenth-century historian named 'Ali b. Husayn, who was born in Baghdad and styled himself as al-Mas'ūdi in honour of a companion of the Prophet Mohammed named 'Abdulláh b. Mas'úd, from whom he claimed lineal descent.[5] In his later life Mas'údi settled in Egypt, but in his more formative years he preferred to wander the length and breadth of the ancient world searching out previously unknown facts of life. In his quest for knowledge, Mas'údi is known to have visited Armenia, Ceylon, India, Madagascar and Zanzibar; he is even said to have reached China.[6] On his travels he would speak to curious and interesting people of every faith and creed, noting down their archaic customs, their ancient beliefs, their alleged sciences and their accepted histories. These were copiously recorded in the many books he attempted to leave behind for posterity. Sadly, only two are now extant, the most important of these being the *Kitāb Murūj al-Dhahab wa Ma'ādin al-Jawhar*, 'The Meadows of Gold and Mines of Gems'.

The *Murūj* states how, while staying in Cairo, Mas'ūdi chanced on a most extraordinary story concerning the pyramids of Giza, revealed during a famous meeting between one Aḥmad ibn Ṭūlūn, the ruler of Egypt between AD 868 and 877, and an unnamed Coptic elder, very probably one of Old Cairo's mysterious priests. This man had sought an audience with Ṭulun intent on defending his persecuted Coptic Christian faith, the adherents of which had received considerable ill treatment at the hands of the Arab authorities. During this lengthy discourse, Ṭūlūn is said to have warmed considerably to the profound wisdom and faith of the elderly Copt, who had proceeded to give his opinion regarding the source of the river Nile and, more important, the construction of the 'great pyramids' of Giza.[7]

In one version of this account, preserved as an appendix to a three-volume work entitled *Operations Carried on at the Pyramids of Gizeh in 1837* by British explorer Colonel Howard Vyse, Mas'ūdi tells us that the builder of the pyramids was an antediluvian king named Saurid Ibn Salhouk (or Surid, Ben Shaluk), who lived 300 years before the Great Flood. He is said to have been troubled by a dream in which he saw that 'the earth was overthrown . . . the inhabitants were laid prostrate upon it', and 'the stars wandered confusedly from their courses, and clashed together with tremendous noise'.[8] At first Saurid mentioned this dream to no one, but he was then troubled by another dream-vision in which he saw 'the fixed stars descend upon the earth in the form of white birds, and seizing the people, enclose them in a cleft between two great mountains, which shut upon them'.[9]

Repairing to 'the temple of the sun', plausibly the famous temple of the sun-god Re at Heliopolis, he rested and in the early morning summoned before him the chief priests of the 130 nomes, or regions, of Egypt. After having heard the contents of Saurid's dream, the most senior among them, a high priest named Philimon or Iklimon, said that he too had been troubled by a strange dream. It had occurred a year before, and in it he had been witness to the same catastrophe. Yet in his opinion, after the disaster had struck, 'the sky would resume its former altitude' – in other words it would return to its former position.[10]

Needing to understand more fully the nature of this impending disaster, Saurid instructed his priests to consult the stars. This was duly done, and on their return they informed the troubled king that a deluge would 'overwhelm the land, and destroy a large portion of it for some years'. Another Arab writer named Ahmad al-Makrizi (1360–1442), who quotes a variation of this story, stated that, in addition to a flood, a 'fire was to proceed from the sign [of] Leo, and to consume the world'.[11]

On learning of these revelations, King Saurid ordered the building of 'the Pyramids', while the prediction of the priests was, he said, to be inscribed 'on columns, and upon the large stones belonging to them'.[12]

Into the pyramids he placed his treasures, his valuable property, 'together with the bodies of his ancestors'. The priests were also ordered to place in them (al-Makrizi states specifically in the 'subterraneous passages' beneath them) 'written accounts of their wisdom and acquirements in the different arts and sciences', which included 'the names and properties of medical plants, and the science of arithmetic and geometry'.[13]

This is the gist of the quaint old Coptic tale related by Mas'ūdi regarding the legendary origins of the Giza pyramids. Other Arab writers, such as the ninth-century historian Ibn Abd Alhokm and the aforementioned al-Makrizi, include variations of the story in their own works, the latter having followed the authority of one 'Usted Ibrahim Ben Wasyff Shah'.[14]

King Saurid himself turns out to be a fictional figure used as a point of focus for what seem to have been a number of quite separate strands of knowledge concerning the supposed events surrounding the construction of the pyramids. While many of these claims are almost certainly a mixture of fact and fantasy, the references to fire and flood devastating Egypt are, as I have attempted to demonstrate elsewhere, almost certainly a distant echo of the geological upheavals and climatic changes, including widespread flooding, which are known to have accompanied the cessation of the last Ice Age.[15]

The association between an age that culminated in fire and flood and the star constellation of Leo is best summed up in a Coptic papyrus apparently found under curious circumstances within a monastery named Abou Hormeis. It was translated into Arabic by Coptic priests and later included in a book written by a historian named Al Kodhai in the year AD 847. The papyrus was said to record that 'The deluge was to take place when the heart of the Lion entered into the first minute of the head of Cancer, at the declining of the star.'[16] The 'heart of the lion' was the name given in classical times to the star Regulus, Leo's 'royal star', which lies exactly on the ecliptic, the sun's perceived path across the sky. Since the constellation of Cancer follows Leo *only* in the precessional cycle (Leo *follows* Cancer in the yearly cycle), then this appears to confirm that this legend preserved not just the memory of actual historical events but also the time-frame in which they occurred.

At my request, electronics engineer Rodney Hale fed the astronomical information contained within the Abou Hormeis papyrus into a computer, using the Skyglobe 3.6 program. With some degree of accuracy, he discovered that the last time Leo's 'royal star' would have risen and been visible on the eastern horizon just prior to the equinoctial sunrise was in around 9220 BC.[17] When the star Regulus, the 'heart of the lion', no longer rose with the sun on the vernal equinox, this would have been seen by the astronomer-priests of Egypt as a signal that the Age of Leo had ended, signalling either that the Age of Cancer was about to commence or that it had already entered its 'first minute' of arc across the sky. This information therefore suggested that the writer of the Coptic text believed that major flooding had occurred in Egypt at around this time, a matter covered in some detail within Chapter Fifteen.

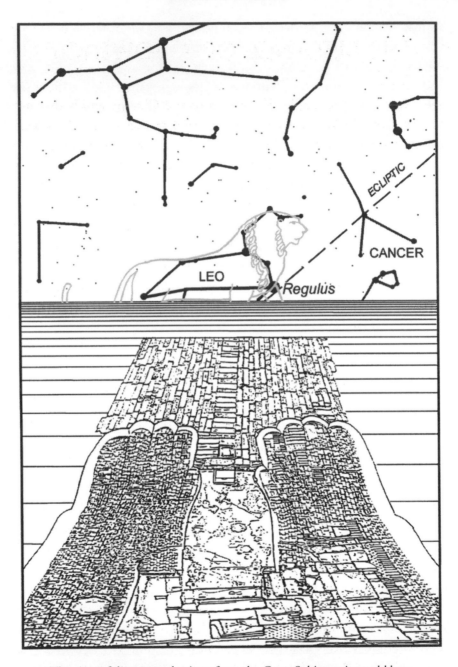

The view of the eastern horizon from the Great Sphinx as it would have appeared in the pre-dawn light on the spring equinox of 9220 BC, the last year that the royal star Regulus would have risen with the sun on this day.

THE DISTANCE OF A BOWSHOT

It is, however, not simply the origins of the Giza pyramids that are discussed by Mas'ūdi, for he goes on to relate the manner by which the monuments came to be built. According to his account, the stone blocks used in the construction of not only the pyramids but also the 'extensive pavement' that surrounded each one of them[18] were transported in the following, rather unique manner:

> In carrying on the work, leaves of papyrus, or paper, inscribed with certain characters, were placed under the stones prepared in the quarries; and upon being struck, the blocks were moved at each time the distance of a bowshot (about 150 cubits), and so by degrees arrived at the Pyramids. Rods of iron were inserted into the centres of the stones, that formed the pavement, and, passing through the blocks placed upon them, were fixed by melted lead.[19]

It is perhaps understandable that the majestic nature of the Great Pyramid, prised open for the first time in AD 820 by the workmen of the caliph al-Ma'moun just a short while before Ṭūlūn's own age, obviously led to much speculation concerning the nature of its construction. For nearly 200 years the Arabs had marvelled at the presence of this great wonder of the world, but since its much-celebrated opening both the Coptic inhabitants of Old Cairo and their Arab rulers had been free to speculate on the seemingly impossible building techniques involved. The presence alone of the 70-tonne granite blocks positioned over the King's Chamber must have struck visitors with an unimaginable awe that could quite easily have conjured visions of supernatural intervention. To anyone at the time, the Great Pyramid must have seemed like the product of, if not a race of spectral origin, one with magical capabilities beyond human comprehension.

Is this why the Coptic priests of Old Cairo, the accepted heirs to the Ancient Egyptians, were forced to create such bizarre stories? Is this all it was: ignorant Copts, or indeed Arabs, conjuring supernatural accounts to explain what they clearly could not understand – or might such traditions have some basis in truth?

Let's look at the facts.

What Mas'ūdi was suggesting in his curious account is that inscribed magical papyri were inserted beneath the stone blocks used in the construction of the pyramids, before the latter were struck by an instrument of some sort, plausibly a rod or stave. Somehow this induced them both to rise into the air *and* travel for a distance of 'a bowshot', the equivalent of 150 cubits, with one 'royal' cubit measuring 0.5773 metres.[20] Even with the most basic knowledge of physics, it is clear that Mas'ūdi was implying that, by striking the stones, the Ancient Egyptians were able to set up some kind of sustained sound vibration that enabled the building-blocks to defy gravity and move over the ground for a distance of around 86.5 metres, before they would have to be struck again to achieve the same result. After producing an initial thrust, they would have been able to take advantage of Newton's first law of motion. This insists that a moving object will continue to travel at the same speed and in the same direction, unless an external force (in this case, the return of gravity) prevents it from doing so.

Historians, when reviewing pseudo-historical works like those of Mas'ūdi, are right to dismiss such wild assertions as idle fantasy, created in this case perhaps by the Copts to elevate the esteem of their noble ancestors. To suggest that some form of sound levitation might therefore have been employed by the pyramid builders to transport large stone blocks over great distances is quite obviously to be seen as complete nonsense.

Yet Mas'ūdi was no fool. He was looked on by later historians as 'the Herodotus of the Arabs' – an appellation seen as 'not unjust' by Arab literary scholar Reynold A. Nicholson.[21] In addition to this, the Arabic writer Ibn Khaldún refers to Mas'ūdi as *imam lil-mu'arrikhin*, 'an Imám for the historians', quite literally the 'father of history'.[22] So it is unlikely that he would have blindly accepted tall yarns without first being given some kind of authentication of their reality.

So what are we to make of the old Copt's tale?

I should perhaps have dropped the matter there and then, but the idea that Egypt's Sphinx-building Elder culture, and/or their pyramid-building descendants, were able to construct cyclopean structures using a form of sound technology unknown in the modern world appealed to me. What if these people really had possessed such unimaginable capabilities? What if ancient cultures really were able to control natural forces in a manner inconceivable today? All we can say for certain is that the most ancient Egyptians were able to move 200- and perhaps even 468-tonne stone blocks with apparent ease, while the Great Pyramid would appear to encode a profound understanding of Pythagorean geometry, ancient metrology, the mathematical value of *pi* and the geodesic measurements of the earth. All of these sciences were known to the Pharaonic Egyptians and then forgotten by all but a few selected initiates of the inner mysteries. Was it possible therefore that the world once possessed an understanding of sound that was lost and *never* recovered?

THEOSOPHICAL SUPPORT

A belief that the Ancient Egyptians were able to move stone blocks using the power of sound is not new. It has often been cited by occult writers as evidence that the pyramid builders inherited a superior technology from a much earlier civilisation, such as the lost continent of Atlantis mentioned in the works of the Greek philosopher Plato. In 1908, for example, a lady named Annie Besant, a follower of the eastern-influenced Theosophical Society, founded in 1875 by the medium and writer Helena Petrovna Blavatsky, wrote in her book *The Pedigree of Man*:

... those stones [used in the construction of 'cyclopean' cities and 'the mighty pyramid of Egypt'] were not raised by mere bulk of muscles, nor by skilful apparatus, strong beyond modern making: they were raised by those who understood and could control the forces of terrestrial magnetism, so that the stone lost its weight and floated, guided by the touch of a finger, to rest on its appointed bed.[23]

Another of Madame Blavatsky's disciples, A.P. Sinnett, came to similar conclusions concerning the technology of the Ancient Egyptians in his 1924 book *The Pyramids and Stonehenge*, when he wrote:

The manipulation of the enormous stones used in this edifice, as also, indeed, the construction of the great pyramid itself, can only be explained by the application to these tasks of some knowledge concerning the forces of Nature which was lost to mankind during the decadence of Egyptian civilisation and the barbarism of the Middle Ages, and has not yet been recovered by modern science.[24] ... The adepts who directed their construction [i.e. the pyramids] facilitated the process by the partial levitation of the stones used.[25]

Whether such views held by the Theosophists of the late nineteenth and early twentieth centuries were based on a translation of Mas'ūdi's account of the construction of the pyramids or on mystical knowledge revealed by Madame Blavatsky has never been made clear. Such claims are important only in so much as they add weight to the idea that the Ancient Egyptians possessed a superior technology far greater than that achieved today.

THE PRIESTS OF ON

As challenging and revolutionary as these ideas might seem, they were never verified with any hard facts or evidence. In spite of these shortcomings, they gave rise to a brief entry in a novel by a British author named Walter Owen which, by means of a curious twist of fate, helped convince a whole new generation of Egypt's lost sound technology.

Owen believed that ever since ancient times an occult or secret tradition had been responsible for the moulding of Western civilisation, and he fictionalised this theme in a book entitled *More Things in Heaven*, published in 1947. Most of the plot is set within a private library in Buenos Aires, and in an attempt to prove the influence across time of this secret brotherhood in human affairs, the central character reads extracts from either genuine or fictional works on religious and occult matters.

At one point in the story, Owen turns his attentions to the Ancient Egyptians and quotes the following statement from a fictitious tome named as 'the *Hieratica* of Hamarchis of Alexandria':

'Certain it is that in ancient times the priests of On [the biblical name for Heliopolis in Lower Egypt] possessed the knowledge of the miraculous art whereby they compelled to their dominion the spirits of the elements and worked many wonders of which the proofs remain to this day . . . and by means of magical words they raised storms, and carried stones for their temples through the air which a thousand men could not lift.'[26]

There the matter might have rested had it not been for the irresponsible actions of an author named Desmond Leslie, who co-wrote a popular book on UFOs and ancient technologies with supposed flying saucer 'contactee' George Adamski. Entitled *Flying*

Saucers Have Landed, it was first published in 1953 and went on to become a major best-seller in many countries of the world.

In a chapter entitled 'Power and the Great Pyramid', Leslie cited Owen's 'priests of On' quotation as evidence of sound levitation in Ancient Egypt, without realising it was pure fiction.[27] Yet by misreading the text on the pages concerned, Leslie managed to attribute this quotation not to 'the *Hieratica* of Hamarchis of Alexandria' but to *La Magie Chez les Chaldeens*, 'the Magic of the Chaldees', a genuine and very authoritative book on Middle Eastern mythology, written by a noted French scholar named François Lenormant and first published in Paris during 1874. This howling error on Leslie's part was never rectified and as a consequence led to some unbelievable literary sloppiness on the part of numerous ancient mysteries writers who went on to use Owen's 'priests of On' statement in their own books without bothering to check whether or not Lenormant's *La Magie Chez les Chaldeens* actually contained this quote.[28] By using this fictitious quotation to back up Mas'ūdi's suggestion that the Ancient Egyptians employed the use of sound vibration to raise large stone blocks, the matter undoubtedly has gained far more attention than it perhaps deserves.

I have to admit that at this stage in my research I was not convinced that sound could have played a part in the construction of either the Valley Temple or the pyramids of Giza. As archaeologists will claim repeatedly, given enough time and manpower anything can be achieved – you don't need to invoke bizarre notions to explain the explainable. I might have agreed had I not discovered that there is compelling evidence to show that the pyramid builders really did possess a highly sophisticated stone technology that throws an entirely new light on the old Copt's tale.

CHAPTER FOUR

PRECISION IMPOSSIBLE

On one stormy day in November 1880, a young and very enthusiastic Englishman, drawn by the mystery and imagination of the Great Pyramids, set sail for Cairo. His intention was to conduct the most studious and exhaustive survey ever undertaken of the temples and monuments of the Giza plateau. Along with the most sophisticated measuring equipment available in his day, he had packed enough supplies to ensure his survival in the hot, barren and very hostile desert, where bandits regularly picked off European travellers as a matter of course.

Sir William Matthew Flinders Petrie (1853–1942) had gained much of his thirst for Ancient Egypt at a tender age. His father, the civil engineer William Petrie, was an ardent supporter of Charles Piazzi Smyth, the famous Astronomer Royal of Scotland, who in the 1860s had drawn immense attention to the Great Pyramid by seeming to confirm the long-held belief that geodetic knowledge of the earth's size could be found in its overall design and measurements. Yet because Smyth had been unable to accredit such feats of engineering to the Ancient Egyptians, who were looked on with disdain in the Bible, he concluded that the pyramid builders had been inspired by God himself, in the same way that the Lord had inspired Noah to build the Ark of the Flood and Moses to construct the Ark of the Covenant. Such assertions had in turn spurred another

Scottish 'pyramidologist' named Robert Menzies to make the claim that the interior measurements of the Great Pyramid contained past, present and future prophecies, including the date of the Second Coming.

This unfortunate situation led to Smyth's theories on the Great Pyramid's precision geometry being lumped together with Menzies' crazy notions of biblical prophecy. His revolutionary findings were dismissed as absurd by the Egyptological community and made a laughing-stock in the popular press. Despite such ridicule, the young Flinders Petrie was undoubtedly fascinated by Smyth's extraordinary claims. He intended to follow in the footsteps of his father's mentor and either confirm or deny Smyth's theories once and for all.

Petrie held a passion for the monuments of Ancient Egypt, born out of a genuine sense of responsibility in recording and not exploiting the wonders of the past, something he accused his contemporaries of in the sternest of words. He was horrified, for instance, at how the ruins of the Sphinx Temple had been shattered by explosives under the direction of so-called Egyptologists who believed that treasure lay buried beneath it in a secret chamber guarded by mechanised devices in human form. 'It is sickening,' he wrote, 'to see the rate at which everything is being destroyed, and the little regard paid to preservation.'[1]

Following his arrival at Giza, Petrie set about surveying and triangulating the entire artificially levelled plateau. Everything was checked and double-checked to ensure the greatest possible accuracy, and as he commented at the time: 'the result of all this mass of checked observations, after duly reducing and computing, was that there was scarcely a point about which one quarter-inch [6.3 millimetres] of uncertainty remained, and most of the points were fixed to within one-tenth of an inch [2.5 millimetres].'[2]

Once Petrie had completed his survey of the Giza plateau, he focused his attentions on the interiors of its temples and monuments with a similar concern for meticulous accuracy ('Instead then of simply measuring from wall to wall, and remaining in ignorance of where the discrepancies lay, I always used plumb-lines for measuring all upright faces, and a levelling instrument for all horizontal faces.')[3] So engrossed did he become in his painstaking work that often he would finish his evening meal and then, once the accursed tourists had departed, enter the darkened interior of one of the pyramids and not emerge again until the early hours, sometimes well past dawn.[4]

The results of all this hard work on Petrie's part were, he realised quickly, 'decidedly destructive' for the theories of pyramidologists such as Smyth.[5] His revised measurements were at odds with those previously used by Smyth to make his calculations. In effect they disproved his findings; this was something Petrie was not happy about, for, as he was later to admit, he would rather it not have been him who had discovered 'the ugly little fact [that] killed the beautiful theory'.[6] Some of Smyth's theories have, however, been ably revived and confirmed in more modern times by the likes of Livio Stecchini and William Fix (see Chapter One).

Petrie did, however, confirm one long-held belief about the Great Pyramid – that 'the angle of the outside was such as to make the base circuit equal to a circle struck by the height as a radius',[7] or in other words the proportions of the structure accurately expressed the mathematical value of *pi*.[8] He also confirmed that the measurements of the King's Chamber displayed a precise knowledge of Pythagorean geometry.[9]

A FEW MEN FAR ABOVE THEIR FELLOWS

That Petrie was in awe of Egypt's pyramid builders is difficult to deny. He came to believe that those originally responsible for this highly advanced technology belonged to a 'New Race', a ruling elite who in Old Kingdom times controlled the construction of pyramids, temples and monuments.[10]

Who exactly this 'New Race' might have been is never made

clear, for the usually conservative Petrie could only conceive of them as a select group possessing technological skills far superior to those of their fellow Egyptians. They were the master craftsmen who decided everything – from which stone to use to what tools should be employed and what angles and measurements were to be incorporated into the building under construction. Once their orders had been given, many jobs would seem to have been left to an Egyptian workforce to complete, a situation that had led Petrie repeatedly to comment on the inexcusable errors so often found alongside the quite magnificent workmanship in buildings such as the Great Pyramid. For example, while Petrie was able to describe the precision involved in the setting out of the Great Pyramid's five-hectare base as 'a triumph of skill; its errors, both in length and in angles, could be covered by placing one's thumb on them',[11] he was dumbfounded by the 'astonishing carelessness and clumsiness' of those left in charge of completing its construction.[12] 'Side by side with this splendid work are,' he admitted, 'the strangest mistakes' in various examples of levelling, dressing, sawing and drilling.[13]

Petrie came to believe that 'the exquisite workmanship often found in the early periods, did not so much depend on a large school or widespread ability, as on a few men far above their fellows, whose every touch was a triumph. In this way we can reconcile it with the crude, and often clumsy, work in building and sculpture found in the same ages.'[14]

So who were these 'few men far above their fellows', and what was this 'New Race' said to have been in Egypt during its earliest days?

Archaeological evidence supports the idea that members of an unknown race of unparalleled sophistication emerged in Egypt as early as predynastic times, *c.* 3500–3100 BC. Late predynastic graves in the northern part of Upper Egypt have yielded 'anatomical remains of a people whose skulls were of a greater size and whose bodies were larger than those of the natives'.[15] Walter Emery, the eminent Egyptologist who made a detailed study of predynastic and early dynastic society in Egypt, was so moved by these discoveries that, in his 1961 book *Archaic Egypt*, he concluded that:

> . . . any suggestion that these people derived from the earlier
> stock is impossible. The fusion of the two races must have
> been considerable, but it was not so rapid that by the time of
> the Unification it could be considered in any way accom-
> plished, for throughout the whole of the Archaic Period the
> distinction between the civilised aristocracy and the mass of
> the natives is very marked, particularly in regard to their
> burial customs. Only with the close of the Second Dynasty do
> we find evidence of the lower orders adopting the funerary
> architecture and mode of burial of their masters.[16]

So who were these 'masters'? Who were these ruling elite of great
stature? Were they Petrie's 'New Race', the 'few men far above their
fellows' responsible for Egypt's stone technology? Emery identified
them with the *Shemsu-hor*, the Companions, or Followers, of the
hawk-headed god Horus whom the Royal Canon of Turin says ruled
Egypt for an incredible 13,420 years *before* the ascent of Menes, the
first recorded Pharaoh.[17]

Emery's words therefore implied that the *Shemsu-hor* were not
only the governing power behind the establishment of dynastic
Egypt but also the descendants of the Sphinx-building Elder gods, or
netjeru, who lived during the First Time, the epoch corresponding
with the precessional Age of Leo. Were they also, then, the master
masons and technologists, the 'few men far above their fellows', who
oversaw the construction of the Giza pyramids and initiated Egypt's
stoneware technology?[18]

DIAMOND-TIPPED SAWS

In addition to his unique findings concerning the advanced techniques, social organisation and ruling elite of the pyramid age, Petrie
also began to make other, more unexpected discoveries. He found that

the stonecutting processes employed in the design and manufacture of the Giza pyramids, their accompanying temples and the sarcophagi inside them, as well as the many items of stoneware found in abundance within many Old Kingdom tombs, were simply unbelievable.

Petrie, for example, examined the remaining casing stones on the northern side of the Great Pyramid and was simply astonished by the incredible precision involved in their manufacture and placement. The mean thickness of joints between stones was on average 0.5 millimetres, an accuracy rivalling, according to Petrie, the 'most modern opticians' straight-edges of such a length'.[19] Each block weighed a cool 16 tonnes apiece and covered an area of 'some 35 square feet [3.25 square metres]', and yet despite their great size the pyramid builders managed to bring them within 0.5 millimetres of each other, even though the joints contained a wafer-thin layer of cement. As Petrie was forced to admit at the time: 'To merely place such stones in exact contact at the sides would be careful work; but to do so with cement in the joint seems almost impossible.'[20]

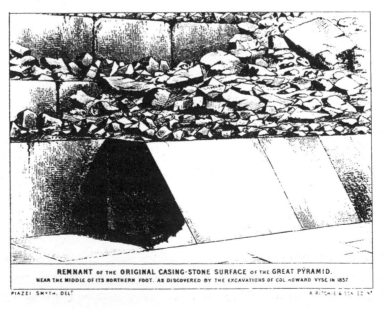

REMNANT OF THE ORIGINAL CASING-STONE SURFACE OF THE GREAT PYRAMID. NEAR THE MIDDLE OF ITS NORTHERN FOOT. AS DISCOVERED BY THE EXCAVATIONS OF COL. HOWARD VYSE IN 1837

PIAZZI SMYTH. DEL.ᵗ   A RITCHIE & SON SC.ᴺ

Remaining casing stones on the northern side of the Great Pyramid.

The techniques employed in this precision engineering clearly baffled Petrie. Yet once he turned his attentions to the sawing and drilling techniques employed in the preparation of the hard igneous rock used so frequently in Old Kingdom times, he found firm evidence of a sophisticated technology unique to the ancient world. Examining the lidless red granite sarcophagus, or coffer, in the King's Chamber, for instance, he noted the presence on its outer surface of horizontal and vertical cut-marks that could have been made only by an extremely long saw. He also observed that in the corner of its northern face, near the west side, the saw had run too deep into the hard granite, which had necessitated it being backed out and the process started again. The next cut was still too deep, so the saw had seemingly been backed out and repositioned for a second time. The whole surface had then been polished in an attempt to hide the errors.[21] Similar saw-marks were also in evidence on the coffer or sarcophagus in the Second Pyramid, as well as on various other cut granite blocks found scattered about the Giza plateau.[22]

As the exterior wall of the sarcophagus in the King's Chamber is a full 2.28 metres in length, Petrie concluded that the 'saw must have been probably about 9 feet [2.7 metres] long'.[23] This is an extraordinary statement for, as Petrie well knew, the only evidence of sawing implements unearthed in Egypt consists of a few bronze knives with serrated edges. These would have had difficulty cutting through a pack of butter, never mind some of the hardest rock in the world.

Egyptologists are not averse to the idea that the masons of Old Kingdom times used bronze saws. Yet in their opinion the sawing of such hard rock was achieved purely through the introduction of a sand-based abrasive that, when placed between the cutting tool and the cutting surface, would grind away the stone, provided, of course, that the correct pressure and sawing action were applied. Petrie accepted that Old Kingdom stonecutters almost certainly used this method to cut softer rocks such as alabaster and limestone, but in his opinion this solution could not account for the sawing processes involved in the cutting of hard igneous rocks such as dark basalt, red granite and black-speckled diorite. After due consideration of the evidence, he proposed that the presumably bronze saws, some up to 2.7 metres long, must have possessed cutting teeth *tipped with jewels*, and that in his estimate: 'The character of the work would certainly seem to point to diamond as being the cutting jewel; and only the considerations of its rarity in general, and its absence from Egypt, interfere with this conclusion, and render the tough uncrystallised corundum [i.e. sapphires, rubies or emery] the more likely material.'[24]

Petrie confirmed the existence of these jewelled cutting points by studying super-hard diorite bowls dating back to the pyramid age. Some of these bore precision-cut hieroglyphs and parallel lines that could have been carved only by an engraving tool with a sharp jewel point. The incisions were always 'regular and uniform in depth, and equidistant' with fluctuations 'no more than such as always occur in the use of a saw by hand-power, whether worked in wood or in soft stone'.[25] He also found evidence for the use of circular saws in Old Kingdom times,[26] as well as lathes. Yes, *lathes*. In fact, he concluded that 'the lathe appears to have been as familiar an instrument in the fourth dynasty, as it is in modern workshops'.[27] The lathe, it must be remembered, is a modern invention born out of our understanding of industrial technology.

Strong evidence of lathework in Ancient Egypt comes from beautifully turned diorite bowls, some 'only as thick as stout card'.[28] These display concave surfaces cut using two separate centre points, or axes. Where the two intersecting curves come together, a slight cusp has been left. Such effects, Petrie decided, had nothing whatsoever to do with grinding or scraping. In his opinion these bowls bore the hallmark of a highly sophisticated lathe, 'fearless and powerful'[29] and totally alien to the ancient world.

PRECISION STONEWARE

This was not, however, the last of Petrie's revelations concerning the stone technology of the Ancient Egyptians, for he also found compelling evidence for a drill that produced tube-like holes in the

A bore-hole and core stem produced by tubular drilling during the
Pyramid age (after Flinders Petrie).

hardest of rocks. Somehow, the cutting tool revolved to create a
thin-walled cylindrical core. Then, when the drill-bit had been
removed, this core was broken away to leave a smooth, circular hole.
The carvers could bore holes many metres in depth using this
method, while the diameter of holes varied between 6 millimetres
and 12.5 centimetres.[30] As in the case of the straight and circular
saws, these tubular drills appear to have employed the use of jewelled
cutting points to bore through the rock. The smallest hole found cut
into granite was five centimetres in diameter. Anything smaller was
found only in softer rocks such as alabaster and limestone. These
holes, so Petrie concluded, had been bored probably using a combination of tubular drill and abrasive slurry.[31]

Tubular drills were used in Ancient Egypt for all sorts of
purposes. For instance, the granite sarcophagus in the King's Chamber contains clear evidence that its interior was burrowed out by
creating rows of tubular holes. Once the lengthy cores had been
broken away, each vertical cusp was flattened and smoothed to
remove any evidence of this technique having been used. Some holes,
however, would appear to have run too deep and, despite polishing
attempts to remove all evidence of their presence, are still visible.[32]

Much smaller drills seem to have been used to bore out the
interiors of beautifully carved vases made of rocks such as alabaster,
breccia, porphyry, serpentine, diorite, rose quartz and even amethyst.
There are literally tens of thousands of these exquisite vessels ranging
in size from a few centimetres upwards. Many have smooth, hollow
interiors with thin walls, burrowed shoulders and long, slim necks
with openings sometimes no more than the size of a little finger.

A granite core produced by tubular drilling in Old Kingdom times (after Flinders Petrie).

Initially, Petrie believed that the high level of workmanship involved in the manufacture of these finely polished stone vases suggested they were unique to Old Kingdom times. Then further examples began to surface in much older levels of occupation belonging to the so-called Archaic period, the First and Second Dynasties of Egyptian history, forcing him to revise the time-frame of their development.[33] As time went on, hundreds more stone vases of incredible workmanship started surfacing in a newly excavated cemetery site at Naqada, 480 kilometres (300 miles) south of Cairo. These examples dated back to the so-called Gerzean or Naqada II culture, *c.* 3500–3100 BC, but by this time Petrie unfortunately had dropped the subject in favour of other, more pressing matters.[34] Somehow this style of stoneware had emerged on to the scene almost overnight in around 3500 BC, a fact that has led some scholars to conclude that the technology behind their manufacture, or indeed the vases themselves, came originally from Mesopotamia.[35]

INVISIBLE EVIDENCE

Scholars have long puzzled over the precision stone-carving tech-niques employed in Ancient Egypt. Modern Egyptologists still con-sider that granite items such as the sarcophagus in the King's Chamber were fashioned using copper tools and a simple sand abrasive.[36] Petrie never denied that an abrasive was used in the cutting of hard stone and openly admitted that sand had been found in saw-cuts stained green through the use of copper tools.[37] What he did deny, however, was whether such techniques could explain the precision cutting, turning and drilling of bowls and vases made of hard rock during Old Kingdom times. In his mind, only the use of much harder, sapphire- or ruby-tipped cutting tools fitted all the criteria set by the evidence at hand. Any rock that equals the hardness of quartz, which is seven on Mohs' hardness scale, is virtually impossible to tackle using a combina-tion of copper tool and sand abrasive. Using this process to carve, grind, drill and polish beautiful vases made of, say, purple amethyst or pink rose quartz, although by no means impossible, would be thwarted by problems and failure. A much harder cutting tool affixed to a mechanical device is the only realistic solution.

The Egyptological community tends to dismiss Petrie's views on the use of jewel-tipped tubular drills during the pyramid age. As in the case of straight and circular saws, no evidence for their existence has ever come to light during excavations.[38] This is something that Petrie attempted to explain in his own day by stating that: 'The great saws and drills of the Pyramid workers would be royal property, and it would, perhaps, cost a man his life if he lost one; while the bronze would be remelted, and the jewels reset, when the tools became worn, so that no worn-out tools would be thrown away.'[39]

Petrie is still a respected hero of early Egyptological exploration. He did much to put the subject on a firm footing by establishing the so-called sequence dating of pottery to discern the ages of different occupational levels at archaeological sites, and he was honoured after his death with the creation of the Petrie Chair of Egyptology at University College, London. He also stopped the ramblings of the 'pyramidiots' such as Smyth and Menzies. His exhaustive surveys of the monuments and buildings of the Giza plateau are still seen as authoritative today; indeed, the 1990 edition of his seminal work *The Pyramids and Temples of Gizeh*, first published in 1883, includes an update by the ultra-conservative Egyptologist Zahi Hawass of the Supreme Council of Antiquities in Egypt.

In spite of the part Petrie played in the pioneering of modern Egyptology, it is also true that Egyptologists today find his assertions regarding sapphire- or ruby-tipped saws, drills and lathes a little embarrassing to say the least. Even the curators of the Petrie Museum in central London, which still houses the tens of thousands of artefacts discovered in Egypt by its founder, refused point-blank to discuss these matters with me, preferring instead either to plead complete ignorance or to refer me to standard textbooks and articles on ancient stone-carving techniques in dynastic Egypt.

DUNN'S HIGH-TECH PHARAOHS

There the matter might have rested had it not been for the entrance into this arena of archaeological conventionalism of an American tool specialist and technologist named Christopher Dunn. Inspired by Petrie's observations in respect to Egypt's advanced stone technology, he wrote a speculative article in 1983 entitled 'Advanced Machining in Ancient Egypt'.[40] By applying his extensive knowledge of tool-making and stonecutting to the mystery, and by consulting unbiased colleagues and work associates, he quickly became convinced of Petrie's findings concerning the use of jewel-tipped saws and lathes in Old Kingdom times. He also found new evidence to back up these claims after examining building-blocks, sarcophagi and stone vessels at Giza, Saqqara and the Cairo Museum.[41] Dunn, however, did not end his research here, for he went on to make what may well turn out to be one of the most revolutionary discoveries ever in respect to Egypt's stoneware technology.

Dunn pondered long and hard over certain inexplicable features that Petrie had noted in connection with an assortment of stone items identified as having been created by the drilling processes employed in Old Kingdom times. They can be summed up as follows.

Petrie found that, first, the granite cores produced by tubular drilling always seemed to taper towards the top, i.e. at the point where the drill entered the stone, while the circular wall of the borehole always appeared to be wider at the top.[42]

Secondly, Petrie noted that on granite cores examined, the jewelled drill-piece left behind perfect grooves that swirled around the circumference to form a regular, symmetrical spiral without waviness or interruption; in one case 'a groove can be traced, with scarcely an interruption, for a length of four turns'.[43]

Thirdly, and perhaps most significantly, Petrie observed that 'the [spiralling] grooves are as deep in the quartz as in the adjacent feldspar, and even rather deeper'.[44] At first reading this might not seem particularly relevant, but to any geologist this is a seemingly impossible statement. Granite is composed of three basic components: quartz, feldspar and mica. Quartz is much harder than feldspar, meaning that a drill should pass through the latter faster than the former. This suggests that the width between each groove should be *greater* as it passes through the feldspar, not the other way around as Petrie was at pains to point out:

> If these [grooves] were in any way produced by loose powder [i.e. abrasive slurry], they would be shallower in the harder substance – quartz: whereas a fixed jewel point would [in Petrie's opinion] be compelled to plough to the same depth in all the components; and further, inasmuch as the quartz stands out slightly beyond the felspar . . . the groove was thus left even less in depth on the felspar than on the quartz.[45]

What possible process could adequately explain all three of these components found in the tubular drilling of hard granite? This was the task that Christopher Dunn set himself using the extensive knowledge and experience he had accumulated as a tool-maker. Yet before coming up with a possible solution to this problem, he had also to take into account one final observation made by Petrie:

> The amount of pressure, shown by the rapidity with which the drills and saws pierced through the hard stones, is very surprising; probably a load of at least a ton[ne] or two was placed on the 4-inch [ten-centimetre] drills cutting in granite. On the granite core, No. 7, the spiral of the cut sinks .100 inch [2.54 millimetres] in the circumference of 6 inches [15.24 centimetres], or 1 in 60, a rate of ploughing out of the quartz and felspar which is astonishing.[46]

Dunn was informed by Donald Rahn of the Rahn Granite Surface Plate Co., Dayton, Ohio, that modern high-tech drills using diamond points rotating at 900 revolutions per minute penetrate into granite at a rate of 25 millimetres in 5 minutes, which works out at 0.0055 of a millimetre per revolution.[47] If this data were to be applied to Petrie's calculations, it would suggest that the Ancient Egyptians were, as Dunn quickly realised, 'able to cut their granite with a feed rate that was *500 times greater* [author's emphasis]'.[48]

This was truly outrageous – the pyramid builders of 4500 years

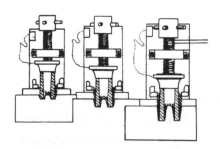

Modern-day tubular drilling process
(after Christopher Dunn).

ago could pierce through granite *500 times faster* than the best diamond-tipped drill-bits on offer today. What in the world were they using to have achieved such extraordinary results? Certainly not flint tools, or copper drill that necessitated the use of a sand abrasive.

Dunn was understandably mystified by this extraordinary revelation, and so thought long and hard about the whole problem. When he did finally come up with what he took to be a plausible solution that fitted *all* the criteria set by himself, he could not wait to share his findings. Yet so bizarre was his solution that he dared not voice it publicly until he received separate confirmation of its logic from other technologists to whom he had also posed the same puzzle.

Patiently he waited for their response. Each studied the available facts and, gradually, all except one shook their heads and gave up the challenge, saying it just could not be done. Every day Dunn would ask the final contestant whether he had come up with a solution, only to be told that he was still working on it. At last he came back to Dunn with a look of satisfaction on his face, having decided that he was being coaxed into admitting the impossible, for in his words: 'They didn't have machinery like that back then!'[49]

So what was it that both Dunn and his unnamed tool-making colleague had independently realised? What was it that had initially stunned them into silence regarding their assessment of Ancient Egypt's drilling capabilities?

Petrie had decided that, to enable a tubular drill to advance 2.54 millimetres into granite per revolution, a constant pressure of one to two tonnes would have to be applied. Dunn disagreed, for in his opinion only one method of drilling fitted all the requirements. The pyramid builders had used a process known today as ultrasonic drilling. This is where the introduction of an inaudible, high-pitched sound causes a diamond-tipped drill-bit to vibrate at an incredibly fast rate.

Ultrasonic drilling works on very similar principles to the more bulky jackhammer or pneumatic drill used in the street to penetrate hard surfaces such as concrete or paving-stones – the rapid vibrations cause the cutting tool to continually bore a hole into the rock. This advanced process is employed today by engineers to precision-machine odd-shaped holes in hard, or brittle, substances such as steel, carbides, ceramics and semiconductors. An abrasive slurry or paste is often used to quicken the cutting pace.[50]

The most poignant evidence in support of this theory is that ultrasound allows the drill-bit, which vibrates at a rate of between 19,000 and 25,000 cycles per second, to cut through quartz much faster than the softer feldspar, because quartz resonates at the same rate as the ultrasonic pulses used to cut the stone. As a sympathetic partner, quartz therefore offers less resistance. In the words of Dunn: 'Instead of resisting the cutting action, as it would when using conventional methods, the quartz would be induced to respond and vibrate in sympathy with the high-frequency waves and amplify the abrasive action as the tool cut through it.'[51]

No other drilling method accounts for all of the features found in the granite cores examined by Petrie. Yet to suggest that the pyramid builders used ultrasound to aid jewel-tipped drills to penetrate hard rock is totally inconceivable to any open-minded individual, never mind a scholar or student of Egyptology. The evidence, however, was clear for all to see, alongside the telltale signs suggesting the presence in Ancient Egypt of straight and circular saws bearing diamond-like cutting points and mechanical lathes; all this in a world that orthodox historians tell us did not even possess the wheel. Most striking of all is the fact that such advanced technology has been invented only in the past 200 years, much of it only in the last 50 years. Petrie could not find a solution to the puzzling clues left in the granite cores and boreholes by tubular drills – it has taken a late-twentieth-century technologist to understand them. How much more are we going to establish about the Ancient Egyptians as further advances are made in this field?

Not only must we force ourselves to drastically revise our understanding of Egyptian technology, but the knowledge that sound played a key role in stoneware manufacture begins to make sense of the suggestion by Mas'ūdi that the pyramid builders, and plausibly even the Sphinx-building Elder culture, utilised sound vibration to levitate and transport large blocks of stone. Drilling holes in granite is one thing, but can sound *really* be used to build walls? Could it be possible that sound once possessed an importance little understood even today? Egypt itself could offer me no further evidence to indicate that our most distant ancestors possessed a form of sound technology alien to our current way of thinking.

Christopher Dunn's findings were ground-breaking, persuasive and plausible, and in many ways he has simply confirmed the extraordinarily high level of sophistication attained by the pyramid builders, whose own legacy shows a command of geodesy, geography, mathematics, metrology and science the world still strives to understand. Yet as I was soon to realise, legends of sound being used to transport building-blocks and to build walls were not confined to Egypt. Such stories could be found not just in antiquity but also among a near-contemporary culture who would appear to have preserved a profound understanding of sonic technology through to the current century.

CHAPTER FIVE

TO THE SOUND OF A TRUMPET

All around the world there are folk-memories that record a time in the past when the founders of civilisation used the power of sound to erect the first cities. Of these, nowhere is more mysterious than the ruins of Tiahuanaco, a great citadel in the Bolivian Altiplano that once lay on the edge of the immense inland sea named Lake Titicaca, and yet, due to severe geological and climatic changes in the region, now lies an incredible 19 kilometres (12 miles) away from its shoreline.

Scattered over a wide area are a series of megalithic structures, mostly temples, as well as many carved monoliths and fallen building-blocks regularly 100 tonnes apiece. Before being reconstructed in modern times, much of what remained of Tiahuanaco was in a recumbent position, as if knocked down by an invisible hand of immense destructive power. In truth, its end was most probably caused by a series of natural disasters that included earthquakes and flooding[1] – events that would also seem to have thrust Lake Titicaca upwards from sea-level to its present position over three kilometres (two miles) above sea-level.[2] Dating the ancient city has proved controversial. It is old, very old. How old no one really knows, although in 1911 a detailed survey conducted by respected archaeologist Professor Arthur Posnansky of La Paz University gave it a foundation date of around 15,000 BC and a date of destruction some time around 10,000 BC, plausibly during the global catastrophes that accompanied the end of the last Ice Age.[3] Other noted scholars then confirmed the immense antiquity of Tiahuanaco,[4] even though conventional archaeologists and historians generally date the site only to AD 700.[5]

The centrepiece in the Tiahuanaco ruins is the Gateway of the Sun, a huge archway of stone weighing around 10 tonnes. Carved on its face in high relief is a male figure holding long staffs. He is Tiahuanaco's legendary founder, Ticci Viracocha, or Thunupa, who emerged from an island in the centre of Lake Titicaca at the beginning of time, and with his followers, known collectively as 'the Viracocha', founded the city of Tiahuanaco before moving north, spreading civilisation wherever they went.[6]

Viracocha, the wisdom-bringer of the pre-Incan peoples, from the so-called calendar frieze on the Gateway of the Sun at Tiahuanaco.

One story told by the local Aymara Indians to a Spanish traveller who visited Tiahuanaco shortly after the conquest spoke of the city's original foundation in the age of *Chamac Pacha*, or First Creation, long before the coming of the Incas. Its earliest inhabitants, they said, possessed supernatural powers, for they were able miraculously to lift stones off the ground, which '. . . were carried [from the mountain quarries] through the air to the sound of a trumpet'.[7]

Bolivia is on the opposite side of the globe to Egypt, and yet here was evidence to suggest that the ancient peoples of the Americas also had an understanding of sound beyond our current comprehension. Where do such myths come from if not based on any kind of historical reality? Might these quite separate traditions be linked in some way? Both Tiahuanaco and Giza have been allotted foundation dates before the end of the last Ice Age, *c.* 15,000–10,000 BC, so was it possible that sonic technology was exported to different parts of the world by a hitherto unknown global culture?

The Aymara Indians of Bolivia and Peru also told the earliest Hispanic travellers and historians that Viracocha was not simply a civiliser and a miracle-worker but also a scientist, a sculptor, an agronomist and an engineer, who 'caused terraces and fields to be formed on the steep sides of ravines, and sustaining walls to rise up and support them'.[8] Yet unlike them, Ticci Viracocha was pale-skinned, blue-eyed, of large stature with fair or white hair and a beard.[9] He would wear a long white tunic with a belt around the waist and was said to have had an 'authoritative demeanour'.[10] Time and time again this is how South America's great wisdom-bringer was portrayed in folklore and legends, emphasising his quite obviously Caucasian appearance. Strange, then, that it was he himself who was accredited with the ability of being able to move stone blocks in mysterious ways. One account speaks of him first creating a heavenly 'fire', which 'was extinguished at his command, though the stones were consumed by fire in such wise that large blocks could be lifted by hand as if they were cork'.[11] Who exactly were the white-skinned Viracocha, and why were they attributed with the ability to be able to move stone blocks by supernatural means alone?

GIVE A LITTLE WHISTLE

Moving northwards into Mexico's Yucatán Peninsula, we find, hidden among the dense jungle landscape, the ancient temples of the Maya, a pre-Columbian civilisation of incredible sophistication and culture. Their extraordinary empire flourished during the first millennium of the Christian era, although it is clear that they inherited their profound knowledge of civilisation from a much earlier culture. The Maya were obsessed beyond belief with not only the cycles of heaven and the movement of the stars but also the passage of time. Their complex Long Count calendar system, for instance, could accurately compute dates hundreds of millions of years ago, stating correctly the exact day and month on which they fell.[12]

One of the most mysterious temple complexes left behind by the Maya is that of Uxmal, which legend asserts was founded originally by a race of dwarfs.[13] More curious, however, is the additional information given about these mythical dwarfs in one Mayan legend, which asserts: 'Construction work was easy for them, all they had to do was whistle and heavy rocks would move into place.'[14] These powerful dwarfs were said to have been responsible for all the earliest foundations at the time of the First Creation, whereby they 'needed only to whistle to bring together stones in their correct positions in buildings or to cause firewood to come from the bush to the hearth by itself'.[15] Despite their apparent supernatural powers, the dwarfs were said to have been destroyed in an all-encompassing flood, even though many of their number had attempted to hide underground in 'great stone tanks like the underground storage reservoirs [which they saw] as boats'.[16]

Here, once again, were abstract, and perhaps confused, stories concerning an antediluvian race that could use the power of sound to construct walls of stone. Such fables are dismissed easily as fantasies of the ignorant, and yet the indigenous peoples of Egypt and the

Americas were not alone in featuring sound in the construction of their most ancient monuments.

BUILT TO THE SOUND OF A LYRE

According to classical Greek writers, Thebes, the capital of Boeotia – an ancient kingdom located north-west of Athens – was founded by Cadmus, a celebrated Phoenician traveller and wisdom-bringer.[17] Known as *Cadmeia* in honour of its founder, this great city was said to have been finished by a son of Jupiter named Amphion. More curiously, it was said of Amphion that he could move large stones to the sound of a lyre, or harp, by which manner he was able to construct the walls of Thebes.[18] In his multi-volume work *Description of Greece*, Pausanias, a Greek geographer of the second century, spoke of Amphion building the city's walls 'to the music of his harp', while his 'songs drew even stones and beasts after him'.[19] Apollonius Rhodius, who lived in the third century BC, poetically recalled in *The Argonautica* how Amphion would sing 'loud and clear on his golden lyre' as 'rock twice as large followed his footsteps'.[20]

Were these stories mere fable, based purely on much earlier literary exaggerations and fabrications, or were they in some way a distorted memory of a time when the first inhabitants of Thebes, united under a founder figure named Amphion, were able to use the song of the lyre to move blocks of stone and erect walls?

It seems incredible, but if such traditions really were based on distorted memories of actual events, then they could well encode important information concerning the origins of this lost technology. The traditions surrounding Cadmus clearly indicate that Thebes was founded by Phoenician migrants who must have settled here in the third or second millennium BC. Cadmus, it is said, introduced Boeotia to both the Phoenician alphabet and the worship of Phoenician and Egyptian deities, so perhaps any knowledge of sonic technology was brought with him from his homeland.[21]

Phoenicia was the great seafaring nation that sprang up in around 2800 BC in the Mediterranean coastal region known as the Levant, which embraces what is today Lebanon and north-west Syria. As a culture it consisted of a series of city-states with their own rulers, cultures and affiliations, and united only in terms of trade, religion and seafaring capabilities. The Phoenicians were the ancient world's greatest mariners. Yet despite this befitting accolade, they themselves spoke of an earlier race of gods from whom they attained their maritime knowledge.

DEVISING BAETULIA

Like classical mythology, Phoenician legend speaks of a golden age before recorded history when gods and men walked hand in hand. The subject is dealt with in the writings of Sanchoniatho, Phoenicia's oldest known historian, who lived just prior to the Trojan wars, *c.* 1200 BC.[22] He spoke of the god Ouranus, or Coelus, founding the first city at a place called Byblos,[23] which even to this day is still a thriving Lebanese port. From here the godly race colonised the entire eastern Mediterranean seaboard. Sanchoniatho even informs us that one of the gods, named Taautus (the Egyptian Thoth, who was the inventor of writing), founded the Egyptian civilisation.[24]

With all this in mind, I was intrigued to find that Sanchoniatho's writings contain a rather ambiguous reference to stone levitation. Without any due explanation, the Phoenician historian states that Ouranus 'devised *Baetulia*, contriving stones that moved as having life'.[25]

The word *Baetulia* in this respect refers to 'rude', or large, uncut stones of a cyclopean nature. By 'contriving', the nineteenth-century English translator of Sanchoniatho's original Phoenician text, preserved in Greek by one Philo of Byblos who lived in the first century AD, seems to have meant 'designing', 'devising' or 'inventing', implying that Ouranus made stones move as if they had a life of their own.

Might the pre-Phoenician culture of Byblos, portrayed by Sanchoniatho as a race of gods, have possessed the ability to raise blocks of stone using the power of sound? Could they have passed on this knowledge to their Phoenician descendants, who in turn carried it into Boeotia at the time of Cadmus and Amphion? And if this is correct, then where might this understanding of sonic technology have come from?

Both the Phoenicians and their Greek contemporaries, the Mycenaeans, employed the use of cyclopean masonry in their architecture. Delphi, Mycenae and Tiryns were all built originally using huge stone blocks of immense size and weight. A nineteenth-century drawing of a gigantic stone wall belonging to the now vanished Phoenician island city-state of Aradus, located off the Syrian coast, shows massive stone blocks, some as large as 3 metres in length and weighing as much as 15 to 20 tonnes apiece (see illustration opposite). Needless to say, there is a distinct similarity between these cyclopean structures and those to be seen on the Giza plateau of Egypt. We also know that as early as *c.* 4500 BC the pre-Phoenician culture would seem to have navigated not only the Mediterranean Sea but also the Atlantic coast beyond the Strait of Gibraltar.[26] Is it possible that this previously unknown seafaring nation somehow inherited the use of sound technology from an even earlier culture, conceivably the Elder gods of Egypt?

Byblos is known to have possessed a thriving township as early as *c.* 4500 BC,[27] and by *c.* 3000 BC it was a seafaring culture trading with places such as Crete and Egypt.[28] Indeed, scholars are open to the idea that Byblos was instrumental in the rise of Pharaonic Egypt.[29] Is it possible therefore that one culture inherited its apparent understanding of sound technology from the other? If so, then which way around might this have been? There is no clear solution to this problem, not at the moment at least. It is, however, worth recalling that it was in around 3500 BC that Egypt began its unbelievable stone-carving industry which, as I have

Nineteenth-century sketch showing the remains of a cyclopean wall at the
site of the ancient Phoenician city of Aradus, off the Levant coast.

already demonstrated, would appear to have included high-tech
power tools such as straight and circular saws, mechanical lathes
and ultrasonic drills.[30]

For the moment it is sufficient to know that traditions connecting sound with building construction are universal and not confined
to any one particular race, culture, creed or continent. Even so, the
sceptic is going to say that all such legends are simply born out of
idle superstition. What's more, even if they were 'real', then they tell
us next to nothing about the methods that might have been
employed in the achievement of sound levitation during ancient
times.

What I needed were more reliable accounts of sonic technology,
and after a considerable amount of archive research I found exactly
what I was looking for – hardcore evidence of sonic technology
having been witnessed by two separate Western travellers in Tibet
during the first half of the twentieth century, both stories being
recorded in the 1950s by Swedish engineer and writer Henry
Kjellson.[31]

THE STRANGE CASE OF DR JARL

The first case concerns a Swedish doctor, whom Kjellson refers to only as 'Jarl', his full name being withheld. During either the 1920s or 1930s – an exact date is not given – Jarl accepted an invitation from a Tibetan friend to visit him at his monastery, which was situated south-west of the capital Lhasa.[32] It was while on sabbatical here that Jarl allegedly witnessed stone blocks, 1.5 metres in length and 1 metre in height and width, being levitated high into the air through the process of sound.[33] These events were said to have taken place in a nearby meadow, which sloped slightly uphill towards north-west-facing cliffs.

Jarl had noticed that around 250 metres up the rocky face there was an opening to a large cave, in front of which was a wide ledge, accessible only by descending ropes hung from the top of the ridge. Here monks were busily constructing a wall of stone. He also noticed that, at an estimated distance of 250 metres from the base of the cliffs, a large flat stone had been embedded in the ground.[34] Its upper surface contained a large bowl-shaped depression 15 centimetres deep. Around 63 metres further back from the embedded stone, a large group of yellow-robed monks seemed to be busily making final preparations for some kind of coordinated operation. Some were tending enormous drums, others supported long trumpets, many more were forming themselves into lines, while one monk used a knotted rope to mark out accurately where everyone and everything should be placed. Jarl counted 13 drums and 6 trumpets – each instrument being positioned approximately 5 degrees apart to form an arc of just over 90 degrees centred on the bowl-stone.[35] Behind each instrument was a line of monks eight to ten deep, making the whole formation appear like a quarter-segment of a huge spoked wheel.[36]

In the middle of the arc was a single monk holding a small drum, supported at waist height by a leather sling worn around his neck.[37] To either side of him were other monks tending medium-sized drums.[38] These were hung from a wooden frame by leather slings affixed to a pair of sticks, inserted sideways through their interiors, which acted as directional levers.

On either side of these two drums were further monks tending enormous three-metre-long trumpets known as *ragdons*. Beyond these, on either side, were a further pair of medium-sized drums, then a pair of even larger drums also hung beneath wooden frames by leather slings attached to protruding sticks.[39]

Completing the veritable orchestra were, progressing symmetrically outwards on either side, two more *ragdon*-trumpets, another four large drums (two on each side), another two trumpets and, lastly, two final large drums (see illustration below). All 13 drums had a skin covering at one end only, the remaining 'open' end being pointed towards the bowl-stone.[40]

Jarl then watched as the first stone block was dragged on a wooden sleigh pulled by yak up to the bowl-stone. Monks quickly manhandled the heavy weight on to the depression before retiring to allow the proceedings to begin.

All 19 instruments were pointed like cannons towards the stone

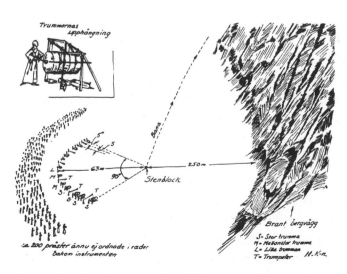

Dr Jarl's detailed sketch showing how Tibetan monks were able to raise stone blocks into the air using the power of sound alone.

block, and, when everything and everybody was in position, the monk with the small drum started chanting rhythmically in a low monotone voice as he began beating the instrument's covered end with one hand. It emitted a harsh, sharp sound that hurt Jarl's ears.[41] In response, the *ragdon*-trumpets were sounded as the rest of the drums were struck with huge clubs 75 centimetres long,[42] their heads covered with leather. Each drum was attended by two monks, who would take turns to beat it. Other than the monk with the small drum, no one spoke a word.

As the strange cacophony progressed, Jarl attempted mentally to record the drum sequence. It began very slowly, but then speeded up so fast that he quickly lost track of the rhythm, which blended to become a solid wall of sound. Unbelievably, the harsh noise made by the little drum managed to penetrate the combined sound produced by the trumpets and drums. This led him to conclude that it was being used to mark time.

Some four minutes passed before anything unusual took place.[43] Then, quite suddenly, the stone block began to wobble slightly, as if gaining partial weightlessness. Finally, it lifted into the air, rocking from side to side.[44] It then rose upwards as the trumpets and drums were tilted accordingly.[45] The stone climbed higher and higher, accelerating in speed and making what Jarl referred to as a 'parabolic arc' as it headed slowly towards the cave mouth.[46] Eventually, with the monks still sounding the trumpets and beating the drums, the building-block reached its final destination before rapidly crashing on to the ledge. It hit the stone platform with such force that it sent dust and gravel flying everywhere and caused an almighty clamour that momentarily echoed across the cliff-face.

All then suddenly went quiet. On casting his eyes back to the assembled party of some 240 monks, Jarl saw that none of them seemed at all moved by the experience. Indeed, they were readying themselves for a repeat performance. Another stone block was quickly brought up to the bowl-stone and, as before, it was man-handled on to the smooth indentation. The whole musical cacophony was then resumed, starting, as before, with the small drum. For some hours Jarl watched as between five and six blocks an hour were transported in this manner.[47] Once in a while a stone would crash on to the platform so hard that it would explode into pieces. When this occurred the monks working in the cave mouth would simply push the fragments over the cliff edge so that they crashed down on to the rocks below.[48]

Jarl admitted that he failed to establish why the 200 or so monks had stood in rows 8 to 10 deep behind the arc of 19 instruments. They made no sound and merely watched the flight-path of the stone blocks as they curved towards the cliff-face. He suggested that they could have been trainees watching the proceedings, or replacements, perhaps, for the monks beating the drums and sounding the trumpets. On the other hand they could have been there, he concluded, either to give the whole show a more religious feel or, more controversially, they had used a form of coordinated psychokinesis, or mind over matter, to aid the flight of the stone.

The most revealing aspect of Jarl's account is the meticulous detail with which he recorded the proceedings in the meadow that day. He wrote down every distance, every angle and every measurement, and even recorded obscure points such as the fact that the large drums consisted of three-millimetre plates in five sections, with approximately seven-millimetre-thick joints holding them together. There is too much information included in this account, preserved by Henry Kjellson, to dismiss it simply as pure fantasy.

The choice of instruments, the specific distances and angles involved, the placing of the stone blocks on a bowl-shaped stone at ground-level, along with the gradual build-up of percussive sounds, all add up to an exact science, a sonic technology, understood by the monastic community visited by Jarl. One of the most poignant statements he makes is in respect of the manner in which all 19 instruments were trained constantly on the target stone, right until it reached its point of destination.

If sound *was* used by Tibetan monastic communities to levitate stone blocks great heights, then how was this possible? What are we to make of the 200 or so monks who stood in lines behind the 19 instruments? What was their purpose? Was it really to attain some form of mass psychokinesis, as Jarl seemed to believe? We cannot say. However, it *is* known that the concept of using the power of the mind to move rocks once formed part of the strict meditational practice known as *dzogchen*, a hidden teaching passed on orally both by the followers of Tibetan lamaism and by shamanic individuals belonging to the pre-Buddhist religion known as Bönpo.[49]

SINGING OUT IN SILENCE

Jarl's account is tantalising evidence of a type of sonic technology now lost to the world. On its own it can be little more than this, but thankfully it was not the only example preserved by Kjellson. In 1939 the Swedish engineer and writer attended a lecture given by an Austrian film-maker named 'Linauer' concerning *his* travels in Tibet. Kjellson was able later to speak to him at length about his claims, and, having obviously satisfied himself as to their authenticity, included them in his book *Försvunnen teknik* ('Disappeared Technology'), first published in 1961. What Linauer supposedly witnessed seems to confirm Jarl's account and also throws new light on what we know about the pyramid builders' apparent ultrasonic capabilities.

Linauer claimed that while at a remote monastery in northern Tibet during the 1930s, he was privileged to witness some very remarkable feats. They included the demonstration of two curious sound instruments which, when used in concert, could defy the laws of nature adhered to so strictly by orthodox science.

The first of these instruments was an extremely large gong mounted vertically in a wooden frame. At 3.5 metres in diameter, it was composed of three separate metals. At its centre was a circular section of solid gold, while around the outside of this was a concentric ring of pure iron. Encircling these two metals was a further ring of extremely hard brass which apparently possessed a certain amount of elasticity.[50] In contrast, the central area of gold was said to have been so soft that it could be marked with a fingernail.[51] In many respects the gong's appearance was not unlike a huge metal target-board. The sound it made when struck was entirely unlike that normally associated with such instruments, for instead of emitting a powerful, sustained note it produced an extremely low *dumph* which ceased almost immediately.[52]

The second instrument was also composed of three different metals, although Linauer was unable to determine their exact identity. It was estimated to have been two metres in length and one metre wide (a depth is not given by Kjellson), while its shape was described as similar to that of a mussel shell, or half-oval.[53] Strings were stretched longitudinally over its hollow surface, and it was supported by a frame that held it fixed in a slightly raised position. Linauer was told by the monks that this curious string instrument was neither played nor touched but simply sang in silence, in that it would emit, in Kjellson's words, an 'inaudible resonance wave' only when the gong was struck to produce its characteristic sound.[54] Used in conjunction with these curious instruments was a pair of large screens that were positioned carefully so as to form a triangular configuration with the two devices. The purpose of the screens would appear to have been to catch, contain and deflect the 'inaudible resonance wave' made by the mussel instrument.

When it came to a practical demonstration, a monk wielding a large club would approach the gong and begin striking it to produce a series of brief, low-frequency sounds that must have had a peculiar effect on the aural senses. With this, the mussel instrument would begin emitting what I can only assume was a range of ultrasonics which, when contained and directed, would induce temporary weightlessness in stone blocks.[55] At such times a monk could lift one of these stones with just one hand. Linauer was informed that this was how their ancestors had been able to build walls of protection around the whole of Tibet. He was also told by the monks (although he did not witness it for himself) that these and other, similar devices could be used to *disintegrate* or *dissolve* physical matter.[56]

Linauer's invaluable account seems to add considerable weight to the belief that isolated monastic communities in remotest Tibet were able to use sound to achieve weightlessness in stone. If we can accept such stories as genuine, then it is surely further evidence to suggest that the archaic legends from Egypt, Bolivia, Mexico and classical Greece, which tell of stone walls, temples and even cities being constructed using instruments of sound, really were based on some kind of distorted truth. Moreover, Linauer's account of an 'inaudible resonance wave' being used to 'dissolve materials' supports Christopher Dunn's findings in respect to the pyramid builders' apparent use of ultrasonics to bore holes through granite.

There seems to be no clear indication why the isolated religious communities of Tibet should have been practising selective forms of sonic technology as late as the first half of the twentieth century. It is possible that they inherited these ideas from some earlier, pre-Buddhist culture, such as the followers of Bönpo, the native shamanic religion that heavily influenced the ritual practices of Tibetan lamaism. On the other hand it is equally possible that, devoid of any real exposure to the outside world, the monastic schools developed these unique scientific skills completely on their own. Perhaps their profound understanding of the universal laws enabled them to discover a means by which they could control the natural forces in a manner completely at variance with our own world view of science.

For the religious peoples of Tibet, Newton's laws of gravity and Einstein's laws of relativity simply did not exist and so could not stand in the way of progress. Yet if we accept this possibility, then we must also imagine that Egypt's Elder culture possessed a very similar approach to life and so was able to develop an understanding of the universal laws far beyond the imagination of the modern scientific world. If this is so, then we must also conclude that it is only our rigid, and very dogmatic, approach to life that holds us back from developing technologies that are not restricted by the barriers of orthodox science.

THE GREATEST LOSS

Acknowledging that Tibetan lamaism may well have developed, or indeed inherited, an advanced knowledge of sonic technology begs the question of why knowledge of its existence never filtered through to the Western world. There is a strange irony in the probable answer to this perplexing question. After Linauer was shown the extraordinary properties of the great gong and the strange mussel-shaped instrument, the monks told him that they had carefully guarded the secrets of their technology to ensure that they did not lose it to the outside world. Foreign travellers were never normally permitted to witness these incredible instruments in operation. The monks further stated that the reason for such safeguards was because they knew very well that once knowledge of this ancient power reached the West it would be exploited for selfish and very destructive purposes, and this could not be allowed to happen.[57] Such a decision by the practitioners of lamaism is entirely understandable; however, it has meant that the testimonies offered by Western travellers, such as Jarl and Linauer, are our only insight into these people's ancient ways. Furthermore, the destruction of Tibetan lamaism at the hands of the Chinese Cultural Revolution during the 1950s has robbed the scientific world of its best possible hope of confirming that sonic technology *was* still being practised as late as the 1930s. Despite Chinese propaganda claims to the contrary, the occupation of Tibet is as brutal today as it has ever been.

Many exiled Tibetans are quite aware of the amazing stories that speak of a time when their forebears had the power to levitate stone blocks and disintegrate rock using sound alone. Such defiance of the natural laws is now little more than a fast-fading memory in the minds of elderly monks and lamas. To know that these profound ancient sciences were preserved across millennia only to be lost within our own modern era is a sad loss indeed. To read Jarl's and Linauer's accounts of witnessing sonic technology in Tibet and then realise that not even the monasteries exist today is tragic in the extreme.

Had the flame of knowledge been extinguished completely? Was there any way of rekindling it by reconstructing the physics behind this apparently lost science known to the ancient world? I intended to find out by whatever means possible.

CHAPTER SIX

CREATING SONIC PLATFORMS

Few people can be unaware of the story about the opera singer who was able to shatter wineglasses simply by attaining a specific note with her voice. The reason why such tricks are possible is that the vocal cords are able to produce sounds that match and, if sustained, exaggerate the inherent vibrational frequency of the glass. This has the effect of causing it to oscillate or shake so violently that eventually it disintegrates.

It is a similar story when panes of glass vibrate as a truck, or a low-flying aircraft, is heard to pass by. The sound-waves produced by their engine, or engines, move through the air and, on reaching the pane of glass, synchronise with its inherent vibrational qualities, causing it to *resonate* in sympathy. Not every aircraft or truck engine will have this effect; only those with engines that match the resonant frequency, or frequency range, of the window, and this can depend on many factors, such as its size, shape, type or position. Just think of the way in which a tuning fork, when tapped and brought up close to another tuning fork of the same length, will induce the latter to hum in sympathy – this is called sympathetic vibration. Bring the same tuning fork up to a second fork with slightly different-sized prongs (and therefore with a different resonant frequency) and the second one will not respond at all.

Sympathetic vibration is completely understood by modern science; indeed, it is this very process that enables ultrasonic drills to cut so easily through quartz. Other minerals do not respond to ultrasonics in quite the same way and so are much more difficult to drill using this process.

The Ancients would appear to have utilised the concept of sympathetic vibration to create sonic processes little understood by the modern world. We can only speculate on how this might have been achieved, although I think it is safe to assume that it involved establishing the resonant frequency of any object they intended to move. Once this was determined, a sustained sequence of sounds would presumably have been directed towards the object, either by playing musical instruments or by using the human voice. To this base chord it is likely that they would have added a sequence of harmonics – sounds based on proportionate fractions of the original note.

To establish an object's natural resonance, the Ancients would probably have used either calculations based purely on audible sounds heard by the human ear or a predetermined knowledge of the resonant sound the object might be expected to make if manufactured to a certain size, shape and pattern. This information could then be matched against the chords produced by different instruments until the object's exact frequency was determined. Provided that the chosen harmonics were pitched so that they did not cancel each other out, this process would have had the effect of creating a wall of sound, a kind of sonic platform, that would have greatly enhanced the oscillations or vibrations achieved within the target object. In turn, this would have caused the air particles around its surface to vibrate in a like manner, creating a kind of cushion effect that might also provide a means to counteract the effects of gravity. All this is, of course, pure speculation and does not explain how the Ancients were able to levitate stone blocks so easily.

IN PERFECT HARMONY

The resonance of an object, or indeed that of a room or building, is defined by a number of quite different factors, such as size, mass, rigidity and symmetry. Together these can greatly affect the quality, tone and availability of sympathetic vibration, something that architects of sacred buildings have been acutely aware of for thousands of years. One of the prime motives in the design of Gothic cathedrals in medieval Europe was to establish a structural resonance in perfect harmony with the human voice. Recent studies in the United Kingdom have indicated that this was also the intention of the Iron Age designers of the mysterious subterranean chambers known as *fogous* found in Cornwall. These have been determined to resonate sound frequencies that match the pitch produced by male vocal cords.[1] The ultimate origin or purpose of this practice is unknown, although the many legends that connect the origins of stone and earthen monuments with music and dance would seem to indicate an original ceremonial function featuring both of these components.[2]

There seems little doubt that music and sound have played a major part in the design of sacred buildings all over the world, and this has especially been so in Egypt, where a profound understanding of sound acoustics is easily detected. Take, for instance, the King's Chamber in the Great Pyramid. A voice sounded in here will resonate in a most extraordinary manner, leading to the conclusion that this effect was created with a specific purpose in mind. Such an assumption might help explain why the pyramid builders incorporated 'Pythagorean' triangles into the chamber's overall design. This particular geometric shape, not officially discovered until the age of Pythagoras some 2000 years later, is known to produce the three most important harmonic proportions, which when brought together produce a fundamental note, or keynote, seen in the combination of the notes D, G and E to produce the keynote C.

Why incorporate such fundamental harmonics into a chamber

built, according to conventional Egyptologists, merely as a tomb for a deceased Pharaoh? The answer, they would say, is simple – it is all just coincidence, without any form of hidden meaning. In which case we must now move on to another example of perfect harmonics in the Great Pyramid – the lidless, dark granite sarcophagus that sits at one end of the King's Chamber. Whether or not this huge coffer once held the mummified body of a deceased king, it has long been known to possess acoustic properties of remarkable quality. It was Petrie who first noted this fact during his meticulous survey of the Great Pyramid in 1881. Having already established that the sarcophagus was fashioned using jewel-tipped tubular drills and 2.7-metre-long saws, Petrie made the decision to raise up the coffer in an attempt to establish its exact size. He also wanted to find out whether it might conceal the entrance into a hidden chamber, a suggestion made by some of his contemporaries.

Movement of the sarcophagus required the help of several *fellahin*, who eventually were able to tilt the enormous rectangular piece of granite a full 20 centimetres off the ground. No opening was discovered beneath it, and once its exact measurements had been taken Petrie struck the empty box. It is said to have 'produced a deep bell-like sound of extraordinary, eerie beauty'.[3] As I have already pointed out, the internal volume of the coffer is precisely one half of that defined by its exterior dimensions, demonstrating the great lengths to which its manufacturers must have gone to achieve the best harmonic resonance. Is this all simply coincidence, or is it, as seems far more likely, that the pyramid builders saw an acute relationship between their own world and that of acoustics?

THUMPING AND A HUMMING

If we now leave the Giza plateau and travel south along the course of the Nile to the seemingly never-ending temple complex at Karnak, we find further evidence of the Ancient Egyptians' profound knowledge of acoustics. Here, among the magnificent ruins, adorned from top to tail in beautifully executed friezes, there are three enormous obelisks made of the finest pink granite extracted from the famous quarries at Aswan, 186 kilometres (116 miles) upriver. Two still stand, one dating to the reign of the Eighteenth-Dynasty king Thutmose I (*c.* 1528–1510 BC) and the other erected during the reign of his daughter Hatshepsut (*c.* 1490–1468 BC). A third obelisk, which lies in a horizontal position nearby, was also raised during the reign of this much-celebrated queen. Although only the upper 9 metres of the fallen monolith remain today, it originally weighed a staggering 320 tonnes and, like its neighbour, stood a mighty 29.6 metres in height.[4]

These colossal obelisks are of a standard size and design for this period of Egyptian history. Their exact purpose is still unclear. They might simply have been commemorative monuments to the Pharaohs in question. On the other hand they may well have served a more functional purpose, as sundials perhaps, used by astronomer-priests to calculate celestial events in the yearly calendar. They might even have been physical representations of the so-called *djed*-pillar, the backbone of the world, which, according to Ancient Egyptian myth, stood on the primeval mound of creation at the beginning of time.[5] Whatever their outward function, their curiously offset horizontal dimensions are thought to embody specific geodetic data preserving the precise latitude and longitude of their place of erection.[6]

It is, however, the broken obelisk of Hatshepsut that is of interest to this debate. Until fairly recently the chances are that, on approaching it, a well-meaning, though possibly costly, Egyptian guide would appear out of nowhere and insist that you repeatedly thump the apex of its perfectly carved and highly polished pyramidion. On carrying out this simple ritual, the whole 70 or so tonnes of obelisk would, with the greatest of ease, start to emit an extremely low drone, almost as if somebody has plugged it into an electrical socket. This curious sound would continue for anything up to 30 seconds before gradually fading away to nothing.[7]

In spite of it being just a third of its original size, Karnak's fallen granite obelisk can be made to give up its resonant frequency, like some giant prong of an enormous tuning fork. If these obelisks were purely commemorative monuments, then why bother to incorporate into their design such a profound knowledge of sound acoustics? Chance does not seem to be a factor here. The builders of the Eighteenth Dynasty would appear to have preserved an ancient art that may well have been linked with the concept of sonic technology.

I am not suggesting that the great obelisks of Egypt were transported or raised into position using sonic platforms, for there is ample evidence to demonstrate that more conventional means were used to transport them from the granite quarries of Aswan to their various points of destination. What I am suggesting is that the knowledge of harmonic proportion originated during a much earlier age when it was utilised for more fantastic purposes, such as the movement of enormous building-blocks and the drilling of holes through hard rock. If such speculation should prove to be correct, then the indications are that this ancient wisdom was part of a legacy passed on to dynastic Egypt by the descendants of the Sphinx-building Elder gods, the elite ruling class of predynastic times spoken of so strongly by the likes of pioneering Egyptologists such as Petrie and Emery.

Are we really to believe that the cyclopean stone blocks used in the construction of monuments such as the Great Pyramid and the Valley Temple were transported into position using sound alone? Their individual measurements vary so much that it would now be impossible to answer this question with any degree of certainty. As we have seen, a profound knowledge of sound harmonics does exist in the design of the Great Pyramid, as well as in the Egyptian obelisks, so it is strongly possible that this goes some way to support Mas'ūdi's claim that sound vibration really was used during the age of the pyramid builders.

In my own opinion, it seems reasonable to suppose that sonic technology was merely an *option* alongside other, more conventional means of moving and positioning huge stone blocks of the sort incorporated so commonly into the architecture of the Giza plateau.

It has always been said that given enough manpower, anything can be achieved, and this is fundamentally correct. As the Egyptian civilisation grew gradually into a huge empire of enormous might and influence, labour would have become far more plentiful. Not only was the Egyptian population increasing, but the many thousands of prisoners of war would have made it that much easier to erect great stone monuments such as the great temple at Karnak. The old ways would have been neglected and finally abandoned, their presence being found less and less in new buildings as the centuries rolled by. In the end, any remaining memory of sound technology would have served a purely symbolic or mythological purpose – the expression perhaps of an inner priesthood that kept alive this ancient wisdom in their initiations, rituals and teachings. Perhaps it was for these reasons alone that the sacred obelisks retained an understanding of harmonic proportion in their overall design.

ACOUSTIC ENTERTAINMENT

What does this new understanding of the relationship between sound and architecture in Ancient Egypt tell us about the legends of sonic technology in other parts of the world? Did the civilisations remembered as having erected walls and cities using the power of sound once possess a similar knowledge of sympathetic vibration and harmonic proportion? Amphion's city of Thebes no longer exists, so little can be said in this respect; however, the sound acoustics of the Mayan temples of the Yucatán are singled out as among the strangest in the world. Top of the list of sites noted for its peculiarities in this respect is the huge temple complex of Chichén Itzá. Its stepped pyramid, known as the Castillo, is noted for its similarity to Djoser's pyramid at Saqqara and for the unique lighting effects incorporated into its design. At the two equinoxes a series of shadow triangles is cast on the northern stairway that ends at the base in serpents' heads. The triangles undulate with the movement of the sun like a snake ascending at the spring equinox and descending at the autumn equinox.

Turning to the Castillo's apparent acoustic anomalies, researched extensively by Wayne Van Kirk of the World Forum for Acoustic Ecology,[8] we find that if a person stands at the base of the Castillo and shouts, the sound will echo as a shriek that comes from the top of the structure. If someone stands on the top of the pyramid and speaks in a normal voice, he or she can be heard clearly on the ground at a distance of 150 metres away. There are no fast explanations for these acoustic properties, and it does not seem that they were created purely by chance alone.

Near the Castillo is the Great Ball Court, which consists of two temples at each end of a huge field, 160 metres in length and 68.6 metres in width. Other structures stand like terraces set within the east and west perimeter walls. A soft whisper at one end can be heard easily at the other end.[9] If you then stand within a circle of stones positioned at a certain spot inside the Great Ball Court, you can have a perfect conversation with a person who stands in a similar circle of stones some 60 metres distance 'as if they were a few feet away'.[10] So popular did the Great Ball Court's weird acoustics become that, during the 1930s, the archaeologist Sylvanus G. Morley impressed guests on moonlit nights by setting up a phonograph in the North Temple and playing Sibelius, Brahms and Beethoven to a spellbound audience who would sit on supplied cushions within the South Temple over 150 metres away.[11] It would seem as if the gods themselves were providing this feast of acoustic entertainment.

Moving away from Chichén Itzá to a Mayan site on the Yucatán coast named Tulum, we find that when the wind is exactly at the right velocity and direction, its temple emits 'a long-range whistle or howl'. A local guide explained that this curious sound acted as an early warning of 'incoming hurricanes and big storms'.[12] At Palenque, another famous Mayan site, we are told that if three people stand one each on the top of its group of three pyramids a three-way conversation can easily be held.[13] Lastly, and perhaps most tellingly, is the knowledge that if a person stands at the base of the pyramid-like

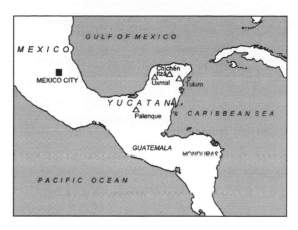

Map of Mexico showing principal Mayan sites featured in this book.

Temple of the Magician at Uxmal and claps his or her hands the stone structure at its top produces an inexplicable chirping sound.[14] This building, as we have already seen, was said to have been built by a race of dwarfs who could just whistle and stones and logs would rise into the air.

None of these unique acoustic effects appears to be simply coincidence. It seems clear that they were purposely incorporated into the design of the buildings under question, and yet despite this their exact cause remains uncertain. One theory suggests that in the case of the Great Ball Court at Chichén Itzá, the strange sound effects could be caused by 'the gaps which are part of the surface of the temple's exterior walls'.[15] Yet in all honesty the experts have no idea what produces these unique acoustic properties. As one Mayan scholar named Manuel Cirerol Sansores was to comment in respect of the strange sound effects noted so often at Chichén Itzá's famous Great Ball Court:

> This transmission of sound, as yet unexplained, has been discussed by architects and archaeologists. Most of them used to consider it as fanciful due to the ruined conditions of the structure but, on the contrary, we who have engaged in its reconstruction know well that the sound volume, instead of

disappearing, has become stronger and clearer . . . Undoubt-edly we must consider this feat of acoustics as another noteworthy achievement of engineering realised millenniums ago by the Maya technicians.[16]

That, like the Ancient Egyptians, the Maya were able to incorporate such a profound knowledge of sound acoustics and harmonic propor-tion into their temple complexes hints at an understanding of sonics over and beyond most other ancient cultures. That legends should also surround their earliest ancestors concerning the use of sonics to raise heavy objects into the air suggests that they really were the inheritors of an advanced technology that parallels the one found in Pharaonic Egypt. Where did it come from? Was it inherited from a much earlier culture, or were they able to develop it themselves over hundreds of years of experimentation? We simply do not know.

MULTI-FACETED STONES

Turning to the magnificent ruins of Tiahuanaco, the mysterious pre-Incan city of the Bolivian Altiplano, we find even further evidence of sound acoustics and harmonic proportion playing an apparent role in the design and construction of its enormous stone temples and palaces. These, as we have previously seen, were said to have been built, according to local legend, by the helpers of the tall, white-skinned wisdom-bringer named Ticci Viracocha, who in Aztec tradi-tion was known as Quetzalcoatl, the great 'feathered serpent', and in Mayan mythology was Itzamna or Zamna (see Chapter Seventeen).

Among the megalithic temples scattered across a wide area at Tiahuanaco is a series of perfectly carved rectilinear monoliths with multi-layered, right-angled sections cut away from their sides. No scholar of pre-Columbian architecture has been able suitably to explain the purpose of these unique stones. It might be suggested that they once acted as support joints for stone or wooden

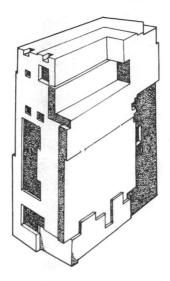

Multi-faceted pillar from Tiahuanaco. Evidence suggests that this stone –
and many others like it at the site – was shaped with acoustic principles
in mind.

cross-beams and horizontal pillars, but the lack of uniformity in their
style and the absence of any surrounding buildings weighs heavily
against this theory. On closer examining these monoliths, it seems
more plausible that they were fashioned deliberately to define the
stone blocks' harmonic proportions, each section being cut away
until the correct resonant frequency was achieved. Whatever the true
purpose of these monoliths, their presence might well be linked to
the stories told by the Aymara Indians of how the city's mythical
builders were able to move the stone blocks of Tiahuanaco from the
local quarries to their place of destination using the sound of a
trumpet. If this is so, then it would mean that the antediluvian
builder-gods of the Bolivian Altiplano would seem to have possessed
an understanding of acoustics similar to that present in Pharaonic
Egypt and Mayan Mexico. It is therefore possible that they used
these extraordinarily advanced principles to create and sustain sonic
platforms on which they could induce temporary weightlessness
within heavy stone blocks in order to steer them effortlessly towards
their point of destination.

EXPERIMENTS IN SOUND

Even in this knowledge, it was still all just circumstantial evidence and theory without any real proof that sound, or any other connected medium, could be used successfully to raise physical objects off the ground. I needed to further my understanding of the effects of sound on a more practical level, and so decided to organise a series of simple experiments to establish whether or not it was possible to induce temporary weightlessness in objects subjected to a barrage of sound. To this end I enlisted the help and expertise of electrical engineer Rodney Hale, who has a wide experience of working in previously uncharted areas of scientific exploration.

An eight-kilogram piece of quartz and a ten-kilogram piece of bunter sandstone were used in the initial experiments conducted at my home in Leigh-on-Sea, Essex, during the second half of 1996. Long recordings of tonal notes based on the musical chords E, G and D – which when combined together form the keynote C – were directed through loudspeakers at each of the stone blocks in the hope of obtaining a measurable variation in weight. The sounds were used individually, together and one after the after, but all to no avail.

On realising that our wall of sound was having little if any effect on either of the blocks, we used different tonal notes to reproduce their individual harmonics in the hope that this would heighten any sympathetic vibration taking place within the rock's crystalline structure. When this proved to be too difficult, we turned our attentions to what might have seemed like a soft option – a Tibetan singing bowl! These beautiful vessels are usually made of polished brass (although some of the older ones are made of three metals beaten together) and vary in size from several centimetres upwards. When a wooden baton is rubbed around their outer rim, their unique shape allows them to produce a sustained note.

I felt sure that if we could reproduce the principal note of the singing bowl (which is one and the same as its main resonant frequency), and then build this up with its corresponding harmonics, we stood a better chance of producing a measurable weight loss. This, of course, was the intention, and even though we found a way to sample and then instantaneously feed back the singing bowl's inherent tones through a loudspeaker positioned nearby, only a very minor weight change was recorded, and even this result was open to question.

Despite the poor success of our experiments in sound, I refused to get downhearted and vowed to continue selling sonics as a forgotten technology of immense importance to our understanding of the past. Even so, I came to realise that I needed more substantial evidence to prove the former existence of this lost science among ancient cultures. At first this had seemed most unlikely, but then somebody mentioned the name John Ernst Worrell Keely . . .

CHAPTER SEVEN

THE GENIUS OF SOUND

One man alone may have found the key to unlocking the mechanics of sound levitation. John Ernst Worrell Keely (1827–98) dedicated his entire life to understanding the concept of sympathetic vibration, which he used to raise heavy weights, power enormous engines, levitate metal balls and disintegrate rock in a most extraordinary manner.[1] Many independent witnesses, ranging from scientific writers to shareholders in the Keely Motor Company, saw the inventor's strange apparatus in operation. Almost all of them went away convinced that Keely had tamed forces of nature never before understood by the scientific world.

Keely was said to have been 'a splendid specimen of the *genus Homo*. Tall, straight, broad-shouldered, and muscular.'[2] He was 'courteous, frank and genial' with friends but cautious among enemies.[3] He sported a distinctive mutton-chop moustache and in surviving pictures is generally shown posing rigidly next to his strange-looking contraptions, like some stern-faced Victorian game-hunter standing proudly over his kill.

To help understand the nature of Keely's bizarre achievements, it will be necessary to recount what some scientific writers witnessed for themselves on visits to his Philadelphia workshop during the 1880s and 1890s. One such person was Mr Plum who, after a visit in 1893, wrote a definitive article on Keely's experiments for a magazine called *Dashed Against the Rock*.[4]

Plum witnessed many strange things that day in the inventor's tiny workroom.[5] Demonstration number one involved an assortment of different apparatus. Standing on a wooden table, covered with a heavy slab of glass, was a 0.3-metre-diameter copper globe, held in place by an upright support and said to have contained a series of metal Chladni plates and 'resonating' tubes. Beneath it was a complete ring of thin metal spikes, several centimetres long, that radiated outwards from a central hub like some sort of sado-masochistic collar. Each one had its own particular length, and when flicked with a finger would sing like the prongs of a tuning fork. Despite the simplicity of this curious device, known as the 'Libera-tor', it was the key to operating all other apparatus in the room.

Trailing from the bottom edge of the Liberator was a long wire consisting of three separate metals – gold around the outside, platinum inside that and silver passing through the core. This line was connected to another device, a so-called 'resonator', positioned on a second table located some 0.6 to 0.9 metres away from the globe. It consisted of a metal cylinder case, some 15 centimetres in diameter and 20 centimetres high, made up of a series of standing metal resonating tubes, on which was placed a brass cup with a glass wall. Inside this was a compass, its dial pointing towards magnetic north.[6]

When everything was ready, Plum watched as Keely moved across to the Liberator and twanged its collar of metal spikes. Once they had begun emitting a sustained note, the inventor twiddled a knob on the side of the globe to tune it properly. Then for a few brief seconds 'a rude harmonicon trumpet' was sounded and, as if by magic, the compass needle on the resonator began to spin wildly, even though nothing magnetic had been used in the construction of the apparatus. Each time the experiment was repeated, the compass would spin for anything between 30 seconds and 3 minutes, some-times much longer, confounding Plum completely.[7]

For the next experiment Keely entered a separate room, which was linked to the main workshop by a small open window. On a table before Plum was a zither, held upright by a support consisting of several carefully tuned metal tubes. Trailing from these was a long thread made of silk which went to another piece of apparatus resting on a separate table covered, as before, by a plate of glass. This new device consisted of a movable framework of 13-millimetre iron rods that held upright a copper globe around 38 centimetres in diameter.[8]

At the given moment, Keely picked up the 'harmonicon trumpet' and blew on it through the open window. This he continued to do for between one and two minutes until the metal globe finally began to turn, slowly at first but then quickly gaining speed. When Keely stopped blowing the horn, the globe gradually slowed to a halt. When he again blew on the horn, the globe once more started to revolve. The stronger and more prolonged the blast, the faster the globe turned. As a final showpiece, Plum was instructed to snip the connecting cord. On doing so, the globe slowly ground to a halt even though the trumpet was still being played, demonstrating how important the connection was between the resonating strings of the zither – tuned perfectly to the chord of the trumpet – and the generation of the force necessary to turn the globe.[9]

METAL THAT SWIMS

More amazing feats were on the way. For the next experiment, Plum was handed a metal ball composed of three different metals. Rolling it around in his hands, Plum was informed that it weighed two pounds (0.9 kilograms) and had earlier been 'sensitised' using the Liberator. Three similar metal balls lay at the bottom of a glass jar filled with water and capped with a metal disc.[10] As before, a wire trailed from this device to the Liberator located on a separate table.

When all was ready, Keely twanged the collar of spikes beneath the Liberator. He then picked up a brass horn and began blasting out a sustained note. Plum watched as one of the balls inside the water-filled jar began to rock gently from side to side. He then gasped as one by one each rose upwards until they hit the glass container's metal cap. More peculiar was the way that, even after Keely stopped playing the horn, the two-pound spheres remained suspended in the water as if they weighed no more than corks.[11] Here they would have remained had not Keely played a quite different note that somehow dissipated their 'charge' and made them sink back down to the bottom of the jar.

The final demonstration involved apparatus that Plum realised was of particular interest to the Keely Motor Company – the commercial enterprise set up by the inventor to provide the necessary finance to fund his years of dedicated research. Every other device demonstrated by Keely was merely a plaything in comparison with his spinning wheel. This time the Liberator, with its copper globe and its spiky ring of prongs, was positioned in the adjoining room with its wire linked via the window hatch to a wheel of eight spokes radiating from a fixed hub. At the end of each spoke was a sensitised disc, and enclosing the whole thing was a stationary rim of metal attached to a series of resonating tubes, each containing an assortment of finely tuned cambric needles that formed a circle around the wheel's central stem. On the inside of the rim were a further nine discs, like those incorporated into the spoked wheel.[12]

Keely twanged the Liberator's ring of spikes, sending a 'stream of sympathetic vibration' along the wire to the metal merry-go-round placed on a table in the main room. After carefully tuning the Liberator, he took up his trumpet and sounded a prolonged note that seemed to vibrate the very room itself. Keely was seen to glance through the window, an approving smile on his face, as he espied the wheel now revolving rapidly, something it would continue to do *so long as the chord was played*.[13]

The inventor's spinning wheel went on to become the main component in the mechanical engine he so wanted to patent.[14] It was to be his *pièce de résistance*, something that could be sold as a new means of power for railway locomotives, road vehicles and even airships. The strange and highly complex engine, which consisted of hundreds of spheres, drums, wheels and metal plates, was witnessed in operation by dozens of people on numerous occasions. All would go away impressed by the sheer power produced by this responsive mechanical monster.[15]

The vibratory force generated by musical instruments, catalysed by Keely's Liberators and boosted by resonators, had other potentials as well. He discovered, for example, that the force of his 'ether' could fire 15-centimetre projectiles through thick pieces of wood. Keely even got so far as demonstrating a vibratory cannon to the United States Navy which, while impressed by the results, rejected the idea on the basis that it was too complicated to operate.[16]

Keely's work has a profound significance to our own understanding of how sonic levitation might have been achieved in ancient times. After much more experimentation, he was able finally to use sound to make the metal balls in the glass jar rise in an environment of *air* instead of water.[17] He then took the idea of levitation further by developing a 3.6-kilogram model of an airship, which, by using the usual combination of Liberator, resonator, musical note and connecting cord, would lift into the air of its own accord.[18] Those who saw this device in 'flight' reported that it could rise, descend, or simply float with a motion 'as gentle as that of thistledown'.[19]

Keely was able to catalyse the vibratory force necessary to make objects move using a variety of different musical instruments, ranging from trumpets to horns, harmonicas, fiddles and zithers. He could even operate the equipment just by whistling,[20] bringing to mind the Mayan legends that told of how the antediluvian dwarfs of Mexico were able simply to whistle and stone blocks and logs of wood would rise into the air.

THE MASS CHORD

That a complex form of sympathetic resonation, and not some unknown etheric force, was the source of power behind Keely's inventions seems blatantly clear. The earliest prototype Liberator was several feet across, but as the years went by he gradually refined its size until in the 1890s he had designed one no bigger than a pocket watch.[21] Despite such advances, the device had an effect only if it were connected to the amplifying resonator by means of a cord, usually the specially developed wire made of gold, platinum and silver and referred to by Keely as a 'Trexar'.[22]

So what exactly did Keely manage to achieve that no one else has ever been able to replicate? What did he discover working alone in his tiny Philadelphia workroom? To suggest that sound acoustics and sympathetic vibration were the sole means of producing the extraordinary force that enabled compasses to spin, globes to revolve, spheres to rise and wheels to turn is oversimplifying the matter to an incredible degree. We know, for example, that the Liberators would always have to be attuned to Keely's own bodily vibrations and could only ever be operated by himself. He also needed to take into account the resonant vibrations of the workroom as well as those of the other apparatus – the principal reason why it was so difficult for him to manufacture a motor suitable for use outside the laboratory. To complicate matters still further, before certain demonstrations could begin, Keely would have to take into account the personal vibrations emitted by his visitors. These he would ascertain and counteract by getting each person to hold a steel tube attached by wire to the resonator being used in the experiment. In this way he could find what he described as the 'mass chord', which was the sum total of all vibrational resonation present in the room at any particular moment in time. For years Keely attempted to find a way of by-passing the personal association of the apparatus to its operator, but in this he failed again and again.[23]

THE DISINTEGRATOR

That Keely understood the mechanics of his sonic technology is difficult to deny. His work is the strongest evidence so far to suggest that the stories and legends concerning the existence in ancient times of a similar technology are very likely to be true. This in itself is an extraordinary realisation, but there is more, much more. Keely made another unbelievable discovery that throws an entirely new light on our knowledge of advanced stone technology in Ancient Egypt and twentieth-century Tibet, for he found that sympathetic vibration could *disintegrate quartz as well as other types of hard rock*. This realisation came to him quite by chance one day in 1887.

Having decided to make a study of 'the actions of currents of ether playing over a floor upon which he had scattered fine sand',[24] Keely set in motion his Liberator and, after satisfying himself that it was attuned correctly, sounded a note on a musical instrument. These actions combined to achieve the so-called mass chord. He then became aware that a large piece of granite being used to fasten back a door was disintegrating before his eyes.

Keely was flabbergasted by this unexpected result and over the next few days experimented further with other pieces of granite. On almost every occasion they would simply crumble to dust as soon as the mass chord was achieved – sound, it seemed, could literally shake the rock to pieces. More significantly, Keely realised that it was the rock's quartz content that seemed to respond more favourably to sympathetic vibration, since it obviously resonated at the same frequency range produced by his apparatus.[25] He even made calculations to this effect and concluded that his mass chord 'on the first octave induces 42,800 vibrations per second', sufficient to disintegrate quartz.[26]

The implications of Keely's rock disintegration cannot be underestimated, for it clearly vindicated the extraordinary findings of technologist Christopher Dunn, who has concluded that the tubular drilling conducted by the pyramid builders was achieved using ultrasonics – extremely high-frequency sound vibrations beyond the audible range of the human ear. He made this quite unbelievable connection after realising that the ancient drills cut through granite with a feed rate *500 times greater* than modern tools and passed through sections of quartz much faster than they had through other, softer minerals. This speed differential occurred because the natural resonance of the quartz exactly matched the sympathetic vibration produced by the ultrasonics used to disintegrate the granite, *exactly* what Keely had discovered over 100 years beforehand.

Keely's discoveries now make more sense of the levitation of stone blocks witnessed in Tibet by Jarl, and the strange devices observed by Linauer during his stay in the country. Both the huge gong and the mussel-shaped string instrument were, like Keely's two-pound (0.9-kilogram) spheres and Trexar wires, made of three different metals, chosen presumably because of their resonant qualities. The string instrument would appear to have acted like one of Keely's resonators in that it produced ultrasonic waves only when the much larger gong was sounded. By containing these emanations, using carefully positioned screens, the monks were able to levitate objects into the air and disintegrate rock in a manner similar to that achieved by Keely.

Keely's discoveries justifiably lend weight to the very real possibility that the pyramid builders also utilised an extremely advanced form of sympathetic vibratory physics to levitate stone blocks and bore holes through the hardest of rock. If this is correct, then it is also likely that any sonic instrument or device used by the Ancient Egyptians would have been personalised in the manner understood by Keely. In other words, any sonic tools they intended to use would first have to be attuned not just to the personal vibrations of the operator, or operators, but also to the acoustics of the room or building in which they were being employed. In this way the pyramid builders would have been able to achieve Keely's so-called 'mass chord' with the aid of musical instruments, tuning rods and amplifying resonators.

So what became of Keely's incredible discoveries?

THE FALL OF A GENIUS

In time the inventor developed a 'rock disintegrator' which he believed could be marketed successfully to the financiers of American gold-mining operations. The demonstration of this device in the Catskill mountains of New York state in early 1888 so impressed the 12 wealthy mining magnates present that its existence not only caused a minor panic on the San Francisco stock market, but also convinced them to fund further research into its commercial potential.[27]

Despite the extra finance, Keely simply continued his work, changing the design of the Liberator and refusing point-blank to reveal the exact nature of the 'etheric' force used in his experiments. This caused bitter antagonism between him and the Keely Motor Company, and in the end its shareholders lost their patience. They withdrew all financial support and threatened Keely not just with a lawsuit but also with imprisonment. The inventor responded irrationally by destroying many of his research papers and dismantling some of his valuable equipment. He also made it clear that he would never reveal his secrets until his work was complete and would rather die than go to jail.[28]

From that time onwards everything seemed to slide downhill for Keely. Although hc continued his experimentation, he was never to achieve commercial success. As with most inventors ahead of their time, this genius of sound died a broken man, the world having turned its back on his revolutionary discoveries.

I do not profess to understand the full mechanics behind Keely's science-fiction-style apparatus, or the true nature of his 'etheric' force. All I have determined is that every last component used in the construction of his equipment was either designed or chosen because of its potential to resonate in sympathy with its surroundings. It was like a domino effect, one sound or vibration triggering the next, then the next, then the next, until everything was buzzing, humming and singing in unison. The precision knowledge used in the manufacture of these acoustic devices was the end product of nearly 50 years of trial and error on Keely's part. All that can be hoped is that at some point in the future, able scientists and engineers will take up the gauntlet and attempt to understand Keely's research into sympathetic vibratory physics using the very latest scientific technology.[29]

Like Keely, the pyramid builders and the more recent monastic communities of Tibet would appear to have understood the processes involved in sympathetic vibratory physics. If this is correct, then they were able to raise stone blocks into the air, precision-cut rock and bore holes through granite, not as great magical feats, but as one small part of a much greater harmonisation with the world around them. Yet as with the basic design of the Great Pyramid, it seems as if this great wisdom was merely the legacy of a much earlier culture identified as Egypt's Elder gods. We are left, then, with a dilemma, for if we accept that the pyramid builders really did have an advanced understanding of sympathetic vibratory physics, then what happened to it – where did it go, and how did it end?

Initially, it seemed as if this was where my quest might come to an end. Then I remembered that there *was* another occasion when sound had supposedly been utilised in a most unusual manner, and, what's more, it was linked firmly with Ancient Egypt. Yet this time trumpets were being used, not to raise stone blocks into the air or to bore holes in rock, but for an altogether more destructive purpose – to bring down the walls of Jericho.

CHAPTER EIGHT

WALLS COME TUMBLING DOWN

Joshua, the son of Nun and the successor to Moses the lawgiver, slept the night at a place named Gilgal within sight of the ancient city of Jericho. His great army, made up of 40,000 able men from each of the 12 tribes of Israel, was encamped ten furlongs distance from its fortified walls, the strongest in Canaan.[1] Having crossed the River Jordan into the Promised Land, only the might of the king of Jericho, and the command of his army, stood between them and the fulfilment of God's word to his chosen people.

The leader of Israel awoke suddenly to find a 'man' standing before him with a sword drawn in his hand. 'Art thou for us, or for our adversaries?' Joshua enquired promptly.[2]

'Nay; but as captain of the host of the Lord am I now come,' the 'man' responded.[3]

Instantly, Joshua fell on his face and gave worship to this messenger of God, asking: 'What saith my Lord unto his servant?'[4]

'Put off thy shoe from off thy foot; for the place whereon thou standest is holy,' he was told, and so Joshua did as was asked of him.[5]

The 'captain of the host of the Lord', speaking as the voice of God, then informed the leader of Israel on how exactly he should take the besieged city. If he carried out these instructions, then 'the king thereof, and the mighty men of valour' would be given unto him.[6]

This is what he was told: 'And ye shall compass the city, all the men of war, going about the city once. Thus shall thou do six days. And seven priests shall bear seven trumpets of rams' horns before the ark: and the seventh day ye shall compass the city seven times, and the priests shall blow with the trumpets. And it shall be, that when they make a long blast with the ram's horn, and when ye hear the sound of the trumpet, all the people shall shout with a great shout; and the wall of the city shall fall down flat . . .'[7]

So it was that Joshua spoke to his priests and the army of Israel concerning these words of the Lord, and, as had been commanded of them, for the first six days the seven priests walked around the city walls, holding aloft their trumpets of rams' horns. At a safe distance in front of them went half of the army, while behind them the Ark of the Covenant was carried on the shoulders of its bearers, behind which came the rest of the army.

All was done in silence, for as Joshua had instructed: 'Ye shall not shout, nor let your voice be heard, neither shall any word proceed out of your mouth, until the day I bid you shout; then shall ye shout.'[8]

The dawning of the seventh day came, and the army and the priests who bore the seven trumpets, along with the carriers of the Ark and the army of men, circumnavigated the city walls as before, but then, on the seventh circuit, as the trumpets blew, all let out an almighty shout and the walls of Jericho came tumbling down.[9]

Once they had seen this great miracle, the army of Israel went up to the city and took it, killing every man, woman and child save for the household of Rahab, the harlot who had sheltered the spies of Israel; only she and her family were saved from the wrath of God.

★

This is the extraordinary account of how Jericho fell to the might of Israel as told in the book of Joshua. Jews and Christians alike accept the Old Testament as the unquestionable word of God, but is there any reason at all to assume that this story is a true relation of historical events? Did the walls of Jericho *really* fall down in the manner described? What we do know is that when the Israelites are supposed to have crossed over the Jordan into the land of Canaan, Jericho had already been a fortified town for at least 7000 years. Its strategic significance lay in the fact that it stood in the path of any invader who entered the country beyond the northern limits of the Dead Sea.[10]

Attempting to prove Joshua's triumphant entry into Canaan with an army of 40,000 Israelites has been the goal of biblical archaeologists for the last 150 years. In the 1930s a British expedition, led by Professor John Garstang, conducted excavations on the site of ancient Jericho and finally uncovered a section in the town wall that appeared to have collapsed outwards, exactly as tradition asserted it had succumbed to the force of the trumpet blows in the well-known biblical story.[11] Against this section of the wall, Garstang also found evidence of a fierce conflagration, suggesting some kind of battle in which the town had been razed to the ground.[12]

Garstang was naturally jubilant, and went on to promote his discoveries as perfect evidence of the way in which archaeology could be used to confirm the historical validity of the Bible. Unfortunately, his celebrations were short-lived, for in the 1950s noted British archaeologist Dame Kathleen Kenyon was back in Jericho excavating a further section of the same stone wall. This time a more methodical catalogue of adjoining strata was made, and it soon became clear that Garstang had got it completely wrong. The collapsed wall did not date to the thirteenth century BC, as he had come to believe, but to around 2350 BC, over 1100 years before the supposed entry into Canaan of the Israelites.

Little evidence of any later violent destruction was uncovered at Jericho by Kathleen Kenyon. She found that the entire top of the mound on which the city was built had eroded away, meaning that all later occupational levels simply did not exist any more. She did eventually uncover evidence of a township destroyed by fire in the first half of the sixteenth century BC,[13] as well as meagre evidence of a single wall and a small clay oven belonging to a building dating to the late fourteenth century BC.[14] In biblical terms this *was* a more important discovery, and after taking into account the dating of various funerary objects found in association with burials uncovered by Garstang in nearby rock-cut tombs, she concluded that there must have been a 'settlement on the tell (or occupational mound) from about 1400 to 1325 BC, or even for a generation or so longer'.[15] After this time, there had been nothing here right through to the eleventh century BC, the era in which King David established the kingdom of Israel.

For those who held true to biblical chronology which implies that the Israelites crossed into Canaan some time around *c.* 1200 BC, Kathleen Kenyon's findings were a staggering blow. Yet as we shall see, revolutionary new findings concerning the dating of the Exodus now suggest that Jericho must have fallen to the Israelites slightly earlier than has always been believed, plausibly around *c.* 1270 BC, bringing the date much more in line with the available archaeological evidence (see Chapter Nine).

THE FATE OF JERICHO

With only the flimsiest of evidence for the destruction of Jericho during the time-frame under review, what, then, are we to make of the story, found in Chapter 6 of the book of Joshua, concerning how the Israelites used just seven trumpets of rams' horns to shatter its city walls? No similar stories exist in the Bible, implying that it is neither a usual expression of God's power over his nation's enemies nor a common means by which the walls of major cities were breached in Old Testament times.

Anyone will tell you that you cannot simply sound trumpets and expect fortified walls to come tumbling down. On the other hand we do know that if a human voice reaches a sufficient volume and matches the resonant frequency of, say, a wineglass, then the glass *will* shatter. The pyramid builders and the monastic communities of Tibet, as well as the nineteenth-century inventor John Ernst Worrell Keely, would all appear to have utilised this principle to disintegrate rock.

Sound as a weapon is not impossible, and yet at a time when the Old Testament was taking its final form in the seventh century BC, such a concept should simply have not existed. Are we therefore to conclude that the earliest Israelites really did have the knowledge and capability to use sound, produced by trumpets, to destroy the walls of Jericho?

Let us examine the facts of the story. For the first six days the seven priests were to circumnavigate the city walls, holding before them the trumpets made of rams' horns. The so-called Ark of the Covenant was to follow in their wake, with half the Israelite army at a safe distance in front of it and the other half keeping a similar distance behind. On these occasions, there was to be complete silence. Then, on the seventh and final day the entire procession was to perambulate the city walls not once but seven times, and when the last, long blow had been sounded by the trumpets the entire army of 40,000 men were to let out an almighty shout.

Is there any reason to suggest that defensive walls could be breached by following this exact procedure? Is there any scientific basis behind such a notion? Looking at the story on a theoretical level, it might well be feasible to breach defensive walls using the power of sound. It might also be possible to create a sustained note that, when combined with a euphoric roar of the sort described in the story, could rupture stonework to the point of collapse. It is possible, but not proven. To date, there is no corroborative evidence whatsoever to suggest that this is how the walls of Jericho were destroyed. Of course, it does not mean that the event did *not* take place, only that currently it is impossible to prove beyond the circumstantial evidence presented in the Old Testament. On the other hand the sheer fact that the Jews of the first millennium BC managed to preserve such a curious story implies that there is at least some basis to the legend. As they say, there is rarely any smoke without fire. In other words, an incident of this nature may well have taken place during the formative years of the Israelite nation, although its exact details are now lost.

If such speculations *should* prove to be correct, then the destruction of the walls of Jericho could have been achieved only through a precise knowledge of sonic technology, and not simply through chance, or the miraculous intervention of God. The key would seem to lie in the fact that the instructions on how exactly Israel should take Jericho came not from Joshua or from the priests or the military advisers but from a mysterious sword-wielding figure known as the 'captain of the host of the Lord'.

What was the identity of this 'man' who possessed intimate knowledge of a destructive, forbidden technology so far beyond the normal capabilities of a Middle Eastern nation in the second millennium BC? Theologians would argue that this divine individual was in fact a messenger dispatched by the Lord to deliver to Joshua the means by which he could defeat his enemies and enter the Promised Land. He was therefore an angel in the *form* of a 'man', who adopted a corporeal body so that he might communicate with Joshua on a one-to-one basis.

Although the terms 'captain' and 'captains' are found on several occasions in the Old Testament, our mysterious 'captain of the host of the Lord' puts in no further appearances, not under this guise at least. In spite of this fact, I became convinced that this 'man' represented a source of forbidden technology made available to the Israelites, primarily through their leader Moses, who led them out of Egypt. If this was so, then how else might this elusive source of arcane wisdom have influenced the destiny of God's chosen people during their formative years?

I could take the matter no further by examining the Old Testament stories concerning the beginnings of the Israelite nation.

If Moses, and later Joshua, really *had* conspired with others at the time of the Exodus, and afterwards during the many years of wandering in the wilderness, then the only way in which I was going to be able to identify these enigmatic individuals was to look more closely at the life and times of Israel's great prophet and lawgiver, and, as might be expected, all roads seemed to lead back to Egypt.

CHAPTER NINE

THE
HERETIC
KING

To discover how the Israelite army under Joshua might have come into
the possession of what appears to have been age-old Elder technology,
we must first understand the genesis of the Jewish nation. We must
ascertain exactly when, and in what context, it came to leave Egypt at
the time of the Exodus. We must also examine the historical evidence
for the existence of Moses the lawgiver, who was supposedly brought
up in the royal courts of Egypt and learnt of its secret wisdom and
magical arts long before he became the Israelites' great spiritual leader.

Moses is unquestionably the most important figure in Jewish
religious history, and his memory has been carefully preserved in Old
Testament tradition. Yet despite his role as lawgiver and prophet to
the Hebrew race, next to nothing is known about his true history.
Furthermore, there is very little to date the events relating to the
supposed Exodus out of Egypt. There are simply isolated quotes here
and there, such as the statement in 1 Kings Chapter 6, Verse 1, which
tells us that Solomon's Temple was built 'in the four hundred and
eightieth year after the children of Israel' had gained their freedom
from Egypt, i.e. 'in the fourth year of Solomon's reign over Israel'.
Since the Revised Version of the Bible implies that Jerusalem's First

Temple was founded in *c*. 977 BC,[1] this provides a date of *c*. 1457 BC for the Exodus.

Another, similar reference, this time in the book of Exodus, states that before its eventual departure from Egypt Israel had 'sojourned', i.e. waited patiently, for a total of 'four hundred and thirty years'.[2] Theological scholars generally consider that the earliest Hebrews were nomadic peoples who entered Egypt from their native Palestine, the biblical land of Canaan, during the reign of a Middle Kingdom king named Senwosret III, *c*. 1878–1843 BC, following a presupposed famine in their own country.[3] Because this attractive, though unsubstantiated, solution parallels the manner in which Moses' illustrious ancestor Joseph, the son of Jacob (or Israel), was sold into bondage by his scheming brothers in the well-known biblical story, some believe that Senwosret's reign marks the beginning of Israel's sojourn in Egypt. If this is correct, then it implies that the Exodus took place 430 years later, in other words somewhere between *c*. 1448 and 1413 BC.

At first this might seem to define a suitable time-frame in which Moses might have been brought up as an Egyptian in the court of the ruling Pharaoh. Biblical chronology, however, is prone to gross numerical exaggeration and should never be taken literally. It is very often contradictory, symbolic in meaning, and can vary from one version of the Old Testament to the next.[4] Yet when dating the events surrounding the Exodus, theological scholars pay particular attention to a statement that appears at the beginning of the book of Exodus and reads:

> Behold, the people of the children of Israel are more and mightier than we [the Egyptians]. Come, let us deal wisely with them; lest they multiply, and it come to pass, that, when there falleth out any war, they also join themselves unto our enemies, and fight against us, and get them up out of the land. Therefore they did set over them taskmasters to afflict them with their burdens. And they built for Pharaoh store cities, Pi-thom and Raamses.[5]

These lines show that at the time they were written, the Israelites were a thriving community of many thousands which had gradually been increasing in number over several generations. More important, they were not forced into slavery until a Pharaoh, who 'knew not Joseph',[6] became increasingly alarmed at their wealth and prosperity (a quite separate Pharaoh is featured in the Exodus story). The whereabouts of the so-called 'store cities' referred to in the passage has long caused consternation among the Egyptological community. It is agreed unanimously that they were located somewhere in Egypt's Eastern Delta, close to the border with what is today Palestine, for it was here, in the biblical 'land of Goshen', that the Israelites are said to have settled at the time of Joseph.

Pi-thom (*pi* is 'domain' or 'estate' in Egyptian) is generally equated with a lost city once situated in the Eastern Delta called Pi-Atum. From an inscription dating to the thirteenth century BC, it is known to have possessed a border fortress, while its surrounding lands were used by nomadic communities to herd and farm cattle.[7] In spite of this information, the exact location of Pi-Atum remains a mystery, and whether or not it really was one of the 'store cities' built by the Israelites remains to be seen.

We are on firmer ground in locating the other 'store' city named as 'Raamses', or Pi-Ramesse as it is known in Egyptian texts. Scholarly opinion places it somewhere in the vicinity of two adjoining villages, Qantir and Tell el-Dab'a, located in the Eastern Delta. Evidence for the former presence here of Pi-Ramesse has come from the excavations between the 1960s and the early 1980s, headed by Dr Manfred Bietak, of an extensive layout of temples, administrative buildings and private residences belonging to the reign of Ramesses II, who ruled *c.* 1290–1224 BC.[8]

Egyptologists view these findings as firm evidence that the mighty Ramesses II, whose colossal ruins litter Egypt to this day, was the Pharaoh of the Oppression, the king who 'knew not Joseph' and set 'taskmasters' over the Israelites to build the 'store cities'. If this were so, then it would mean that his son and successor, Merenptah, who reigned *c.* 1224–1214 BC, was the Pharaoh of the Exodus, who

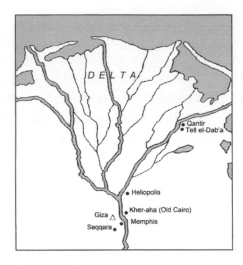

Map of the Nile Delta showing principal sites featured in this book.

along with his army was drowned when he attempted unsuccessfully to follow Moses and the Israelites across the Red Sea after the waves were parted by the hand of God.

There is, however, no firm evidence whatsoever to back up this bold assertion, which is almost immediately thrown into considerable doubt by a much-debated reference to the peoples of 'Israel' found on a victory stela (or proclamation stone) discovered by Flinders Petrie in 1895 west of the old royal capital of Thebes (modern Luxor), and dated to Year Five of Merenptah's 10-year reign. Its inscription, which lists successful military campaigns supposedly undertaken by the Pharaoh, reads as follows:

> The princes are prostrate, saying: 'Peace!'
> Not one raises his head among the Nine Bows.
> Desolation is for Tjehenu, Hatti is pacified;
> Plundered is the Canaan with every evil;
> Carried off is Askelon; seized upon is Gezer;
> Yanoam is made as that which does not exist;
> *Israel is laid waste, his seed is not;*
> Kharu [Syria] has become a widow for Egypt!

All lands together, they are at peace.
Everyone who was restless has been bound by [Merenptah].[9]

This is the first time that the name 'Israel' appears on any form of inscription, which is significant in its own right. Yet the so-called 'Israel Stela' makes sweeping assertions that are now known to be slightly inaccurate, such as the reference to Hatti, the Hittite empire of Anatolia (modern Turkey) and northern Syria, being 'at peace'. Merenptah's father, Ramesses II, filled 20 walls of a temple pronouncing the defeat of the Hittites in a decisive battle fought during his own reign, and not during that of his son Merenptah, who simply cribbed the glories of his father for his own purposes. Moreover, extant documents drawn up between the two kingdoms show that the battle, fought at Kadesh in northern Syria, was in fact *a draw*.[10]

So whether or not Merenptah really did lay waste to the Israelite nation is uncertain in itself. Of more immediate importance was the fact that the stela implies that by Year Five of his reign the 'seed' of Israel was already well established in Canaan. Yet the Old Testament tells us that before the Hebrews entered the Promised Land they wandered in the wilderness of Sinai and Paran for a full 40 years, meaning that the Exodus must have occurred at least 35 years *before* the fifth year of Merenptah's reign; conceivably, many decades before even that. This realisation throws the whole contentious issue back into the reign of his father Ramesses II, but there are major flaws in assuming that the Exodus took place during his reign as well.

Recent excavations at Qantir and Tell el-Dab'a, the site of the Egyptian city of Pi-Ramesse, by Dr Manfred Bietak have shown conclusively that the city had first been occupied at least 500 years *before* the age of Ramesses;[11] in other words it was not built as a 'store city' by enslaved Israelites. Moreover, there is also ample evidence to identify this same city with Avaris, the ancient capital of the Hyksos, the so-called 'shepherd kings' of Canaanite origin whose warring nomadic tribesmen controlled Egypt for approximately 155 years from around 1730 BC onwards. It therefore seems certain that, although Ramesses II engaged in major building projects at Pi-Ramesse, it had existed long before the commencement of his reign and gained its name simply in honour of this king. Furthermore, since the Semitic-speaking Hyksos were forerunners and possibly even the antecedents of the Israelites, their presence at Pi-Ramesse, the old Avaris, had little, if anything, to do with forced labour; it was their ancestral homeland where their forefathers had settled many hundreds of years beforehand.

From the information provided in the Old Testament we can say only that the Exodus out of Egypt, and the Israelites' subsequent 40 years in the wilderness, occurred some time between *c.* 1450 BC and the middle years of Ramesses II's 67-year reign. There is, however, a growing body of evidence to suggest that *all* of these events were in some way connected with the tumultuous period of Egyptian history known as the Amarna age, which was marked by the succession to the throne in around 1367 BC of an enigmatic king named Amenhotep IV.

THE ENEMY OF AKHETATEN

During the later years of the reign of his father, Amenhotep III, Amenhotep IV became Pharaoh and quickly took the unprecedented step of attempting to introduce a form of monotheistic (one-god) worship. Its unnamed deity's only representational image was to be the multi-rayed sun-disc, the Aten, seen as omnipotent, life-giving power of the double horizon. It is depicted in surviving reliefs as a reddy-orange solar orb encircled by the so-called *uraeus*-snake – a sign of eternity – around the neck of which hangs the *ankh*-cross, the Egyptian symbol of life. Narrow rays of light radiate down from the sun-disc and terminate in hands, some offering life in the form of *ankhs.*

In addition to proclaiming the Aten disc as the sole symbol of godhead, the king changed his name from Amenhotep – which honoured the god Amun – to Akhenaten, meaning 'glory' or 'spirit' (*akh*) of the Aten. He also transferred his seat of power from the city of Thebes to a virgin site some 277 kilometres (173 miles) downriver, located on the east bank of the Nile and known today as Tell el-Amarna. Here he constructed beautiful palaces, great administrative centres and open-air sun temples totally unique to Egypt. He gave it the name Akhetaten, meaning 'the horizon of the Aten', and administrators, priests, sculptors, architects, artists, builders and loyal subjects from every part of the kingdom joined him in his bold endeavour.

From the extensive excavations conducted at Amarna, many scholars have looked on Akhenaten as a great artist, a poet, a mystic and a philosopher. Certainly, he was unlike any other Pharaoh that had ever ruled Egypt. He had artists depict both himself and his

Map of Ancient Egypt showing principal sites featured in this book.

family in natural poses that were in complete contrast to the powerful regal and militaristic art of the previous 1700 years. Day-to-day scenes showed Akhenaten and his famous queen and wife, Nefertiti, relaxing in the company of their six daughters. Akhenaten also changed the whole manner in which he was represented in reliefs and statues. The Pharaoh (and, to a lesser degree, immediate members of his family) was now shown with an enlarged cranium, elongated facial features and oversized lips, as well as female hips and breasts. Why exactly he chose to adopt this image is a matter of much speculation. Some scholars have suggested that he suffered from a form of endocrine deficiency, caused by constant inbreeding, which can produce an assortment of acute physical abnormalities – hence the exaggerated features. Against this view, however, is the sheer fact that no evidence of any of these characteristics has been found in connection with the mummified remains of individuals thought to have belonged to Akhenaten's immediate family.

Akhenaten ruled for just 17 years, 12 to 13 of those in his dream city at Tell el-Amarna, before vanishing completely from history. He is presumed to have died, most probably a victim of the plague that is thought to have swept across Egypt and the Near East during the later half of his reign.[12] Akhenaten was replaced for a few brief months by a mysterious figure named Smenkhkare, his co-regent for the final two years of his life. Following Smenkhkare's untimely death at a young age, the boy-king Tutankhaten succeeded to the throne of Egypt and, under the influence of the priests of Amun at Thebes, changed his name to Tutankhamun, which, of course, honoured their god. The relationship between these three royal personages is still unclear, although it seems possible that Smenkhkare and Tutankhamun were brothers and that their father was Akhenaten's own father, Amenhotep III, who may well have lived on as a co-regent right through until the eleventh year of his son's reign.[13]

The young Tutankhamun reigned for just nine years, and following his death at the age of 18 the throne of Egypt fell first to

Akhenaten's old vizier, Aye, and then to Tutankhamun's military commander, Horemheb. He immediately set about erasing all trace of not only Akhenaten's reign but also every other so-called Amarna king – Smenkhkare, Tutankhamun and Aye. Horemheb outlawed any use of their names, while the years ruled by Akhenaten became simply the time of 'the rebel', 'the rebellion'[14] and 'the enemy [or criminal] of Akhetaten'.[15]

Horemheb targeted everything and anything connected with the Amarna kings and their now reviled faith of the Aten. He destroyed their temples, toppled their statues, defaced their reliefs and chiselled out their inscriptions. Worse still, tombs located in the cliffs on the edge of the city and built for Akhenaten's family and courtiers were systematically despoiled and looted, their enshrined mummies being desecrated and cast out to disintegrate in the scorching desert heat. Horemheb's final act against the Amarna kings was the destruction of Akhenaten's gleaming white citadel, which by the commencement of his reign, *c.* 1335 BC, had become a shanty town, home only to a few nomadic tribesmen. Buildings were dismantled systematically, their stones carted away for construction use elsewhere in Egypt.

Horemheb's actions were a gross humiliation to the memory of the one Pharaoh who had attempted to unite Egypt in a single faith. If anything, the fanatical suppression of everything that represented the Amarna age merely demonstrated the effect Akhenaten's monotheism must have had on the pages of Egyptian history. Why go to such lengths to wipe out the past? Why should Akhenaten and his successors have been denounced as heretic kings?

It was perhaps with these thoughts in mind that some scholars had begun to note the comparisons between Akhenaten's Aten faith and the religion of Moses, adopted by the Israelites after the Exodus out of Egypt. For example, it had long been realised that a certain hymn to the Aten, once thought to have been composed by Akhenaten himself, bore distinct similarities to the verses of Psalm 104, first recorded in Solomonic times, *c.* 980 BC.[16] Was this simply coincidence, or had one influenced the other?

Then in 1937 the by then elderly Sigmund Freud, inventor of modern psychology, published an important article which proposed that the biblical figure of Moses had been an Egyptian linked to the court of Akhenaten.[17] He provided much stimulating evidence to support his argument, including the fact that the Jewish word for 'Lord', *Adonai*, becomes 'aten' when its letters are transformed into Egyptian.[18] This realisation actually makes considerable sense of a curious statement in Exodus Chapter 12, Verse 12, in which God informs Moses that, once the first-born of Egypt are slaughtered during the night of the Passover, 'against all the gods of Egypt I will execute judgements: [for] I am the Lord'.[19] Since the word for 'lord' is here cited as 'Adonai', God is in effect saying 'against all the gods of Egypt I will execute judgements: [for] I am the Aten'.

Freud also pointed out that the act of circumcision, a requirement of Hebrew law for every new-born child, was first practised by the Ancient Egyptians, and not by any other Asiatic or Middle Eastern culture. In his opinion it seemed obvious that the Jews had inherited this tradition via Moses from the Ancient Egyptians.[20]

Freud's controversial views did not go down well with the elders of the Jewish faith, and when in early 1939 it became known that he was about to release a book clarifying these controversial views, he was urged by senior Jewish officials to withdraw its publication as they feared it would undermine the ethics of Judaism.[21] Freud died just a few months after the book, *Moses and Monotheism*, appeared in the shops, and whatever the correctness of his opinions there is no doubt that it set the tone for scholars to begin reassessing Akhenaten's life and ideals in respect to the establishment of Jewish monotheism. It was not, however, until 1990 that the most influential of all the books on this subject reached the bookshelves. *Moses Pharaoh of Egypt* by Egyptian-born historian Ahmed Osman was to cause far more of a stir than the polite waggle of a finger received by Freud some 50 years earlier.

Osman, who now lives in London, came right out and said what most people, including Freud, had never dared suggest: that Akhenaten was *one and the same person* as Moses. Osman's seemingly outrageous theory infuriated Muslim leaders, especially in his native Egypt. Since Moses is an important prophet in the Koran, and Osman is a Muslim by birth and thus bound by its holy laws, they saw his extreme views as a blasphemy in the sight of God. In much the same way that the Islamic world greeted the publication of Salman Rushdie's *Satanic Verses* in 1989, copies of Osman's book were openly burned in the streets of Cairo. Such, it seems, is the price of radically questioning the consensus opinions concerning the characters and events of the Koran.

So what are we to make of Osman's wild views?

Unfortunately, there is no conclusive evidence to prove that Akhenaten *was* one and the same person as the Israelite leader of the Exodus, and in all probability it seems more likely that Moses – who is said to have lived a staggering 120 years[22] – was a composite character created out of the faded memories of a variety of different individuals, some Hebrews, others Egyptian in origin. What seems more certain, however, is that the events of Akhenaten's life, especially his adoption of the Aten faith, reflect stories concerning the figure of Moses preserved *outside* of the Bible.

THE IMPURE PEOPLE

The earliest non-Jewish source that mentions Moses and the Exodus is the writings of an Egyptian priest and historian named Manetho, who lived *c.* 320 BC. His works included a history of his country written in Greek and entitled *Aegyptiaca*, which, although now lost, was much quoted by later writers such as Flavius Josephus, a Jewish historian of the first century AD, and early Christian writers such as the Greek historian Sextus Julius Africanus (*d.* AD 232) and Eusebius of Caesarea (AD 264–360).

Manetho seems to have been acutely aware of the legends circulating Egypt during his own day concerning a great prophet and leader known to the Jews of Alexandria as Moses. Yet his version of the life and times of Israel's great prophet and lawgiver, recorded rather disparagingly by Josephus in a text entitled 'Treatise Against Apion', contrasts greatly with the one revered by whole nations in the Old Testament.[23]

Manetho tells us that a king of Egypt named 'Amenophis', who desired to see the gods, sought advice from a 'wise man' and 'prophet' named 'Amenophis, the son of Papis'. Having listened to these words, the wise man informed the king that his wish would be fulfilled only if he rounded up all 'the lepers' and 'impure people' who lived in the kingdom and made them work in the quarries on the 'east side of the Nile'.[24]

The king, on hearing the good words of his trusted seer, duly rounded up 80,000 unfortunate individuals who were made to work in the aforementioned quarries. Aware of the consequences of the advice he had just given to the king, the seer then predicted that 'certain people would come to the assistance of these polluted wretches', who would then rise up, depose the Pharaoh and stay in charge of the country for 13 years.[25] Unable to face the consequences of this eventuality, the seer conveyed these words to others before committing suicide.

On learning of the death of his wise man and of the prophecy he had left, the king attempted to reconcile his improprieties towards 'the lepers' and 'impure people' by allowing them to take over Avaris, the city left deserted after the departure of the 'shepherds', or Hyksos kings (who were defeated and run out of Egypt by the forces of a Pharaoh named Ahmose, c. 1575 BC).[26] It was then that the 80,000 'impure people' elected for themselves a leader 'out of the priests of Heliopolis' named Osarsiph, who afterwards took the name Moses. He instituted many new laws and customs quite opposite to those of Egypt and told his people that they should not 'worship the Egyptian gods'.[27] They were also *not* to abstain from killing those animals sacred to these gods and were to 'join themselves to nobody but to those that were of this confederacy'.[28]

Manetho records that Osarsiph-Moses then told the 'impure

people' to stop working in the quarries and instead build walls around their city and make ready for a war against the king. Osarsiph-Moses then secured the 'friendship' of 'the other priests [of Heliopolis] and those that were polluted with them' and dispatched ambassadors to 'Jerusalem' in an attempt to persuade the 'shepherds', i.e. the Hyksos peoples, to support their cause, promising them in return their old capital, Avaris.[29]

The Hyksos are said to have accepted this offer, and so, with the aid of 200,000 of these 'shepherds', Osarsiph-Moses seized control of Egypt, banishing the king and the remainder of his army to Ethiopia. Thirteen years pass by, and, finally, after amassing an almighty force of 300,000 men, the Pharaoh, with the assistance of a second great army raised by his son, named as Ramesses or Sethos, returns to Egypt and finally manages to defeat Osarsiph-Moses, along with the 'impure people' and the Hyksos 'shepherds', who are driven to 'the bounds of Syria'.[30]

This is the basic story of Moses as presented by Manetho, who informs us that these events took place 518 years after the expulsion of the Hyksos,[31] a somewhat meaningless date which, if calculated, falls around 1057 BC, some 200 years after the traditional date of the Exodus. Yet encrypted within this web of confused pseudo-history, orientated in favour of the Egyptians, is, I believe, historical information of immense importance. The Pharaoh named as 'Amenophis' is said to have desired to see the gods, clearly implying some kind of religious proclamation or reform, perhaps an allusion to the polytheistic worship abandoned by Akhenaten and reinstated shortly before the reign of Horemheb. More significantly, this 'Amenophis' also seems synonymous with another king referred to in the account as 'Hor', or 'Oros', the name by which Horemheb is referred to in Manetho's king-list. Although the Osarsiph-Moses story cited by Josephus actually refers to 'Hor', or 'Oros', as an 'ancestor' of Amenophis, it is clear that the two were originally one and the same Pharaoh, a fact convincingly argued by noted Amarna scholar Donald Redford.[32] Since the name 'Amenophis' was also an alternative name given to Akhenaten's father, Amenhotep III, this seems to suggest that the Pharaoh who confronts Osarsiph-Moses is based partly on Akhenaten's father and partly on the events surrounding Horem-heb's 27-year reign. The seer known as 'Amenophis, the son of Papis', is also a historical character, based on Amenhotep-son-of-Hapu, Amenhotep III's Minister of All Public Works, who lived till the age of 80 and was last mentioned in Year Thirty-four of the king's reign.

The 'lepers' and 'impure people' forced to work in the quarries on the 'east side of the Nile' seem to correspond with the Hebrews of Goshen, who the book of Exodus tells us were put to work on the construction of the 'store cities' located in the Eastern Delta. One of these was, of course, Pi-Ramesse, or Avaris, the former capital of the Hyksos peoples, which Manetho tells us was returned to them by Osarsiph-Moses in exchange for their assistance in helping him to run the king out of Egypt.

Manetho also tells us that Osarsiph-Moses instructed his people in laws and customs 'opposite' to those of Egypt, and commanded them not to worship the Egyptian gods and to 'join themselves to nobody but to those that were of this confederacy'.[33] These words seem to parallel closely the manner in which Akhenaten outlawed the worship of the Egyptian pantheon of gods, shifted his seat of power from Thebes to Tell el-Amarna and invited those dedicated to his faith to join him in his bold endeavour. His actions could easily be construed as those attributed to Osarsiph-Moses, who withdrew from the outside world to communicate only with those of 'the confederacy'. Furthermore, the 13 years in which Osarsiph-Moses is said to have taken charge of Egypt parallels exactly the period of time in which Akhenaten ruled from the city of Akhetaten, following his move here in around Year Six of his reign.

Not only were these the conclusions drawn by Ahmed Osman,[34] but support for this supposition has come from Egyptologist Donald Redford, who sees in the Manetho account of Osarsiph-Moses a straight reflection of the religious reforms instituted by Akhenaten and preserved both orally and in written form within the temple annals of Egypt.[35] In his book *Pharaonic King-Lists, Annals and*

Day-books he was prepared to admit that: 'The occupation of a deserted area, set apart (though in the modified form of the story replaced by Avaris), sounds like the hejira to Amarna; and the 13 years of woe wrought by lepers and shepherds can only be the term of Akhenaten's stay in his new city. The figure of Osarsiph-Moses is clearly modelled on the historic memory of Akhenaten.'[36]

Like Osarsiph-Moses, Akhenaten is also known to have had close ties with Hebrews, one of whom was his Chief Minister, Aper-el (or Abd-el), 'servant of El', whose intact tomb was discovered beneath the hot sands of the Saqqara necropolis in 1988 by Belgian archaeologist Alain Zivie.[37] That Aper-el was a Semite is known from the hieroglyphs used to denote his name, for the suffix *el*, or *ia*, was the name of the Canaanite high god who went on to become associated with the god of the Hebrews.[38]

Might Aper-el have helped influence the young and perhaps impressionable Akhenaten during his formative years? Did this close liaison lead to the king conferring some kind of special status on the Hebrew tribes of the Eastern Delta? Was this realisation also an indication of Akhenaten's involvement in the events that eventually culminated in the Old Testament account of Israel's departure from Egypt?[39] If so, then does this new knowledge shed greater light on the events of the Exodus?

Manetho speaks of a son of King Amenophis named Ramesses (Rampses) or Sethos, who helped his father expel from Egypt Osarsiph-Moses, along with the 'impure people' and the Hyksos. Since he also states that the son of this Ramesses-Sethos was *also* named Ramesses, and that this son reigned as king of Egypt for 66 years,[40] we know for certain that it has to be a reference to Seti I, whose son, Ramesses II, did indeed reign for a period of either 66 or 67 years.

PHARAOHS OF THE EXODUS

Manetho states that when Osarsiph-Moses rose up against King Amenophis, his son Ramesses, or Sethos, was just five years old. Since we know that Seti I was 40 to 45 years of age when he ascended to the throne in around 1307 BC,[41] it points clearly towards the fact that Osarsiph-Moses, if he existed as a historical character, must therefore have risen to prominence at around the beginning of Horemheb's reign, *c.* 1335 BC. This shows that although he may well have embodied some of Akhenaten's character and deeds, Osarsiph-Moses, like his biblical counterpart, was a composite figure with more than one identity.

If these events really did begin during Horemheb's reign, then it seems likely that this king, who is known to have persecuted Akhenaten's followers, is to be equated with the Bible's Pharaoh of the Oppression, who 'knew not Joseph'. This would mean therefore that Horemheb's successor, Ramesses I, Seti's predecessor and the first king of the Nineteenth Dynasty, was the subsequent Pharaoh who reigned at the time of Exodus – a conclusion drawn by Ahmed Osman in his book *Moses Pharaoh of Egypt*.[42]

Had Ramesses I allowed the Israelites – as well as surviving members of Akhenaten's outlawed cult of the Aten, many of whom were incarcerated as political prisoners in the Eastern Delta during Horemheb's reign[43] – to leave Egypt of their own free will soon after he ascended the throne? If so, then why should he have done this? The answer seems to lie in the fact that Ramesses I was himself an adherent of the Aten faith, as is evidenced from an important stela found during excavations in 1904 by Flinders Petrie at Serabit el-Khadim, a sacred mountain in the Sinai Peninsula. The stela shows the king in a style of dress that resembles 'the work of Akhenaten'[44] and bears an inscription that proclaims him 'prince of every circuit of the Aten'.[45] The fact that the dreaded Aten should appear on an inscription in the Sinai was difficult enough to understand, but that it should also be linked directly with Ramesses I seemed quite inexplicable, for as Petrie commented at the time: 'To find the Aten mentioned thus after the ruthless Amunism of Horemheb is remarkable. Hitherto the latest mention of it was under King Ay.'[46]

Was this an indication that worship of the Aten had been kept alive from the death of Aye in *c.* 1335 BC right down to the reign of Ramesses I some 22 years later? Might this have been a motive for his allowing the Exodus to take place, in the knowledge that convicted followers of the Aten still lived among the enslaved Hebrew labourers of the Eastern Delta?

When Ramesses succeeded to the throne of Egypt following the death of Horemheb, he was already an old and very frail man. The king was therefore in no position to prevent his rival, Seti, from taking control of the kingdom. It is strongly possible that a co-regency existed between the two kings during the short one year, four months of Ramesses's reign.[47] If this is really what happened, then it could well explain the confusion in Manetho's account of Osarsiph-Moses between the names Ramesses and Seti, or Sethos – the memory of both kings having been blended together to form one single character named Ramesses-Sethos. It also suggests that Seti I might have had a firm hand in the events surrounding the Exodus and that it was him, and not his predecessor, who, in Manetho's words, provided military aid to help king 'Amenophis', i.e. Horemheb, to expel the 'lepers' and 'shepherds' from Egypt. As a great military general, like Horemheb before him, Seti would have ruled Egypt with an iron fist, adhering to strict moral and civil laws and patronising the old gods, especially the cult of Amun at Thebes, which had suffered greatly under the rule of Akhenaten and his successor Smenkhkare. Anything that had been beloved of Akhenaten and the Amarna kings would have become the enemy of Seti I, and this would have undoubtedly included the Semitic peoples of the Eastern Delta.

Was Manetho therefore fusing together very real events that occurred during the short period of co-regency that apparently took place between Ramesses I and Seti? If so, does this throw further light on the historical reality of the biblical Exodus? Accepting Manetho's account of Osarsiph-Moses as a confused record of real events that took place at the end of Horemheb's reign, it would appear as if some kind of uprising occurred among the Canaanite peoples of the Eastern Delta. United under a former priest of Heliopolis named Osarsiph, who had adopted the name Moses, they clashed with the Egyptian army under the leadership of Sethos, i.e. Seti I, and were finally driven out of Egypt. This supposition is supported in the knowledge that during Year One of Seti's reign he is known to have embarked on a military campaign against the *Shasu*, the name given to Bedouin or nomadic peoples of Palestine, Syria and Sinai, in other words the descendants of the Hyksos. An inscription, dating to this period, brings news to the king of the *Shasu* uprising, and reads:

> The Shasu enemies are plotting rebellion. Their tribal leaders are gathered in one place, standing on the foothills of Khor [a term for Palestine and Syria], and they are engaged in turmoil and uproar. Each of them is killing his fellow. They do not consider the laws of the palace.[48]

These incidents, which could well have sparked similar uprisings among their Semitic cousins in Egypt's Eastern Delta, initially led to Seti capturing the city of Pa-Kanaan, modern Gaza. The king then pushed further and further north through Palestine until eventually he reached the eastern Mediterranean coast, opposite the Sea of Galilee. The cities of Yanoam (mentioned in the Israel stela of Seti's grandson Merenptah's reign), Beth-Shan and Hammath all fell before him, until finally he reached the Hittite strongholds in northern Syria – victories celebrated on the walls of the Temple of Amun at Karnak.

These are the events that Manetho appears to have been alluding to in his account, implying therefore that it was as a result of Seti's anti-Semitic campaign that the Hebrew peoples of the Eastern Delta had fled Egypt, plausibly because they had risen up in support of their suppressed cousins in Canaan. The Israelites' choice to go to the wilderness of Sinai and Paran, as opposed to the Promised Land of Canaan, can thus be construed as a strategic move, perhaps in the knowledge that Seti would never have pursued them into the desert – his mind being set on taking Palestine.

So what led to the 'impure people' and 'shepherds' of Manetho's account, the Israelites of the Old Testament, being allowed to depart from Egypt?

Is it possible that Ramesses I, in his dying days, gave the Semitic peoples of the Eastern Delta permission to leave Egypt, due to his reverence for the outlawed Aten faith, and yet, on hearing of their release, Seti went in pursuit of them with an army in an attempt to make them return to the land of Goshen? After all, they did form a major part of Egypt's labour-force. Such a view might help explain why the book of Exodus tells us that, after having first let the Israelites have their freedom, the ruling Pharaoh then changes his mind and pursues them with an army as far as the Red Sea, where the latter are supposedly drowned. I do not believe that Seti's demise was in this manner. However, the implications of these realisations suggest that there was not one but two Pharaohs of the Exodus – Ramesses I and Seti I, a supposition strongly hinted at in Manetho's account of Osarsiph-Moses.

In summary, it seems highly likely that the story of Moses and the Exodus out of Egypt, as portrayed in the book of Exodus, began with the reign of the Pharaoh Akhenaten, *c.* 1367 BC, and came to a head some 60 years later during Year One of Seti I's reign, *c.* 1307 BC, the proposed date of the Exodus. To pursue the matter further is beyond the scope of this book, but if these ideas prove to be correct, then they provide us with a completely new insight into the events surrounding the foundation of the Israelite nation.

Having established these facts, it is reasonable to assume that any forbidden technology in the possession of the Israelite army under the leadership of Joshua, Moses' successor, almost certainly originated in Egypt. More precisely, it must have been connected in some way with those responsible for the emergence of Akhenaten's faith of the Aten at the beginning of his reign. They perhaps inherited these age-old ideas from a priestly group who had preserved them across millennia before they finally reached the ears of Joshua and his army before the fall of Jericho. So who might these individuals have been, and how, if at all, were they linked to the mysterious personage referred to in the Bible as the 'captain of the host of the Lord'? The answer appears to lie in the words of Manetho, who tells us that Osarsiph-Moses belonged to an elite religious group known as the priests of Heliopolis. Who exactly were these priests of Heliopolis, and what part did they play in the rise of Akhenaten, the heretic king? As we shall see in the coming chapters, the role they played in the development of Ancient Egyptian religion becomes crucial in our quest to discover the Elder gods' ultimate legacy to mankind.

CHAPTER TEN

FIRST CREATION

A Greek grammarian of the first century AD named Apion of Alexandria made some quite remarkable statements about the life of Moses, the biblical lawgiver. In a quotation taken from his now lost work *Aegyptiaca*, fortunately preserved by the Jewish historian Flavius Josephus, he tells us:

> I have heard of the ancient men of Egypt, that Moses was of Heliopolis, and that he thought himself obliged to follow the customs of his forefathers, and offered his prayers in the open air, towards the city walls: but that he reduced them all to be directed towards the sun-rising, which was agreeable to the situation of Heliopolis; that he also set up pillars instead of gnomons [obelisks?], under which was represented a cavity like that of a boat, and the shadow that fell from their tops fell down upon that cavity, that it might go round about the like course as the sun itself goes round in the other.[1]

Apion was writing 1300 years after the Exodus out of Egypt, and yet it is clear that even in his own age the memory of Israel's great religious reformer was still strong in the minds of the Egyptian people. Like Manetho before him, Apion goes on to state that this wise man 'of Heliopolis' united the 'lepers' and 'impure people'

125

against the might of Egypt before being driven out of the country by the ruling Pharaoh.[2] And, like Manetho, Apion cites Moses as having championed a new style of sun-worship 'agreeable' to the age-old priesthood at Heliopolis.[3]

Where did this recurring theme that Moses had been a priest of Heliopolis actually come from? Why accredit this role to the biblical lawgiver who, until Sigmund Freud casually pointed out his obvious Egyptian background in the 1930s, was understood to have been born an Israelite of the house of Levi? In the knowledge that the character we know as Moses would appear to be integrally linked with the religious reforms instigated by Akhenaten at the commencement of the Amarna age, the association between Moses and the priests of Heliopolis becomes tantalisingly more apparent.

When Akhenaten succeeded to the throne of Egypt as Amenhotep IV in around 1367 BC, he proclaimed himself to be First Prophet of his new faith of the Aten, and yet he did not refer to his omnipotent one-god under this name, not yet at least. For the first nine years of his reign it was known as Re-harakhty, Horus of the Horizon. This was a falcon-headed form of the sun-god Re that embodied the dual aspects of the double horizon – the solar disc in the west at sunset and in the east at sunrise. The centre for the cult of Re was the city of Heliopolis, in Lower Egypt. The Arabic name for Heliopolis is 'Ain-Shams, literally the 'sun eye' or 'spring of the sun', while in the Bible it is referred to as On, a very close rendering of its original Egyptian name *Aunu*, *'Ounû* or *Iwnw*, the 'pillared city'.[4] It is a title linked intrinsically with the towering obelisks that once stood in the forecourt of its ancient sun temples, the last remaining of which, erected during the reign of Senwosret I (Twelfth Dynasty, *c.* 1991–1962 BC), can be seen today amid the hustle and bustle of the el-Matariyah suburb of modern Cairo, close to the international airport.

Akhenaten championed the Heliopolitan cult of Re, adopting its religious ideals, its teachings, its priestly titles and its unique style of worship, which included, as Apion stated, open-air temples where the sun would be ceremonially welcomed at dawn each day.[5] In plain terms, the Heliopolitan doctrine became the principal Egyptian cult religion for the seventeen years of Akhenaten's reign, for the brief three-year reign (two as co-regent) of his successor, Smenkhkare, and for the first three years of Tutankhamun's reign (under the name Tutankhaten). Although any reference to Re-harakhty disappeared from royal inscriptions after Year Nine of Akhenaten's reign, it is clear that behind the development and spread of the Aten faith was the extremely influential priesthood of Re. Somehow the priests were responsible for Akhenaten's unprecedented departure from the traditional polytheistic worship, as well as his desire to dedicate his life to one single, all-encompassing deity. So strongly did he believe in this omnipotent, nameless god that he was prepared to change his name to honour its symbol, the sun-disc. It also made him relocate his entire capital city, forbid the worship of any other god and, as we shall see, alter the entire face of Egyptian civilisation. What could possibly have motivated him to make such drastic changes in a matter of a few short years?

KEEPERS OF THE SECRET

Heliopolis was a great centre of learning, a 'university' known throughout the ancient world. Greek writers and travellers would come to spend time with its learned priests, who were apparently versed in the ancient wisdom. Before the time of Alexander in the fourth century BC, the city was a magnificent sight with an enormous temple complex, complete with administrative buildings, schools of learning and open courts all surrounded by an almighty double wall 13 metres in width and 9 metres in height. Heliopolis is its Greek name and means, quite literally, the 'city of the sun' – a reference to its priesthood's much-celebrated cult of the sun-god Re, which evolved from the more ancient cult of the god Atum, who was known as the Great One of Perfection. It was not until the advent of the pyramid age, c. 2678 BC, that the cult of Re overtook Atum in popularity at Heliopolis, almost certainly because of its royal patronage during Old Kingdom times. Yet the history of Heliopolis goes back way beyond the age of the Pharaohs to a time when Egyptian religious texts tell us that the enigmatic *Shemsu-hor*, the Followers of Horus, ruled as priest-kings from this ancient seat of power.[6]

The ancient heritage and wisdom of the Heliopolitan priesthood were renowned. Herodotus, the famous Greek historian of the fifth century BC, visited Heliopolis and subsequently recorded that in his opinion its priests had 'the reputation of being the best skilled in history of all the Egyptians'.[7] Not only were they versed in geometry, medicine, mythology and philosophy, but they were also looked on as 'masters of astronomy'.[8] Herodotus alludes to this in his *History* by stating that the priests of Heliopolis, along with those of Memphis and Thebes, 'were the first to discover the solar year, and to portion out its course into 12 parts [i.e. the 12-fold division of the ecliptic and the 12 lunar months, each of 30 days]'[9] – knowledge, he said, they obtained 'from the stars'.[10] The priests also informed him that the Egyptians were the first to use the 'names of the 12 gods, which the Greeks adopted from them' and the first to erect 'altars, images and temples to the gods' and that 'in most cases they proved to me that what they said was true'.[11]

So revered were Heliopolis' ancient libraries that a Thirteenth-Dynasty Pharaoh named Khasekhemre-Neferhotep, *c.* 1750 BC, left for posterity a stone stela at Abydos on which he recorded how he had 'desired to see the ancient writings of Atum' so that he might know 'how he was created, and how the gods were fashioned, and so that I may know the god [Osiris Khenti] in his [true] form, and may make [a statue of] him as he was of old, at the time when they [the gods] made the images [of themselves] at their council for the purpose of establishing their monuments on earth'. The inscription goes on to state that the king accepted an invitation from the priests, the 'keepers of all the secret [books]', to visit the libraries of Atum at Heliopolis, where he was able to view likenesses of Osiris Khenti that enabled his craftsmen to make a statue of his 'ancestor', whom he firmly believed was buried like a mortal man in a royal cemetery within Abydos' western necropolis.[12]

The age-old libraries of Heliopolis contained many ancient books hoary with age even in Khasekhemre-Neferhotep's day. It was from these that Manetho, who was himself a priest there, undoubtedly obtained much of the material that appeared subsequently in both his king-lists and his now lost three-volume history of Egypt.[13]

Other writers who are known to have consulted the libraries at Heliopolis include Pythagoras, Thales, Democritus and Eudoxus.[14] Plato (429–347 BC), the noted Greek philosopher and author of various literary works of great importance, wrote that the priests of Egypt (perhaps those at Heliopolis) had observed the stars 'for 10,000 years or, so to speak, for an infinite time'.[15]

That the priests of Heliopolis were 'masters of astronomy' is impossible to deny. The holy of holies deep inside the temple complex was known as the 'Star Room',[16] while its high priest bore the title 'Chief of the Astronomers'. Apparently, he wore a robe adorned with stars and carried as an emblem of office a long staff which terminated in a five-pointed star.[17]

The Heliopolitan brotherhood did not, however, confine its astronomical interests simply to noting the positions and courses of the stars. It would also seem that, as Plato suggested, they used the heavenly bodies to monitor the passage of time. This is strongly indicated by the role once played by Heliopolis' needle-like obelisks, for as the fourteenth-century Arab chronicler al-Makrizi noted:

> 'Ain-Shams is the temple of the Sun at Heliopolis where there stand two columns so marvellous that one has never seen anything more beautiful . . . They are about 50 cubits high . . . The points of their summits are made of copper . . . At the moment when the Sun enters the First Point of Capricorn, that is to say on the shortest day of the year, it reaches the southernmost of the two obelisks and crowns its summit; and when it reaches the First Point of Cancer, that is to say on the longest day of the year, it touches the northernmost obelisk and crowns its summit. These two

obelisks thus form the two extreme points of the solar swing
and the equinoctial line passes between them . . .[18]

This ancient tradition, recorded by Makrizi long after Heliopolis had
fallen into ruin, seems to echo the opinion of Apion, who spoke of
the rebel priest and religious reformer named Moses as having 'set up
pillars instead of gnomons' so that their shadow 'might go round
about the like course as the sun itself goes round'. It seems certain
that at least some of the obelisks of Heliopolis were set up to mark
the course of the sun as it shifted gradually back and forth from
solstice to solstice via the two equinoctial days. The necessity of such
precision knowledge was to monitor the movements of the stars as
they slowly altered their positions against the backdrop of the
celestial horizon.

HORUS OF THE HORIZON

Although few scholars would deny that Akhenaten hijacked the
Heliopolitan cult of Re to initiate his own religious revolution, to
understand how this came about will necessitate going back in
history nearly 50 years to the reign of his grandfather, Thutmose IV
(c. 1413–1405 BC), for it was this king who began elevating the
sun-god to the role of supreme deity for the very first time.

It is said that when Thutmose was no more than a prince,
something very strange happened when he was out hunting one
day. Having become weary, he fell asleep against the towering head
of the Great Sphinx. In a dream its spirit addressed the young
prince, telling him that if he were to clear away the sand that
clogged its body, then he would become king of Egypt. The Sphinx
remained true to its word, for after carrying out its request, the
prince of Egypt, perhaps inevitably, ascended the throne to become
Thutmose IV. Both the dream and its fulfilment are commemorated
in an important inscription carved on a red-granite stela, erected by

Thutmose during his reign and found today between the out-stretched paws of the leonine monument.[19]

Whatever the reality of Thutmose's prophetic dream, it affirms two things: first, that the king would appear to have patronised the Heliopolitan cult of Re, and, secondly, that its priesthood would appear to have supported him. The key to Thutmose's devotion to the sun cult of Re is the Great Sphinx, for although the principal form of Re-harakhty, Horakhty or Horus of the Horizon was the falcon-headed god (the manner in which he was depicted in the earliest temples built by Akhenaten at Karnak), the name would also appear to be linked to the Great Sphinx. The Sphinx, or Dream, Stela as it is popularly known, names the *genius loci* of the leonine monument as *Har-em-akhet-Khepri-Re-Atum*. Re and Atum we have already encountered. Khepri is the sun-god in the form of the dung beetle, while *Har-em-akhet*, 'Horus-in-the-Horizon', is essentially another form of Re-harakhty.[20] The granite stela also tells us that Thutmose IV was the protector of Harakhty, 'living image of the All-lord', seemingly a reference to the Sphinx itself.[21] For, as the eminent Egyptologist Sir E.A. Wallis Budge was to note:

> The largest known monument or figure of Heru-khuti [i.e. Horakhty, or Re-harakhty] is the famous Sphinx, near the Pyramids of Gizeh, which was his type and symbol.[22]

As we have already seen, the Great Sphinx stands as sentinel guardian close to the south-eastern corner of the Giza plateau, just 22.5 kilometres (14 miles) south-west of the old religious centre at Heliopolis. Ever since Old Kingdom times, when the various pyramid fields were being constructed, Giza, or Rostau as it was known in Egyptian, came under the jurisdiction of the Heliopolitan priesthood. To them it was a necropolis of the dead and featured heavily in their mythological doctrine of the underworld (see Chapter Twelve). The fulfilment of Thutmose's revelatory dream, along with his erection of the Sphinx Stela following the clearance of sand from around the body of the Sphinx, is to be seen therefore as an attempt by the king to affirm some kind of mutual alliance not just with the priests of Re at nearby Heliopolis but also with their god Re-harakhty, Horus of the Horizon.

Thutmose's royal patronage of the Heliopolitan doctrine was unprecedented in New Kingdom times. All previous kings of the Eighteenth Dynasty, which had begun with the expulsion of the Hyksos in around 1575 BC, had honoured the god Amun, whose powerful priesthood controlled state affairs and rites of kingship from their cult centre at Thebes (modern-day Karnak in southern Egypt). No one can deny this powerful connection between Thutmose IV and Heliopolis, for he also took the unprecedented step of erecting a single obelisk that honoured Re-harakhty on the east–west axis line of Karnak's Temple of Amun.[23] That Thutmose was beginning to revere the Heliopolitan sun-disc over and above any other deity is proved by the discovery of a huge stone scarab beetle issued during his reign. Its inscription refers to the Aten as the god of battles who 'makes pharaoh mighty in his dominions' and brings all his subjects under its sway.[24]

Thutmose IV's son, Amenhotep III (c. 1405–1367 BC), Akhenaten's father, continued this renewed royal patronage of the Heliopolitan cult of the sun, under the influence of which he began to change the whole emphasis of Egyptian religion. Pushing further than his father before him, Amenhotep became the first king to elevate the Aten sun-disc into a divinity with its own temples and priesthood.[25] He also named his royal barge *Aten Gleams*, or the 'radiance of Aten',[26] and even adopted the name Akhenaten, 'spirit of Aten', as a praenomen.[27]

There was nothing unusual about kings placating and venerating one particular cult centre or deity over and above another, and so the fact that both Thutmose IV and his son Amenhotep III developed an open affinity with the gods of Heliopolis should not be seen as strange, simply a case of personal preference. Yet when Akhenaten took the throne of Egypt after his father, Amenhotep III, he did not simply patronise the temples at Heliopolis and promote their solar faith; he became *utterly obsessed* with their doctrines over and above every other cult. Not only did both Re and Re-harakhty merge to become important aspects of the Aten, but Akhenaten also cast aside his own rules in forbidding the use of animalistic symbols so that he could depict himself as a human-headed sphinx.

It is in this manner that Akhenaten is portrayed in a little-known wall relief in the possession of the Kestner Museum at Hanover in Germany. Here the king is shown in a scene typical of the Amarna style of art as a human-headed sphinx making offerings to the multi-rayed Aten sun-disc. Its existence, when seen alongside his utter devotion to Re-harakhty, hints at the possibility that, like his grandfather Thutmose IV before him, Akhenaten possessed a special interest in the Sphinx monument of Giza. What might this have been? What could he have possibly learned from the priests of Heliopolis concerning the leonine monument's hidden mysteries? Only by understanding the depth at which Akhenaten adopted the Heliopolitan doctrines can we even begin to contemplate these questions.

Animal worship and the adoration of idols were, as we have seen, forbidden by Akhenaten and yet, in addition to depicting himself as a human-headed sphinx, he also revered the sacred Mnevis bull of Heliopolis, which was seen as an incarnation of the god Ur-mer, described in ancient texts as the 'life of Ra'.[28] Each bull would be afforded a life of luxury by its presiding priests, and after its natural death the carcass would be mummified and interred in a specially prepared tomb at Heliopolis. Yet after his move to Amarna, Akhenaten is known to have commissioned the construction of a grand tomb in the so-called Royal Wadi – where he also constructed a tomb for himself – which was intended to house the mummified remains of the current Mnevis bull when it died.[29] It is uncertain whether the tomb was ever used for this purpose, although its mere existence once again affirms Akhenaten's great reverence for the Heliopolitan religion.

MANSIONS OF THE BENBEN

More significant was Akhenaten's veneration of what was perhaps the most important element of the Heliopolitan sun-cult: the so-called *benben* (*bnbn*). This was a sacred stone shaped like a cone, a pyramid or a stepped object, which had been mounted on a stone perch located in an open court adjoining a temple at Heliopolis known as the Mansion of the Benben or the Mansion of the Phoenix.

In Year Four of his reign, Akhenaten initiated the construction of a huge temple at Karnak, Thebe's religious centre, called, in similarity to its counterpart at Heliopolis, the Mansion of the Benben. As with its 'mother' temple, Akhenaten is likely to have set up a huge sandstone representation of the *benben*-stone in its vast open-air court. In addition to this, following his relocation to what is today Tell el-Amarna in Middle Egypt in Year Six, he set about building within the confines of his new city another huge open-air temple called the Great House of the Aten. This, too, included at its eastern end, closest to the morning sunrise, a Mansion of the Benben which is known to have housed a *benben*-stone. This sacred pillar took the form of a round-topped stela of quartzite, surmounted on a stone dais.[30] Akhenaten even erected a stylised stela with the appearance of a round-topped *benben*-stone at Heliopolis, where his father had already built a temple to the Aten during his own reign.[31] On this stone Akhenaten and his family were shown prostrating themselves before the sun-disc.[32]

The origin of this strange practice is obscure. It has been theorised that the original *benben*-stone might have been composed of meteoric iron, a precious substance highly revered by the Ancient Egyptians and connected by them with the worship of the stars.[33] This supposition, advanced by a number of authors, is, however, still a matter of conjecture, for the texts are silent on the matter. Furthermore, the original *benben*-stone had disappeared long before the pyramid age, and plausibly even before the advent of dynastic

Egypt. No one can be sure what it might have been, although it is generally accepted that the priests of Heliopolis replaced the original item with a conical-shaped stone surmounted on a needle-like pillar, which may well have been the prototype for the much later obelisks so familiar to Egyptian architecture.

Akhenaten's apparent obsession with *benben*-stones almost certainly explains the curious statement made by Apion of Alexandria, who spoke of Moses, the religious reformer 'of Heliopolis', erecting 'pillars instead of gnomons'. The word 'gnomons' is a reference to needle-like obelisks, while the word 'pillars' seems to imply something else, very likely the round-topped dais stones thought to have been erected by Akhenaten at Karnak, at his new city in Amarna and at Heliopolis. The fact that Apion also refers to this Moses offering 'his prayers in the open air, towards the city walls' and directing everyone that they should worship 'towards the sun-rising' in a manner 'agreeable to the situation of Heliopolis'[34] points to one clear conclusion. It is that Apion was preserving some kind of distorted memory, still prevalent in Egypt during the first century BC, concerning the religious changes implemented during the reign of Akhenaten under the influence of the Heliopolitan priesthood.

THE DIVINE SOULS

How might we explain Akhenaten's strange fascination with the *benben*-stone? What did it mean to him, and why did he feel it necessary to place within the heart of his temple complexes cult objects that could easily have been construed as idolatrous fetish stones? As Egyptologist Donald Redford felt obliged to comment on this subject:

> That Amenophis IV should, in the light of his well-attested aversion to polytheistic symbolism in mythology, have permitted this icon to a naive account of creation to find a

prominent place in his thinking, is strange to say the least. Obviously the *bnbn* did not conjure up for the king the objectionable connections with mythology that we might have expected.[35]

To understand Akhenaten's reverence of the *benben*-stone we must look at exactly what this cult object meant to the Ancient Egyptians. In very basic terms it was the crystallisation of the primeval mound, or hill – the first solid ground that emerged from the primeval ocean in the darkness that preceded the light of the first morning. It was a representation of the *djed*-pillar, or perch, on which the primeval god Atum, a role adopted later by Re, was able to effect acts of creation in the world.[36] A more detailed description of the *benben*-stone is given in the Pyramid Texts, found inscribed on the tomb walls of various Fifth- and Sixth-Dynasty pyramids, such as the Pyramid of Unas (*c.* 2370–2340 BC) at Saqqara. This extraordinary collection of cosmo-logical writings and magical spells constitutes what is perhaps the oldest body of magical-religious material anywhere in the world. More significantly, Egyptian language scholar R.T. Rundle Clark concluded that they were composed 'in the main' by the astronomer-priests of Heliopolis.[37] Their repeated references to the solar cult of Atum-Re and Annu (Heliopolis), as well as their direct connection with the kings and pyramids of Old Kingdom times, all point clearly towards a Heliopolitan origin for this material.

The original *benben*-stone positioned on a stone pillar in the court adjoining the Mansion of the Benben at Heliopolis was in effect a marker that symbolised the Point of First Creation, the place of *sep tepi*, the First Time, where the initial group of nine *netjeru* gods, known in Heliopolitan tradition as the Great Ennead, made their entry into the world. In time, these divine beings were followed by a second group of nine gods known as the Lesser Ennead, who were in turn followed by a third and final group of nine variable gods. Finally, these were replaced by a further group of 'mythical' individuals known in the Pyramid Texts as the Divine Souls.[38]

Egyptologist Abdel-Aziz Saleh recorded in his definitive work

Excavations at Heliopolis that the Divine Souls are to be equated with the *Shemsu-hor*, who he described as 'the pre-dynastic lords, or monarchs, of the city'.[39] These demi-gods were, he wrote, viewed by the priests of Heliopolis as the true founders of its first physical temple, known as the Mansion of the Princes or the Mansion of the Nobles.[40] Indeed, the priesthood would seem to have been convinced that the Divine Souls had ruled from Heliopolis and its environs during a golden age prior to the coming of the mortal Horus-kings.[41]

To these astronomer-priests of great wisdom and understanding, such concepts were not simply myths; they were a tangible reality conveyed in poetic terms within their cosmological doctrine. To them Heliopolis *really was* the home of the gods, who really *had* built the first temples both here and at nearby Giza.

Our knowledge of the Giza plateau's immense antiquity, along with its astronomical alignments and high technology, points clearly towards the fact that the astronomer-priests of Heliopolis were somehow preserving the memory of the Sphinx-building Elder culture, who reigned supreme in Egypt during the First Time, the age of the lion, which had passed many thousands of years before the ascension of the first Pharaoh. It seems plausible that if anyone inherited the advanced technology of the Elder gods, then it was the priesthood of Re at Heliopolis. Could the knowledge of sonic levitation and ultrasound drilling have passed into their sphere of influence at the beginning of dynastic history? If so, were they behind its use during the pyramid age, and did they in turn convey at least some semblance of this sound technology to Akhenaten?

Before answering these pressing questions, it will be necessary to understand the manner in which the arcane myths surrounding the golden age of the gods influenced the establishment of Egypt's royal dynasties and religious cults from the time of the pyramid builders to the ascent of Akhenaten. Only then will a much clearer picture begin to emerge.

CHAPTER ELEVEN

SPIRIT OF THE AGE

Heliopolis might well have staked its claim as being the Point of First Creation but there were rivals – other powerful cult centres that could also claim to be the place of the First Time, the domain of the gods. The chief among them was Thebes, the powerful seat of the cult of Amun, the 'hidden' god. Its mighty priesthood believed Thebes to be the oldest city, built on the site of the primeval mound that rose out of the watery abyss at the beginning of time.[1] The Temple of Amun even had its own form of *benben*-stone – a hemi-spherical stone, or *omphalos* (a Greek word meaning 'navel'), that marked the centre of everything and acted as an oracle of great renown, proclaiming the rise and fall of kings.[2]

There were many *omphali* in the ancient world, the most famous being the one at Delphi in Greece. Of this it was said that the mighty sky-god Zeus, wishing to learn the whereabouts of the exact centre of the earth, sent forth two eagles from its eastern and western limits.[3] They flew without stopping until they met at Delphi, and here the gods erected a navel-stone, on either side of which was carved a golden eagle.[4] Ancient tradition spoke of it as having been fashioned from a single piece of marble and shaped like an egg – a symbol of creation in mythologies around the world.

Thebes' claim to be Egypt's oldest cult centre was largely ignored in Old Kingdom times, due to the royal patronage bestowed on

Heliopolis. It was not until the Middle Kingdom, *c.* 2134–1786 BC, that the myth and ritual surrounding the cult of Amun began to take on a national importance, for it was at this time that a dynasty of Theban kings rose to prominence and eventually took control of the kingdom.[5] Four of them even chose the name Amenemhet, 'Amun is foremost', in honour of their local god.[6] At the same time the influence of Heliopolis was on the wane, in sharp contrast to the enormous respect its priests had commanded during the pyramid age.

It was a battle of religious provenance, and Thebes was taking the upper hand. Yet this clear north–south divide between the two most dominant priesthoods of Egypt was itself deep-rooted and probably went back to the tribal wars that had been waged in predynastic times between the legendary Horus-kings of Heliopolis and the Seth-kings (after the god Set) of Nubt (Naqada) in the south.[7] Even after Menes, the first Horus-king of a united Egypt, brought peace to the country in around 3100 BC, feelings must have run deep, causing a cultural and religious division that prevailed in some form right down to Roman times. This situation might be compared with the blatant differences that still prevail between the northern and southern states of America, over a century and a half after the American Civil War, or the fierce political and religious divide that continues to exist between the Catholics and Protestants of Northern Ireland, even though the root of the problem is centuries old.

Such was the situation at the beginning of the so-called Second Intermediate Period, *c.* 1786–1575 BC, when the collapse of the ruling dynasty of kings led to most of Egypt, including the capital Memphis, being overrun by the Hyksos, or 'shepherds' – the nomadic peoples of Canaan. In spite of their very different cultural backgrounds, these people quickly settled into an Egyptian lifestyle and established a seat of power at Avaris in the Eastern Delta, *c.* 1730 BC. The Hyksos kings also adopted the myths and rituals of the Egyptian Pharaohs and, most pertinently, enlisted the aid of the priests of Heliopolis to conduct rites of kingship;[8] indeed, inscriptions record that at least four of the listed Hyksos kings bore

EGYPTIAN PERIOD	DYNASTIES		RELEVANT KINGS	HIGHEST DATED YEAR	CONJECTURAL DATES BC	SUGGESTED DATES BC OF CORRESPONDING BIBLICAL EVENTS
PREDYNASTIC (GERZEAN/ NAQADA II)					3500–3200	
PROTODYNASTIC	0				3200–3100	
ARCHAIC	I–II				3100–2700	
		I	NARMER		c. 3100	
			HOR-AHA (MENES)	62	c. 3050	
OLD KINGDOM	III–VII				2700–2137	
		III	DJOSER	29	2678–2649	
		IV	SNOFRU	29/24	2620–2596	
			KHUFU	63/23	2596–2573	
			KHAFRE	66/23	2550–2525	
			MENKAURE	28/18	2512–2484	
FIRST INTERMEDIATE	VIII–X				2137–?	
MIDDLE KINGDOM	XI–XII				2134–1786	1921† – ABRAHAM TRAVELS FROM UR VIA HARRAN TO EGYPT
			SENWOSRET I	48/19	1991–1962	
			SENWOSRET III	33	1878–1843	
	XII		AMENEMHET III	45	1842–1797	
			AMENEMHET IV	6	1798–1790	
			SOBEKNOFRURE	3 YRS 10 MONTHS	1789–1786	
SECOND INTERMEDIATE (INCL. HYKSOS)	XIII–XVII (XV–XVI)				1786–1575 (1730–1575)	
		XIII	KHASEKHEMRE-NEFERHOTEP	11	c. 1750	
NEW KINGDOM	XVIII–XX				1575–1308	
	XVIII		AHMOSE	22	1575–1550	
			AMENHOTEP I	21	1550–1528	
			THUTMOSE I	9/4	1528–1510	
			THUTMOSE II	18	1510–1490	
			HATSHEPSUT	22/20	1490–1468	
			THUTMOSE III	54	1490–1436	
			AMENHOTEP II	23	1436–1413	
			THUTMOSE IV	8	1413–1405	c. 1400–1350*–RISE OF MOSES
			AMENHOTEP III	39.38	1405–1367	
			AMENHOTEP IV (AKHENATEN)	17	1367–1350	
			SMENKHKARE	3	1350–1347	c. 1350*–MOSES EXILED TO SINAI
			TUTANKHAMUN	9	1347–1339	
			AYE	4	1339–1335	
			HOREMHEB	28/27	1335–1308	
	XIX		RAMESSES I	2	1308–1307	1307?*–EXODUS FROM EGYPT
			SETI I	14/11	1308–1291?	
			RAMESSES II	67	1290–1224	1267?*–ISRAEL'S ENTRY INTO CANAAN. FALL OF JERICHO
			MERENPTAH	10	1224–1214	
LATE DYNASTIC PERIOD	XXI–XXXI				1087–332	1020†–ASCENT OF DAVID 980†–ASCENT OF SOLOMON 977†–FOUNDATION OF SOLOMON'S TEMPLE

NOTE: All Egyptian dates are based on the chronology of 'The Kings of Egypt from Manetho, the King-Lists, and the Monuments', included as an appendix to Gardiner, *Egypt of the Pharaohs*. Suggested dates for biblical events are based on the findings of this current work* and *The Illustrated Bible Treasury*, edited by William Wright.†

Chronology of Ancient Egypt.

praenomens that honoured the sun-god Re,[9] clearly demonstrating their devotion to the Heliopolitan doctrine.

With the Hyksos kings firmly established in Lower Egypt, a new, though at first very feeble, dynasty of Egyptian Pharaohs began to emerge under the wing of the Amun priesthood at Thebes. Gradually these Theban rulers gained enough strength and knowledge of warfare – much of it stolen from the Hyksos – to expel the enemy, which finally they succeeded in doing shortly after the ascension to the throne of a king named Ahmose in around 1575 BC. Freedom returned to Egypt, and Ahmose became the first Pharaoh of not only the Eighteenth Dynasty, *c.* 1575–1308 BC, but also the so-called New Kingdom period. Yet instead of returning to its old residence in Memphis, the royal family stayed on at its new palace in Thebes and continued to allow the Amun priests to conduct rites of kingship, for both the living and the dead. A new necropolis was henceforth established on the west bank of the Nile (even though Theban kings had been buried in the area since the Middle Kingdom), and here the Pharaohs of Egypt were interred in rock-cut tombs. Royal burials continued in this fashion throughout the whole of the New Kingdom period, and today this necropolis is most famous for its Valley of the Kings, where the tomb of Tutankhamun was discovered by Howard Carter in 1922.

Under the mighty kings of the Eighteenth Dynasty, Thebes became the most influential cult centre of Egypt, a situation that Heliopolis must have loathed. Yet the indications are that the Re priesthood had no intention of accepting this loss of royal favour without a fight. Its ancient cosmology was too old, too well established, too important for it to be simply ignored, so a compromise was finally reached between the two cult centres. Henceforth Amun, the principal god of Thebes, would absorb, and thus acknowledge, the superior aspects of the sun-god Re, and in so doing would create a new hybrid god-form known as Amun-Re. In this role the twin deity would become the supreme deity of Egypt, embodying both the hidden virtues of Amun and the greatness and primordial sanctity of Atum-Re, the god who had alighted on the primeval mound at the beginning of time.

THE MIDDLE OF NOWHERE

Despite the apparent agreement made between the two rival priest-hoods some time during the early Eighteenth Dynasty, Heliopolis realised that it had lost out to Thebes,[10] and there was really very little it could do about the situation until the arrival of the future Thutmose IV. It was his dream-inspired clearance of sand from around the body of the Great Sphinx, *c.* 1420 BC, that had led to the establishment of a new alliance between the royal family and the Heliopolitan brotherhood – a situation that had grown gradually over a 50-year period until the succession to the throne of Akhenaten in around 1367 BC. Not only did he adopt wholesale the Heliopoli-tan doctrine, but his decision to build a Mansion of the Benben smack in the heartland of the Amun temple complex at Thebes can only be seen as a blatant attempt to usurp the political and spiritual dominion of its *omphalos*-stone, its own Point of First Creation.

Egyptologists believe that Akhenaten built his city simply to give the Aten a cult centre of its own. This is questionable, especially as the Aten was merely an upgraded form of the god Re-harakhty, who already had a home at Heliopolis. Even if this solution were correct, it does not explain the king's decision to build his city on the edge of the eastern desert, close to what is today Tell el-Amarna. If the king really did view Heliopolis in terms of Egypt's all-important Point of First Creation, then his erection of a brand-new Mansion of the Benben, complete with its own *benben*-stone, within the grand temple to the Aten at Akhetaten, suggests that he was attempting to establish not just a new seat of divine rule but an entirely new Point of First Creation.

The only realistic explanation offered by any scholar of Egyptol-ogy was the one put forward by the late Cyril Aldred, a well-respected scholar of the Amarna period. He pointed out that the gap in the eastern hills above the Royal Wadi, where the sun is seen to rise from the position of the city at certain times of the year, seems to resemble a saddle-back indentation, similar to the hieroglyph used to denote the word *akhet*, 'horizon'.[11] It was therefore conceivable that Akhenaten may have witnessed the sun emerging between this gap on a visit to the region, and, seeing this as some kind of sign given to him by the Aten, sealed his decision to build a city here and name it Akhetaten, the 'horizon of the Aten'.

It is an interesting theory, and if Akhenaten really had been witness to a sunrise of the description given by Aldred, then I feel it would certainly have appealed to his religious spirit. On the other hand it hardly explains why the Pharaoh saw this bleak location as important in the first place. In my opinion there had to be a more realistic, and perhaps more profound, purpose behind his move to Amarna. Yet since the decision to build here would not appear to have been purely political or religious in nature, then it had to be linked in some way with Akhenaten's belief in the Aten. So what really did inspire him to build his city in the middle of nowhere?

One possible clue to unravelling this perplexing mystery is the boundary stelae that once marked the outer limits of Amarna's jurisdiction.[12] There were 14 of these immovable round-topped stones carved out of solid rock at different places either on the edge of the eastern desert, up against tall cliffs, or close to the fertile banks of the Nile. Each one bore a relief and hieroglyphic inscription that proclaimed the king's conviction to Re-harakhty-aten and the construction of the intended city, along with details of the stela's dedication ceremony at which the king and members of the royal family had been present.

The boundary stelae also tell us that the site chosen for the new city was revealed to Akhenaten by the Aten itself, and that no one, no matter who it was, would persuade him to build his city elsewhere.[13] This enigmatic statement implies that some kind of divine revelation might have been involved in the Pharaoh's choice of location. It also reveals that at least some people close to Akhenaten, perhaps even members of his own family, had questioned his decision to relocate here. In addition to this, the inscriptions also state quite clearly that if this proclamation should ever be removed or defaced, then it would

One of the boundary stelae which marked the city limits of Akhetaten
(after N. de G. Davies).

immediately be replaced by another.[14]

Strangest of all, the stelae tell us that Akhenaten is now 'living in
maat' (*ankh-em-maat*).[15] Again and again they proclaim the same
thing – Akhenaten is 'living in *maat*'. Exactly what did this mean –
'living in *maat*'? No other Pharaoh referred to himself in quite such a
manner, so what or who was *maat*? Might this provide us with some
clue as to why Akhenaten wanted to re-establish Egypt's Point of
First Creation at a virgin site on the edge of the eastern desert?

LIVING IN *MAAT*

Maat was an important Egyptian goddess who personified all that
was proper – justice, truth, the right way of doing things. In many
respects Maat might be seen as the prototype of the woman holding

the scales associated with the sign of Libra in the modern zodiac. She might also be equated with the female figure with an upright sword in one hand and the scales of justice in the other, who watches over the Old Bailey lawcourts in London. Maat's distinguishing symbol was the white ostrich feather that she wore tied to a band around her head. This same device was used as the counterbalance on the scales of justice when the hearts of the dead were weighed in the presence of Osiris, the god of the underworld. From the very beginnings of dynastic Egypt, Maat was worshipped as a female counterpart to the moon-god Thoth, and, like Thoth, she was especially venerated at Heliopolis.[16]

Maat as a cosmic principle was, however, very much more than simply a goddess of truth and justice. In Egyptian art she is often seen standing on a wedge-shaped pedestal, generally taken to be either a unit of measurement, a 'cubit', or 'some instrument used for measuring purposes'[17] – a conclusion only emphasised by her name, which translates as 'that which is straight'.[18] When viewed in association with the goddess's white feather, this curious device signifies Maat's primary role as the embodiment of cosmic order by divine rule both through the establishment of the canon or rule of the Horus-king as *ruler*[19] and as the *measured* lines of geographic extent defined by the location of the centrally positioned seat of kingship.

The concept of divine kingship might seem complex and even pointless in our own day and age, but to the Ancient Egyptians the idea of establishing cosmic order was a fundamental part of divine rule. Fail to enact the correct myth and ritual, and the links between the celestial and physical realms would be severed, resulting in chaos. To ensure that cosmic order was maintained, the king would have to rule in majesty from his chosen seat of power, which would be seen not just as the point where the terrestrial and celestial worlds met but also as the centre of everything and the point of beginning. The king's role was then to adopt the mantle of the primeval god and continue the act of creation in the world – only by doing this could he be seen as truly 'living in *maat*'.

Akhenaten's adoption of the principle of *maat* on the establishment of his new city is explainable in this context but, as Amarna expert Cyril Aldred commented, his obsession with this religious concept seems to have gone far beyond that understood by any other Pharaoh:

> A more profound examination of the 'maet' in which Akhenaten professed to live has shown that its earlier translation [by Egyptologists] is an over-simplification, and it refers rather to that harmony prevailing when the universe left the hands of the creator at the beginning of time.[20]

This statement implies that in addition to establishing cosmic order at Amarna, Akhenaten was attempting to create a pattern of divine rule in the manner he conceived as having existed during the First Time, the primeval age when the *netjeru* gods lived in the world. That the king had a special interest in the concept of the First Time is not in doubt, for as Aldred goes on to say in respect to his decision to leave Thebes: 'Inspiration had come to the king to seek the place in Egypt where the Aten had manifested himself at the First Time when the world had come into existence.'[21]

What did Akhenaten really know about the First Time? What did it really mean to him? Is there some way in which he could have become convinced of the physical reality of the *netjeru* gods and the Divine Souls of Heliopolis? Could this have inspired him to change the face of Egyptian religion and relocate his entire world to the edge of the eastern desert? More pressing, how did he come to believe that the place of the First Time was a more-or-less isolated location away from any other cult centre putting claim to this prestigious title?

THE BOUNDS OF EGYPT

All the indications are that by Year Four of his reign, Akhenaten had somehow come to realise that the ancient beliefs held by existing cult centres in respect to their being Egypt's true Point of First Creation were simply inadequate. What he needed was something more. Something more powerful. Something that would permit him to instigate his new aeon from a place of immense spiritual potency and yet at the same time would still enable him to embrace the claims being made by its two most powerful cult centres. In many ways he wanted to rule over Egypt like some kind of enormous giant with one foot on Thebes, the other on Heliopolis, and his head, mind and spirit positioned firmly within the bounds of his planned utopic paradise.

So how did he exact his master plan?

The answer would appear to be through a profound understanding of ancient geography.

It is a plain fact that the site of Akhenaten's city is located midway between Heliopolis in the north and Heliopolis in the south, the latter being a name applied to Thebes from the Eighteenth Dynasty onwards.[22] Each location is exactly 275 kilometres (172 miles) from Akhenaten's city, a relationship that cannot be coincidence. This geographical association between the three sites is not denied by Egyptologists, although its significance has never been properly understood.

One man alone seems to have grasped a true understanding of Akhenaten's taste for landscape geometry, and this is Livio Stecchini, the metrologist and mathematician who was the first to define the exact geodesic relationship between the Great Pyramid and the northern hemisphere. Having become fascinated with the life and times of Akhenaten, Stecchini turned his attention to the subject of the siting of the city. This quickly led him to realise that its placement seemed carefully planned in accordance with a precise ground-plan involving the lines of latitude and longitude of the earth. As he explained in the long appendix he contributed to Peter Tompkins' milestone work, *Secrets of the Great Pyramid*:

> The new capital for the god Aten . . . was set at latitude 27° 45′ north, at the middle point between the northernmost point Behdet [in the Nile Delta] and the southern limit of Egypt at latitude 24° 00′ north [Aswan, or Elephantine]. The longitude could not be equally as significant, since the capital had to be on the banks of the Nile. It was one degree east of the western axis of Egypt, that is, 30° 50′ east.[23]

Stecchini also realised that this placement, which defined the precise midway point between the most northerly and southerly limits of Egypt, could not have occurred by chance alone. This same age-old system of geodesy Stecchini had found embodied in the measurements of the Great Pyramid, as well as in the positioning of the east–west demarcation line defining the division between Upper and Lower Egypt, which had supposedly been established by Menes *c.* 3100 BC.[24]

Stecchini also noted that if a line, the same distance as that between Amarna and Behdet, be swung eastwards from the site of Akhenaten's city towards the Red Sea, it would take you to the island of Ghānim, situated off Cape Az Zaytīyah – the so-called Drepanon promontory referred to by Ptolemy, the Alexandrian astronomer and geographer of the first century AD. The importance here is that both Cape Az Zaytīyah and the island of Ghānim, which lies slightly to the south, were seen by the Egyptians as the southernmost extent of the Gulf of Suez.[25]

Intrigued by these discoveries, Stecchini turned his attentions to the dimensions of the city, as defined by the 14 boundary stelae. He soon concluded that their placement conformed to a geodesic system that pre-dated even the foundations of Pharaonic Egypt. For example, on the two stelae that marked the city's most northerly and southerly limits, the distance between them is given specifically as

6 *atur*, ¾ *khe* and 4 cubits.[26] Using these measurements, Stecchini then made some careful calculations and eventually concluded that they were an exact proportional representation of 106 *atur*, the figure traditionally given as the length of Egypt from its most northerly point at Behdet to its designated most southerly point at Aswan, the twenty-fourth parallel. Furthermore, by conforming to this rigid geodesic system, the measurements of the city expressed an exact microcosmic form of the average degree of latitude of the earth, *as well as* the length of the arc of meridian based on the figure of 12 × 106 *atur*.[27]

As Stecchini was justifiably able to comment:

> Akhenaten wanted to prove that Thebes could not properly claim to be the geodesic center of Egypt and that he had chosen [in Amarna] the geodesic center conforming to an absolutely rigorous interpretation of *maat*, the cosmic order of which the dimensions of Egypt were an embodiment. In order to follow absolutely exact standards of measurement, he reverted to the predynastic geodetic system which counted in geographic cubits starting from [the ancient capital of] Behdet.[28]

This is an astonishing statement to make, as it implies clearly that in choosing the location and dimensions of his new city Akhenaten had, if I might use Cyril Aldred's words, attempted to re-create the 'harmony prevailing when the universe left the hands of the creator at the beginning of time.' He was, of course, referring to the First Time, when Egypt was still in the hands of the *netjeru* gods. Stecchini fell short of actually making this link. However, he did suggest that, in the light of these findings: '. . . one should re-evaluate the entire historical role of Akhenaten, taking as the starting point what he himself considered the initial step in his program to establish true and just conformity with *maat*'.[29]

FLIGHT OF THE PHOENIX

Even further confirmation of Akhenaten's obsession with divine kingship and its association with the concept of the First Time is the royal name he adopted in honour of the Aten. The usual interpretation of Akhenaten is 'glory' or 'spirit of Aten' and, more recently, 'that which is beneficial to the Aten'.[30] Yet the prefix *akh* means much more than this, for it was used in hieroglyphic inscriptions to denote the spirit of a Pharaoh which, after its release in death, rises rapidly into the sky to become a circumpolar star – a star that revolves for ever around the celestial pole and is never seen to set.[31] Collectively, these divine souls or *akhu* (the plural of *akh*) thereafter become one with the cosmic force that is seen to revolve around the pole of the ecliptic, defining the passage of time.[32]

The concept of the *akh* was bound up integrally with the Heliopolitan view of recurring cycles of time, and together they were themselves linked with the Egyptian myth concerning the grey heron or *bennu*-bird – the purple-plumed phoenix of Greek tradition. This mythical bird of great fable and renown figured exclusively in the Heliopolitan creation myth, where it was seen as the aspect of the god Atum (and later Re) that alighted on the primeval mound, or hill, at the moment of sunrise on the first morning.

As the sun's rays burst forth on the sacred *benben*-stone, the *bennu*-bird took flight, making its way to the Isle of Fire – a mythical destination seen as the place of birth and regeneration of the gods.[33] When it returned to Heliopolis, the original site of the primeval mound (in their tradition, at least), it signalled the death of the First Time, the golden age of the gods, and the commencement of a new world epoch. Each time the *bennu*-bird was seen to return to Heliopolis, it would signal the end of one aeon and the commencement of the next.

Herodotus, the noted Greek historian, received a rather distorted version of the tradition surrounding the *bennu*-bird when he visited

The Egyptian *bennu*-bird, which was transformed into the phoenix of
Greek tradition, seen perched on the *benben*-stone – a symbol of the
mound of creation.

Heliopolis in the mid-fifth century BC, for as he tells us in his *History*:

> They [the Heliopolitans] tell a story of what this bird does,
> which does not seem to me to be credible: that he comes all
> the way from Arabia, and brings the parent bird, all plastered
> over with myrrh, to the temple of the Sun, and there buries
> the body. In order to bring him, they say, he first forms a ball
> of myrrh as big as he finds that he can carry; then he hollows
> out the ball, and puts his parent inside, after which he covers
> over the opening with fresh myrrh, and the ball is then of
> exactly the same weight as at first; so he brings it to Egypt,
> plastered over as I have said, and deposits it in the temple of
> the Sun. Such is the story they tell of the doings of this
> bird.[34]

It is a quaint old legend that bears very little resemblance to what is
known of the *bennu*-bird from original Egyptian sources. The myth
of the phoenix does, however, emphasise the idea that the end of an
aeon is heralded by the appearance of the mythical heron, which in

real life returned to rest on the Nile around midsummer each year. Its mythical counterpart, however, marked the culmination of a much longer time-cycle, variously described by scholars as 500 years or 1460 years (the latter being the so-called Sothic year, which begins when the first annual appearance at dawn of the star Sirius coincides with the commencement of the Egyptian new year – an event that occurs only once in every 1460 years).[35] There is no set length for a divine year of the phoenix in Egyptian myth, although its close association with the idea of the *akh*-spirit strongly suggests a link with the turning of the pole of the ecliptic, as well as the concept of the Great Year,[36] or precessional age, which would seem to have been part of the hidden wisdom passed on to the Heliopolitan priests by their forerunners, the *Shemsu-hor* and the Divine Souls.[37]

By combining this principle of the *akh* with his decision to create a seat of *maat* at Amarna, designed to reflect the divine order as it had been during the epoch of the First Time, Akhenaten had attempted to become the living expression not only of *maat* but also of the returning *bennu*-bird. In many ways he would appear to have consciously set himself up as the 'spirit of the age', so that, in some strange fatalistic way, he could change the course of Egyptian history.

Yet what motivated Akhenaten? From where did he obtain such extraordinary ideas? Who gave him this knowledge – this inspiration to create a new cosmic aeon? Certainly not the Amun priesthood, as he was strictly opposed to their cosmological doctrine that contradicted much of what was taught by his priestly brothers at Heliopolis. There seems to be just one realistic answer, and this is the astronomer-priests at Heliopolis who, as we have seen, were so intimately associated with everything about Akhenaten's life.

The priesthood at Heliopolis believed whole-heartedly that their earliest temples and monuments had been constructed by a much earlier divine race that ruled Egypt many millennia before the rise of the first Horus-king. The Royal Canon of Turin, for instance, speaks of the *Shemsu-hor* as having reigned 13,420 years before the unification of Upper and Lower Egypt, *c.* 3100 BC.[38] The validity of such incredibly long time-spans need not detain us, for they are based on oral tradition alone. More important is the fact that the Egyptians believed in a chronology that began with the *netjeru* gods and *Shemsu-hor* and ended with the first mortal kings.

This was not all that the Horus-kings gained from their divine ancestors, for it would also appear that they inherited their physical localities as well. The environs of Heliopolis, the original seat of power of the Horus kings, were looked on as the place of the ancestor gods, where they had erected the first temples and monuments. Included within these sacred environs was, of course, Giza, which is referred to on the Sphinx Stela of Thutmose IV as 'Rostau . . . the horizon west of Heliopolis',[39] and 'the splendid place of the First Time'.[40] To them the location of the Great Sphinx and the pyramids of Giza was quite literally the horizon of the gods.

The cosmological doctrine formulated by the Heliopolitan priesthood was linked not just with the design and purpose of the Great Pyramid but also with its neighbours in the other pyramid fields built between the Third and Sixth Dynasties as part of a vast necropolis linked with the Old Kingdom capital of Memphis. We know, for instance, that Imhotep, the great architect of the step pyramid built for Djoser, *c.* 2678 BC, was high priest of Heliopolis,[41] while the Pyramid Texts inscribed on the tomb walls of Fifth- and Sixth-Dynasty pyramids, also at Saqqara, originally derived from principal elements of the Heliopolitan doctrine.[42]

If, as seems likely, the Heliopolitan priesthood really were the prime inheritors of age-old traditions and secret wisdom that originated with Egypt's Elder culture, then it seems clear that Akhenaten was certainly privy to these inner mysteries. Whether this was through initiatory degrees or personal tutoring, we do not know, although whatever the means by which he obtained this hidden knowledge it would appear to have seriously affected his whole outlook on life.

Is it possible that Akhenaten's father, Amenhotep III, and his grandfather, Thutmose IV, who likewise patronised the Heliopolitan sun-cult, were also privy to this same hidden tradition? A major clue to this enigma must be Thutmose's clearance of sand from around the base of the Great Sphinx and, presumably, the adjacent Temple of the Sphinx. Such an act, under the auspices of the Heliopolitan priesthood, cannot have been for devotional or aesthetic purposes alone. Did the priests need some kind of royal sanction to excavate the Sphinx enclosure? More important, were they looking for something, and, if this is so, did they find it? Curiously enough, the relief on the Sphinx Stela set up by Thutmose IV in front of the stone monument shows him venerating the Sphinx, which appears to be resting on an underground temple or building with a large entrance door.

Could this image have been alluding to some kind of hidden temple or chamber located beneath the Great Sphinx? Was it this that the priests of Heliopolis were seeking to discover?

Without any hard evidence, we can take the matter no further. However, it is highly likely that it was this hidden knowledge, or discovery, directly connected with the priests of Heliopolis, that secured the royal patronage of three successive kings – Thutmose IV, Amenhotep III and Akhenaten. This great revelation might even help explain why Akhenaten flouted his own religious laws to have himself

Section of the so-called Sphinx, or Dream, Stela of Thutmose IV which shows the king adoring the leonine form of Re-harakhty, who stands on a temple-like structure. Might this image signify the presence of hidden chambers located beneath the Sphinx enclosure?

depicted in relief as a human-headed Sphinx.

For reasons that may never become totally clear, Akhenaten would seem to have made a serious attempt to re-create the lost world of the Elder gods. History suggests that his one-man revolution failed. There was little chance that he would ever succeed, as his own acts of creation were destined to upset too many people. But did he really fail?

In the aftermath of his reign he was cast as a rebel, a heretic, an accursed one whose name was to be struck from the annals of history. No one was ever to speak his name again. Yet they did – under the names Osarsiph and Moses. The writings of Manetho and Apion, as well as the testament of the ancient Hebrew scribes, all ably demonstrate that it was this man above any other who was the inspiration for the revolution we know today as Judaism, the religious faith of Israel. Moreover, it was from the strict adherents of the laws of Moses, who lived austere, though highly reactionary, existences on the shores of the Dead Sea during the first century BC, that the Jerusalem Church arose. If the Gospels are to be believed, then this new faith was brought into the world by someone else who wanted to be the 'spirit of the age'. On this occasion, however, the bird of the holy spirit was not the phoenix but the white dove.

Out of chaos comes order, and out of order comes chaos, and so the world and the stars go around and around.

The priests of Heliopolis played an essential role in attempting to turn Egypt into a monotheistic kingdom during the reign of Akhenaten. Some of them undoubtedly became the first Aten priests, and these in turn would have become teachers to the trainee priests present at Amarna during its final years. It is almost certain that surviving followers of the Aten would have accompanied the Hebrew masses as they departed from Egypt at the time of the Exodus, plausibly during the co-regency between Ramesses I and Seti I, c. 1307 BC. How many Heliopolitan priests also accompanied them into the wildness of Sinai and Paran? One, certainly, if we are to believe the word of Manetho and Apion – the religious reformer named Osarsiph-Moses.

Before the Israelites' triumphant entry into Canaan, precise instructions on how the sound of trumpets could pull down the walls of Jericho were supposedly imparted to Joshua, Moses' successor, by the mysterious personage known as the 'captain of the host of the Lord'. If this incident, and the subsequent fall of Jericho, really is based on actual events, then there has to be a possibility that this character was no divine messenger of God but a quite mortal informant well versed in the art of sonic technology. Could he have been a priest of the Aten or even a priest of Heliopolis who had been closely monitoring the progress of the Israelite army?

If the ancient science and technology of the Elder culture had been inherited by anyone, then it was the Horus-kings and astronomer-priests of Heliopolis. This much we can perhaps accept, but was there more? What else might the Heliopolitans have preserved concerning the former existence of this divine race of individuals? What else might they be able to tell us about the abodes of the Elders, those places where the *netjeru*-gods and the Divine Souls founded the first temples and monuments?

The Sphinx Stela tells us that 'the sacred road of the gods' led from Heliopolis to Giza-Rostau, the horizon in the west.[43] I wanted to know what lay at the end of that 'sacred road', and why exactly the Heliopolitan priests so boldly saw Giza as the 'splendid place of the First Time'.

CHAPTER TWELVE

 # THE SECRET OF ROSTAU

For the world today, the sun rises in the morning and sets in the evening. There is no mystery in this knowledge, and where the solar orb disappears to at night is of little concern to us. To the Ancient Egyptians it was quite another matter. They were concerned especially about where the sun went after dark and even built a whole mythological doctrine based on this very problem. For them, once the sun had set down into the western horizon, it began a complex journey through an underworld realm of darkness known as the *am-duat*, or just simply *duat* (sometimes spelled *tuat*), which they saw as divided into 12 equal parts, known as divisions or 'hours' of the night.

Taking on the form of a ram-headed figure, the sun-god, now referred to in this guise as the Great God Atum, was pulled along in his high-prowed barque, or barge, by a crew of lesser deities as he passed through each 'hour'. Whole pantheons of gods and goddesses, demons and shades resided in this realm. Moreover, the sun-god would be obliged to avoid various obstacles such as pits of fire, murderous knives, streams of boiling water, foul stenches, fiery serpents and hideous animals.[1] He would also be required to utter magic spells that would allow him exit from one hour and enter into the next. Ethereal light that illuminated the darkness would be provided by helpful *uraei*-serpents positioned on the ship's prow.[2] After all 12 'hours' had been completed successfully, the sun would be reborn anew at dawn on the eastern horizon – the whole process being repeated night after night until the end of time.

As in the case of the Pyramid Texts on the tomb walls of the Fifth- and Sixth-Dynasty pyramids, the accounts that deal specifically with the sun's passage through the *duat* were meant as star-maps or guides for the soul-spirit of the deceased Pharaoh as it passes through the underworld on its way to becoming at one with the god Osiris, in his form as the constellation Sahu, or Orion.[3] The symbolism used to describe the *duat* incorporates a number of starry themes which imply that its underworld component is in essence a reflection of the celestial realm through which the sun passes during the hours of darkness.[4]

Yet if this were all that the myths of the *duat* represented, they could be dismissed as cosmological jargon created initially by the Heliopolitan priesthood to explain away the daily disappearance of the sun. And perhaps this is what these myths actually became in late Pharaonic times. But if we take a closer look at the origins of these arcane traditions, then we begin to find key elements that hint at a symbolic record of a strange chthonic world that existed in Egypt long before the dawn of dynastic times.

GUARDIANS OF THE GATES

Deciphering the ancient books of the underworld[5] creates a strange though slightly familiar picture. We quickly discover, for instance, that the *duat* has two gates to the outside world – an entrance in the symbolic mountain of the west, where the sun sets, and an exit on the eastern horizon, where the sun rises in the morning. Each is guarded by a reclining lion or sphinx known as an *aker*,[6] which is usually shown in illustrations as a leonine head and fore legs only. Together, the double *aker*, or *akeru*, was depicted in illustrations either as two lions back to back or as a single beast with two heads. Like the cave in the Disney film 'Aladdin', the entrance to the *duat* was through the lion's open mouth, and only by crossing this threshold could the sun god enter within the subterranean realm.[7]

Such a basic concept of guardianship might at first seem to be of little relevance to our debate. Stone lions are found as guardians to entrance gateways all over the ancient world; the famous Lion Gate at the Bronze Age citadel of Mycenae in Greece or the bull-lions of Assyrian Nineveh being perfect examples. Yet the presence of twin lions on the double horizon begs the question of what exactly they might have represented originally. Were they purely symbolic beasts or did they have a more tangible reality on the celestial horizon around dusk and dawn?

Since the *aker*-lions were to be found in the path of the rising and setting sun, and thus on the line of the ecliptic, they *must* represent one of the 12 zodiacal constellations. It does not take much imagination to realise that the most obvious choice is Leo, but does any of this make sense of what we know about Egyptian astrology?

When the ancient books of the *duat* were set down in writing for

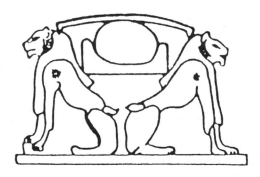

The sun-disc resting on the hieroglyph for horizon, which is itself supported by the *aker*-lions that mark the entrance and exit to the *duat*-underworld.

the first time, the constellation of Leo would have accepted the dying sun into its care on the west-south-western horizon only at sunset on midsummer's eve. It would then have released the reborn sun from its guardianship at dawn the next morning on the east-south-eastern horizon, when Leo would have risen heliacally (i.e. with the sun) for the one and only time of the year. At first this knowledge would seem to accord well with what we know of the *duat*, for the Pyramid Texts speak of the celestial sky as it would have appeared from the ground in the reddish glow before sunrise on the summer solstice.[8] This is evidenced by the fact that the Pyramid Texts allude to the heliacal rising of the star Sothis, or Sirius, which also occurred only at midsummer and coincided with the annual inundation of the Nile, when the melting of snow on the mountains of equatorial Africa brought necessary flooding to the river's fertile valleys.[9]

This solution also matched well with the observations of the fourteenth-century Arab chronicler al-Makrizi, who spoke of the priests of Heliopolis using obelisks to define the longest and shortest days of the year. More important, in their book *Keeper of Genesis*, authors Robert Bauval and Graham Hancock demonstrate that certain utterances alluding to Harakhty, or Re-harakhty, and found in the Pyramid Texts actually refer to the movement of Leo in the 70-day period prior to the summer solstice during the pyramid age.[10]

At first there might seem good grounds to conclude that the sun-god's journey through the 12 'hours', or divisions, of the *duat* relates to the sun's course through the 12 constellations of the zodiac, beginning and ending with Leo at the time of the solstice. This makes a lot of sense, but unfortunately there is a major obstacle preventing us from accepting this interpretation of the Egyptian underworld.

Egyptologists consider that the 12 'hours' of darkness in Egyptian mythology derive from an astronomical system that features no fewer than 36 constellations collectively known as the *bakiu*. Using as a starting-point the first heliacal appearance of the star Sirius on the summer solstice, each constellation was allotted a period of 10 consecutive days as it rose with the sun before making way for the next of the *bakiu*, which would then reign for a period of 10 days before giving way to the next *bakiu*, and so on, until the full 36 constellations had come and gone.[11] These 10-day periods were known in Greek as 'decans'. Thirty-six of these decans, each composed of 10 days, makes a calendar year of 360 days, leaving the five so-called epagomenal days to be dedicated to five of the principal *notjoru* gods belonging to the Heliopolitan pantheon.

It was the night-time procession of the *bakiu* that was seen to have defined the 12 'hours' of the *duat*. Apparently no fewer than 12 of them would have been seen in the hours of darkness before the first rising of Sirius. So although the *duat*-underworld was segmented into 12 divisions, or houses, known as 'hours', this term bore *no relation whatsoever* either to real time or to the sun's course through the 12 signs of the zodiac.

This, at least, is the orthodox view of Ancient Egyptian astrology held by today's astrologers, astronomers and Egyptologists. However, the nocturnal calendar system based on the 36 decans is thought to date only to the Middle Kingdom of Egyptian history, *c.* 2100 BC–1796 BC,[12] and there is some evidence to suggest that Upper and Lower Egypt possessed different views on the importance of star constellations and calendar systems.[13] Even though the summer solstice is known to have played a key role in the cosmological myth and ritual of Ancient Egypt, there seemed to be an alternative solution to the dark mystery of the 12 'hours' that the sun-god spent each night within the *duat*.

As we have already determined, the priests of Heliopolis viewed the Great Sphinx as a leonine embodiment of Harakhty, Re-harakhty, the sun-god in its aspect as Horus of the Horizon. It also seems clear that the Sphinx was seen as a physical representation of one of the two *aker*-lions, quite possibly the one guarding the exit of the *duat* on the eastern horizon.[14] These links, with both Re-harakhty and the *aker*-lions, imply therefore a direct relationship between the Sphinx monument and its apparent celestial counterpart – the constellation of Leo.

Yet as we also know by now, the Great Sphinx gazes out not at the position on the horizon where the celestial lion and the reborn sun would have been seen together at dawn on the summer solstice during the pyramid age but where they would have been together as one at dawn on the spring equinox during the precessional Age of Leo, some 8000 years beforehand.

If the sun's journey through the *duat* was conceived originally as having taken place not at the time of the summer solstice but on the spring equinox, it would make much more sense of its 12-fold division, for it is only on the equinoxes that we achieve exactly 12 hours of daylight and 12 hours of darkness – equal day and equal night. Should this be so, then it implies that the sun was originally conceptualised by the astronomer-priests of Heliopolis as having been received into the custodianship of the *aker*-lions, the constellation of Leo on the western horizon at sunset on the eve of the spring equinox. Then – having passed through the 12 'true' hours of darkness – the reborn sun would have been released from the lion's care on the eastern horizon at dawn on the equinox itself.

At no time other than in the Age of Leo would the sun have been seen to set into the stars of Leo and then rise with them at dawn exactly 12 hours later. This, then, is why the Great Sphinx was seen as a physical embodiment of both Re-harakhty *and* one of the *aker*-lions – because it gazed out at its starry counterpart on the eastern horizon *only* during the astrological Age of Leo. In my opinion, this option better explains the *duat*'s relationship to the celestial horizon and the 12 hours of darkness through which the sun is seen to pass at night. Since the spring equinox not only defines the astrological influence of an age but also the true zero-point in the year's 12-fold zodiacal calendar, it also makes more sense of the *duat*'s clear connection with the 12-fold division of the ecliptic.

Everything comes together perfectly when the night of the spring equinox is introduced as the original time-frame in which the sun was ideally conceptualised as having passed through the *duat*-underworld. Yet it only makes sense if it is placed within the confines of the Age of Leo. Does this therefore mean that the whole concept was developed during this early epoch by the Elder gods, when the Great Sphinx is now thought to have been carved out of the limestone bedrock as an equinoctial marker? If so, then it implies that at a much later date, plausibly during the pyramid age, the whole mythological tradition concerning the *duat* was altered radically to take into account the precessional shift of the heavens, which now meant that Leo rose and set not at the time of the spring equinox but on the summer solstice, coincident to the heliacal rising of Sirius and the inundation of the Nile.

These factors alone must have signalled a complete change of emphasis in the whole way that the astronomer-priests of cult centres such as Heliopolis viewed the significance of the celestial horizon. Yet since the orientation of the Great Sphinx was fixed for ever on the equinoctial horizon, it remained as a legacy of the more ancient concept of the *duat*, which also retained certain other themes, such as the twin *aker*-lions and the 12 'true' hours of the night, which henceforth were equated with the 36 constellations known as the *bakiu*, instead of what we might refer to today as the 12 signs of the zodiac.

THAT WHICH IS IN THE DUAT

Establishing the astronomical connection between the Great Sphinx and the *duat* has been essential, for we can now move on to examine the relationship between the Egyptian underworld and the Giza plateau as a whole. To do this we must trace the course of the sun-god as he makes his journey through the 12 divisions of the *duat* as told in the *Shat-ent-am-tuat* – 'The Book of that which is in the Duat', translated by noted British Egyptologist Sir E.A. Wallis Budge and included in his three-volume work *The Egyptian Heaven and Hell*.

After entering the underworld via the mountain, or 'horn', of the west, the sun-god finds himself within the First Hour, described as an

The solar barque carrying the ram-headed sun-god in the form of Atum,
the Great One of Perfection. It is supported by the *aker*-lions, which are
positioned above the mummified body of the deceased Pharaoh. Above
him is a hawk-headed sun, symbol of Re-harakhty, Horus of the Horizon,
as well as an arch of stars. These signify the sun-god's journey through
the twelve hours of darkness, reflected in the concept of the twelve
divisions, or houses, of the *duat*-underworld.

arrit – an antechamber or entrance hall.[15] As darkness overcomes
him he encounters various groupings of gods, animals and serpents
before he can utter the magic spell to allow him passage into the
Second Hour. More trials and tribulations occur here before he is
permitted to enter the Third Hour of the night.

Then something odd occurs in the *Am-duat* text. As the sun-god
begins his descent into the Fourth and Fifth Hours of the night, the
narrative appears to take on a completely different format. Instead of
passing directly *through* this twinned realm, seen as the central region
of the *duat*, the solar barque is obliged to pass *over* the top of the
main obstacles which lie in its path. This hidden domain also has its
own title, since it is described as the 'kingdom', 'land' or House of
Seker, or Sokar,[16] who was the patron god of the Memphite
necropolis, which encompassed all the major pyramid fields including, of course, Giza. Indeed, the Sphinx Stela of Thutmose IV
actually refers to the Great Sphinx as sitting 'beside Sokar in

Rosta',[17] with Rostau being the Egyptian name for Giza. Not only is this hawk-headed deity the guardian influence of the Fourth and Fifth Divisions of the *duat*, but he is also a form of Osiris, the god of the underworld who, as we shall see, is linked intrinsically with both the *duat* and the mysteries of Giza.[18]

The solar barque enters the Land of Sokar via a long descending corridor, with a large ribbed rectangular section in its roof, very reminiscent of the Great Pyramid's Ascending Passage and Grand Gallery when seen in cross-section – a connection noted by a number of authors.[19] This long descending passage is named specifically as Re-stau, or Rostau,[20] while the narrative tells us that it is the 'road of the secret things of Re-stau . . . the road by which entereth the body

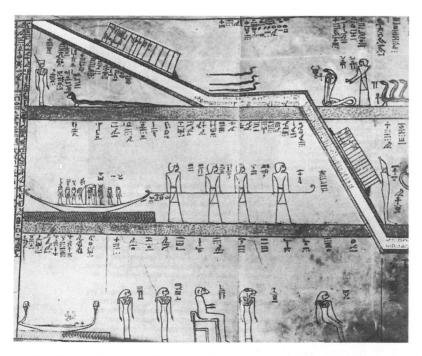

The Fourth Hour, or Division, of the *duat*-underworld showing the descending corridor known as the 'road' of Rostau – Rostau being the ancient name given to the Giza necropolis. Note the rectangular chambers in the roof, which bear an uncanny resemblance to the Grand Gallery inside the Great Pyramid.

of Seker, who is on his sand, the image which is hidden, and is neither seen nor perceived'.[21]

This is another intriguing statement, for as we already know the Sphinx Stela of Thutmose IV tells us that Giza-Rostau lay at the end of the 'sacred road of the gods', suggesting therefore that the 'road' was some kind of underground passageway or corridor along which the *netjeru* gods were thought to travel. More pertinently, it hints at the possibility that although the rest of the 12 divisions of the *duat* were perhaps symbolic in origin, based on celestial imagery linked with the precessional Age of Leo, the Fourth and Fifth Hours, otherwise known as the House of Sokar, seem to refer to Giza itself. This was a conclusion drawn by noted Egyptologist Selim Hassan, who observed that: 'the Fifth Division (as well as the Fourth Division) was originally a version of the Duat and had its geographical counterpart in the Giza necropolis'.[22]

Rostau's sacred 'road' of the gods continues to descend in stages as it passes from the Fourth to the Fifth Hour of the night. Here too are rectangular compartments cut into the roof of the descending passageways. Beyond these the sun-god enters the very heart of the House of Sokar, where he finds the ground rising to form a hollow mound that terminates at its highest point in the head of a woman, over which his solar barque must be towed by its attendants.[23] Directly above the mound the ancient texts show the *khepri*-scarab beetle, a form of the sun-god Re. This is seen descending out of a round-topped object, like a bell, on which two birds, described by Budge as 'hawks', cling to either side. He identified this strange object as 'some form of the dark underworld of Seker',[24] as the Egyptian symbol for 'night' or 'darkness' appears on top of its curved surface. Yet in the opinion of Livio Stecchini and myself, this fiery-orange bell-like object is unquestionably a representation of a *benben*-stone or *omphalos*, like the examples known to have existed in ancient times at Heliopolis, Thebes and Delphi. Its presence in the centre of the House of Sokar therefore signifies not only the precise centre of the *duat* but also the Point of First Creation, making the mound below this object the primeval mound, or hill, on which the

Great God initiated the first acts of creation at the beginning of time.

Stecchini also identified the two so-called 'hawks' clinging on to the side of the bell-shaped *omphalos*.

> Usually on top of Sokar, as on top of any *omphalos*, there are portrayed two birds facing each other; in ancient iconography these two birds, usually doves, are a standard symbol for the stretching of meridians and parallels.[25]

Immediately beneath the mound, yet seemingly contained within its form, an elongated ellipse is seen. Inside this is a hawk-headed individual who stands on the back of a two-headed (sometimes three-headed) winged serpent. The name given to this god is Sekri, simply another form of Sokar,[26] while the ellipse itself is referred to, confusingly, as the 'Land of Sekri'.[27] According to Budge, this curious curved shape signifies 'an oval island in the river of the

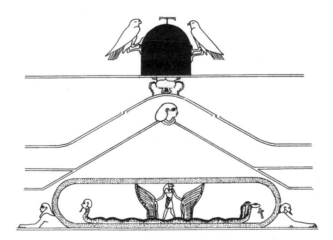

The central part of the Fifth Hour, or Division, of the *duat*-underworld, showing the hawk-headed god Sekri (a form of Sokar) standing on a winged cosmic serpent, which is itself surrounded by an oval-shaped island protected by twin sphinxes. Above it is the mound of creation, capped with a human head, as well as the bell-like *bnnt* (embryo, seed) or *benben*-stone. On this are perched twin pigeons or doves – symbols of geographical centres or *omphali*.

Tuat'.[28] Two human-headed sphinxes, each facing outwards with only their forequarters visible, cradle the island or 'land of Sekri' on their backs. The purpose of this double sphinx, known as the *Af*, is to 'keep ward over his [the sun-god's] image',[29] yet it is clear that they are in effect alternative forms of the twin *aker*-lions that guard the entrance and exit to the *duat*. This realisation is yet further evidence that the mythology concerning the House of Sokar is, as Hassan has suggested, a condensed, yet quite separate, rendition of the Egyptian concept of the *duat*-underworld, a kind of microcosmic variation contained within a more general account of the 12 hours of the night.

Yet the House of Sokar seems to have been much more than this, for somehow it reflected a tangible underworld domain associated directly with Giza-Rostau. The twin lions that support the elongated ellipse or 'island' positioned beneath the pyramidical mound at the heart of the Fifth Hour appear to reflect the presence at Giza of the Sphinx monument. Furthermore, the passageway of Rostau, and the *duat* as a whole, hint at the existence beneath Giza's limestone bedrock of tunnels, corridors and hidden chambers, the knowledge of which was preserved, either by accident or design, in the symbolic account of the *duat*-underworld composed by the astronomer-priests of Heliopolis.

The idea that some kind of physical representation of the *duat*-underworld awaits discovery beneath the sands of Giza should come as no surprise to Egyptologists, for it has long been known that the limestone plateau is riddled with natural cavities and tunnel systems carved out by underwater erosion. Furthermore, a cave-like structure, or 'Secret Mansion', actually described in ancient accounts as an 'underworld', is known to have existed in Pharaonic times at a place called *Kher-aha*, a cultic site attached to the sacred domains of Heliopolis. Today the entrance to this Secret Mansion can be found beneath the streets of Old Cairo.[30] Indeed, Egyptologist Abdel-Aziz Saleh records a local tradition that asserts that it was reached via the now water-filled crypt below the ancient church of St Sergius.[31] According to Coptic tradition, this site was visited by the Virgin

Mary and the infant Jesus during their flight through Egypt.[32]

Kher-aha's quite separate 'underworld' domain has no connection with the one thought to exist beneath the bedrock of Giza, although it does show that this actual term was used by the Ancient Egyptians to describe an underground shrine once used for religious purposes.

More important still is the development of the myths concerning the sun's journey through the *duat*. Egyptologists consider that they derive their origin from the solar cult prevalent in Egypt during Old Kingdom times. Only after this time were they transformed into the concept of a purely symbolic underworld domain.[33] Yet Selim Hassan crucially points out that in addition to these elements, the myths include facets of an ancestor cult, personified in later times by the god Osiris, which placed the *duat* in direct association with the tombs of the dead.[34] These beliefs he saw as quite separate to, and perhaps even older than, the solar elements that, as we have seen, derive in the main from the Heliopolitan doctrine. It is therefore quite feasible that the physical representation of the *duat*-underworld was looked on as a 'tomb', linked directly with Osiris, or Sokar, and Rostau, the ancient name for Giza.

So is it really possible that somewhere in the vicinity of the Great Sphinx there exists an entrance to an underground complex dating back to the epoch of the First Time? Might this have been what the priests of Heliopolis expected to find when Thutmose IV gave orders for the clearance of sand from around the body of the leonine monument? Did these excavations reveal tangible evidence of hidden chambers that convinced Thutmose, Amenhotep III and finally Akhenaten that the *netjeru* gods and Divine Souls really did build Giza-Rostau's first temples and monuments? Could this be why these three kings patronised Heliopolis over and above all others, because they had learned the secret of Rostau? These were tantalising possibilities that may well turn out to have some basis in truth.

A HALL OF RECORDS

Modern-day psychics, occult societies and new-age mystics all believe firmly in the existence at Giza of an underworld labyrinth of concealed corridors and hidden chambers, which they see as having been constructed by survivors of the lost continent of Atlantis, or even by aliens. They refer to it as the 'Temple' or 'Hall of Records', after the psychic 'readings' given to 'patients' by American 'sleeping prophet' Edgar Cayce during the early 1930s.[35] In the previous decade, a similar underground complex, referred to as the 'Chambers of Initiation', was independently proposed by English medium Hugh C. Randall-Stevens.[36]

Such ideas, although highly fascinating, are, as we have seen, not entirely new. As early as Roman times, legends abounded in Egypt concerning the existence in the vicinity of the Giza pyramids of 'subterranean fissures and winding passages called syringes', built so that they might preserve 'the memory' of 'ancient rites' which it was feared would be destroyed in a coming 'deluge'.[37] Similar traditions were also preserved by the Coptic Church, and recorded in writing by later Arab historians.

In 1993 these wild ideas suddenly became more than simply the

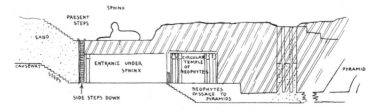

Mystics, psychics and new-agers alike believe that a series of concealed chambers awaits discovery beneath the Giza plateau. Are they correct? This image of temples and passageways thought to be located below the Great Sphinx was drawn by British medium H.C. Randall-Stevens following apparent visionary experiences in 1927.

delusions of the new-age community. Not only was a previously unknown chamber found at the end of the southern shaft of the Queen's Chamber inside the Great Pyramid by a tiny high-tech robot designed, built and controlled by Munich-based engineer and robotics expert Rudolf Gantenbrink, but another, even more enigmatic discovery was made public for the first time.

During the autumn of that year, it was announced that seismic soundings of the hard bedrock beneath the Sphinx enclosure had revealed the presence, some five metres down, of a large rectangular room some nine metres by twelve metres in size. Dr Thomas L. Dobecki, the geophysicist and consultant in charge of the operations, which were conducted in 1991, was cautiously optimistic about the discovery, admitting that: 'The regular, rectangular shape of this [chamber] is inconsistent with naturally occurring cavities, so there is some suggestion that it could be man-made.'[38]

In 1996 a team of geophysicists, working under the direction of the University of Florida and the Schor Foundation – an organisation set up by Dr Joseph Schor, an American businessman and life member of the Edgar Cayce Foundation – began a new round of seismic testing in the Sphinx enclosure. The official reason given for the exploration by Dr Zawi Hawass of the Supreme Council of Antiquities in Egypt was to examine the limestone bedrock in order to pinpoint faults and cavities that might present a potential hazard to visitors if they were to collapse.[39] It was, however, patently clear to anyone with any knowledge of the subject that the real purpose of this work was to confirm Dobecki's findings and to see whether an entrance could be found into the 'Hall of Records', which the Egyptian presidential family and the Egyptian authorities firmly believe to exist.[40]

Before they too were ordered to cease their exploration of the Sphinx enclosure in late 1996, for alleged irregularities in their methods of surveying, Schor's team was able to detect the presence of no fewer than *nine* further tunnels or chambers located beneath the bedrock. Geophysical sensing equipment also produced readings that strongly suggested the presence in all of them of metal.[41]

What might these geophysical teams, led respectively by Dr Dobecki and Dr Schor, have actually found? Have they detected natural cavities caused by underground water erosion, or were they man-made structures created either by the Pharaonic Egyptians or by the Sphinx-building Elder culture? Until further exploration is permitted by the Egyptian government we must all wait with bated breath for an answer. There are, of course, suggestions that these chambers might be linked in some way with the entrance to the proposed 'Hall of Records'. Cayce predicted that it would be found and opened shortly before the end of the millennium (see Chapter Twenty).[42] Furthermore, he said that the 'connecting chambers' leading into the 'Hall of Records' were located 'between the paws of the Sphinx', or more precisely below its 'right paw',[43] the reason for the recent testing in this area of the sunken enclosure.

Only time will tell whether Cayce's predictions are accurate.

What seemed more important to me was to ascertain exactly what might be contained inside these chambers. Were they in any way linked with Giza's lost underworld domain, and, if so, who constructed them, and why? Did they really constitute a 'Hall of Records' – some kind of museum to the memory of a lost culture containing, among other things, a 'history of Atlantis', 'historical writings', 'dietary information', 'medicinal compounds' as well as 'musical instruments and compositions',[44] as Cayce's latter-day followers seem to believe, or did they have a more profound purpose?

Since the texts accredited to the Heliopolitan priesthood concerning the House of Sokar and the 'road' of Rostau found in the Fourth and Fifth Hours of the *duat*-underworld are silent on such matters, we must now turn our attentions to an entirely different source of inspiration – the myths and rituals that celebrate the gods of the First Time found inscribed in hieroglyphic form on the walls of a Ptolemaic temple at Edfu in southern Egypt. It is here that we must continue our quest to discover the ultimate legacy of the Elder gods.

CHAPTER THIRTEEN

ISLAND OF THE GODS

What remains today of the temple at Edfu, some 87 kilometres (54 miles) south of Luxor, is an imposing edifice founded during the reign of Ptolemy III, one of the Greek dynasty of kings introduced in the wake of Alexander's triumphant entry into Egypt in 332 BC. Records tell us that it was begun in 237 BC, and yet it was not completed until 57 BC. According to legends carved on its stone walls, the current temple replaced a much earlier structure designed in accordance with a divine plan that 'dropped down from heaven to earth near the city of Memphis'.[1] Its grand architects were, significantly, Imhotep – a native of Memphis and, of course, a high priest of Heliopolis – and his father Kanefer.[2] They combined their skill and expertise to produce the site's first dynastic temple during the reign of the Third-Dynasty Pharaoh Djoser, for whom Imhotep had built the step pyramid at Saqqara in around 2678 BC.

Yet if even older legends can be believed, then the origins of the once important city of Edfu are to be accredited to the mysterious *Shemsu-hor*, the Followers of Horus, who were said to have established the cult centre here in honour of their leader, Horus of Behdet, the capital of Lower Egypt, long before the coming of the Pharaohs.[3] In the religious literature of Ancient Egypt they are said to have become the god's *mesniu*, 'workers of metal', or blacksmiths, fashioning the weapons that enabled their leader to achieve ultimate supremacy.[4] Traditions that imply that the *Shemsu-hor* once inhabited this region may prove to be crucial in our understanding of the jewel in Edfu's crown – its so-called Building Texts which adorn whole walls in various sections of the existing Ptolemaic temple.

I was first made aware of the existence of the Edfu documents as early as 1985. American ancient mysteries writer Joseph Jochmans was championing them as evidence for the past existence of Egypt's antediluvian race, and this subsequently led me to read Dr E.A.E. Reymond's fascinating work, *The Mythical Origin of the Egyptian Temple*. As an Egyptologist, she was one of the few people who seemed to have grasped the profound nature of the Edfu texts and realised that they contained accounts of a strange world that existed in Egypt during what might be described as the primeval age.

The texts at Edfu are many and varied, and it seems certain that much of their contents was derived from several now lost works, with titles such as the *Specification of the Mounds of the Early Primeval Age*, accredited to the god Thoth, the *Sacred Book of the Early Primeval Age of the Gods* and one called *Offering the Lotus*.[5] All of these extremely ancient works begin with the gradual emergence out of the Nun, the primeval waters, of a sacred island, synonymous with the primeval mound of Heliopolitan tradition. This event is said to have occurred during a time-frame spoken of by Reymond as the 'first occasion' – her interpretation of the Egyptian expression *sep tepi*, or the First Time.[6]

Surrounding this mound or hill, known then as the Island of the Egg, was a circle or 'channel' of water,[7] and by the edge of this lake was a 'field of reeds' and a sacred domain named Wetjeset-Neter[8] (sometimes Wetjeset-hor). Here were erected posts or columns referred to as *djed*-pillars, which served as perches for the domain's first divine inhabitants, said to number 60.[9] These mysterious beings were led by a group of individuals known as the *drty*-falcons, or Sages, who were ruled by an enigmatic figure called the *Pn*-god, or, simply, This One.[10] Other groups and individuals also bore peculiar names such as the Kas, the Flying Ba and *Heter-her*. These faceless forms were said to have been the seed of their own creation at the time when the rest of the world had not yet come into being. The most astonishing fact about this strange collection of characters is that they are said to have *preceded* the appearance of the *netjeru*,[11] the gods of the Greater and Lesser Ennead revered so highly in Heliopolitan tradition.

The Edfu account speaks at length of the events surrounding the Island of the Egg and the Wetjeset-Neter, collectively referred to as the 'homeland', and alludes to some kind of violent conflict which brought to a close the first period of creation.[12] An enemy appears in the form of a serpent known as the Great Leaping One.[13] It opposes the sacred domain's divine inhabitants, who fight back with a weapon known only as the Sound Eye, which emerges from the island and creates further destruction on behalf of its protectors.[14] No explanation of this curious symbol is given, although Reymond felt it to be 'the centre of the light that illumines the island'.[15] As a consequence of this mass devastation, the first inhabitants all die,[16] and darkness returns to the world, as it had been before the moment of First Creation. Death and decay are everywhere – a fact recorded in the alternative names now given to the Island of the Egg, which include the Island of Combat,[17] the Island of Trampling[18] and, finally, the Island of Peace.[19]

More important, after the violent conflict with the enemy serpent, a major transition occurs in the conception of the sacred island. For a time it vanishes beneath the primeval waters of Nun amid the perpetual darkness that has consumed the world, yet then it emerges again and henceforth is given the title Underworld of the Soul.[20] It also becomes known as the Place of the First Occasion in memory of the death of the *drty*-falcons and their leader, This One, the *Pn*-god, who are now collectively referred to as the *ddw*-ghosts and the Ancestors of the First Occasion.[21]

We are told that the only 'relic' of the first period of creation to survive the time of conflict is a single *djed*-pillar located in the Field of Reeds, situated by the side of the waters of Nun.[22] It is subsequently replaced by a new 'perch', or *djeba*, which becomes the focus of a renewed period of creation involving a second generation of divine inhabitants. They include an important group of individuals known as the Shebtiu,[23] the leaders of which are named as Wa and 'Aa, who are described as the 'Lords of the Island of Trampling'.[24] Another group of eight Shebtiu – corresponding with the eight Ogdoad, or builder gods, of the Theban creation myth – are given enigmatic titles such as 'The Far Distant', 'The Sailor' and 'The Lord, mighty-chested, who made slaughter, the Soul who lives on blood'.[25]

These gods of Wetjeset-Neter are joined by other important divinities, such as the god Ptah-Tanen, and his 'Children of Tanen',[26] as well as an enigmatic figure named the Falcon, who is known as the 'Lord of the Perch' and 'The Winged One'.[27] He commands a further group of individuals called the 'crew of the Falcon'.[28] Collectively, these ancestral gods are also described as the Senior Ones or the Eldest Ones,[29] from which we derive the term 'Elders' 'Elder gods' and 'Elder culture' to denote Egypt's divine race.

This second generation of divine individuals, known for the first time as *netjeru* gods, henceforth become the new rulers of Wetjeset-Neter. They are also seen as 'living deities', who live 'in the company of Re',[30] the first real link with the sun-cult of Heliopolis.

The Shebtiu and their companions set about constructing a 'shelter' or enclosure on the edge of the sacred lake, close to Wetjeset-Neter.[31] This is followed by the appearance of the first temple, known as the 'Mansion of Wetjeset-Neter',[32] which is also referred to as the Grand Seat or Temple of the Falcon[33] (the Ancient Egyptians were, it seems, obsessed with the idea of giving things a multitude of names and titles). According to the Edfu documents, this imposing building stood 'in a vast enclosure surrounding another inner enclosure which was the real temple'.[34] Specific details are given as to its measurements, which are said to have been '30 cubits west to east, and 20 cubits from south to north'.[35] A large courtyard was located in front of this sanctuary, while smaller structures were to be found along the 'two inner sides of this courtyard'.[36] Did this building really exist in the mists of time? What became of it, and where exactly might it have been situated?

After an undisclosed period, rising waters again threaten the Island of Trampling, causing the original temple or Mansion of Wetjeset-Neter to be damaged or destroyed. Yet then something curious occurs. The Shebtiu Wa and 'Aa are instructed by the God-of-the-Temple to enter within the enigmatically named Place-in-which-the-things-of-the-earth were-filled-with-power,[37] another name for the water-encircled island, and here they conduct 'magic spells' which make the waters recede.[38] To this end they appear to have used mysterious power objects, named *iht*, 'relics', which are stored *within* the island.[39] Then, according to Reymond's summary of the events under question, the Shebtiu, or Ogdoad, appear to have simply 'sailed' away[40] 'to another part of the mythical world to continue their creative task'.[41]

Various subsequent stages in the creation of the world involve a gradual progression in the design and appearance of the Temple of the Falcon, while a further building, named as the Solar Temple, is said to have been built on the site of an earlier battle,[42] plausibly one connected with the destruction of the first divine inhabitants by the enemy serpent. Before the commencement of each new building phase, a series of consecration ceremonies is conducted by the Shebtiu using the *iht*-relics. These also involve familiar figures such as the gods Thoth and Ptah-Tanen, the goddess Seshat, the sun-god Re and the eight builder gods known as the Ogdoad (who were simply another form of the Shebtiu).[43] It must be pointed out, however, that these additional building phases are not necessarily to be seen as later events, since the texts are often mixed up, duplicated and confused and may therefore refer to events relating to the first two periods of creation.

Gradually the world evolves and the divine inhabitants of Wetjeset-Neter are replaced by the *Shemsu-hor*, the predynastic ancestors of the Egyptian race led by Horus of Behdet. These in turn give way to the first Horus-kings, bringing the story conveniently up to the foundation of the First Dynasty of a united Egypt, *c.* 3100 BC. This, then, is the Edfu account of the creation of the world and, we must assume, the origins of Egyptian culture during the epoch of the First Time.

OSIRIS OF ROSTAU

The incredible significance of the Edfu material cannot be overstated, for the Egyptian priests, scribes and artists involved in preserving these traditions saw them as very real events that preceded the rise of their own civilisation. Their stories of first creation not only formed the basis of their myths and rituals but also influenced the design, construction and consecration ceremonies of their own temples and monuments, which were looked on as exact representations of the structures erected by the divine ancestors during the primeval age.[44]

Dr Reymond was certain that the texts preserved the memory of a forgotten culture that built Egypt's first temples in a misty epoch long before the ascent of the first Pharaoh, for as she was prepared to admit:[45]

> . . . these traditions and beliefs were made into a myth of creation which became familiar to other religious centres of predynastic and protodynastic times.[46]

In other words, the events of the mythical age were themselves instrumental in defining the mysterious origins of Egyptian civilisation. However, she also made it clear:

> . . . that there is no scrap of archaeological evidence that such a temple ever existed at Edfu, nor have remains of such a primitive shrine as yet been found elsewhere in Egypt . . . Against all this, the account of the appearance of the temple and of its eventual expansion is clear and specific, and certainly built on real facts . . . We incline to the opinion that

experiences of a far distant past lie at the heart of the Edfu myth of creation.[47]

Reymond considered that the spread of these creation myths during predynastic times helped establish various individual forms of the same basic story-line among cult centres all over Egypt, each of which came to believe that the core creation myth related in some way to their *own* temple foundation.

Yet where did these myths concerning the creation of the world, the coming of the gods and the foundation of the first temple actually originate? The answer appears to be somewhere in the locality of Memphis, the Old Kingdom capital of Egypt, for, as Reymond herself noted, the Edfu records 'preserve the memory of a predynastic religious centre which once existed *near to Memphis*, on which the Egyptians looked as . . . the *homeland* of the Egyptian temple [author's emphases]'.[48] In a separate article on the same subject Reymond, under her maiden name of E.A.E. Jelinkova, added that its priestly scribes 'might have used an earlier tradition which originated *outside* of Memphis [author's emphasis]'.[49]

But where 'outside of Memphis'?

The Edfu account states clearly that after the re-emergence of the Island of the Egg from beneath the primeval waters of Nun, following the period of conflict, it became a tomb for the 'ghosts' of the first divine inhabitants, who had been led by the *drty*-falcons, or Sages. More significantly, it now bore the name Underworld of the Soul and became the first resting-place of the body of Osiris, the god of the underworld.[50]

The term 'underworld' is the same here as that used in the Heliopolitan texts to describe the journey of the sun-god through the *duat*-underworld, while the resting-place of Osiris, although linked with the necropolis of Abydos in southern Egypt, was intimately associated with various divisions of the *duat*, including the Fourth Hour, which forms part of the House of Sokar.[51] Osiris is also connected with Giza-Rostau in the famous Inventory Stela, discovered at Giza during the nineteenth century by French Egyptologist

Gaston Maspero. Now in the Cairo Museum, it records the visit to Giza of King Khufu, the believed builder of the Great Pyramid. Not only does this important text of the Twenty-sixth Dynasty make reference to various structures on the plateau, including the Great Pyramid and Great Sphinx (showing its extreme antiquity, since Khufu reigned before Khafre, in whose reign academics suppose the monument to have been carved), but it also makes reference to the 'House of Osiris, Lord of Rostau'.[52] Since the Sphinx is cited as being 'north-west' of this 'House of Osiris', it is thought by some writers to be a reference to the Valley Temple, which lies roughly east-south-east of the Sphinx monument.[53]

There is enough evidence to link Osiris, the deceased god of the underworld, both with Giza-Rostau and with the House of Sokar, the region of the *duat* connected with the proposed subterranean world thought to exist beneath the Old Kingdom necropolis. Furthermore, the Inventory Stela links Osiris with the Valley Temple, which is perhaps the best surviving example of Elder architecture on the whole of the plateau. It therefore seems certain that the mythical realm of Wetjeset-Neter and its environs – with its field of reeds, water-encircled island and temple complex – *was almost certainly located at Giza.*

Giza as the true Point of First Creation, where Egypt's megalithic race began several thousand years before the pyramid age, is a very attractive supposition. There is, however, one major problem – how might we reconcile the appearance of the plateau today with the description of Wetjeset-Neter as a temple complex located beside a field of reeds, situated on the edge of a primeval lake containing a small mound-like island?

A SORT OF ISLAND

Looking at the plateau today, with its desert backdrop and its striking sentinel-like pyramids that cannot help but exude a stark sense of permanence, it is hard to imagine Giza any different. Yet in the past

1. The Great Sphinx of Giza from the north. The Valley Temple of Khafre can be seen on the left. Who built these monuments, and for what purpose?

2. The Great Sphinx, with the pyramids of Khafre (right) and Menkaure in the background. Between its paws is the so-called Sphinx, or Dream, Stela of Thutmose IV. Does this reveal clues concerning Giza's underworld domain?

3. The Valley Temple of Khafre, adjacent to the Sphinx monument. The huge blocks used to construct the core walls of this building were extracted from what became the Sphinx enclosure. Does this therefore make it as old as its leonine guardian?

4. Black granite sarcophagus inside the King's Chamber of the Great Pyramid. Long saw marks are clearly visible along its sides, even though no sizeable saw has ever been found during excavations in Egypt.

5 & 6. Two views of what is arguably one of the most enigmatic buildings in Egypt – the Osireion of Abydos. Who constructed it, and when? Why did it become the focus for the worship of Osiris, the god of the underworld?

7. Small statue of Khufu, the traditional builder of the Great Pyramid. This is the only known representation of this Fourth-Dynasty Pharaoh and it was found at Abydos, close to the Osireion. Does this hint at a link between Khufu and this mysterious structure?

8. Life-size statue in diorite of Khafre, the supposed builder of Giza's Second Pyramid. The falcon, a symbol of the Horus king, protects him. Why are Khafre's funerary monuments attached to the Great Sphinx and the adjacent Valley Temple by means of a stone causeway? What interest did he have in these archaic structures?

9. An extraordinary stone triad showing Menkaure, the believed builder of Giza's Third Pyramid, standing between a provincial goddess on his right and Hathor, the goddess of joy and love, on his left. How did the Ancient Egyptians develop such remarkable artistic talents so early in their country's history?

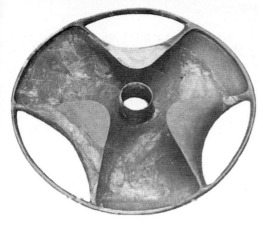

10. A curious fly-wheel-like object, carved from a solid block of schist and found at Saqqara in Lower Egypt. It is beautifully finished and highly unique, and yet it dates to the First Dynasty of Egyptian history, *c.* 3100–3000 BC. How was it made using, if we are to believe the academics, simple copper tools?

11. Sir William Matthew Flinders Petrie (1853–1942). His study of the monuments of Giza in 1881 revealed the extraordinary capabilities of the pyramid builders, including their use of enormous jewel-tipped saws, mechanical lathes and space-age-style tubular drills.

12. Beautifully carved stone vases dating to the Gerzean or Naqada II period of Egyptian history, *c.* 3500–3100 BC. Literally tens of thousands of these hard-stone vessels have been unearthed at predynastic and early dynastic sites across Egypt. Where did this extraordinary talent for making such precision objects come from?

13. Section of the famous Gateway of the Sun at the ancient city of Tiahuanaco on the Bolivian Altiplano, showing a figure thought to be Thunupa, or Ticci Viracocha. Local tradition asserts that he had the power to raise rocks in the air using magic alone, and that heavy stone blocks used to build the city were transported from local quarries to the sound of a trumpet.

14. The Temple of the Dwarf, in the Mayan city of Uxmal in the Yucatán. Local tradition once spoke of it being constructed by dwarfs who could simply whistle and blocks of stone would rise into the air. Where do such traditions originate, and what factual basis might they have?

15. Amphion (*right*), the son of Zeus, with his twin brother Zethus. In classical mythology it was said that when Amphion played his lyre stone blocks moved of their own accord, in which manner he was able to fortify the walls of Thebes, the Boeotian city north-west of Athens. What is the truth behind such curious fables?

16. Tibetan monks shown holding long *ragdon*-trumpets of the type supposedly seen being used, in concert with drums, to raise stone blocks into the air by Swedish traveller Dr Jarl during the 1920s or 1930s.

17. Fallen granite obelisk dating to the reign of Hatshepsut (*c.* 1490–1468 BC) at the Temple of Karnak in Upper Egypt. Until recently, it was possible to make it hum for anything up to 30 seconds simply by repeatedly thumping its apex. Why were such precision acoustics incorporated into the design of commemorative pillars of this type?

18. John Ernst Worrell Keely (1827–98), the inventor of sympathetic vibratory apparatus that allowed objects to rise into the air and granite to disintegrate.

19. An illustration by nineteenth-century Victorian artist Gustave Doré of Jericho's walls tumbling down to the sound of trumpets blown by the Israelite army. Is there any reality behind this well-known biblical story, and if so does it preserve a knowledge of sonics kept alive by the priestly followers of Moses?

20. Enigmatic face of Akhenaten, the heretic king of the so-called Amarna age of Egyptian history, *c.* 1367–1335 BC. Through his actions he brought the empire to the brink of collapse, and yet his religious reforms were inspired by a profound understanding of *sep tepi*, the epoch of the First Time.

21. The city of Akhenaten at Tell el-Amarna in Middle Egypt, built on the edge of Egypt's eastern desert in accordance with exact geographical principles set out during predynastic times.

22. Billie Walker-John's striking impression of the Chief of the Astronomers, an important priestly title at the cult centre of Atum-Re at Heliopolis in Lower Egypt. It seems certain that the Heliopolitan priests preserved traditions concerning Giza's proposed underworld domain, popularly known as the 'Hall of Records'.

23. The Pharaoh Akhenaten shown as a human-headed Sphinx making offerings to the multi-rayed Aten sun-disc. This wall-relief, currently in the possession of the Kestner Museum, Hanover, seems to confirm that, just like his grandfather Thutmose IV, the heretic king possessed a special interest in Giza's leonine monument.

24. The strange bell-shaped object that stands in the Fifth Hour of the *duat*-underworld, above the mound of creation. Does this object represent the *bnnt*-embryo, *swht*-egg or indeed the *benben*-stone, now thought to be located at the heart of Giza's underworld domain?

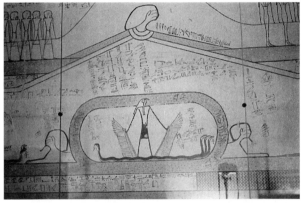

25. The mound of creation with the Island of Sekri found in the central region of the *duat*-underworld. They are placed beyond the 'road' of Rostau – the Egyptian name for the Giza necropolis. Is this image the visual key to understanding Giza's topography during the epoch of the First Time?

26. Maat, the goddess of truth, justice and cosmic order, from a wall relief at Denderah in Upper Egypt. Why did Akhenaten believe he could become a vessel for the expression of *maat* by establishing a new Point of First Creation at his city of Akhetaten?

27. A photograph taken in 1874 showing the annual Nile inundation lapping at the base of the Giza pyramid field. Since we know that the river was much nearer to the plateau in antiquity, it is extremely likely that Giza once possessed a sacred lake that surrounded a primeval island as the Edfu Building Texts suggest.

28. Colossal headless statue thought to represent the serpent Kematef – later Chnoubis or Chorzar – found recently in the Temple of Amun at Luxor, ancient Thebes, and now in the Luxor Museum. As the soul of the primeval island, it symbolised the cosmic intelligence connected with the *duat*-underworld.

29. A necklace of ten burgundy 'agate' beads from a neolithic grave-site at Ashikli Höyük in central Turkey (ancient Anatolia), dated to *c.* 7000 BC. Each one is longitudinally perforated even though the largest of the beads are 5.5 cms in length. Those who fashioned them were clearly accomplished artisans with an immense knowledge of the lapidary trade. From whom did the neolithic peoples inherit such specialised skills?

30. The extraordinary standing monolith and surrounding cult building unearthed at Nevali Çori in south-eastern Turkey and dated to *c.* 8000 BC. Note the five-fingered hands on the front face of the pillar and the clear resemblance to the Kalasasaya palace court at Tiahuanaco, Bolivia.

31. Serpent-headed 'vulture' statue found at Nevali Çori and dated to *c.* 8400 BC. This beautiful piece, which would not look out of place in a modern art gallery, is just one of the anthropomorphic bird statues found in its cult building, clearly implying the presence of a shamanic based religion.

32. Owl-faced bone pendant found at Çayönü, south-eastern Turkey, and dated to *c.* 7000 BC. Note the tears coming from the eyes, reminiscent of Hurrian and Mesopotamian creation myths which tell of how the tears that flowed from, respectively, Kumarbi and Tiamat created the waters of the Euphrates and Tigris rivers. Is this what this 9000-year-old pendant represents?

33 & 34. Two views of a bird-man statue found in Nevali Çori's cult building and dated to *c.* 8000 BC. It is 23 cm high and shows a hammer-headed individual with closed wings. It seems to represent a bird shaman in ceremonial dress, and yet its crudity is in stark contrast to the snake-headed vulture statue which pre-dates this example by as much as 400 years.

35. Carved stone bowl found at Nevali Çori, showing two ecstatic figures standing either side of an upright turtle, the primary symbol of the nearby Euphrates river. In later Mesopotamian mythology, the pond turtle became the familiar of Enki, or Ea, while in Hurrian tradition it was a form of the creator god Kumarbi.

36. A hawk-headed statue of the god Horus in the Louvre, Paris. Are the myths surrounding the *Shemsu-hor*, the Followers of Horus, proto-memories of a race led by a ruling elite who returned to Egypt, their ancestral homeland, from the Near East in predynastic times, *c.* 4000–3100 BC?

38. An egg-shaped human head with snake-like pony-tail, found in a niche within Nevali Çori's cult building of *c.* 8000 BC. What does it represent, and why did it gaze out through the stone entrance gateway towards the south-west horizon?

37. The famous step pyramid of Saqqara, built for the Third Dynasty king named Djoser, *c.* 2678 BC. With its distinctive seven tiers why does it bear an uncanny resemblance to the ziggurat structures of Mesopotamia?

39 & 40. Many people now believe that a 'Hall of Records' exists beneath the sands of Giza. One individual who has captured the ambience of what we might expect to find down there is British psychic Bernard G., who in 1985 was inspired to paint a series of pictures following dreams involving the Sphinx's underworld domain. Above, the *arrit*, or entrance room, referred to as the 'Hall of the Twelve', and, below, the first of twelve chambers grouped around a thirteenth 'Chamber of First Creation'.

things were not as they appear today. It is now known, for instance, that over the past 12,500 years the Nile, which currently lies nine kilometres (five and a half miles) east of the plateau, has shifted its course gradually eastwards, and that as late as Old Kingdom times it was much closer to the pyramid field.[54] Indeed, recent excavations in the vicinity of the Valley Temple have revealed the presence of an Old Kingdom stone quay used by boats coming in from the Nile.[55]

The Nile floods have also changed over the course of time. The work of Egyptologist Fekri Hassan of University College, London, who specialises in the effects of climate and geology during predynastic times, has ably demonstrated that in the eleventh millennium BC the Nile suffered extremely high floods. These were probably caused by the gradual rise in water-levels at the end of the last Ice Age, c. 10,500–9500 BC.[56]

It is also a little-known fact that the annual inundation of the Nile, triggered each midsummer (until the Aswan dam blocked its path) by the sudden melting of snow and ice in the mountains of central Africa, would often cause high floods that occasionally reached right to the foot of the Giza plateau. In past ages this connection with the Nile floods was so strong that one Arab legend even asserts that the Sphinx monument was built 'to express the fertility occasioned by the overflowing of the Nile'.[57]

All these facts point clearly to the conclusion that in the eleventh millennium BC, low-lying areas east of the Giza plateau were regularly, if not permanently, flooded to create a shallow lake that may have encircled a small rocky island. It is also important to recall that prior to the desiccation of the eastern Sahara in around 3000 BC, Egypt experienced a much wetter climate that would have made large areas into a rich savannah, more akin to the terrain of equatorial Africa. Tropical undergrowth and tree cover would therefore have surrounded the land closest to the Nile, including, we must presume, Giza's lake and central island. This, then, provides us with an entirely new picture of how this location might have looked when the first divine inhabitants settled in the region during the epoch of the First Time.

So much for hydrology and geography, but what about ancient tradition? Might sources outside of the Edfu account preserve knowledge of the former existence at Giza of an island surrounded by a lake? The answer is yes, for the Arab historian Ibn Abd Alhokm, in his own variation of the Coptic tale concerning the legendary king Saurid Ibn Salhouk, alluded to the presence of a man-made water channel at Giza, when he recorded:

> And there remained a certain number of years to come, and he [King Saurid Ibn Salhouk] commanded in the mean space to build the pyramids, and that a vault [or cistern] should be made, into which the river Nile should enter, whence it should run into the countries of the west, and into the land Al-Said.[58]

Turning to my Standard English Dictionary, I found that the word 'cistern' denotes either a 'man-made receptacle for water' and/or 'a natural reservoir'.[59] In which case Alhokm seems to have been implying that in past ages some kind of water channel linked either a man-made or natural reservoir in the vicinity of the Giza pyramid field to the nearby river Nile. Like Mas'ūdi, who also mentions water being channelled to the pyramids, Alhokm probably gained such facts from Coptic sources in Old Cairo, so there is every chance that he was recording a very real tradition handed down by word of mouth since Pharaonic times.

A much more important tradition was preserved by Herodotus following his visit to Giza in the mid-fifth century BC. Having described how Cheops (i.e. Khufu) had ascended to the throne of Egypt and forced shifts of 100,000 men to build a causeway on which the stones for the pyramids were to be conveyed, he went on to state that:

> To make it [the pyramid of Cheops] took 10 years, as I said – or rather to make the causeway, the works on the mound where the pyramid stands, and the underground chambers,

which Cheops intended as vaults for his own use: these last were built *on a sort of island, surrounded by water introduced from the Nile by a canal* [author's emphasis].[60]

Further on in the text he speaks about the construction of Chephren's (i.e. Khafre's) pyramid, and here again confirms his earlier words:

Chephren imitated the conduct of his predecessor, and, like him, built a pyramid, which did not, however, equal the dimensions of his brother's. Of this I am certain, for I measured them both myself. It has no subterranean apartments, nor *any canal from the Nile to supply it with water*, as the other pyramid has [author's emphasis].[61]

It can be determined from these statements that in Herodotus' time it was commonly believed that the Great Pyramid had been constructed on 'a sort of island', fed by a 'canal' linked to the Nile; moreover, that 'underground chambers, which Cheops intended as vaults for his own use' were incorporated into the original design. Egyptologists have, as a whole, completely ignored these statements when assessing the historical validity of Herodotus' claims about the Giza pyramids. Yet those who have considered them worthy of speculation generally see them as evidence of an as yet undiscovered chamber containing the tomb of Khufu, around which is an 'island, surrounded by water'.

I really do not think this is what the Greek historian was saying at all, for independent evidence suggests that a water channel of some kind really did once link the Giza plateau with the Nile. It comes from British physician and traveller Robert Richardson (1779–1847) who in 1816 noted that:

There is a broad deep trench cut in the rock at the middle of the east front of the large [i.e. Khufu's] pyramid, and running parallel with it. It is rather broader than a carriage road; it

descends toward the middle from each end, and resembles a
carriage entrance to and from a pond. It is half full of sand,
and is entered on the east side by a channel like a canal for
the conveyance of water. I am disposed to consider this is the
channel by which water of the Nile entered the pyramid.[62]

Since we know that the annual Nile floods once reached the very
edge of the Giza plateau, Richardson's observations are indeed of
interest, for they imply that some attempt was made either in the
pyramid age or perhaps earlier to channel water to the edge of the
plateau. If this is so, then did this reservoir, or lake, contain a natural
island which in Egyptian myth was seen as the primeval mound, hill
or island situated in the middle of the waters of Nun?

According to the Edfu account, the island of creation was known
by an assortment of names that included the Isle of the Egg (the egg
being a universal symbol of creation) and the Island of Trampling,
while in the cosmological doctrine developed at Thebes it was known
as the Island of the Two Flames.[63]

There is also one other significant reference to an island
surrounded by water in Egyptian myth, and this is the one found
in the Fifth Division of the *duat*-underworld, otherwise known as
the House of Sokar.[64] As previously mentioned, Budge, in his
book *The Egyptian Heaven and Hell*, identified this curious
elliptical shape in which the god Sekri (i.e. Sokar) stands on a
multiple-headed winged serpent as 'an oval island in the river of
the Tuat'.[65] In illustrations it is shown sitting on a long narrow
'lake' called Netu,[66] which is accompanied by an inscription
linking it with the waters of Nun.[67] This island is also shown
directly beneath both the primeval mound and the fiery-orange
bell-shaped *omphalos*, confirming its association with the idea of
First Creation. As previously explained, the area of the *duat* known
as the House of Sokar is said to have been accessed through a
long descending passageway named as the 'road' of Rostau,
bringing us back to the Giza necropolis. Most telling of all is the
fact that the island of Sekri is supported by the twin sphinxes

called *Af* who, as variations of the *aker*-lions that guard the entrance and exit to the *duat*, are found embodied in the carved form we know today as the Great Sphinx.

All this strongly suggests that an island surrounded by a man-made reservoir, or lake, really did once exist in the vicinity of the Giza plateau. Furthermore, it was originally established as a sacred domain not during the pyramid age but much earlier – during the epoch of the First Time, the very fact acknowledged by the inscription on the Sphinx Stela which proclaims Giza-Rostau as the 'splendid place of the First Time'. Exactly where this sacred lake may have been located is discussed in the next chapter.

During the dynastic age the mammoth stone structure known as the Valley Temple would seem to have been associated with Osiris, the god of the underworld. It cannot therefore be coincidence that one of Egypt's only other cyclopean buildings, the mysterious Osireion at Abydos, should also be linked with the island of creation. Reymond referred to its rectangular stone 'island' surrounded on all sides by a water channel fed by a well and proposed that it was a representation of 'the primeval land which was believed to be the first to emerge from Nun, and on which the first sacred place was created'.[68] If this strange megalithic structure was indeed constructed by the Elder gods, then it would appear that one of their principal obsessions was the idea of First Creation which they felt inclined to represent as much as possible. That they may have landscaped the area around the Giza plateau to create a reservoir around an actual primeval mound, or hill, appears to demonstrate the level of importance which they accorded this location.

Even though the Edfu texts would seem to have a slightly different origin from the cosmological doctrine preached by the priests of Heliopolis, there are clear crossovers of ideas and themes in many places. For instance, the fact that one of the main groups of divine inhabitants present at Wetjeset-Neter during its second stage of creation was the so-called Company of Re hints at a line of transmission from the First Time through to the first foundations of the cults of Atum and Re in predynastic and early Pharaonic times. If this is so, then was it via this route that the Heliopolitan priests gained their highly sophisticated knowledge of astronomy, geometry, medicine, sculpture, time-cycles, landscape geometry and, just possibly, sound technology?

MEN IN THE FORM OF BIRDS

Having tentatively established the historical authenticity of the Edfu Building Texts, a whole new range of questions arises. What, for instance, are we to make of the various different groups of divine beings said to have inhabited the Wetjeset-Neter? Were they really key individuals who lived around the Giza area during some primordial age, or were they merely symbols of 'natural powers' as Dr Reymond was finally to conclude in her authoritative commentary on the Edfu texts?[69]

I was intrigued by the number of references in the documents to the divine inhabitants bearing names and titles connected with birds. In predynastic times warlords of Egypt would adopt names and titles that reflected their personality, deeds or appearance. One perfect example is the Egyptian king known only as Scorpion, who reigned at the very end of the protodynastic period, c. 3100 BC.[70] He was followed by a king called Narmer, and then by Hor-aha, or Menes, traditionally the first king of a united Upper and Lower Egypt. His name translates as 'fighting hawk (or falcon)', expressing perhaps his skill in battle.[71]

Many of the titles borne by Edfu's curious menagerie of divine beings appear to reflect an age when so-called 'totemic', or animalistic, names were applied either to individuals, tribes or groups of people. Attempting to interpret specific examples might prove a little difficult without any first-hand knowledge of who exactly the inhabitants of Wetjeset-Neter might have been. Yet the continued references to birds and, more specifically, falcons struck me as particularly significant. As Reymond herself admitted, the individual known as the Falcon, who bore the title of the 'Winged One', 'was conceived as a divine being in the form of a bird'.[72] Substitute 'human being' for 'divine being', and it seems clear that we are dealing with an individual who has clearly taken on the guise of a bird. Reymond also admits that the figure known as This One, or the *Pn*-god, of the first period of creation is to be seen as 'a physical personality conceived as a bird'.[73]

In Dr Reymond's valued opinion, the Edfu cosmological texts contained traditions 'that connected the very spot of creation . . . with the realm of the falcons', and, furthermore, that these 'Sages assumed the form of falcons, and . . . foretold the creation of the world'.[74]

Just who were these 'Sages' who 'assumed the form of falcons' and 'foretold the creation of the world' during the primordial age?

Is there some special meaning behind these continued references to birds?

Individuals who generally take on the appearance of birds usually fall within the category of persons known to anthropologists as shamans – those who have walked between worlds since time immemorial. Such individuals have been considered capable not only of conversing with ancestral spirits and tribal deities but also of travelling to otherworldly domains in astral form. For this role they would take on the shape of a bird or animal, generally indigenous to the region in which they lived. For the shamans of Siberia it was the reindeer; for the bushmen of South Africa it was the spring-heeled reebok; and as we shall shortly see, for the prehistoric shamans of western Asia, it was the vulture.

In order to live out their chosen totemic image, shamans would adorn themselves in magically charged items such as necklaces of bones, the skin of an animal or, in the case of birds, severed claws, selected feathers or even whole cloaks or head-dresses made of feathers. More important, such individuals would become known to their community by a name that reflected their shamanic associations. Many myths and legends describing encounters between mortal kind and alleged supernatural beings – spoken of either as animals or birds

– are almost certainly abstract accounts of meetings with shamans.

It is also clear that some kind of shamanic root lies behind the foundation of the *hebsed*-jubilee festival conducted by the Horus-kings of Ancient Egypt during the thirtieth year of their reign and periodically afterwards, in an attempt to rejuvenate their ailing bodies and souls. According to ancient writings this archaic ritual, so indelibly linked to the concept of divine kingship, was said to have taken place 'since the Time of the Ancestors'.[75] During the proceedings the king would be carried in a state palanquin from his palace to a place of proclamation, where he would address representatives from all over Egypt. For the occasion he would be dressed in a jewelled vestment that imitated the feathered plumage of the falcon-god Horus. Those invited as ambassadors from the various regions of the country would parade around the enthroned king making offerings of rich gifts brought especially for the occasion.[76] The fact that this tradition was said to go back to the 'Time of the Ancestors' supports the view that this ceremony is at least as old as predynastic times, and may even date back to the age of the Elder gods.

Should these observations prove correct, then we are left with the distinct possibility that some of the divine inhabitants of Wetjeset-Neter and its environs were bird shamans who associated themselves with the falcon and adorned themselves in garments of feathers. If true, then it would also mean that some semblance of this shamanic tradition was later inherited by the Horus-kings of Heliopolis, who felt it important to continue incorporating garments of imitation feathers into their jubilee festivals right through to Pharaonic times. Furthermore, there is every chance that the *Shemsu-hor*, the Followers of Horus, the hawk-headed god, were direct descendants of the Elder gods who first occupied Egypt thousands of years before the generally accepted genesis of civilisation.

So if the Falcons of the Edfu texts are to be seen as bird shamans, then what about the rest of Wetjeset-Neter's divine inhabitants? What can be gleaned about these individuals? Only one other personal feature is mentioned in the Edfu account, and this is their facial countenance. Reymond notes that the companions of This

One, the *Pn*-god, who was himself a 'bird',[77] were given names that contained the component *hr*, 'face, countenance'.[78] What could this possibly mean? Did it imply that these primeval beings bore a facial radiance of the kind associated with divine individuals found in various Near Eastern mythologies? In Persian myth, for example, the first god-kings of Iran were said to have borne a facial countenance known as the *farr*, or Divine Glory.[79] Without this sign of divinity a king could not rule, and if he were to misappropriate this sacred power during his reign then the *farr* would leave him in the form of a bird, never to return.[80] Many of the early patriarchs of the Bible also possessed shining countenances – individuals such as Enoch, Noah and Abraham are all described in textual accounts as having faces that shone like the sun. Countenances were necessary symbols of divinity and divine beings, and so their presence in the Edfu texts may well express a very real attribute thought to have been possessed by Egypt's earliest inhabitants.

Are these true reflections of those who inhabited Egypt during the epoch known as the First Time – groups and individuals, some almost certainly shamans, who bore shining countenances and adorned themselves in garments of feathers? Does the Edfu account give us our first real glimpses of Egypt's Elder culture and of the individuals responsible for carving the Great Sphinx, building the first temples and carving out water channels at the tail end of the palaeolithic age, *c.* 10,500 BC?

The prehistoric 'creation myths' of Edfu appear to recall specific individuals, events, locations and building projects from the epoch of the Elder gods. Yet encoded in these ancient textual accounts is much more than this – clues that, if interpreted properly, will reveal the nature, appearance and meaning of what has remained in darkness beneath the bedrock of the Giza plateau for the past 11,500 years.

CHAPTER FOURTEEN

UNDERWORLD
OF
THE SOUL

The Edfu account enables us to construct a remarkable picture of how the Giza plateau might have looked during the epoch of the Elder gods. Yet if we were to find ourselves a time-machine and travel back to the year 10,500 BC, what would we *really* find? The chances are that we would enter a hot, humid environment alive with lush green vegetation of the type you might come across today in equatorial Africa. Eventually, we would come to the edge of a shallow lake lined on one side with a field of reeds, home to flocks of freshwater birds such as the grey heron. Before us would be the first evidence of sophisticated human habitation – tall polished pillars, carved perhaps in dark stone, standing on the banks, and beyond these we would see the outer enclosure wall of a gleaming white temple. In the shallow waters nearby would be a small island, the symbolic Point of First Creation, the primeval hill, crowned with a simple stone structure that proclaimed its ancient sanctity (see p. 192). This, then, was the Island of Trampling within the waters of Nun.

Locally we would find indigenous peoples of the late palaeolithic age tending cultivated areas of wild cereals, herding domesticated

Conceptual image of how the Giza plateau might have looked with its
island and Nile-fed lake, as suggested by textual information contained in
both the Edfu building texts and the books of the *duat*-underworld.

wild animals, making beautiful flint tools and using wooden spears to
harpoon fish in the nearby river Nile. Yet behind the tall stone wall of
the sacred enclosure was an altogether different kind of person –
commanding figures adorned in bird feathers with radiant faces that
made them striking in appearance. These individuals, who perhaps
numbered no more than 60 at any one time, were seen as *netjeru*,
divinities, Elders, and their memory was destined to be carried across
many thousands of years by their semi-divine descendants, who
would preserve for ever the memory of the age of the ancestors, the
sep tepi, or First Time.

An idealistic view, based on scant evidence and too much
speculation?

At this point maybe. But as we shall see, the image we have
formed of Egypt's Elder gods strengthens dramatically when we
attempt to determine the ultimate fate of this lost culture. However,
for the moment our more immediate assignment is to attempt to
understand what might await discovery on the island itself.

As we have seen, two of the most important inhabitants of
Wetjeset-Neter's second period of creation were Wa and 'Aa, the

leaders of the so-called Shebtiu. They would appear to have been allotted very special duties in the Mansion of Wetjeset-Neter, for they were the custodians of certain power objects referred to only as *iht*, an Egyptian word meaning 'relic' or 'substance'.[1] These items were said to have embodied the creative power and could be used either in the temple or within the Underworld of the Soul, which appeared to be some kind of subterranean domain accessed via the summit of the island.

There is every indication that the Underworld of the Soul – which is considered to be the primary source behind the legends of the *duat*-underworld[2] – was some kind of physical realm situated *beneath* the island. In the Edfu texts, this chthonic domain is given the alternative title of *bw-ḥnm*,[3] which provides further evidence for this supposition. The prefix *bw* translates as 'place', while the suffix *ḥnm* is a little more difficult to determine. It can mean 'to assume kingship', as in a coronation,[4] a 'coming together', as in a royal jubilee festival, or it can mean a constructed 'well', a translation that led Reymond to conclude that its closest approximation in English was 'Place of the Well'.[5] On the other hand, *ḥnm* can also mean 'to construct', a fact that led Joseph Jochmans to translate *bw-ḥnm* as 'a deep underground place that is constructed',[6] suggesting the presence of some kind of subterranean structure.

That the uninspiringly named *bw-ḥnm* was some kind of physical structure is not in doubt. Reymond proposed that it might have been a 'primeval well' situated actually *on the island*.[7] Since we know that the part of the *duat*-underworld connected with Giza-Rostau is associated not only with a sacred island and human-headed lion sphinxes but also with a long descending passageway, then might we be dealing with some kind of underground complex accessed via a stairwell located on the mound-like island?

We are then told that the *iht*-relics were 'stored'[8] in the *bw-ḥnm*, which their Shebtiu guardians were able to enter to conduct magic spells that furthered the act of creation in the outside world. It is also stated that these strange rituals involving the *iht*-relics could, if necessary, make the waters recede from the edges of the sacred lake.

Since the water-levels would have been controlled by the rise and fall of the Nile, the Edfu texts were implying that these people believed they could actually control the tides, perhaps even the annual floods, which is a quite extraordinary concept to grasp whatever way you look at it.

Our picture of Wetjeset-Neter's sacred island is becoming clearer. If we were able to cross over the clear blue waters of the lake and descend into the *bw-ḫnm*, the underground structure apparently accessed via the island, then our next move would be to find out what lay at the bottom of the 'primeval well'. Could we be about to enter the so-called 'Hall of Records', containing the lost legacy of a forgotten race of great antiquity? The evidence seems to suggest that the inner mysteries of the island complex are much more profound.

The earliest name given to the primeval mound in the Edfu documents is the Island of the Egg. Exactly what the *swḥt*, 'egg', might have been is never made clear, although it is described in the texts as the creative force responsible for the formation of the earth.[9] Like the island itself, this power source would appear to have been known by a number of different names, and would also seem to have been synonymous with something referred to in the Edfu account as the *bnnt*, 'embryo',[10] or 'seed',[11] which was seen as the 'nucleus' of the *iht*-power objects used inside the underworld complex by the Shebtiu.[12] The egg would also appear to have been one and the same as the so-called 'Great Lotus', or 'throne', which were both said to have been located within the island and to have emitted a 'radiance',[13] a fact that had led Reymond to comment:

> It looks as though the Egyptians believed that during the first period of the island the nucleus of the radiance remained on the ground, and that from the island the radiance illuminated the primeval waters.[14]

What kind of power source was this 'nucleus' that could radiate divine light from the heart of the island, and how might it have been linked with the movable *iht*-relics used by the Shebtiu in their so-called acts of creation?

A further name for the 'nucleus' of the island appears to have been the Sound Eye,[15] which was also said to have been the 'centre of the light which illumined the island'.[16] This therefore linked its function with the Great Lotus or throne. It was, of course, the destruction wrought by the Sound Eye that contributed to the period of conflict and darkness that engulfed Wetjeset-Neter and submerged the sacred island at the end of the first period of creation. In other words, the potency of the 'nucleus' was looked on as linked directly to the stability of the sacred domain.

Perhaps inevitably, Dr Reymond was of the opinion that *all* the terms used to describe the sacred island's power source were merely abstract expressions of natural forces believed by the Ancient Egyptians to have been responsible for the creation of the world. I disagree, for with our new knowledge of the Elder gods' apparent historical reality during the primeval age, the symbolic account given in the Edfu texts suddenly takes on a whole new dimension. Specific details concerning people, places and events hint strongly at the fact that we are dealing with the deeds and actions of a forgotten culture of extraordinary capability. Only in this under-standing can we determine the true meaning of what these texts contain.

As we stand at the base of the stairwell awaiting entry into the long passageway known as the 'road' of Rostau, I cannot help but wonder what might lie at the heart of the underworld complex. What was the nucleus, the divine power source spoken of in the Edfu texts? Was it still there beneath the limestone bedrock awaiting discovery, or had it been removed and destroyed long ago? Let us look at the evidence.

Firstly, the Egyptian word *bnnt*, translated by Reymond as 'embryo', is in fact a female rendering of the masculine root *bnn*, meaning 'to copulate, to beget, to be begotten, virile, phallus'.[17] It also derives from the same root as *bnbn*, or *benben*, the name given to the stone, obelisk or pyramidion associated with the primeval hill.[18] This, as you may recall, was seen in the Heliopolitan doctrine as a form of *omphalos*, a centre of all things and a symbol of divine creation. Since we know that the sacred mound appears to have been synonymous with the Island of the Egg of the Edfu documents, then it implies that the underground complex thought to have been located beneath it actually contained some kind of physical representation of a *benben*-stone, embodying both male and female elements in its character.

Secondly, as we saw in Chapter Twelve, the detailed description of the Fourth and Fifth Hours of the *duat*, collectively known as the 'land' or House of Sokar, strongly hints at the presence of an underworld realm beneath the sands of Giza-Rostau. Not only is the concept of the *duat* linked by Reymond with references in the Edfu texts to the Underworld of the Soul, but illustrations of the House of Sokar show a fiery-orange bell-shaped *omphalos* on which two birds, identified by Stecchini as doves, cling to its surface. This object is placed in direct relationship with both a sacred island, called the 'land of Sekri', and the mound of creation, suggesting therefore that it was synonymous with the 'embryo', 'seed', 'egg', etc. of the Edfu and Theban creation myths, as well as with the Heliopolitan concept of the *benben*-stone.[19]

Were we therefore dealing with the presence at the heart of the underworld complex of some kind of enormous sacred stone associated with the potency of cosmic creation? Did it embody the coming together, the crystallisation, of the universe's creative power source?

If so, then its appearance and purpose would be strikingly similar to the sacred lingams of Hindu tradition which were seen as phallic embodiments of the creative and regenerative power of the god Shiva. Generally smooth-surfaced and conical-shaped, these sacred stones were usually placed in shrines or recesses located at the heart of a temple, and often in some kind of subterranean sanctuary. One perfect example is the lingam located in the rock-cut cave temple at Elephanta, near Bombay, described in the following manner by German Indologist Dr Heinrich Zimmer in his scholarly work *Myths and Symbols in Indian Art and Civilisation*:

> The central sanctuary of this extensive temple is a simple, monumental, square shrine, with four entrances on the four sides, each guarded by a pair of divine door-keepers. Within is the austere symbol of the lingam, emanating to the four quarters its all-productive energy. This lingam, as the main stone image, forms the center of the innermost cella, the holy of holies or 'womb house' (*garbha-griha*). In the innermost recess of the organism of the temple it serenely stands, constituting the life-center of the subterranean cave.[20]

Like the *omphalos* of Greek mythology and the *benben*-stone of the Heliopolitan doctrine, sacred lingams are seen as the 'axis mundi', an imaginary Point of First Creation at the centre of everything.[21] Furthermore, in keeping with the *bnnt*-embryo or seed located in the Underworld of the Soul, the lingams expressed the regenerative powers of both the male phallus and the female yoni, which were often blended together in sculpted form. More often than not, however, lingams were simply conical-shaped stones that blatantly resembled the male member, emphasising its regenerative powers.

THE SEALED THING

There is one more tantalising piece of evidence which hints at the presence of something of extreme magical potency beneath the bedrock at Giza-Rostau, in the hidden domain of Sokar-Osiris. It can be found among the Heliopolitan-influenced literature known as the Coffin Texts, which are magical spells that were inscribed on funerary coffins. Spell 1080 reads as follows:

> This is the sealed thing, which is in darkness, with fire about it, which contains the efflux of Osiris, and it is put in Rostau.

It has been hidden since it fell from him, and it is what came
down from him onto the desert of sand . . .[22]

What is this 'sealed thing' with 'fire about it', which was placed in
Rostau and is in 'darkness', concealed out of sight, beneath the
'desert of sand'?

The resting-place of the body of Osiris is, as we have seen,
integrally linked with both the *duat*'s House of Sokar and the Edfu
texts' Underworld of the Soul. It is, I suspect, therefore another
allusion to the nucleus of the sacred island, the *omphalos* or *benben-*
stone at the heart of Giza-Rostau's subterranean complex. The
illustrations depicting the fiery-orange bell-like *omphalos* in the heart
of the House of Sokar show above it the hieroglyph for 'night' or
'darkness', leading Budge to conclude that it was 'some form of the
dark underworld of Seker'.[23] To me, however, it points clearly to the
fact that this powerful object has been sealed away in total darkness.
Yet despite its solitary confinement, Spell 1080 still tells us that it has
'fire about it', implying that it emits some form of divine fire or
radiance, exactly what is stated in the Edfu texts in connection with
the nucleus of the underworld complex. That 'the sealed thing' is
said to have been 'put in Rostau', where it now lies hidden, seems
doubly to confirm that we are dealing with an actual physical object
inside an underground world that exists to this day beneath the sands
of Giza.

On first reading Spell 1080 I was struck instantly by its great
similarity to a passage in a Judaic pseudepigraphal (i.e. falsely
attributed) text entitled the Book of Enoch. Compiled in stages by
Hassidic Jewish reactionaries between the second century BC and the
first century of the Christian era, this fascinating work purports to be
an account of the life of the patriarch Enoch, whose great-grandson
was the biblical Flood hero Noah. Our interest in this work – lengthy
fragments of which were found among the Dead Sea Scrolls in 1947
– is its graphic account of Enoch's visit to the so-called seven
heavens.

In the seventh and final heaven Enoch finds himself alongside the wall of a 'house' built of 'crystals' and surrounded by strange 'tongues of fire'.[24] Its 'ground-work' is also said to have the appearance of 'crystal', while of the building's interior the narrator says: 'Its ceiling was like the path of the stars and the lightnings . . . A flaming fire surrounded the walls, and its portals blazed with fire.'[25] Moving on to a second 'house' which 'excelled in splendour and magnificence and extent', Enoch found himself prostrating before a 'lofty throne' of 'crystal'.[26] On this were moving wheels as bright as the 'shining sun', and from beneath it came 'streams of flaming fire' so bright that he could not look on them. And 'sat thereon' the throne was the Great Glory, whose 'raiment shone more brightly than the sun and was whiter than any snow'.[27]

Although there is no obvious link between this descriptive narrative from the Book of Enoch and the Coffin Text quoted above, the repeated references to heavenly fire seen to surround the floor, walls and contents of the rooms made of crystal help us to envisage the 'sealed thing' with 'fire about it' hidden beneath the desert sands of Rostau. Is it possible that the fire being referred to in both cases was merely the shimmering radiance that might be expected when orange torchlight is refracted through transparent, crystal-like surfaces? Was the *omphalos* or *benben*-stone of the underworld complex some kind of enormous crystal lingam? Might this be what we can expect to find at the end of the long passageway of Rostau's subterranean world?

MOVABLE CRYSTALS

In the light of this knowledge concerning the supposed nucleus at the heart of Giza's underworld domain, what, then, are we to make of the *iht*-relics used inside it by the Shebtiu to conduct acts of creation? The Edfu documents refer to these movable power objects as expressions of the *bnnt*-embryo, or 'egg', from which originally they gained their creative power.[28] If this is the case, then might the *iht*-relics have been hand-held lingam-style crystals resonating the cosmic energy contained within the nucleus located at the heart of the complex?

The idea is not unique, for there are certain similarities between the purpose and appearance of the *iht*-relics and the hand-held conical-shaped crystals used for meditational purposes by the practitioners of *dzogchen*, an ancient teaching of Tibet found almost exclusively among the *Nyingma-pa*, perhaps the oldest school of Buddhist lamaism.[29] In the past large uncut quartz crystals would be used for this purpose, but in the last 40 years most *dzogchen* practitioners living and teaching in the West have tended to use manufactured prismatic cut-glass crystals. Not only are these conical-shaped stones used by initiates as a means of mental focus, but they are also believed to act as a channel through which the practitioner can communicate with the creative forces of the universe.

Curiously enough, there exist certain legends featuring the antediluvian patriarch Enoch that speak of some kind of sacred stone being placed in hidden chambers beneath the Giza pyramids. To the Jews who lived in the cosmopolitan city of Alexandria during the Ptolemaic period, the Great Pyramid was looked on as having been constructed by Enoch, who was himself equated with the figure known as Hermes Trismegistus ('Thrice Greatest Hermes'), the Graeco-Roman or 'Hermetic' form of Thoth, the Egyptian god of books and writing. Enoch was even said to have been the inventor of the 12-fold division of the starry canopy,[30] which is reflected in the astrological sections of the pseudepigraphal books accredited to the antediluvian patriarch. Somehow Enoch went on to become confused with the stories that later circulated among the Copts of Old Cairo which featured the legendary king Saurid Ibn Salhouk, who, being warned of the coming deluge, built the pyramids of Giza and constructed secret chambers in which all the arts and sciences of his race were preserved.

As confusing, and perhaps misleading, as these legends of Enoch might seem, they are worth quoting for they contain some intriguing elements which do not reappear in other Egyptian literature. According to one lost tradition, Enoch constructed, with the help of his son Methuselah, nine hidden vaults, each stacked one on top of the other.[31] In the lowest of these he deposited a 'white oriental porphyry stone' (a 'gold triangular tablet' in another version), bearing the Ineffable Name of the Hebrew God, while a second tablet, inscribed with strange words Enoch had gained from the angels themselves, was given into the safekeeping of his son. The vaults were then sealed, and on the spot Enoch constructed two indestructible columns, one made of marble, so that it might 'never burn', and the other made of *Laterus*, or brick, so that it might 'not sink in water'.[32]

On the brick column were inscribed the 'seven sciences' of mankind, the so-called 'archives' of speculative Masonry, while on the marble column he 'placed an inscription stating that a short distance away a priceless treasure would be found in a subterranean vault'.[33]

How or where these legends originated is completely unknown. They have no connection whatsoever with Enoch's few brief mentions in the book of Genesis, and they do not appear in any other early Hebrew sources. It is, however, extremely likely that they were the creation of Alexandrian Jews, and therefore relate to the enigmas attached to the Great Pyramid even in Ptolemaic times. Were they a highly simplified memory of the Underworld of the Soul, the concealed complex that the Edfu texts clearly say existed within Giza-Rostau's sacred island?

PSYCHIC ASSAULT COURSE

Continuing our imaginary journey along the descending passageway of the Underworld of the Soul, we have now tentatively established that somewhere in its heart there might exist a large conical-shaped *omphalos* or *benben*-stone, plausibly a crystal-like structure, as well as smaller, hand-held sacred stones, or crystals, like the Shiva-lingams of

India. Yet what does the layout of the interior look like? What sort of rooms or chambers might we expect to encounter? Is there any kind of overall ground-plan to this place, and, more pressingly, does it contain any artefacts?

The first real clue concerning the layout of the complex comes from the account of the *duat*-underworld in Heliopolitan cosmological tradition. This speaks of the First Division, or Hour, consisting of 'an *arrit*, i.c. a hall, or a sort of ante-chamber of the Tuat'.[34] Could this refer to some kind of entrance hall where the Shebtiu guardians would have to prepare themselves before moving into the main descending passageway? If so, then to where might this have led?

Having successfully traversed the imagined entrance hall and descending passageway, we can only assume that the initiate, in his role as the sun-god, would be made to navigate the 12 divisions in the correct sequence. In each of these it must also be assumed that he or she would undergo a series of trials and tribulations in which they would encounter a plethora of astral forms in the guise of serpents, monsters, demons and solid-looking obstacles. Only by successfully penetrating each section using a mixture of mental endurance and magical utterances would they be allowed to pass into the next chamber. In many ways the whole quest would have been rather like going on a psychic assault course. Only after having traversed each chamber would the guardian, or initiate, have been permitted to come face to face with the *bnnt*-embryo, or cosmic egg, the original Point of First Creation and *benben*-stone, plausibly contained within its own special chamber. Should this supposition be correct, then it is conceivable that the Underworld of the Soul consists of a series of interconnecting chambers linked to a long passageway entered through some kind of antechamber or underground hall.

Since we know that the twin *aker*-lions, as guardians of the entrance and exits of the *duat*, appear to have reflected the influence of their celestial counterparts on the equinoctial horizon during the precessional Age of Leo, it is tempting to suggest that the chambers represent the 12-fold division of the ecliptic, beginning with the house of Leo. Should this be so, then might each of the 12 'houses' or chambers have reflected a different astrological influence?

Despite what some might believe, the *duat* was actually conceived of as being round, like the path of the sun, and not straight like a river. In a quotation from one of the seventy-five Praises of Re found inscribed on the walls of royal tombs dating to the Nineteenth and Twentieth Dynasties, the sun-god is referred to as 'Ra, exalted Sekhem [Power], lord of the hidden circles [of the Tuat], bringer of forms, thou restest in secret places and makest thy creations in the form of the god Tamt.'[35] This is typical of the manner in which the *duat* is so often described as being composed of circles.

If this supposition is correct, then it is likely that the *iht*-relics reflected the creative influences of the 12 chambers which were themselves individualised emanations of the centrally positioned 'embryo' or 'egg' of creation. The Edfu texts tell us that acts of creation were conducted by the Shebtiu using the *iht*-relics in concert with magic spells inside the underworld complex.[36] To me this seemed to imply that it was only when the Shebtiu acted in perfect concert with both their chosen power objects and their corresponding chambers that this creative process could take place. It might therefore be suggested that these guardian figures were each chosen for the role because they were seen to reflect the resonance, or cosmic influence, of specific chambers and power objects.

Whether or not Egypt's Elder culture were aware of the zodiac as we know it today remains a matter of speculation. In my opinion this seems most unlikely, for there is ample evidence to suggest that the zodiacal constellations derive from Mesopotamian originals created at some point in the mists of prehistory. This is not to say that the Sphinx-building Elder culture did not divide up the line of the ecliptic into 12 divisions or houses, and did not see their own precessional age as governed by the terrifying influence of a cosmic lion or lioness (seen later variously as the stars of Leo, the goddess Sekhmet and the Great Sphinx), only that the signs of the zodiac commonly used today were devised at a much later date.

We might therefore imagine that before us now is the first of a large circle of interconnected chambers. In here we might expect to find one of the *iht*-power objects, with the appearance perhaps of a lingam stone, 'stored' away in a recess or cavity. The room would probably be empty, for its shape, dimensions and appearance would have to reflect specific sound acoustics that would differ in each chamber, so that every one would reflect a predetermined cosmic influence matched only by its Shebtiu guardian. Collectively, the influences of the 12 chambers would perhaps have been seen to blend together as one in the heart of the complex, where the nucleus, *omphalos*-stone or egg of creation was positioned.

This, then, is the type of information offered by a radical reinterpretation of the Edfu Building Texts, in view of our current knowledge concerning the role of the *duat*-underworld and the survival in Egypt of the Elder culture's advanced technological capability.

THE SERPENT KEMATEF

More difficult to determine is the exact function of the underworld complex at Giza-Rostau, and for this we must move away from the Temple of Horus at Edfu and travel 89 kilometres (56 miles) or so upriver to Thebes' religious centre at Karnak and here make our way to the Temple of Khonsu, the moon-god. Beside it is a small temple named in the inscriptions as the 'House of Creation' of Osiris,[37] where we will find a series of mythological texts that contain important clues to the origins of the Egyptian civilisation not found among either the Edfu or Heliopolitan literature.

Like other creation texts, the Theban account begins with the emergence out of the primeval waters of the sacred mound at the beginning of time. It also speaks of the *bnnt*-embryo, or 'seed', located at the heart of the island, and equates this with the 'egg' of creation.[38]

One feature unique to the Theban creation myth is the so-called 'soul' of the island, personified as a primordial snake called Kematef,[39] the coils of which were seen to be the stepped terraces that wound their way around the primeval hill.[40] More important, this serpent, who is described in the inscriptions as 'he whose moment of living had ended or was thought buried',[41] seems to have been connected directly with the Theban variation of the under-world.[42] It is also linked both with the eight Ogdoad,[43] the Theban counterparts to the Shebtiu mentioned in the Edfu account, and with the egg of creation. Even more intriguing is that the 'great soul' of Kematef – although adopted by the cult of Amun as an aspect of their principal god – was also connected with the body of Osiris, the god of the underworld, who is referred to as 'in the Chamber of the Kingdom of the Dead with the eight great gods'.[44]

Kematef was said to have been 'self-begotten' or the 'creator of his own egg', in other words the self-begetter in the act of impreg-nation.[45] Another inscription speaks of Kematef as 'the *bnnt* in Nun who fashioned [i.e. brought forth] the *bnnt* on the First Occasion [*sep tepi*]',[46] so in effect the serpent was seen as the core intelligence and even the creator of the nucleus, or *omphalos*, at the heart of the island complex that rose from the waters of Nun at the beginning of time. It was therefore looked on as having produced its own egg over which it also became guardian – an image familiar in much later Graeco-Roman Hermetic tradition, where the serpent of wisdom was often depicted coiled around the cosmic egg.

Ancient legend spoke of a snake of two horns (the horned viper) sacred to Thebes, which was said to have been buried after its death

The Pharaoh seen enthroned as the god Osiris and as a mummy, located in the *duat*-underworld beneath the mound, or hill, of creation. Its steps were said to have been the coils of Kematef, the cosmic serpent of the ancient Theban creation texts.

'in the temple of Amun'.[47] This, however, seems to be a misinterpretation of Kematef's association with the oracle or *omphalos*-stone, housed inside the Temple of Amun. This can be seen by the fact that the more famous *omphalos* of Delphi was believed to be not only a stylised egg but also the headstone of a grave that contained a sacred snake,[48] suggesting that a comparative legend may have built up around Kematef at Thebes.

In Graeco-Roman times, Kematef became fused with myths regarding other serpentine deities. He also became associated with a creator-god named Khnum,[49] as well as another Theban deity named Kneph,[50] and finally Chnoumis or Chnoubis,[51] the deity worshipped by the followers of Hermetica (after the teachings of Hermes Trismegistus) and frequently carved on magical gems used to cure patients of stomach pains![52] This hybrid form of Kematef was usually depicted with the body of a coiled snake and the head of a lion, an affiliation taken from the division of 36 constellations known as the *bakiu*, where Chnoumis was seen as the First Decan of the Lion.[53] More significantly, he bore a mane that generally consisted of either twelve or seven spoke-like rays, which undoubtedly represented respectively the twelve signs of the zodiac and just possibly the seven pole stars of the 26,000-year precessional cycle.

Very little is known of the myth and ritual surrounding Chnoubis, although what little has been preserved can be found in the writings of the Peratae, or Peratics, a gnostic Christian sect belonging to the second century AD. One relatively unknown, and quite obviously blasphemous, Peratae text speaks of the serpent Kematef under the name Chorzar in the following, quite extraordinary, manner:

> I am a voice of awaking from sleep in the aeon of the night, [and] now I begin to lay bare the power from Chaos. The power is the mud of the abyss, which raises the mire of the imperishable watery void, the whole power of the convulsion, pale as water, ever-moving . . . taking advantage of the things thrown up by the 12 eyes of the Law, showing a seal to the power which arranges by itself the onrushing unseen water

which is called Thalassa . . . Ignorance has called this power
Kronos . . . [The] power to whom Thalassa is entrusted is
masculo-feminine, who traces back the hissing [water] from
the twelve mouths of the 12 pipes and after preparing distrib-
utes it . . . The Typhonic [i.e. 'monster serpent']^54 daughter of
this [power] is . . . Chorzar. He [*sic*] that is encircled with the
12-angled pyramid and darkens the gate into the pyramid with
divers colours and perfects the whole blackness.^55

An interpretation of this powerful piece of forgotten prose is
necessary in our search to understand the true function of Giza's
underworld complex. The 'unseen water' or 'watery void' that
emerges in the 'aeon of the night' is, of course, the Nun – the
boundless watery mass that existed in a state of eternal darkness
before the first rays of light reached the primeval mound at the
beginning of time. 'Thalassa' is to be seen as the intelligence or
personification of this primordial chaos, which being female matches
the gender originally attributed to the Nun under the name Nut.^56

The '12 eyes of the Law' referred to in the Peratae text are
interpreted not as 'eyes' of sight but as 'eyes' in the landscape – wells
in the ground^57 – immediately implying some kind of 12-fold
structure located underground. More significant is the 'monster
serpent' named as Chorzar, who 'traces back the hissing [water] from
the 12 mouths of the 12 pipes'. Initially, I found this line a little
difficult to decipher. The '12 pipes' seemed to imply the 12
individual aeons, or 'Great Years', of classical tradition, which correspond to the precessional cycle of 26,000 years and were seen as the
celestial mechanism for measuring time.

In the cult of the Roman god Mithras, which first appeared in
what is today southern Turkey during the first century BC, the
so-called *kosmokrator*, or keeper of cosmic time, was represented by a
lion-headed figure with a male human body, a pair of keys in one
hand and either the earth or the cosmic egg beneath its feet. Coiled
around its torso was the cosmic serpent, its head rising up over the
top of the mane (occasionally shown entering the mouth), while

studded either on to its chest or carved in an arc above its head would be the 12 signs of the zodiac, showing it to be an image both of Chnoubis and of the much earlier Kematef. I believe that the 12 'pipes' mentioned in the Peratae text refer symbolically to 12 umbilical cords nourishing the navel, or *omphalos*, of each coming world aeon, which was seen in terms of an unborn 'child'.

As strange as these gnostic beliefs might seem, they appear to have been influenced by the cosmological doctrines taught among the Hermetic schools of Alexandria in the centuries prior to the birth of the Christian era. This is made clear by the fact that the Peratae text quoted above states that Chorzar is a form of Kore,[58] an important Graeco-Roman goddess whose festival at Alexandria on 6 January each year celebrated the birth of the child of the aeon.[59]

The most peculiar statement in the Peratae text is the reference to Chorzar being 'encircled with the 12-angled pyramid' which 'darkens the gate into the pyramid with divers colours and perfects the whole blackness'. Even though the '12-angled pyramid' has been interpreted by some commentators as referring simply to the 12-fold

Gnostic gem showing the lion-headed Chnoubis, or Chorzar, the
Graeco-Roman form of Kematef, the cosmic serpent and *kosmokrator* of
the Theban creation texts.

division of the zodiac, these strange words seem to be implying that the lion-headed and/or serpentine *kosmokrator* of precessional aeons, or ages, and known variously as Chorzar, Chnoubis or Kematef, was viewed as the protector of the '12 eyes [or wells] of the Law' and the '12-angled pyramid', terms which I feel express knowledge regarding the underground complex thought to be present beneath the sands of Giza.

CHAMBERS OF FIRST CREATION

There seems to be little doubt in my mind that the sequence of chambers making up Giza's underworld domain were once considered to have been microcosmic representations of the creative forces that split into 12 parts at the beginning of time, a concept reflected in the idea of the 12-fold influence of the zodiac. The *bnnt*-embryo, or 'seed', was understood originally to have been a crystallisation of the moment of creation, what we refer to today as the Big Bang – the starting-point of the universe. From that point onwards time existed, and will continue to do so in recordable cycles for ever, explaining perhaps the Elder gods' apparent obsession with first creation and long time-cycles.

To the modern world the idea of constructing a huge subterranean complex to perpetuate the act of cosmic creation might seem nonsensical, if not a little absurd. In many ways it might be argued that these Chambers of First Creation have more in common with the vast underground complex used as a particle accelerator at the CERN establishment in Geneva than a hall of records containing the writings, artefacts and lost teachings of an antediluvian civilisation. To the Elder culture such a location would seem to have been essential to ensure, and even effect, the process of creation. If I am correct, then it implies that the Elders – seen in terms of the Shebtiu or Ogdoad – believed that by entering the Chambers of First Creation and ritually interacting with the essence of the hand-held *iht*-relics they could perpetuate, or even accelerate, evolution in the outside world.

Whether or not this assessment of the cosmic influences and divine powers connected to the underground domain beneath the Giza pyramid field is accurate will be known only if and when an entrance is finally uncovered by the spades of the Egyptologists.

For the moment our imaginary journey inside the island complex has come to an end. We have passed through the suggested ring or 'pyramid' of 12 outer chambers, each reflecting individual cosmic influences and linked by interconnecting gateways. We have also encountered the great *bnnt*-embryo, or 'egg', at the heart of the complex, so must now retrace our steps back along the descending corridor to the *arrit*-hall or antechamber. From here the stairwell will take us back out into the outside world.

In the Age of Leo the initiate would have emerged from the Underworld of the Soul to stand on the sacred island, surrounded by the primeval waters of Nun. Yet with the desiccation of the eastern Sahara and the rise of Pharaonic Egypt in around 3100 BC, the setting has changed quite dramatically. No longer are we able to look out over the shallow lake, created by the waters of the nearby river Nile, and see beyond it the gleaming white Mansion of Wetjeset-Neter nestling behind tall enclosure walls. In its place is the hot

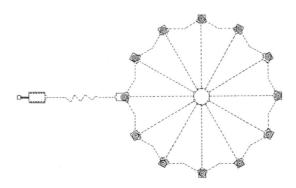

Suggested 12-fold ground-plan of the Chambers of First Creation, based on the contents of the Edfu Building Texts and the books of the *duat*-underworld.

desert sun, its blistering heat interrupted only by the *khamsin*, the fierce wind storms that occasionally blow in from the south and engulf everything in their path.

Gone too is the sacred island, with its structured enclosure and concealed entrance to the Underworld of the Soul. Instead, we find ourselves somewhere in the vicinity of the Giza pyramid field. Yet where exactly? Having recently examined the layout and altitude of the various monuments on the plateau, it is my conclusion that the sacred lake can only have lain to the east or north-east of the Great Sphinx and the Valley Temple of Khafre. In no way can it have been located on or around the plateau itself, for it rises up too steeply beyond the pyramid of Menkaure on its western side. Only on its eastern side can we find a low-lying area sufficient in size to have created either a temporary, or more permanent, lake or reservoir. This observation is supported by the recent discovery of a stone quay on the eastern side of the Valley Temple, which may itself be the last remains of the Mansion of Wetjeset-Neter constructed by the Elder gods, next to the Field of Reeds on the edge of the sacred lake.

If I am correct in these assumptions, then it could well mean that the Island of the Egg, the mound of First Creation, now lies beneath the streets of the Nazlet el-Samman village, situated beyond the eastern edge of the plateau. This is a sad realisation, for if access to the Underworld of the Soul was via the water-bound island, then its entrance may never be found.

In many ways I hope I am wrong in this assessment of the evidence available to us at the present time. However, these findings appear to concur precisely with the inspired readings of American psychic Edgar Cayce. On being asked in 1933 to provide details regarding the contents of the Hall of Records, he revealed the actual whereabouts of the subterranean complex by stating that:

> In position, this lies – as the sun rises from the waters – as the line of the shadows [or light] falls between the paws of the Sphinx; that was set later as the sentinel or guard and which

may not be entered from the connecting chambers from the Sphinx's right paw until the time has been fulfilled when the changes must be active in this sphere of man's experience. Then [it lies] between the Sphinx and the river.[60]

'Between the Sphinx and the river' – in other words, to the east of the Sphinx and the Valley Temple. If he was right in this respect, then let us also hope that he was correct in his belief that connecting chambers led from the underground complex to a position coincident to the right paw of the Sphinx monument. If this is so, we still stand a reasonable chance of locating a second entry point using modern-day sounding equipment.

Whether or not the nine chambers beneath the Sphinx enclosure discovered in 1996 by the team put together by the University of Florida and the Schor Foundation are actually connected with Giza's underworld complex remains to be seen. It may well be that, although of man-made construction, and therefore of profound interest to our knowledge of Egyptian history, they lie too near the surface to be connected with the Elder culture's Underworld of the Soul. On the other hand they might well contain the ultimate proof of the former existence in Egypt of a high culture of almost alien mentality, whose knowledge of ancient technology and natural sciences will change the entire way we perceive human evolution. As the clock ticks nearer and nearer to millennial midnight, the pressure is mounting for the Egyptian government to allow professional, university-linked archaeological terms to continue the search for Giza's lost legacy (see also Chapter Twenty), for only then will the real truth be known.

Let us look forward to that day.

CHAPTER FIFTEEN

THE CRADLE OF CIVILISATION

It is clear that at the commencement of the pyramid age the monuments remaining on the Giza plateau were in advanced states of decay. Yet in this same great epoch the architects and engineers of Fourth-Dynasty Pharaohs such as Khufu, Khafre and Menkaure would appear to have repaired, redesigned and resanctified structures such as the Valley Temple and the Great Sphinx, which were then incorporated into the gradually emerging pyramid field. If this were indeed the case, then why had this resurrection of the Elder gods' ancient places of power not been done thousands of years earlier? Why did it take so long for the great sanctity of the Giza plateau to be recognised for what it was – the Splendid Place of the First Time? Did the earliest dynastic Egyptians simply not have the means to embark on such enormous building projects, or were the likes of Khufu and Khafre inspired by visionary ideals, in the same way that Thutmose IV was compelled by a dream to clear away the sand from around the base of the Sphinx over 1000 years later?

If lineal descendants of the Elder culture really did remain in Egypt following the geological upheavals and climatic changes that brought to a close the last Ice Age, *c.* 10,500–9500 BC, then why were their great temples allowed to fall into a state of ruin? The only explanation that makes any real sense is that the few Elders left in Egypt were unable to perpetuate or maintain the building activities with which they had been preoccupied for perhaps thousands of years. Since we have very little knowledge of any major building construction in Egypt between the end of the Age of Leo, c. 9220 BC, and the tail end of the predynastic period, c. 3150 BC, then it would imply that those Elders who possessed the technological skills necessary to construct temple complexes were simply no longer present.

Perhaps cyclopean structures, such as the Valley Temple and the Osireion at Abydos, were like the ruined medieval abbeys of Britain today, revered yet never repaired, until some as yet uncertain impetus appeared on the scene and initiated the Pharaonic age in around 3100 BC. All the indications are that at this very time a whole plethora of new cultural ideas, new styles of worship and new designs in architecture were gradually being introduced into Egypt by Eastern invaders. Who were these people, and how might they have inspired Egypt's ruling elite to initiate major building projects, such as the construction of the various pyramid fields around the ancient city of Memphis? Were they in any way connected with the Elders who are presumed to have left Egypt over 5000 years beforehand? Did they retain myths and legends that spoke of Egypt, or more precisely the Giza plateau, as being their ancestral homeland? Could it have been these peoples who, with the aid of the Heliopolitan priesthood, helped revitalise Giza's ancient sanctity?

The identity of this unknown culture, and how exactly it might fit into the overall picture, is a problem currently being studied by a number of leading Egyptologists, and will be discussed in a later chapter. More important for the moment is to establish the probable fate of the Elder culture, beginning with its demise.

SAILING AWAY

The Edfu texts are specific on what became of at least some of the divine inhabitants of Wetjeset-Neter and its sacred domain. They say that, at the end of their time, the Shebtiu simply 'sailed' away to what Reymond suggested was 'another part of the primeval world'[1] where they could 'continue their creative task' undisturbed.[2] Further evidence that these mythical beings were mariners or navigators of some sort comes from the fact that one Shebtiu is named as 'the sailor',[3] while, collectively, the followers of the divine individual known as the Falcon are referred to as 'the crew'.[4]

This clear allusion to maritime activities among the Nilotic Egyptians of the palaeolithic age is hard to grasp, since the oldest accepted seafaring culture was that of the Phoenicians, who first navigated the Mediterranean coast, and very probably the eastern Atlantic seaboard, no earlier than the third millennium BC. No other seafaring nation is known to have existed before them. However, as we saw in a previous chapter, Sanchoniatho, the Phoenician historian who lived just before the Trojan War, *c.* 1200 BC, recorded that before the rise of his peoples there had existed a divine race who founded Byblos, Lebanon's first city.[5] He spoke of them possessing 'light and other more complete ships', clearly implying that they were a culture with maritime capability.[6]

That such a culture existed in the Mediterranean some time prior to the birth of the Phoenician race is also supported by the findings of the late Professor Charles Hapgood of Keene College, New Hampshire, in his classic work *Maps of the Ancient Sea Kings*. He made an extensive study of early portolan maps, such as the famous Piri Reis map of 1513, which he saw as being constructed from more ancient prototypes dating back many thousands of years. Hapgood found that almost all of those examined by him and his students showed large areas of coastline in different parts of the world, including the Mediterranean Sea, as they would have been at least

6000 years ago. After due consideration, he concluded that those who had originally compiled these maps must have belonged to '*one culture* [author's emphasis]' of extreme antiquity with maritime connections across the globe.[7]

The famous early dynastic boat burials uncovered both at Giza and at Abydos in the south of the country have revealed powerful seagoing vessels with high prows; this being despite the fact that Ancient Egypt is not believed to have had any obvious maritime capabilities during the early dynastic period. These enormous vessels, which are seen by Egyptologists as having been made for purely ceremonial purposes, were clearly designed for the navigation of rough seas, not the gentle waters of the Nile.

Exactly where this advanced maritime knowledge came from need not detain us. It is cited only to demonstrate the feasibility of the divine inhabitants of Wetjeset-Neter having sailed away to some foreign land after their time had ended in Egypt. If this is what really happened, then how are we to determine exactly where in the primeval world the Shebtiu might have ended their time? With seafaring abilities they could have set sail for any part of the world. However, I felt it would be safer to confine my search to the countries bordering the Mediterranean coastline to see what this might produce. More important, I would need to find hard evidence of a high culture that:

a) showed distinct signs of the level of sophistication and technology accredited to Egypt's Sphinx-building Elder culture;
b) had risen to prominence shortly after the final throes of the last Ice Age, *c.* 10,500–9500 BC, a time-frame that also corresponds with the fall of the astrological Age of Leo and the commencement of the Age of Cancer;
c) possessed cosmological doctrines that matched those found in Ancient Egypt;
d) preserved myths and legends which spoke of Egypt as its true homeland; and finally
e) practised a shamanic religion of the kind expressed in Egyptian creation texts, such as those preserved at Edfu.

Only by finding a high culture that complied with each and every one of these points could I claim to have found the remnants of Egypt's Elder culture. In my opinion, I was looking for a line of transmission that would take me to the genesis point of a culture that inherited the capabilities, and perhaps even the mentality, of its Egyptian forebears. Having searched long and hard for a possible solution, I realised eventually that the key to the mystery was the sudden emergence in the Near East of what might be described as the neolithic revolution, and in particular the appearance of agriculture.

DOWN BY THE RIVER

The earliest known examples of proto-agriculture to be found anywhere in the Old World come from the late palaeolithic communities of the Nile. At four sites belonging to the so-called Isnan or Qadan peoples – at Isna (modern Esna), Naqada, Dishna, and Tushka, 200 kilometres (125 miles) upriver from Aswan – Egyptologists have unearthed evidence that their occupants cultivated wheat grass, wild barley and other types of grasses as early as 12,500 BC.[8] Stone sickle blades were used to reap the harvests, while grinding stones enabled them to extract the maximum amount of grain.[9] In addition to possessing a primitive form of agriculture, the Isnan and Qadan had mastered animal husbandry. They also possessed a sophisticated microblade technology and lived in communal villages that seem to pre-empt the lifestyles later adopted by the very first neolithic peoples.[10]

It was, however, the sudden decline of the Isnan's and Qadan's technological skills that interested me, for in around 9500 BC the grinding stones and sickle blades used in the production of cereals suddenly disappear to be replaced by much cruder stone implements of the sort used by other, less advanced cultures of the Nile valley.[11] Agriculture then vanishes entirely from Egypt for a full 4500 years, until it is finally reintroduced, probably via Palestine, in around 5000 BC.[12]

Egyptologists such as Fekri Hassan have suggested that the extraordinary reversal in lifestyle among the Isnan and Qadan was caused by extremely high Nile floods that continually engulfed the Nile valley between 10,500 BC and 9500 BC.[13] Hassan has argued that this heavy flooding discouraged the Nilotic communities from continuing their agricultural lifestyle, settling instead for a more basic hunter-gathering means of existence, like that observed by all their neighbours.[14]

The dates given for the mass flooding in Egypt correspond exactly with the global catastrophes that would seem to have accompanied the end of the last Ice Age. In North America alone the geological upheavals and climatic changes that occurred during the eleventh millennium BC claimed an estimated forty million animals. Many of these species – which included giant beavers and sloths, mammoths, mastodons, sabre-tooth cats and woolly rhinoceroses – became extinct virtually overnight. It was these events, which included volcanic eruptions, periods of darkness, tidal waves and severe flooding, that appear to have been preserved in folk-memory all around the world.[15]

How or why the Isnan and Qadan developed their notions of primitive agriculture remains a mystery. It could be that they evolved faster than their rivals by chance alone. This is certainly a possibility, although just maybe there is an altogether different solution. Instead of simply having the intellectual capacity to learn faster than everyone else, perhaps the Isnan and Qadan were taught their superior skills by even more advanced individuals. I speak, of course, of the Elder culture who would seem to have been responsible for the cyclopean structures built along the Nile during this very same epoch. To accept this theory, we must assume that, in addition to their many other advanced capabilities, these individuals also pioneered the cultivation of wild cereal crops and then supplied this knowledge to the local Nilotic peoples, who at that stage were little more than simple fishermen.

Maybe the Elders collaborated with these communities for purposes of mutual benefit and cooperation. It could be that they needed manpower for help in construction projects such as the building of temples and enclosure walls, and the digging of water channels like the one at Giza. Should this be the case, then it implies that the cessation of agriculture among the Isnan and Qadan was caused when the Elder culture's encouragement and technical know-how was suddenly withdrawn. Without constant supervision, the primitive farming communities of the Nile simply lost all interest in agriculture and reverted back to their hunter-gatherer lifestyles. This is not to say that the extremely high floods during this period were not a factor involved in the abandonment of their agricultural lifestyle, only that they were secondary to the main cause of these changes.

The fact that after 9500 BC agriculture disappears completely from Egypt for a full 4500 years really does hint at a clean break in continuity. Was it therefore possible that the Elders carried their knowledge of a settled agricultural-based lifestyle to a new place of settlement? If so, then it is important to establish when and where cereal cultivation emerged outside Egypt.

THE FIRST FARMERS

As has previously been stated, the emergence of the neolithic age marked the transition of the palaeolithic hunter-gatherer into a more settled way of life where instead of moving from settlement to settlement, humankind began working in cooperation with nature. The key element of this major change in lifestyle was, of course, the development of agriculture and animal husbandry, which necessitated the establishment of more permanent settlements where a community could work together to produce enough food and livestock to sustain itself through the winter months. Removing the element of uncertainty from the daily lives of the inhabitants enabled the neolithic peoples to start developing technical capabilities and to regulate their lives for the first time.

This, at least, is the orthodox view of how the gradual change from palaeolithic to neolithic began in a humble manner, some time after the end of the last Ice Age. Yet there are major flaws in this supposition, for it is clear that the transition from hunter-gatherer to settled farmer did not occur everywhere at the same time. Indeed, it would seem to have emerged first in one region alone and to have remained in virtual isolation here for at least 1000 years before spreading very slowly outwards. The genesis point of the so-called neolithic revolution is the fertile river valleys of the Upper Euphrates of northern Syria and eastern Anatolia, modern-day Turkey. Here, from around 9500 BC onwards, evidence for the cultivation of wild cereals, as well as animal husbandry, starts to appear at important sites such as the extensive 'farmers' village' at Tell Abu Hureyra on the Upper Euphrates in northern Syria.[16] As in the case of the Isnan and Qadan communities of Egypt, evidence of cereal cultivation has come from the discovery here of stone pestles, rubbing stones and milling stones. In addition to this, archaeologists also found an abundance of seeds from three different types of cereal grains – a form of wild barley, a wild wheat called einkorn and wild rye[17] – two of which had previously been grown by the Nilotic communities of palaeolithic Egypt. Since none of these cereal plants was indigenous to Abu Hureyra, it meant that they must have been purposely selected and brought to the area and then subsequently grown and harvested by the village's earliest inhabitants.

The clear fact that agriculture appears in the Near East at around the very same time that it vanishes from the Nile valley is striking and cannot be overlooked. In my opinion, there seems to be a direct link between these two quite different farming regions separated by over 900 kilometres, and the most obvious solution is the transmission of agricultural knowledge and skills through the migration of individuals from Egypt to the Near East.

So is it possible that some of the remaining Elders departed from Giza for the fertile valleys of the Upper Euphrates, carrying with them their technological capabilities, some time in around 9500 BC? Let us look a little more closely at the emergence of civilised society in the Near East.

UNCERTAIN FORCES

Eastern Anatolia forms the westernmost flanks of a vast snow-capped expanse of mountains that stretches north to the remote rocky regions of Russian Armenia; eastwards to the shores of Lake Urmiah in western Iran, and south-east along the length of the Zagros mountains as they descend towards the Persian Gulf and act as a more-or-less impenetrable barrier between Iraq and Iran. This enormous, mostly desolate part of the earth, home in the most part to bands of warring rebels, isolated religious communities and the occasional bombed-out village, town or city, is known to the world as Kurdistan – the cultural and political homeland of the much-troubled Kurdish peoples.

It was in this geographical region of the globe that the first neolithic farmers cultivated everything from peas to lentils, alfalfa and grapes.[18] Yet a settled agricultural lifestyle brings with it time for experimentation, and this resulted in a whole number of 'firsts' for the peoples living in the mountains, foothills and fertile river valleys of the Near East. In addition to the development of crop cultivation and animal husbandry, the first evidence anywhere for the use of metals comes from this region. At a huge cave in Iraqi Kurdistan, situated high above the Greater Zab river, some 520 kilometres (325 miles) east-north-east of Abu Hureyra and known locally as Shanidar, palaeontologist Ralph Solecki unearthed a slim, almond-shaped piece of copper. This object had two equally spaced perforations at its end so that it could be worn as a pendant around the neck.[19]

The context in which it was found indicates a date of around 9500 BC, making this the earliest example of a copper artefact. Its presence at the site was almost certainly connected with the nearby settlement of Zawi Chemi, whose inhabitants are known to have used grinding stones to produce flour from wild cereal grains as early as the late tenth millennium BC.[20] The workmanship of this hammered object made from unsmelted copper ore is quite extraordinary and suggests an extremely long time-frame during which this style of copper work was developed – telling evidence that this trade began long before 9500 BC. There is even a possibility that it might have been an heirloom from an earlier culture, as there is no evidence for the use of hammered copper objects until 7200 BC, some 2300 years later, when they seem to reappear quite suddenly at an important neolithic village, located some 400 kilometres (250 miles) west-north-west of the Shanidar cave. Known today as Çayönü, it lies some 60 kilometres (37 miles) north of Diyarbakir, the present capital of Turkish Kurdistan. Here archaeologists Robert Braidwood and Halet Çambel discovered four early copper items – two pins, one bent fish-hook and a reamer or awl – showing that its inhabitants had become proficient metalworkers by this age.[21]

The noted craftsmen of Çayönü went on to produce many other copper items, including oval-shaped beads,[22] as the trade spread gradually to other major sites in the region. One of these was the important neolithic village of Jarmo, situated on a tributary of the Lesser Zab river in the foothills of Iraqi Kurdistan. Here, at an occupational level corresponding to 6750 BC, Robert Braidwood and his team uncovered various copper items, as well as a single bead made of smelted lead, the oldest evidence of metallurgy anywhere in the Old World.[23] It has been suggested that smelting developed first in the foothills and valleys of Kurdistan for the simple reason that its mountains are literally teeming with ore deposits. Indeed, the inhabitants of Çayönü have been producing smelted copper and bronze objects for at least 7000 years.[24]

Also from Çayönü comes the Old World's[25] earliest known piece of cloth, which was found still wrapped around an antler, possibly to provide a better grip. It is 9000 years old and is thought to be a linen fabric, woven from locally grown flax.[26] At another early neolithic site called Mureybet, located on the west bank of the Upper

Euphrates in northern Syria, the earliest examples of 'lightly fired clay vessels' have been found. Radiocarbon tests have revealed that these vessels date to around 8000 BC.[27] At another site named Ganj Dara, near Kermanshah in Iranian Kurdistan, archaeologists have unearthed fired pottery and tiny clay figurines which date to the early eighth millennium BC, far in advance of the stone, wood, plaster and basketry work typical of this period.[28] Back at Abu Hureyra, where cereal cultivation first appeared in around 9500 BC, we find what is perhaps the earliest evidence for the use of cosmetics. A large cockleshell dating to the early neolithic period, c. 7000 BC, was found to contain traces of powdered malachite, a green natural substance known to have been used by women in predynastic Egypt as eye shadow.[29] Like many other materials found at early neolithic sites in northern Syria and eastern Anatolia, malachite is not native to the region, so its presence is positive evidence of trading with distant communities, even at this early stage in the development of mankind.

The list of 'firsts' for Kurdistan goes on and on. The widespread cultivation in the region of grapes inevitably led to the production, around 5400–5000 BC, at a site named Hajji Firuz Tepe in the Zagros mountains of Iranian Kurdistan, of the first alcoholic beverage. This came in the form of a wine similar to the retsina still popular in Turkey today.[30] More significantly, the earliest evidence of writing has come to light recently in the form of a series of pictogram carvings on flat, oval-shaped stones unearthed at Jerf el Ahmar on the Upper Euphrates of northern Syria. These markings consist of lines, arrows and animals and are believed to date back 10,000 years. Danielle Stordeur of the Institute of Oriental Prehistory near Nîmes in France believes they are an intermediary between palaeolithic cave art and more modern forms of writing.[31]

It has long been known that clay tokens, used for bartering and trading between different communities, were first developed in the foothills of Kurdistan during the eighth millennium BC.[32] These, of course, went on to become smaller and more complex, and by 3000 BC they had been replaced by sequences of markings inscribed on clay cases. Shortly afterwards, the first known examples of baked clay tablets bearing what are known today as ideograms began appearing on the plains of ancient Iraq.[33]

So many advances were made throughout Kurdistan, and most particularly in the region of the Upper Euphrates, between 9500 BC and 5000 BC that something rather unique must have been occurring across the region, long held to be the cradle of civilisation. No one has satisfactorily accounted for why exactly the neolithic revolution began where it did – a puzzle that prompted Mehrdad R. Izady, Professor of Near Eastern Studies at New York University, to comment in his essential work *The Kurds – A Concise Handbook*:

> The inhabitants of this land went through an unexplained stage of accelerated technological evolution, prompted by yet uncertain forces. They rather quickly pulled ahead of their surrounding communities, the majority of which were also among the most advanced technological societies in the world, to embark on the transformation from a low-density, hunter-gatherer economy to a high-density, food-producing economy.[34]

What does this mean – an 'accelerated technological evolution' by 'yet uncertain forces'? What kind of 'uncertain forces' was Izady alluding to here – changes in regional flora and fauna, brought on by

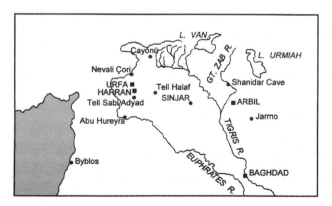

Map of the Near East showing the principal sites featured in this book.

post-Ice Age climate changes conducive to the gradual emergence of a cultural revolution, or the sudden appearance in the region of highly talented individuals who brought with them an entirely new way of life? In private conversations I have had with Mehrdad Izady in respect of the observations made in his book, he is happy to accept the latter solution as a very real possibility.[35]

THE FIRST STONE BEADS

Another important area of study which seems to demonstrate that the early neolithic peoples of the Upper Euphrates possessed an extraordinarily advanced level of technology is the discovery at various sites of extremely long beads made of hard stone substances such as agate, carnelian and quartz. These have been found at locations such as Abu Hureyra, which has yielded agate beads up to 5.5 centimetres in length,[36] and at Ashikli Höyük, near Aksaray in southern Turkey, where in 1989 a burgundy agate necklace consisting of 10 oval and butterfly wing-shaped beads, all between 2.5 and 5.5 centimetres in length, was uncovered during salvage operations by a team headed by archaeologist Ufuk Esin.[37] The most astonishing fact about these beads is that they all date to between 7500 and 7000 BC[38] and have been perforated longitudinally, even though agate is perhaps the hardest substance known to have been used in the lapidary trade of the Old World.

The level of technical sophistication necessary to drill holes less than 5 millimetres in diameter and up to 2.5 centimetres in depth at either end of a long, slim agate bead no more than 7 or 8 millimetres in thickness is almost beyond comprehension. To drill similar holes in agate today requires the use of a highly specialised diamond-tipped tungsten-carbide drill, and even this has to be constantly cooled by running water. At places such as Jarmo in Iraqi Kurdistan, c. 5500–4750 BC,[39] and various sites in the Indus Valley, c. 2600 BC,[40] specialist artisans were able to perforate hard stones, such as agate, carnelian and quartz (which are all seven on Mohs' scale of hardness), only by using a cylindrical drill-bit made of a type of stone that either equalled or was harder than the mineral being drilled.[41]

For this they would have had to use a wooden bow drill,[42] better known for its use as a means to make fire, and an equally inventive wooden vice clamp.[43] Sometimes tiny emery chips or quartz sand would have been introduced as an abrasive, while on other occasions the hardness of the stone drill-bit (particularly in the cities of the Indus Valley)[44] would have been sufficient to cut into the bead, provided that it was first heated up and running water was used as a coolant. As a point of interest, it was in around 600 BC that craftsmen at a site called Nagara, near Cambay (Khambhat) in western India, first developed the so-called double-diamond drill – in which two large uncut diamonds (each an almighty 10 on Mohs' scale) were inserted into the cutting edge of the drill tip – to perforate hard carnelian beads.[45] There is, however, no evidence that diamond-tipped drill-bits were ever used at prehistoric sites anywhere else in the Old World.[46]

That neolithic man was able to bore 2.5-centimetre perforations in hard stone such as agate is not in question. What is interesting is that the evidence of a lapidary industry at Jarmo in Iraqi Kurdistan and in the city-states of the Indus Valley civilisation in northern India and Pakistan strongly suggests that the innovative methods employed to drill long beads made of hard stone were developed *only* as a result of the gradual demand for more stylised items of jewellery, as well as an extremely long period of slowly evolving lapidary skills. At Jarmo it would appear that hard stone beads began appearing only after a period of 1250 years of producing literally thousands of beads in materials such as copper, bone, pottery, shell and soft stones,[47] while in the Indus Valley the ability to produce highly prized hard-stone beads started only after a period of perhaps 3000 years of bead manufacture.[48]

Since the occupational levels in which the remarkable beads of Abu Hureyra and Ashikli Höyük were found both date to between 7500 and 7000 BC, it hints at an extremely long period of perhaps thousands of years during which this particular trade evolved from making beads out of shells, clay, bone and soft stone to drilling long holes in some of the hardest substances ever used in jewellery manufacture. In eastern Anatolia, the main bead-producing centre during the early neolithic period was at Çayönü,[49] attesting to the high level of sophistication achieved by its specialist artisans even in the village's formative years.

Academics tell us that in around 8000 BC 'humans first began to change from a semi-nomadic life of hunting and gathering to a more settled lifestyle based on the rearing of animals and the harvesting of crops'.[50] If this is true, then it is difficult to imagine where exactly its earliest artisans gained their extraordinary lapidary skills, which must have involved mechanical devices, such as bow drills, wooden vices and specialist drill-bits, as well as a unique knowledge of jewellery manufacture. So unique, in fact, that this knowledge disappeared completely and did not reappear until the later stages of Jarmo's own bead-making history, some time in around 5500 BC.

Is it feasible that the lapidary skills found among the neolithic peoples of eastern Anatolia and northern Syria were inherited from highly evolved individuals who entered the region shortly after the end of the last Ice Age? Did these individuals bring with them a profound knowledge of jewellery production, including the means to bore holes in agate beads over five centimetres long?

RETURNING TO THE SOURCE

If I am correct in assuming that there really were as 'yet uncertain forces' behind the neolithic explosion that had begun on the Upper Euphrates in around 9500 BC, then could I find clearer links between what we knew of the Sphinx-building Elder culture and the earliest neolithic sites of the Near East? I pondered over this problem for some while and began examining the folklore and mythologies of the various tribal cultures that inhabit Kurdistan,

Mesopotamia and Iran today and still adhere to indigenous forms of religion based on an *ad hoc* mixture of Christianity, Islam, Judaism and Iranian Zoroastrianism.

Searching through the religious traditions of the Mandaeans, a neo-Babylonian tribal-based religion found mostly among the Marsh Arabs of southern Iraq and the isolated communities of western Iran, I discovered something of immense value to our debate. The Mandaeans believe that their distant ancestors came originally from a mythical location known as the Mountain of the Madai, which they locate to the north or north-east of the ancient city of Harran, modern Altinbasak, which lies just over the Syrian border in south-eastern Turkey on a tributary of the Euphrates, some 125 kilometres (78 miles) from Abu Hureyra.[51]

Confirmation that the Mandaeans originated in this region is easy. Their distinctive style of mud-plaster buildings has been compared by Mesopotamian scholars with those known to have been constructed by the Ubaid, an important culture that inhabited the Kurdish highlands between 4500 and 4000 BC[52] (see Chapter Seventeen). What seemed infinitely more interesting was the fact that the Mandaeans also claim that the Mountain of the Madai is not the *true* place of origin of their race. They say that their most distant ancestors came originally from *Egypt*.[53] One Mandaean manuscript even speaks of 'the interior of Haran [i.e. Harran] admitting them' on their arrival in this land, shortly after which they 'entered the mountain of the Madai, a place where they were free from domination of all races'.[54]

Admittedly, the Mandaeans associate their migration out of Egypt with the Exodus of the Jews, *c.* 1300 BC, but mythological time-frames suggested by their religious traditions cannot be taken literally. Like so many other races of the Middle East, the Mandaeans have attempted to equate their tribal ancestry with biblical history, and often this has produced a distorted hotchpotch of legends and folk-tales which are further confounded by the introduction here and there of Babylonian, classical and Persian mythology.

The Mandaeans' insistence that their most distant ancestors came to Kurdistan from Egypt does not seem to be pure fantasy, either, for certain words used in their vocabulary are clearly of Ancient Egyptian origin. They include Pthahil, or Pthah (the suffix *il* simply means 'god'), the name given to their demiurge, who gains his name from the Egyptian creator-god Ptah. Another is *ntr*, a word used to signify the root 'watch', which can be applied to 'watch-houses'[55] or 'watchers'.[56] In Egyptian, the word-root *ntr* or *netjer*, 'divinity' or 'divine', is a title applied to the Elder gods.

THE STAR-WORSHIPPERS

Sceptics might rightly suggest that any connection between the Egyptian and Mandaean languages almost certainly stems from contact between the two quite separate cultures during the Eighteenth Dynasty of Egyptian history, *c.* 1575–1308 BC. It was then that an alliance existed between the ruling Pharaoh and the king of the Mitanni, an Indo-European-speaking culture that occupied the region lying between the Upper Tigris and Upper Euphrates rivers of northern Syria and eastern Anatolia from around 1500 BC onwards for approximately 200 years. Their territories included the ancient metalworking and religious centre at Harran, which was also the home of the star-worshipping cult known as the Sabians. It was from these mysterious peoples that the Mandaeans claimed direct descent[57] – hence their alternative titles of Subba, Sabba or Sa'Ba, which are all thought to derive from the Egyptian word *sba*, meaning 'star'.[58]

Yet it is clear that the Mandaeans are wrong about their chosen affiliation with the peoples exiled from Egypt at the time of the Exodus of the Jews. Their blood brothers, the Sabians, would appear to have revered Egypt as their ancestral homeland as early as the first half of the second millennium BC, many hundreds of years before the birth of Moses.

During his extensive excavations in and around the Sphinx

enclosure during the 1930s, noted Egyptologist Selim Hassan came across various votive stelae with inscriptions which showed that during the occupation of Egypt by the Hyksos peoples, *c.* 1730–1575 BC, Semitic-speaking peoples from Harran, unquestionably star-worshipping Sabians (see below), established a township named after their home city, near Giza, and made special pilgrimages to the Great Sphinx.[59] More important, this devotion to the monuments of Giza does not seem to have been confined to the Hyksos period. The eleventh-century Arab historian Yakut-el-Hamawi recorded that in his own day the Sabians made pilgrimages to both the Great and Second Pyramids.[60] Following a discourse concerning the origin of the word 'Sabian' or 'Sabba', Hassan admitted that, in his opinion, 'the fact remains that they [the Sabians] fully recognized the Pyramids . . . as being monuments connected with the stellar cult, and revered them as places of pilgrimage'.[61]

The real question is whether or not the clear link between the star-worshipping inhabitants of Harran and the monuments of Giza goes back any further than the first half of the second millennium BC. Hassan suggested that the Sabians revered the Great Sphinx as a representation of their own hawk-headed god *harana* or *hol*, whom they equated with the Egyptian sun-god Re-harakhty,[62] while the pyramids were venerated because of their legendary associations with stellar-worship. This might well be so, but these pilgrimages to Giza from far-off Harran embody something far more symbolic than simply a respect for another culture's ancient monuments. Since the Mandaeans insist that their most distant ancestors travelled from Egypt to the Mountain of the Madai via Harran during some mythical age, it seems plausible to suggest that the Sabians saw Egypt, and Giza in particular, as their ancestral homeland.

The circumstantial evidence to suggest that Harranians saw their most distant ancestors as having come originally from Egypt is very strong indeed. It also makes some sense of the story told in the book of Genesis of how the prophet Abraham journeyed with his Semitic-speaking peoples from the city of Harran to Egypt,[63] an event that biblical scholars believe took place some time between 2000 and

1800 BC, around the time when the Hyksos first entered Egypt. In the age of Abraham, Harran was a cult centre for the worship of the Babylonian moon-god Sin, who was later equated with the Egyptian god Thoth.[64] This association with the moon was carried through to Graeco-Roman times, when the Hermetic teachings of Hermes Trismegistus, the Greek form of the moon-god Thoth, were promulgated by initiates who would descend on Harran from all over the ancient world to learn of its innermost mysteries.[65] They would come from such far-flung places as India, Persia, Mesopotamia and, most revealing of all, Heliopolis in Egypt.[66] It takes very little imagination to realise that its astronomer-priests must have had much in common with their Sabian counterparts!

Despite the long-held tradition that the celebrated city of Harran was one of the oldest religious centres anywhere in the ancient world, archaeological evidence to back up such bold claims is a little thin on the ground. Nothing has been discovered beneath its age-old streets to suggest that it dates to any earlier than 3000 BC, when the first Mesopotamian city-states were beginning to appear down on the fertile plains of ancient Iraq. To discover the greatest achievements of the very first neolithic communities of the Upper Euphrates, we will have to leave Harran and travel north just 93 kilometres (58 miles) to a neolithic site in the district of Hilvan, where in 1983 a German archaeologist chanced on a bizarre cult centre that may well contain the most important evidence yet for the presence in the Near East of Egypt's Elder gods.

CHAPTER SIXTEEN

GATEWAY TO EDEN

And the Lord God planted a garden eastward, in Eden; and there he put the man whom he had formed. And out of the ground made the Lord God to grow every tree that is pleasant to the sight, and good for food; the tree of life also in the midst of the garden, and the tree of knowledge of good and evil. And a river went out of Eden to water the garden; and from thence it was parted, and became four heads.[1]

This is how the Bible introduces the concept of Eden in the book of Genesis. Although most biblical scholars consider this place to have been purely mythical in origin, there is every reason to believe that in ancient times Eden was a geographical locality in its own right. In the book of Ezekiel Eden is mentioned alongside 'Haran [Harran] and Canneh' and 'Assur [Assyria] and Chilmad' as 'the traffickers of Sheba',[2] whom the author says dealt in riches such as spices, gold, precious stones and 'choice wares, in wrappings of blue and broidered work, and in chests of rich apparel, bound with cords and made of cedar'.[3]

Exactly where Eden was located can be determined from the fact that four individual rivers took their source from its central region and flowed out to four separate countries, delineated, very approximately, by the cardinal points. In much later times Eden's basic geography was expanded to place the 'garden' of Eden in the centre of a world watered by the four rivers of paradise, a concept also found among the rich mythology of Akkad, the Semitic-speaking kingdom that rose to prominence in northern Iraq during the second half of the third millennium BC.[4]

The first of these rivers is cited as the Perath (*Pirat* in Arabic and Turkish), known today as the Euphrates, which rises as a series of tributaries in the mountains west and north-west of Lake Van and flows out into Turkey before curving around to flow through northern Syria. It then enters Iraq and heads south-eastwards to finally empty into the Persian Gulf.

The second river cited is the Hiddekel, known since Greek times as the Tigris. This also emerges from a series of tributaries, these ones located south-west of Lake Van. They converge to form a fast-flowing river that snakes its way down through the foothills of the eastern Taurus mountains before entering the plains of northern Iraq. It then runs in a south-easterly direction, east of and roughly parallel to the Euphrates, until it too finally empties into the Persian Gulf – the land between them being known as the Fertile Crescent.

The third river is given as the Gihon, which has long been connected in Armenian tradition with the Arak, or Araxes (Arabic *Gaihun*).[5] This rises to the north-east of Lake Van and flows in an easterly direction, through the kingdom of Armenia, the ancient land of Cush,[6] into the Caspian Sea.

The fourth and final river, the Pishon, is more difficult to determine. Some scholars have seen fit to associate it with the Uizhun,[7] which rises south of Lake Urmiah in western Iran and, like the Arak, flows eastwards to empty into the Caspian Sea. It is equally likely, however, that the Pishon was the Greater Zab river, which rises south-east of Lake Van and becomes a mighty watercourse that flows through Iraqi Kurdistan before joining the Tigris close to the ancient Assyrian capital of Nineveh in northern Iraq. Indeed, so strongly did the local Nestorians, or Assyrian Church, believe that the Greater Zab was the River Pishon that, as late as the early twentieth century, its Patriarch would often sign off his official letters 'from my cell on the River of the Garden of Eden'![8]

It can thus be determined that each of the rivers of paradise flows out from one of the four quarters of Eden, with the central focus being the mighty Lake Van. This is a huge inland sea some 96 kilometres (60 miles) in length and around 56 kilometres (35 miles) wide, which is today situated on the borders between Turkish Kurdistan and the former Soviet Republic of Armenia. Confirmation that Lake Van was the central focus of the land of Eden comes from an Armenian legend, which asserts that its 'garden', where Adam and Eve were raised, is now at the bottom of its depths, where it has lain since it was submerged at the time of the Great Flood.[9]

The Akkadians and earlier Sumerians, who held together southern Iraq with a series of city-states during the third millennium BC, possessed their own rendition of the Eden story. In the mythologies of both cultures the paradisical realm, where gods, human beings and animals lived together in peace and harmony, was known as Dilmun. Here the water-god Enki, the great civiliser, was placed with his wife, an act that initiated 'a sinless age of complete happiness'. Dilmun was said to have been a pure, clean and 'bright' 'abode of the immortals' where death, disease and sorrow were unknown and mortals were given 'life like a god'.[10] This story seems to echo, and yet also contradict, the Genesis story of Adam and Eve in the Garden of Eden. Here, after being tempted by the serpent to eat of the fruit of the 'tree of the knowledge of good and evil', humanity's First Parents are expelled lest they also eat of the fruit of the 'tree of life' and 'live for ever', in other words become immortal like gods.[11]

Although scholars present sound evidence to demonstrate that Dilmun was the name given to the island of Bahrain in the Persian Gulf, there is also good reason to show that much earlier it was a geographical realm located in the mountains above what is today northern Iraq. For example, there is one reference to 'the mountain of Dilmun, the place where the sun rises'.[12] Since there is no 'mountain' in Bahrain, and in no way can this island be described as lying in the direction of the rising sun in respect to Iraq, it seems certain that there were two Dilmuns. Confirmation that the mythical location of this name was somewhere in the mountains of Kurdistan comes from the fact that the 'tabooed' Dilmun was referred to in ancient texts as the 'land of cedars'.[13] Noted Kurdish historian Mehrdad Izady has shown conclusively that the 'land of cedars', which was also seen as the abode of the gods, was placed by the ancient Akkadians and Sumerians among the mountains of the Upper Zagros, which stretched from the borders between Iraq and Iran to the very banks of Lake Van, and even further west into the eastern Taurus range.[14]

Mehrdad Izady has traced the origins of the mythical Dilmun, which has much in common with the biblical concept of Eden. His scholarly research associates the original Dilmun with a tribal region, located south-west of Lake Van in eastern Anatolia, known as Dilmân, or Daylamân, where the so-called Dimila, or Zâzâ, Kurds made their home.[15] Ancient Church records found at Arbil (ancient Arbela) in Iraqi Kurdistan cite this same geographical region as the land of Dilmân. They assert that *Beth Dailômâye*, the 'land of the Daylamites', was to be found 'north of Sanjâr', in other words among the foothills of the eastern Taurus range, between the Upper Euphrates and the tributaries of the Tigris.[16] Izady found confirmation of these assertions in 'The Zoroastrian holy book, *Bundahishn*, [which] places Dilmân . . . *at the headwaters of the Tigris* [author's italics]',[17] the very region in which the early neolithic peoples developed a high level of culture between 9500 and 5000 BC. It seemed no coincidence, then, that this same region was also synonymous with the biblical land of Eden.

THE ROAD TO EDEN

This, then, was the cradle of civilisation, the gateway to Eden, according to the most ancient traditions of the Hebrews, the Akkadians and the Sumerians, and it was through this very region

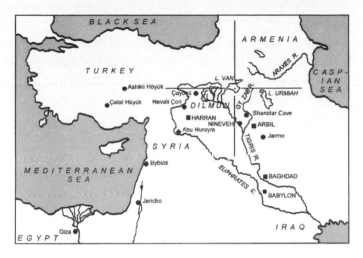

Map of the Near East showing the four rivers of paradise and the
four-fold division of the biblical land of Eden. The site of Dilmun, the
mythical domain of Mesopotamian tradition, is also marked.

that we would now have to travel on our journey to the district of
Hilvan in the province of Sanli Urfa. North-east of here the
snow-capped heights of the eastern Taurus mountains pierce the
sky and enter the realms of heaven, while towards the south-east is
the little-used road to Iraq. It was along this route that in April
1997 the Turks launched the latest of their so-called spring
offensives against soldiers of the Kurdish Workers' Party (PKK),
who inhabit strongholds deep within Iraqi Kurdistan. Over 50,000
troops, 250 tanks, massive air support and a battery of heavy
artillery were dispatched into Iraq to track down just 4000
freedom fighters.[18]

Our destination is the edge of the modern Ataturk reservoir, west
of the town of Hilvan, created as recently as 1992, when the waters
of the Upper Euphrates were dammed to create hydroelectric power
for Turkey. Many such dams have been built at various places along
both the Euphrates and the Tigris, and every one has succeeded in
flooding important archaeological sites which are now lost for ever.
The greatest loss by far is Nevali Çori (pronounced *chor-ree*), a site of
immense archaeological significance dating back to the stage of

235

human development known as pre-pottery neolithic B (PPNB), which in eastern Anatolia took place roughly between 8800 BC and 7600 BC.[19]

THE MONOLITH

I first came across Nevali Çori by chance during the autumn of 1996 when I received an informative letter from a correspondent named Mark Burkinshaw. Attached to it were various photocopies, one showing an enormous sculptured monolith standing in the middle of a sunken temple, with walls composed of packed dry stone interspersed by a series of upright pillars.[20] I thought at first that I was looking at one of the carved standing stones at Tiahuanaco in Bolivia (see below). To me everything about the picture said South America. It was not until I looked more closely at the accompanying text that I realised I was looking at a site in eastern Anatolia.

Not only were the sides of the great monolith seen in the picture precisely rectangular, but the whole thing appeared to be set into a perfectly smooth floor, which I later found was composed of a lime-based mortar known as 'terrazzo', something quite unique to neolithic sites in this region. Strangest of all were the extraordinary carvings on the two-metre-high erect pillar, which had quite obviously lost its uppermost section. In low relief on its two longest faces were extended arms, bent upwards so that they formed a horizontal V-shape. These terminated on the front, narrow face of the monolith in stylised hands, each with five fingers of equal length – a peculiar sight that gave the immediate impression of flippers, like those of a sea mammal such as a seal, a whale or a dolphin. Above the 'hands' were two long rectangular strips that ran from beyond the visible break at the top of the stone to about half-way down its length, giving the impression of extremely long hair hanging over the shoulders of a human form that had lost its head.

Most important of all was the age of this extraordinary mono-lithic temple. The accompanying text, taken from the book *Anatolia: Cauldron of Cultures*, published by Time-Life in 1995, spoke of Nevali Çori as a 'time-machine' over 10,000 years old! If this were correct, then it had been constructed in around 8000 BC, 5000 years before the emergence of civilisation in ancient Mesopotamia. Could this be true – a culture on the Upper Euphrates of eastern Anatolia, the unquestionable cradle of civilisation, sophisticated enough to produce carved stone pillars so beautiful that they were more in keeping with the megalithic art of Malta or Western Europe, executed many thousands of years later?

To say that the picture of Nevali Çori's cult building fascinated me is an understatement. I could not stop staring at this compelling image which so perfectly captured the strange ambience of the location. In my opinion, there was a level of sophistication here comparable with the monuments left behind by Egypt's Elder culture. As I was quickly to discover, even greater surprises awaited me at Nevali Çori.

HAUPTMANN'S DISCOVERY

The settlement itself was first identified during a systematic survey of occupational mounds in the Kantara valley by archaeologist Hans Georg Gebel in 1980.[21] At the time he was working on excavations at another site some nine kilometres (five and a half miles) away, so was able to do little more than report the existence of a previously unknown occupational terrace approximately ninety by forty metres in size, some three kilometres (two miles) from the southern bank of the Euphrates and east of the village of Kantara Çayi (37° 35′ N, 38° 39′ E). Three years later, in 1983, Harald Hauptmann of the University of Heidelberg began the first of several seasons of excavation at Nevali Çori, which takes its name from the surrounding terrace. He returned in 1985 and again during various subsequent seasons. He was last at Nevali Çori in 1991, when the recent completion of the Ataturk dam turned the excavations into a salvage operation to preserve whatever he could from the site. Shortly afterwards, the rising waters of the Euphrates lapped at the edge of the occupational terrace, and very quickly Nevali Çori was tens of metres beneath the Ataturk reservoir. Mercifully, the aforementioned monolith was taken down and transferred to nearby Urfa museum, where it has now been re-erected and placed on display.

What is abundantly clear from Hauptmann's excavations at Nevali Çori is that from the very earliest occupation of the site which began, according to carbon-14 dating, in around 8400 BC,[22] who-ever settled here already understood the basic principles of agricul-ture. Cereals were cultivated and animals domesticated at the very earliest stages of its development. From then on the site was occupied at various times right down to the middle of the sixth millennium BC. Yet despite this extremely long occupation, it is Nevali Çori's earliest phases, during the pre-pottery neolithic period, that are of special interest to the archaeological world.[23]

Why exactly Nevali Çori was built where it was is unclear today. There were obviously agricultural considerations involved in the decision, although it is clear that this was no simple farming community. Of the 22 dwellings uncovered, only one appears to have been used for domestic accommodation.[24] Many of the site's rectangular-shaped, grid-planned buildings were used for storage purposes alone. One seems to have acted as a workshop for the making of flint implements, while others bore evidence of cultic use in the form of buried skulls[25] (see Chapter Seventeen).

Nevali Çori's primary function would appear to have been as a religious centre, focused around a rectangular stone structure which Hauptmann named the 'cult building'. All that remained of its earliest building phase was a piece of wall just four metres long. However, several superb sculptures from this period of occupation were preserved by the inhabitants and later incorporated into the subsequent buildings constructed on the same site.[26] The next cult house, known as Building II, was built some time around 8100 BC, with its rear end partially set into the rock-face, giving the whole thing a cave-like feel.[27] Inside an earthen bank, four walls were constructed of dry stone which rose to a height of 2.8 metres and were as much as half a metre thick.[28]

Hauptmann noted that the walls of Building II had originally been covered with a limestone mortar, and here and there traces remained of a grey-white plaster that bore evidence of black and red paint, showing that the walls had once been decorated with murals, presumably of a religious or symbolic nature.[29]

TEMPLES AND BIRDS

As already noted, Nevali Çori's cult building possessed a hard terrazzo floor, which must have given it the appearance of a building thousands of years ahead of its time. Into the walls themselves were positioned 13 upright stone pillars located at regular intervals. Each one was originally capped with a T-shaped capital, a fact that led Hauptmann to conclude that they had acted purely as supports for a roof.[30] Flanking the steps that formed the entrance down into the south-western quarter of the building were two huge standing stones, while in the wall on the opposite side Hauptmann found a niche for a cult statue. Most important were the various stone statues found at this level. One was a broken limestone sculpture of a bird found 'walled up' in Building II, implying that it was in secondary use and had almost certainly come from an earlier phase of construction, plausibly that of Building I. In my opinion, it has a clear snake-like head that resembles the stylised features of the Aztec god Quetzalcoatl, the feathered serpent. Its beak is broken, but despite this its large eyes, rounded breast and stylised wings are so beautifully executed that this statue would not look out of place in a modern art gallery.[31]

The third and final phase of Nevali Çori's cult house, Building III, seems to have been constructed in around 8000 BC. A bench-like platform, topped with enormous stone slabs, was added to three out of four of the interior walls (the exception being the south-western section within which the stepped entrance was located), considerably reducing the size of the terrazzo floor.[32] Twelve slim pillars – carved on their widest faces with arms, bent and hunched at the elbows, that ended on their front narrow face with five-fingered hands – replaced the thirteen standing stones of the second phase.[33] Matching these 'support' pillars, as Hauptmann refers to them, were two (not one, as I had first presumed) three-metre-tall rectilinear monoliths on which were also carved anthropomorphic forms in low relief.[34] These formed an enormous gateway and stood one each side of the centre of the building, their front narrow faces directed towards the south-west.

It was the remaining portion of one of these two monoliths that had so fascinated me in the picture included in the Time-Life

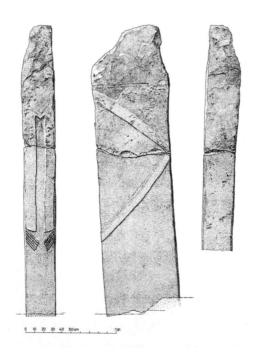

Side-plan of the remaining monolith at Nevali Çori, eastern Turkey, courtesy of Harald Hauptmann.

publication *Anatolia: Cauldron of Cultures.* The weathered apex of this particular stone was found by Hauptmann lying face down at a higher level, indicating that, unlike its lower section, it had been exposed to the elements for some considerable time, perhaps even thousands of years. Curiously, the remaining monolith had been inserted just five centimetres into the terrazzo floor, which makes very little sense whatsoever. If we recall that this slim carved pillar was originally three metres in height, then it does not take a genius to work out that a depth of just five centimetres would have made it so unstable that someone merely leaning on it would have pushed it over. Hauptmann believes the monoliths were capped with lintel stones and were simply decorative roof supports without any obvious mystical significance. As we shall see in Chapters Eighteen and Nineteen, it seems more likely that, in the minds of the priesthood at Nevali Çori, they served a very important religious function.

Also found in Building III was a carved clean-shaven head, 37 centimetres in height and shaped like an egg! Although the face is missing, it still bears carefully executed ears and, most extraordinary of all, a long single 'plait' or pony-tail that flows down from the crown to the neck and must also represent a curling snake. This astonishing piece of sculpture is unlike anything else that has been found at any other neolithic site in the Old World. It was positioned in the north-east wall, facing south-west, and appears to have been taken from a full-sized statue belonging either to Building I or Building II.[35] Hauptmann believes that this skull-like form represents a 'heavenly celestial being',[36] although in my opinion it represents either an ancestor spirit or a member of a priestly caste. If this is correct, then it might well imply that members of the community sported bald heads with pony-tails. Its distinctive egg shape and curling snake device also appear significant, since both the egg and the serpent were universal symbols of fertility, wisdom and first creation.

In addition to the shaven head, Building III also produced a 23-centimetre-high limestone statuette of a bird-man with an extremely elongated head, almost the shape of a hammer. On its back were large closed wings and the stumps of arms, confirming that it is a human dressed as a bird.[37] It was found face down in a recess within the wall, and once again it seems to have been preserved from an earlier building phase.

The subsequent levels of occupation are not so interesting to our debate. They have, however, produced various curious statues that could conceivably have been purloined from the first three levels, *c.* 8400–7600 BC. These include a composite figure that shows 'two female figures crouching back to back surmounted by a bird',[38] as well as a mysterious female head marked with hatching to represent feathers.[39] This seems to have once formed part of a kind of totem pole composed of different carved forms, more in keeping with North America than eastern Anatolia.

HUMAN SACRIFICE

Something a little more disturbing found to be present at Nevali Çori is the clear evidence of human sacrifice. In one of the buildings, designated House 21, Hauptmann found a female burial with flint tips still embedded in the skeleton's neck and upper jaws, as if the woman had been repeatedly struck with stone projectiles. Hauptmann admitted that the evidence pointed towards the deliberate killing of the individual; moreover, that the house in question could well have been a 'sacrificial building' used specifically for this purpose.[40] This is obviously a chilling prospect, especially as we have accredited the incoming wisdom-bringers of the early neolithic peoples with a high level of sophistication and technological know-how.

It would be easy to dismiss the discovery of a sacrificial victim at Nevali Çori as an isolated incident. Unfortunately, however, there is firm evidence of an even more vicious sacrificial cult at Çayönü, just 100 kilometres (60 miles) away to the north-east. Here we find a large number of rectangular stone buildings with grid-plan foundations, like those found at Nevali Çori, as well as other buildings with special functions. One, for instance, has a terrazzo floor, while another – the so-called Flagstone Building – has a floor made entirely from large polished flagstones into which were set megalithic stones (further standing stones were set up in rows nearby),[41] giving it an appearance not unlike the interior design of Giza's Valley Temple.

It is, however, Çayönü's so-called Skull Building that is of the greatest interest. This stone structure – which is 7.9 by 7 metres in size and has a round apse at one end that gives it the uncanny appearance of a ruined eleventh-century Norman church – possesses very dark secrets indeed. Here, in two small antechambers, archaeologists unearthed some 70 skulls, all of which had been slightly charred,[42] while overall excavations in the Skull Building revealed the bones of no fewer than 295 individuals.[43] In all likelihood they featured in some kind of localised ancestor worship, although no one can be certain.

More difficult to explain was the unexpected discovery at Çayönü of a large chamber that was found to contain an enormous one-tonne cut and polished stone block, which almost certainly acted as an offering table. Nearby, excavators found a large flint knife, which would eventually lead them to a macabre realisation. Microscopic analysis of the altar stone's smooth surface revealed a high residue of blood that was found to come from aurochs, sheep and *human beings*.[44] There can be little doubt what this implies. The Skull Building was not only used for strange ancestral rites but also human sacrifice,[45] an element of their society never dwelled on by the archaeological world. It would seem that although the neolithic peoples of Nevali Çori and Çayönü lived extraordinarily advanced lifestyles, comparable with a world that existed on the plains of Mesopotamia thousands of years later, the ruling priesthood led a somewhat amoral lifestyle more in keeping with the civilisations of Meso-America, *c.* AD 1000, than with the earliest communities of eastern Anatolia, *c.* 8000 BC.

I can recall when I first set eyes on the picture of the towering monolith in the centre of the cult building at Nevali Çori. Despite its stark simplicity, the structure exuded a feeling of absolute dread. There seemed to be some kind of subtle relationship between this monument and the compelling art of South America, in particular that of the Chavin culture of Peru and the Tiahuanacan culture of the Bolivian Altiplano. Here, in Tiahuanaco, thought to have been built somewhere between 15,000 and 10,000 BC,[46] we find mega-lithic temples closely resembling the one at Nevali Çori. As at Çayönü, these were accompanied by rows of standing stones, as well as carved stone pillars of unusual quality and design.

One carved monolith, known locally as *El Fraile* (the Friar), stood in the south-west corner of the Temple of the Sun in a section of the ruins known as the Kalasasaya,[47] the enclosure walls of which *greatly* resemble those of Nevali Çori. Chiselled from a solid block of red sandstone, this two-metre-tall figure has an anthropomorphic head and low-relief arms that hug its sides and end on the front face of the pillar in hands that clutch strange objects. In the right hand is what appears to be a wavy-line blade, like an Indonesian *kris*, while in its left hand is something akin to a vase (perhaps a locally made *keru*).[48] More peculiarly, from the waist downwards *El Fraile* sports a garment meant to represent fish scales, each one individually carved into a tiny fish head.[49] Adding to the effect is a waistband decorated 'with stilized crustaceans', identified as a type of crab known as *hyalela*, found in nearby Lake Titicaca.[50] There seems little question that this monument represents some kind of fish-man, a connection made all the more poignant by the existence of archaic local folk-tales recorded by archaeologist Arthur Posnansky which spoke of 'gods of the lake with fish tails, called "Chullua" and "Umantua" '.[51]

Somehow there appeared to be some kind of subtle relation-ship between South America's carved statues, such as Tiahuanaco's *El Fraile*, and the remaining monolith at Nevali Çori. What's more, the link seemed both cultural and aquatic in nature. Other examples of sculpted art from Nevali Çori also seem to possess pre-Columbian influences. But how could this be so? Nevali Çori lay on a completely different continent, many thousands of miles away from the Americas.

It was a problem without any obvious answers. For the moment it seemed more important to establish who exactly the prime movers were at sites such as Nevali Çori and Çayönü. I needed to know who built Nevali Çori's cult temple, with its finely carved monoliths. Who officiated at its ceremonies and rites, which would seem to have included human sacrifice? Who was behind the sudden emergence of the extraordinary technology found in association with the earliest neolithic sites of eastern Anatolia, and how might any of this link back to the Egyptian Elder culture?

CHAPTER SEVENTEEN

FEATHERED SERPENTS

The remarkable cult buildings and carved monuments of the earliest neolithic sites of eastern Anatolia appear to resonate the same strange ambience as the stone structures of Egypt now accredited to the Elder gods. This much seems clear. Yet if we now turn our attentions to Nevali Çori's enigmatic carved statues and compare them with the image conveyed of the divine inhabitants of Wetjeset-Neter in the Edfu Building Texts, then an even greater picture emerges. The Edfu account speaks repeatedly of falcons, or Sages, adorned with the wings and feathers of this bird of prey, suggesting perhaps that these individuals were men dressed as birds, or bird shamans. At Nevali Çori this is evidenced in the mysterious statues of birds and bird-men unearthed by Hauptmann and belonging to all three building phases of the cult house, from 8400 through to around 7600 BC.

According to Harald Hauptmann, the beautifully carved statue of a bird with enormous eyes and the head of a serpent, which he found 'walled up' in a section of Building II, can be identified with the vulture.[1] He was unwilling to place the same interpretation on any more of the bird carvings,[2] although in my opinion the 23-centimetre-high standing figure of a bird-man, with large closed wings and stumps for arms, found face down within a walled recess in Building III, shows every sign of being a vulture. Its bizarre elongated head seems highly reminiscent of the long-necked vulture, and if this is indeed the case, then it seems likely that some, if not all, of the other bird-linked sculptures also depict men and women either dressed as vultures or wearing head-dresses made of vulture feathers.

If so, then what was so special about the vulture?

Vultures are creatures much reviled by the modern world. These enormous birds, many species with wingspans greater than 3.5 metres across, are carrion-eaters, in that they feast on the flesh of the dead. They will gorge on the carcasses of animals, birds or human beings, very often climbing inside the ribcage to tear out internal organs. Despite this highly repulsive activity, they are actually very clean birds and were greatly revered in ancient times as symbols not only of mortality but also of death-trances and mental transformation induced by psychotropic drugs, sensory deprivation and near-death experiences (NDEs). By taking on the guise of the vulture, shamans and initiates were thought to be able to attain astral flight, enter otherworldly realms, communicate with ancestor spirits and bring back universal knowledge and wisdom.

The mighty vulture, once the primary symbol of death, transformation and rebirth throughout the neolithic world.

PICKING THE DEAD CLEAN

Of equal importance in the cult of the vulture was the bird's role in the funerary practice known as excarnation, also called 'sky burials', where dead bodies would be exposed on high wooden platforms in charnel areas located well away from settlements. Carrion birds such as the vulture and the crow would then be allowed to feast on the human carcass until all that remained was a denuded skeleton – a process that would have taken as little as 30 minutes. The remaining bones would then be left to dry before being collected up and buried either in stone chambers or beneath the ground, often in the floor of the deceased's relatives' own home!

Very often excarnation would have involved what is known as fractional or secondary burial, whereby the bones would be separated out and concealed at more than one location. For instance, at many sites in the Near East, skulls would be removed from the skeleton and placed beneath the floors of buildings usually with some kind of cultic significance. Other skulls would be preserved, either by the deceased's relatives or by shamanic priests, and used for oracular purposes, in other words communicating with the spirit of its former owner, which was believed to inhabit the skull, even in death.

Many skulls used for such purposes were first covered with mortar and given decorative eyes made from cowrie shells or shell fragments, as if to emphasise the embodied power and presence of their earthly owners. This form of ancestor worship was common throughout the neolithic period in many parts of the Near East.[3] At Nevali Çori skulls were buried in pairs along with so-called long bones (human femurs), and many of these were positioned so that they faced each other.[4] Evidence here of secondary burial also implies that excarnation took place; however, the skulls Hauptmann and his team unearthed do, in fact, date to a slightly later period than the cult building.[5]

BIRDS TO MEN

A more spiritual dimension to the cult of the vulture was the belief that after death the bird would accompany the deceased into the next world as its guide, or *psychopomp*. This heavenly location was generally considered to be in the direction of the pole star, i.e. to the north, and once here the discarnate soul would be judged by the gods, following which it would either achieve immortality or wait in a limbo state for reincarnation.

Our knowledge of the significance of excarnation in ancient times derives mainly from the funerary rites and beliefs of Zoroastrianism, the religion of Iran, which continued to practise sky burials through to the twentieth century. One branch of the Zoroastrians, the Parsees of India, may well still practise excarnation today, and it is from these people that we have learned much about the very ancient rituals and customs surrounding this archaic tradition, which almost certainly originated among the neolithic peoples who inhabited the mountains of Kurdistan. This rugged, mountainous region once formed part of the ancient kingdom of Media, and it was here that, in the fifth century BC, the Greek historian Herodotus witnessed members of the priestly caste known as the Magi (from which we derive words such as 'magic' and 'magician') officiating at rites of excarnation.[6]

The Mandaeans, who following their arrival from Egypt are supposed to have settled in the area of Harran, also record that their most distant ancestors practised sky burials.[7]

Excarnation was widespread throughout Eurasia during neolithic times. Wherever evidence of its existence has been found, the cult of the vulture is also generally present. The obscure origins of these religious practices are, however, particularly relevant to this debate. Aside from the evidence we now have for the existence of the death cult of the vulture at Nevali Çori during the late ninth millennium BC, other evidence for its presence in the region during this same early period has come from an important discovery made at the

Shanidar cave in Iraqi Kurdistan. This enigmatic location overlooks the Greater Zab river, which was seen as one of the four rivers of paradise. As mentioned earlier, it was here that during the 1950s the earliest known evidence for the use of hammered copper came to light in the form of an oval-shaped pendant dating to 9500 BC.

During these same excavations, palaeontologists Ralph and Rose Solecki uncovered, alongside a number of goats' skulls, a large quantity of bird remains, consisting mostly of entire wings of large predatory birds covered in patches of red ochre, which was sprinkled over burials in neolithic times.[8] Carbon-14 dating of organic deposits associated with the bones produced a date of 8870 BC (+/–300 years),[9] 400 years prior to the accepted foundation date for Nevali Çori.

The bird wings were shipped off to the United States, where they were examined by Dr Alexander Wetmore of the Smithsonian Institution and Thomas H. McGovern, a graduate student in the Department of Anthropology at Columbia University. They identified four separate species present and as many as seventeen individual birds: four *Gyptaeus barbatus* (the bearded vulture), one *Gyps fulvus* (the griffon vulture), seven *Haliaetus albicilla* (the white-tailed sea eagle) and one *Otis tarda* (the great bustard) – the last being the only species still indigenous to the region. There were also the bones of four small eagles of indeterminable species.[10] All except for the great bustard were raptorial birds, while the vultures were quite obviously carrion-eaters, and, as Rose Solecki was later to comment, were 'thus placed in a special relationship with dead creatures and death'.[11]

Of the 107 avian bones identified, 96 (i.e. 90 per cent) were from wings, some of which had still been in articulation when buried. Slice marks on the bone ends also indicated that the wings had been deliberately hacked away from the birds by a sharp instrument, and that an attempt had been made to remove the skin and feathers covering at least some of the bones.[12]

Rose Solecki believed that the bird wings had almost certainly formed part of some kind of ritualistic costume, worn either for personal decoration or on ceremonial occasions.[13] She also realised that they constituted firm evidence for the presence of an important religious cult at the nearby neolithic village of Zawi Chemi, for as she was to conclude in an important article written on the subject:

> The Zawi Chemi people must have endowed these great raptorial birds with special powers, and the faunal remains we have described for the site must represent special ritual paraphernalia. Certainly, the remains represent a concerted effort by a goodly number of people just to hunt down and capture such a large number of birds and goats.[14] . . . [Furthermore, that] either the wings were saved to pluck out the feathers, or that wing fans were made, or that they were used as part of a costume for a ritual. One of the murals from a Çatal Hüyük shrine . . . depicts just such a ritual scene; i.e., a human figure dressed in a vulture skin . . .[15]

Çatal Hüyük is the name of what is plausibly the most important neolithic site in the whole of Anatolia. First identified in 1958 by a British archaeological team headed by prehistorian James Mellaart, this double occupational mound near Konya in central Anatolia revealed a vast sub-surface metropolis which Mellaart began excavating in 1961. It was found to consist of a whole network of interconnecting dwellings and cult shrines belonging to an extraordinarily advanced community that thrived between 8500 and 7700 years ago.[16] Nothing like this had ever been anticipated, let alone found, before in the Near East. The magnificence of its art, tools, weapons and skilfully fashioned jewellery showed a level of technology and sophistication which has forced archaeologists to review completely their understanding of the development of civilisation.

Following four seasons of excavations at Çatal Hüyük, Mellaart had managed to uncover and restore a series of extraordinary shrines that formed an integral part of the city complex and could be accessed only from adjoining rooms. They revealed all kinds of strange reliefs and murals that included life-size bulls' heads (or *bucrania*) with horns emerging from plaster-covered walls; leopards in high relief, either stamped with trefoil designs or spread-eagled in the birth position; and human breasts moulded from plaster – in the walls behind which archaeologists found actual griffon vulture skulls, their bills protruding to form nipples.

Most important of all was that in many of the shrines the walls were adorned with enormous skeletal-like representations of vultures. Some were shown alighting on wooden-framed excarnation towers, in the process either of devouring the flesh of the dead or taking into their care the head of the deceased, which was looked on as the seat of the soul.[17] The birds' characteristic bald heads, short legs and visible crests easily identified them as griffon vultures.[18] Other wall-scenes showed not vultures themselves but men or women adorned in the paraphernalia of the vulture. These could easily be identified as shamans, and not birds, by virtue of the fact that they had articulated legs – a conclusion openly drawn by those who have made careful studies of these extraordinary murals.[19]

Alan Sorrell's evocative image of vulture shamans performing magical rites in one of the underground shrines at Çatal Hüyük, *c.* 6500 BC.

The cult of the vulture thrived at Çatal Hüyük, while further evidence of excarnation has come from the discovery of secondary burials.[20] As at Nevali Çori and several other neolithic sites in the Near East, the presence of decorated skulls found inside the shrines shows that ancestor worship and oracular communication were also practised here.[21]

Harald Hauptmann does not accept that there is any link between the vulture shamanism of Çatal Hüyük and the clear vulture and bird-men imagery that predominates the art of Nevali Çori.[22] This is despite the fact that he admits openly that there is a clear connection between birds and human beings intended by the sculptures and statues, and that birds and mixed beings 'appear to have taken a special meaning in cult events' within the community.[23]

We know from the evidence of bird wings found in the Shanidar cave that a highly developed form of vulture shamanism was present among early neolithic villages during the ninth millennium BC. Furthermore, the high culture present at Kurdish sites such as Nevali Çori and Çayönü during this period was also present in central Anatolia, as the agate bead necklace from Ashikli Höyük clearly demonstrates. This item, and others like it, was almost certainly manufactured by the skilled bead-making artisans of Çayönü. It suggests that the cult of the vulture developed in the fertile valleys and foothills of Kurdistan before being carried into other regions, including central Anatolia, where it was inherited by much later communities such as the one at Çatal Hüyük, c. 6500 BC.

With this knowledge, I feel it unreasonable to suggest that the cult of the vulture was not present at Nevali Çori during the ninth millennium BC, especially as the Shanidar cave is only 465 kilometres (290 miles) away. Indeed, it is highly likely that it was present among many more of the neolithic communities of Turkish and Iraqi Kurdistan.

If this is so, then I find it beyond coincidence that in the Edfu Building Texts the ancestral gods, or divine Sages, are referred to specifically as birds, with titles such as the Falcon and the Winged One. Were the Elder gods not falcons at all, but vulture shamans?

Could it be possible that the death cult of the vulture originated among the Sphinx-building culture of palaeolithic Egypt before being carried into the Near East by its descendants?

Should this be so, then we must explain the specific references, not to vultures but to falcons, in the Egyptian texts. In my opinion, the transition from carrion-eater to bird of prey may well have occurred long after the age of the Elder gods, perhaps as late as predynastic times, when the falcon, or hawk, became an important totem in the wars between the Horus-kings of Heliopolis and the Set tribes of southern Egypt. Perhaps it became more appropriate to see the ancestral gods not as reviled vultures but as fighting falcons. It is certainly known that the Hebrews deliberately edited out the vulture from early stories and replaced it with the more acceptable image of the eagle,[24] so perhaps the same thing happened in Egypt as well. The vulture was in fact an important bird in Ancient Egyptian myth and ritual, where it became the symbol of Mut, the wife of Amun, Meretseger, goddess of the Theban necropolis, and Nekheb, the principal goddess of Upper Egypt. Unfortunately, their respective cults, all centred in the south of the country, appear to have been latecomers to the Egyptian scene, and probably originated with foreign invaders who entered the Nile valley from the east during predynastic times.

The evidence emerging from Nevali Çori hints strongly at the fact that its sculpted statues and carvings depict shamanic individuals adorned in coats and head-dresses of vultures' feathers. They, it seems, were the community's prime movers during the early neolithic period, c. 8400–7600 BC. Yet despite the firm presence of vulture imagery in the cult building throughout its three different phases of construction, many of the anthropoid bird statues seem almost naive, crude even, when placed alongside the aforementioned serpent-headed vulture statue, or compared with the minimalistic art of the great monolith.

It would appear that, living alongside the highly skilled artisans who designed and created the earliest sculptures and carvings at Nevali Çori, there existed another class of individual responsible for the somewhat cruder art, which included many of the later human bird statues. By representing them in artistic form, it seems almost as if they were attempting to please the elders, priests or rulers of the community. It points clearly towards the conclusion that there were two distinct groups of people present at Nevali Çori, and presumably at other early neolithic sites as well. One was a ruling body, who seem to have been synonymous with the human bird, or vulture shamans, depicted in art form, while the other was made up of the remainder of the community, which probably consisted of an assortment of builders, labourers, farmers and shepherds, as well as more specialised artisans and craftsmen.

THE SERPENT-HEADED ONES

A more detailed profile of the neolithic ruling elite, who are likely to have been behind many of the innovations and technological achievements at sites such as Nevali Çori and Çayönü, has proved difficult. To learn more we must bring the clock forward another 2000 years.

The pre-pottery phase of the neolithic era was followed by the gradual emergence all over the Near East of fired and painted pottery. The date of its first appearance varies from area to area, although in eastern Anatolia it was introduced some time between 7600 and 5750 BC. The latter date marks the entrance-point of an entirely new culture known as the Halaf, after Tell Halaf, an occupational mound situated above the Khabur river near the village of Ras al-'Ain on the Syrian–Turkish frontier. It was here just before the First World War that a German archaeologist named Max Freiherr von Oppenheim first identified the presence of their distinctive glazed pottery and gave them this title.[25] The Halaf culture thrived all over Kurdistan between 5750 and 4500 BC, and they are thought by archaeologists to have been the prime movers behind the much-prized trade in the black volcanic glass known as obsidian. This was obtained in a raw state from an extinct volcano known as Nemrut Dağ situated on the south-western shores of Lake Van.[26]

In around 4500 BC a new culture entered the Near Eastern arena. Known as the Ubaid, they began to occupy many of the sites previously held by their predecessors, the Halaf. From here the Ubaid spread gradually southwards to form new communities, including one at Tell al-'Ubaid, near the city of Ur in southern Iraq, from which their name derives. Their lengthy presence in the Fertile Crescent almost certainly influenced the spread of Mesopotamian civilisation between 4500 and 4000 BC.

The Ubaid are perhaps most remembered for the strange anthropomorphic figurines, several centimetres in height, which they placed in the graves of their dead. These were either male or female (although predominantly female), with slim, well-proportioned naked bodies, broad shoulders, as well as strange, elongated heads and protruding snouts, which scholars generally describe as 'lizard-like' in appearance.[27] Each has slit eyes, made of elliptical pellets of clay pinched together to form what are known as 'coffee-bean' eyes. On top of the head, many examples originally bore a thick, dark plume of bitumen, thought to represent a coil of erect hair. Each one also displays either female pubic hair or male genitalia.

Every figurine is unique. Some of the female examples stand erect with their feet together and their hands on their hips. At least one male statue holds what appears to be a sceptre of office, plausibly a symbol of divinity or kingship. Oval-shaped pellets of clay that cover the upper chest, shoulders and back of some of the statues are almost certainly representations of beaded necklaces, which may act as symbols of authority.

The most compelling of all the Ubaid figurines are the ones that show a naked woman cradling a baby to her left breast. The infant's left hand clings on to the breast, and it seems to be suckling milk. More curious is the fact that the children also have reptilian heads, implying that, for some strange reason, the Ubaid would appear to have been making representations of individuals whom they believed

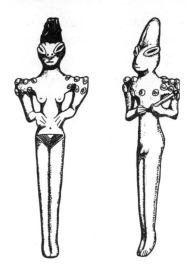

Two examples of Ubaid figurines – one male and the other female –
c. 4500–4000 BC.

actually possessed these distinctive features.

The Ubaid figures have often been identified by scholars as representations of the Mother Goddess[28] – a totally erroneous assumption since some examples are clearly male. Sir Leonard Woolley, the British archaeologist who first identified the Ubaid's existence in Mesopotamia following his excavations at Tell al-'Ubaid during the 1930s, concluded that they represented 'chthonic deities' – i.e. underworld denizens associated with rites of the dead.[29] Furthermore, it seems infinitely more likely that they do not represent lizards, as has always been thought, but serpents. Lizards play no role whatsoever in Mesopotamian mythology, which was undoubtedly influenced by the much earlier beliefs of the Ubaid.

Although these distinctive serpentine figurines were unique to the Ubaid, less abstract representations of snake-faced individuals with huge almond-shaped eyes have been found at the neolithic village of Jarmo in Iraqi Kurdistan.[30] If you recall, it was during excavations here in the 1950s that the earliest known evidence of lead smelting was unearthed by Robert Braidwood and his team.

These lightly baked heads date to as early as 6750 BC, and so suggest that this distinctive form of serpentine art developed first in the highlands and foothills of Kurdistan before gradually being transferred down on to the Iraqi plains some time around 4500 BC.

Much can be said about the snake in Mesopotamian mythology. It is known to have been associated with divine wisdom, sexual energy and guardianship over otherworldly domains. The Ubaid's belief in serpent-headed individuals implied either that they felt there existed individuals who bore physical features that could be construed as serpentine in nature, or that they represented shamans whose practices focused on the cult of the snake, something I have shown elsewhere to be integrally linked with the culture and customs of the Kurdish tribal religions over the past several thousand years.[31]

To compare a person's face with that of a snake, whether it be in an abstract or direct manner, seems a rather peculiar thing to do, unless, of course, there is good reason to do so. Among the American jazz-clubs of the 1930s, the term 'viper' was used to describe musicians who played for long hours, sustaining their creativity by consuming vast amounts of marijuana. Amid the smoky haze, their long, gaunt expressions and puffed-up eyes, further highlighted by low light, would give the appearance of snake-headed people playing on the stage. The term 'viper' was so common among the jazz community between the 1930s and 1950s that it became more generally used to describe 'pushers', those who actually sold or dealt in illicit narcotics.[32] In this knowledge, it seems clear that if a person were considered to have had a face like a viper, then it implied

An example of the curious baked clay anthropomorphic heads found at Jarmo in Iraqi Kurdistan, and dated to *c.* 6750–5750 BC. Note the elongated facial features and almond-shaped eyes.

that he had long, gaunt features with slit-like eyes comparable with the earliest baked-clay figurines found at Jarmo and dating to 6750 BC.

Was it possible that among the inhabitants of the neolithic, as well as the subsequent Halaf and Ubaid, cultures of Kurdistan there existed a class of individual with facial features that were thought to resemble those of a snake?

If the Ubaid figurines were therefore created to represent these characters, then who might these people have been? Why did the community feel it necessary to appease them in this manner? Was it a similar case at Nevali Çori, where the ruling priests would seem to have been artistically represented in a naive manner by those who treated them almost like gods? Could the same thing have been occurring in the case of the serpent-headed figurines found both at Jarmo *and* among the much later Ubaid graves? Were they too attempting to portray their ruling elite, or at least some memory of them, in a highly abstract form?

Such wild ideas are not stated lightly, for there is firm evidence to suggest that among the Halaf and later Ubaid communities of Kurdistan there really did exist a ruling elite of quite striking appearance and character.

LONG-HEADED ELITISM

Tell Arpachiyah is an occupational mound located near Mosul in the foothills of Iraqi Kurdistan. It dates to the Halaf period and is looked on by archaeologists as a specialised artisan village that produced painted polychrome pottery of exceptional quality. It is known to have had cobbled streets, rectangular buildings, some for religious purposes, like those at Nevali Çori and Çayönü, as well as round buildings with domed vaults like the *tholoi* burial houses of Bronze Age Mycenaean Greece. Finds have included steatite pendants and small discs marked with incised designs that have been interpreted as early examples of the more well-known stamp seals used so much by later Mesopotamian kingdoms such as Akkad and Sumer, and, after their fall, Assyria and Babylon.

During excavations at the site of the tell by the archaeologist Max Mallowan in 1933, a large number of human burials were uncovered, many in an extensive cemetery that dated to the late Halaf, early Ubaid period, *c.* 4600–4300 BC.[33] Most of the skeletons were badly crushed or damaged, but 13 skulls in a slightly better state of preservation were shipped off to Britain, where they were forgotten about for over 30 years. Then, in 1969, Mallowan published an article on these skulls, and this prompted two anthropologists, Theya Molleson and Stuart Campbell, to conduct their own examination of the remains. What they found concerning the appearance and genetic background of the skulls' owners changes our entire perspective of the mysterious world in which these people lived around 6500 years ago.[34]

Molleson and Campbell found evidence to show that six out of the thirteen skulls had been artificially deformed during the life of the individual, the purpose being to increase the length of the cranium and create a more sloping forehead.[35] Such deformations are usually achieved by skilfully wrapping circular bands, sometimes containing wooden boards, around the skull of an individual when still in infancy. In the past this practice was widespread in many parts of the world, particularly South America, and was conducted either for religious or superstitious purposes, as well as to distinguish a person from others not of his or her rank, caste or class.[36]

Knowledge of skull deformation at Tell Arpachiyah came as no surprise, for it had earlier been suspected by Max Mallowan, the original excavator, who even before the study made by his two younger colleagues concluded:

> . . . we appear to be confronted with long heads, and there are certain pronounced facial and other characteristics which appear to imply that the possessors of this [Ubaid] pottery had distinctive physical features, which would have made them exceptionally easy to recognise.[37]

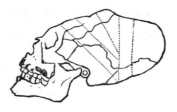

Elongated skull, showing the outline of bands used to create deformation
during infancy. This strange process was practised in the Near East
among the ruling elite of the Halaf and Ubaid peoples during the late
neolithic period.

Skull deformation in prehistoric Kurdistan was itself interesting;
however, Molleson and Campbell went on to realise something else
of importance about the skulls. Some of the cranial abnormalities had
not been induced artificially using head bands and blocks of wood,
but were instead clearly genetic in nature,[38] leading them to observe
that 'several of the individuals (including some without deformations) were related to each other'.[39] In their opinion, this discovery
showed that since the skulls derived from individuals coming from
both the Halaf and Ubaid periods of occupation at the site, then the
two cultures must have been genetically linked in some way.[40] More
significantly, they concluded that artificial deformation at Arpachiyah
had been practised by 'a particular group' who must have been
'genetically related'.[41] They further added that the abnormalities
present among this group suggest a degree of 'inbreeding comparable to the prescribed cross-cousin marriages prevalent in the area
today'.[42] From the anatomical evidence available, it seemed clear to
Molleson and Campbell that they were dealing with a family group
who deliberately elongated their craniums to make themselves stand
out from other groups in the community, almost like some kind of
body uniform.

Cranial deformation among the Halaf and Ubaid peoples of the
sixth and fifth millennia BC has been determined at several sites in
northern Iraq,[43] as well as at others in eastern Anatolia.[44] Its exact
purpose among these cultures who helped create the Mesopotamian
races, and, in the case of the Ubaid, were the direct forerunners of

the Mandaeans, is still a matter of speculation among anthropologists and archaeologists. Molleson and Campbell pointed out that such a 'distinctive appearance would render the individual identifiable as to class or group even if taken prisoner and stripped of other visible accoutrements of status'.[45] They also noted that this practice 'has considerable potential for elitism'.[46]

Molleson and Campbell have proposed that the strange serpent-like figurines of the Ubaid period are *abstract representations of these long-headed individuals* – the tall bitumen 'head-dresses' and flat-tened faces being clear evidence of this association.[47] They also point out that members of this same elite group are depicted in a highly stylised form on fired pottery dating to both the Halaf and Ubaid periods.[48] Many of these images have, in addition to long heads, flattened, protruding faces, over and beyond that caused purely by skull deformation.[49] Another, equally important characteristic is the presence on one example from the Halaf period, *c.* 4900 BC, of two individuals who have elongated heads from which trail curved lines that represent feathered head-dresses.[50] Curiously enough, this painted pottery comes from a site called Tell Sabi Adyad, located on the Syrian–Turkish border, just 20 kilometres (12½ miles) south-south-east of Harran and 113 kilometres (70 miles) south of Nevali Çori.

CULT OF THE RATTLESNAKE

Molleson and Campbell suspected that the skull deformation found among both the Halaf and Ubaid societies was being used to 'demarcate a particular elite group, either social or functional', who were of 'close genetic relationship' and 'hereditary and closely inbred'.[51] Furthermore, the 'shapes of the head may have had specific meaning'.[52] Who were these long-headed individuals depicted in clay as anthropomorphic serpents and on pottery as priests or shamans wearing feathered head-dresses?

Artist's impression of skull deformation among the Chinook tribes of
North America. Note the boards and bands used to achieve this effect. A
similar process took place among the *chane* priests of Mayan Mexico.

In an attempt to answer this question, we must switch our
attentions to another part of the world altogether. Among the
Mayan culture of Mexico's Yucatán Peninsula, a hereditary line of
priests known as *chanes*, 'serpents', would apply bands to deform
the heads of infants in order to give them what was known as a
polcan – an elongated serpentine head. By doing this at an early
age, the child became eligible for acceptance into the family of
chanes, the people of the serpent who perpetuated the cult of the
rattlesnake.[53] The priesthood honoured Itzamna, or Zamna, a form
of *Ahau Can*, 'the great, lordly serpent', who was believed to have
taught their earliest ancestors the Mayan calendar system.[54] In the
corresponding tradition of the Aztecs, Zamna became Quetzalcoatl,
the great 'feathered serpent' and divine wisdom-bringer. Just as the
followers of Ticci Viracocha, the great civiliser of South America,
were collectively known as the Viracocha, so the 'king-priests' of
Quetzalcoatl were referred to in legend as *Quetzalcoatls*, 'feathered
serpents'.[55]

Is it possible that a priestly elite – like the *Quetzalcoatls* of the Aztecs
and the *chanes*, or 'serpents', of the Maya – once existed among the
foothills and fertile valleys of Kurdistan? If so, then did they also
purposely elongate their heads like serpents and wear feathered head-
dresses in honour, or in memory, of ancient wisdom-bringers who

entered their world at the beginning of time?

If, as seems likely, the ruling elite of the Halaf and Ubaid peoples saw themselves as descendants of this proposed group of anthropomorphic serpents, then it provides us with a meaning behind their use of skull deformation. Maybe they felt the need to resemble their divine ancestors, whom they saw as serpentine bird-men with viperous faces and elongated craniums that were likened to the shape of an egg – a primary symbol of first creation. Could this be why we find a carved stone head shaped like an egg and with a serpentine pony-tail facing out from a niche in Nevali Çori's cult building? Was it meant to represent one of the shamanic descendants of the Elder gods, perhaps even one of the

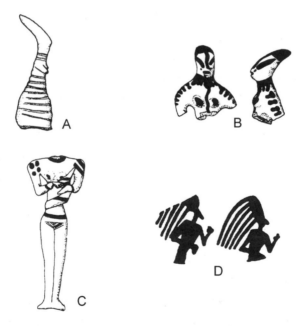

Four abstract examples of probable skull deformation found among Halaf and Ubaid art (after Theya Molleson and Stuart Campbell): a) A Halaf statue from Yarim Tepe, *c*. 5750 BC; b & c) Striking Ubaid figurines from Ur in southern Iraq, *c*. 4200 BC. Note the baby's almost chilling features; d) Halaf pottery from Tell Sabi Adyad, *c*. 4900 BC. Note the stylised feathered head-dresses, plausibly denoting the practice of bird shamanism.

Elder gods themselves? Might the same be said of the beautifully executed serpent-headed 'vulture' statue and the hammer-headed bird-man that were also found in the building?

There is evidence to suggest that oversized craniums, or long heads, were a genetic feature of the elite group present among the Halaf and Ubaid cultures outside of skull deformation. All they did was accentuate what was already present. This is an important realisation since there is firm evidence for the presence among the Isnan and Qadan settlements of Egypt, c. 12,500–9500 BC, of individuals with oversized, long-headed craniums who have been likened to the Cro-Magnon *Homo sapiens* who thrived in this world many millennia before the rise of these advanced communities.[56] Although these are unlikely to be representative of the Elder gods, it does prove that elongated craniums were a genetic feature of the Nilotic communities during the time-frame under question. If the Elder gods *were* genetically related to the Isnan and Qadan peoples, then it seems highly probable that they themselves possessed unique cranial features which included elongated heads. Could this be why their proposed Near Eastern descendants were seen as bird-men with the faces of serpents, because of their distinctive shaped skulls?

Other than the references to their appearance as birds, the Edfu texts tell us only that the primeval ones bore some kind of facial countenance,[57] like the god-kings of Iran and the antediluvian patriarchs of Hebrew tradition. If this too related in some way to their facial features, then with their cloaks of feathers, both the Elder gods and their presumed neolithic descendants would have possessed quite striking appearances that may well have contrasted greatly with the indigenous peoples of Kurdistan.

If the earliest priest-shamans at Nevali Çori and Çayönü really were the descendants of Egyptian Elder gods, did they also introduce the neolithic peoples to the practice of human sacrifice? Does this reveal a darker side to the Elder gods – one that by today's standards would be considered as amoral and almost inhuman? Might this explain why one of the Shebtiu was known as 'The Lord, mighty-chested, who made slaughter, the Soul who lives on blood'?[58] Did

Billy Walker-John's impression of a Neolithic priestly shaman like that
thought to have formed the ruling elite at neolithic cult centres such as
Nevali Çori and Çayönü in eastern Anatolia.

they also help establish elitism based on a belief in divine ancestry?
This idea – which I have outlined in great detail elsewhere – almost
certainly went on to become the roots of divine kingship among the
earliest civilisations of the Near East.

Although not so grand, the megalithic structures of eastern
Anatolia bear a clear resemblance to both the Valley Temple at Giza
and the Osireion at Abydos. Should it ever be proved that these
neolithic structures really were the product of the same high culture,
then it begs the question of what else the Elder gods might have
introduced to the earliest neolithic communities of the Near East,
and what exactly their role was in the genesis of civilisation. It is these
pressing questions that we must now address in the next two
chapters.

CHAPTER EIGHTEEN

THE BLACK LAND

From the moment I first set eyes on Nevali Çori's beautifully sculpted stone monolith, I felt it was a very special place. I became convinced that the site had been founded by the direct descendants of Egypt's Elder gods, whose ancestors – named in the creation texts as the Shebtiu or Ogdoad – had journeyed from the Lebanese or Syrian coast and across the Levant to reach the fertile valleys of the Upper Euphrates some time around 9500 BC.

Testing such a wild theory seemed an almost impossible task, especially as the entire settlement at Nevali Çori was engulfed by the rising waters of the Euphrates river following the construction of the Ataturk dam. Short of hiring a boat and diving down to examine what remained of the ruins, or simply visiting Urfa museum, where much of the cult building has been reconstructed, there seemed little I could do to take the matter any further.

If, however, Egypt's Elder culture really did incorporate intricate astronomical data into the overall design of the monuments and plateau at Giza, as so many researchers now believe, then what were the chances that this same knowledge had been brought across from Egypt and incorporated into the design of Nevali Çori's extraordinary cult building? Many megalithic temples throughout the world incorporate an array of different solar, lunar and stellar alignments, so there was no reason to doubt the possibility that astronomy and perhaps even geomythics (geographically linked mythology) had once played a role at Nevali Çori. If this could be proved correct, then it might reveal more of the beliefs held by the earliest priest-shamans of the Upper Euphrates.

To examine any possible alignments at Nevali Çori, I needed a surveyor's plan of the cult building. This proved impossible to procure, so instead I used accurate ground-plans of the building from what is to date the only detailed report of Hauptmann's excavations, found along with a number of unrelated papers in an obscure, limited-edition monograph entitled *Between the Rivers and over the Mountains*, published in 1993.[1]

Looking at the ground-plan of the cult building during its third and final phase, *c.* 8000 BC, it is plain to see that it is angled almost perfectly south-west, the exact orientation of the Kantara valley which draws the eyes towards the mighty Euphrates river, clearly visible in the distance. Indeed, computer analysis of the internal structure of this particular building phase confirms beyond reasonable doubt that, based on Hauptmann's ground-plan, the north-western and south-eastern interior walls are aligned to within 0.1 of a degree of true south-west, i.e. 225 degrees azimuth. The same orientation of 224.9 degrees is achieved if a line is taken from the centre point of the terrazzo floor through the temple's south-western entrance stairway.

The north-eastern and south-western interior walls are almost as precise in their orientation. The former has a bearing of 134.1 degrees azimuth, which is 0.9 degrees short of true south-east, while the latter is 135.8 degrees, which is an error of just 0.8 degrees. These figures alone should be enough to set alarm bells ringing throughout the archaeological community, for they show conclusively that the 'primitive neolithic farmers' of 8000 BC accurately laid out buildings in strict accordance with the four compass points, a technical skill that would have required an advanced understanding of either the circumpolar stars and/or the yearly course of the sun.

The preoccupation among the people of Nevali Çori with the

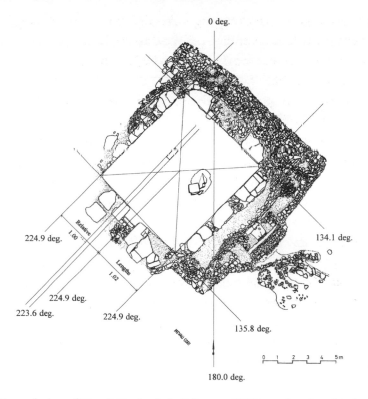

Ground-plan of Nevali Çori cult building, *c.* 8000 BC, showing the clear
south-westerly orientation of its interior walls and remaining standing
monolith, courtesy H. Hauptmann.

south-west does not end here. The carved stone egg-head also stared
out from its niche towards this direction, while the remaining
sculpted monolith is angled at 223.6 degrees azimuth, just 1.4
degrees south of true south-west. Was this slight alteration in
orientation pure clumsiness, or did it serve some kind of exact
purpose? From the existing ground-plan, it is clear from the position
of the stone fragments found within the terrazzo floor that the
second monolith would have stood at an equal distance on the
opposite side of the centre line, facing out towards the same
direction. Together they would have formed an enormous, three-
metre-high portal almost perfectly aligned towards the south-west,
where the steady-flowing Euphrates could be seen disappearing off

into the distance. Since the arms, hands and long hair carved in low relief on the side and front faces of the two sculpted monoliths would also have looked out towards the south-west it begs the question of whether or not there was some connection between the building's quite specific orientation and the celestial horizon at some point in the solar year.

The most common alignments at megalithic sites were fixed on the equinoxes and solstices. It was therefore important to inspect the positions of stars in relation to the south-western horizon at all of these different times of the year. After careful study of a whole range of computer printouts, only one date and time made complete sense, and this was the pre-dawn period before sunrise on the spring equinox.

If you were to stand between the two huge sculpted monoliths and gaze out beyond the entrance stairway towards the south-western horizon in 8000 BC, just one constellation would dominate the early morning sky. This was Cetus, the Latin name given to the fabled sea-monster or kraken turned to stone by the hero Perseus who exposed it to the head of the gorgon Medusa. This was after it had been dispatched by the water-god Neptune (Poseidon in Greek myth) to devour the beautiful Andromeda. What exactly this sea-monster might have been is a matter of some speculation. Some have seen it as a sea-serpent, although it is more likely to have been a whale, the form in which it is often depicted on ancient star-maps.[2] Generally it is shown in association with the river of heaven[3] known as the Eridanus, in which it either swims or is shown with its fore quarters on one bank and the rest of its bulbous body in the water.[4]

RIVER OF THE NIGHT

The curious star-lore surrounding the constellation of Cetus makes intriguing reading, and yet added very little to this debate. My suspicions were, however, aroused when I realised that the celestial

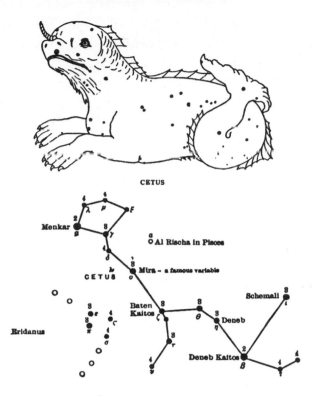

Ancient conception of Cetus, the kraken, whale or sea-monster of mythology, next to its starry counterpart. Note the proximity of the constellation known as Eridanus, the starry stream, identified by Robert Brown Jnr with the Euphrates river.

river named Eridanus was in fact a constellation in its own right known variously as 'the river' or the 'starry stream'. Usually it is shown as flowing from the star Rigel, which forms the left foot of the constellation of Orion, across to the 'paws' of Cetus (hence the mythological and artistic associations). More important, it can be shown that Eridanus is a celestial counterpart not only of the river Nile, to which it is often compared, but also of the Euphrates.[5] Robert Brown Jnr, the noted nineteenth-century scholar of star-lore and its relationship to Mesopotamian mythology, wrote much about this subject, his findings being published in 1883 within a book entitled *Eridanus: River and Constellation*.[6] In this classic work he

The sea-monster Cetus swimming in the mythical Eridanus, the starry
stream of the southern sky.

argues in favour of the Eridanus being the celestial counterpart of the
Euphrates by citing the following evidence:

> [The two rivers are] . . . frequently alluded to, from very early
> days to the classical age, as The River, the Euphrates origi-
> nally being Pura or Purat . . . that they resemble each other as
> long and winding streams with two great branches; that each
> is connected with a Paradise – Eden and Heaven; that the
> adjoining constellations seem to be Euphratean in origin; and
> that each is in some way associated with the Nile, and each
> with the overthrow of the sun-god.[7]

In addition to this, the name Eridanus seems to be a Latinised
form of Eridu, a very ancient city at the mouth of the Euphrates.[8]
Professor George Smith, the noted nineteenth-century scholar of
Assyrian studies, who first translated the Mesopotamian account of
the Great Flood, believed that he had found reference to the starry
stream of Eridanus in ancient cuneiform tablets, where it is named
as the *Erib-me-gali*.[9] Robert Brown Jnr agreed with him,[10] yet
added that the root of the name Eridanus derived from the
Akkadian word *aria*, meaning 'the river'.[11] This, in the words of

French Mesopotamian scholar François Lenormant, was 'the ocean of the celestial waters . . . viewed under the form of a river'.[12] Using the same word-root, Brown also demonstrated that the Eridanus was the same as the Assyrian *nahru*, meaning 'river', from which was derived the word Naharin, the name given by the Egyptians of the Eighteenth Dynasty to the land of the Mitanni, the kingdom between the Upper Euphrates and Tigris rivers in northern Syria, eastern Anatolia.[13]

In Mesopotamian myth, both the Eridanus and the Euphrates were also synonymous with the River of the Night, or the River of the Underworld, which was named as the Ḫubur.[14] This in turn was seen as the River of Creation, which was yet another form of the celestial Euphrates.[15]

By themselves, such speculations were of little use. My curiosity had, however, been raised by Brown's assertion that 'adjoining constellations' in the vicinity of the constellation of Eridanus were also seen as 'Euphratean in origin'.[16] I soon found that they included Cetus, which, as already stated, was often shown on star-maps in association with the Eridanus. Since Cetus hung low in the south-western sky in the pre-dawn light of the spring equinox in 8000 BC, below which the Euphrates was seen to flow out towards the Syrian

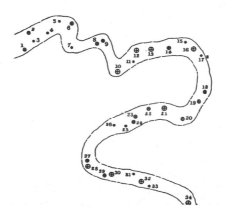

The constellation of Eridanus, the starry stream, as perceived by Ptolemy and drawn by Robert Brown Jnr.

plains, this seemed too much of a coincidence. Might the constellation of Cetus have had a counterpart among the rich mythology that eventually developed down on the plains of ancient Mesopotamia?

The answer is unquestionably yes. The stars of both Cetus and Eridanus are intrinsically linked with the sea-monster known as Tiamat, which was looked on in Mesopotamian myth and legend as the female personification of the dark watery abyss.[17] One part of her, the Upper Tiamat, governed the waters of the subterranean ocean, the *apsû*, while the other half, the Lower Tiamat, presided over the terrestrial waters in her role as *Ummu-Ḫubur*, 'the Mother Ḫubur', the name given to the Euphrates as the River of the Underworld.[18]

The story of Tiamat's fall is recorded in the Mesopotamian Epic of Creation known as the *Enuma Elish*. It states that before the creation of the world only two great beings existed – Apsû, the personification of the subterranean waters that nourished the sources of springs and ponds, and Tiamat, who presided over the salt waters. The union of these two natural forces resulted in the appearance of the first gods, including An (or Anu), 'heaven', and Anu's son Enki (or Ea). They began a new world order, or 'way', which caused so much animosity that Apsû, with the aid of his minister Mummu (meaning 'chaos'), plotted to destroy them. Very quickly the god Enki uncovered their plot, and so frustrated it by informing the other gods of the intended revolt.

The primeval sea-monster Tiamat as depicted on a Babylonian cylinder seal currently in the possession of the British Museum.

Enki went against Apsû and Mummu, slaying them both, and as a consequence of these actions Tiamat, wishing to avenge the deaths of her former allies, threatened to cause a deluge that would cover the earth. She also spawned a brood of 11 'monster vipers' of 'lofty stature',[19] which included a scorpion-man, a lion-demon, a raging lion, a bull-man and a *kulullu,* or fish-man[20] – all almost certainly early forms of star constellations.[21] Led by Tiamat's minister Qingu, this demon-brood engaged the god named Marduk (sometimes Bel-Marduk or Bel) in battle, who duly dispatched each one before destroying Tiamat by splitting open her skull and standing on her 'lower parts'. Having sliced her in two, like 'a dried fish', one half of her body became the starry canopy, while the rest of the body was used to form the earth. It was said that her breasts became the mountains, her spit became the clouds, while her tears formed the sources of the Tigris and Euphrates.[22] After the destruction of the 'monster vipers', the god Marduk then completed his act of creation by allowing Enki to cut off his head so that the blood could form the first animals and human beings.

This is a basic translation of the creation myth revered among the great Mesopotamian cultures of Akkad, Sumer, Assyria and Babylon. Its origin remains obscure, although plausibly it was handed down from the earliest days. That the celestial representations of Tiamat and the River of the Night were to be seen on Nevali Çori's south-western horizon at dawn on the spring equinox in 8000 BC really does suggest that its elite group of priest-shamans were blatantly aware of this stellar alignment. The curling necklace of 34 stars defined by Ptolemy,[23] the Alexandrian astronomer who flourished *c.* AD 139, as making up the constellation of Eridanus seems to mimic the winding course of the southerly flowing Euphrates as it steers around the cities of Urfa and Harran before entering northern Syria.

In many ways the starry stream would appear to have been an exact mirror of the terrestrial Euphrates. This theory is made all the more pertinent in the knowledge that the celestial waters of the Eridanus were looked on as flowing downwards towards the southern horizon,[24] i.e. in the same direction as the Euphrates if viewed from the vicinity of Nevali Çori, close to its headwaters. Is this what the priest-shamans of Nevali Çori saw and understood from the position of their cult building around the year 8000 BC? Is this why the whole structure, including its anthropomorphic monoliths and egg-headed statue, is angled south-west towards the Euphrates river?

We cannot, however, be certain exactly how old the cult building, or indeed the settlement at Nevali Çori, might actually have been. The carbon-14 testing of organic materials can provide only approximate dates of contextually placed stone structures. Indeed, looking at the star-charts for dawn on the spring equinox for the years 8500 BC, 9000 BC and 9500 BC, the celestial horizon is seen to turn gradually clockwise, bringing the constellation of Eridanus closer and closer to a position directly above its terrestrial counterpart, while at the same time still leaving the wide body of stars that make up Cetus-Tiamat lingering above the south-western horizon. The later dates all left the stars of Eridanus slightly out of kilter with its earthly counterpart. It is my opinion that the celestial mirror synchronises perfectly with the terrestrial horizon in around 9000 BC, which, if correct, clearly implies that the cult building was constructed at least 600 years earlier than has previously been imagined. Yet as we have no supportive evidence to this effect, I will continue to use the date of 8000 BC when reviewing Nevali Çori's proposed astronomical alignments.

If the members of the ruling elite at Nevali Çori really were aware of the geomythical relationship between the horizon and the sky in 8000 BC, then how might they have interpreted such alignments? Are we really expected to believe that they were aware of important aspects of the Mesopotamian creation myth over 5500 years before it first surfaced in written form down on the plains of ancient Iraq?

THE GATE OF THE DEEP

One clue may come from a fragmentary astrological text, seen as a supplement to the creation epic, which seems to relate the myth of Tiamat to a specific area of the celestial horizon. On the subject of Marduk's triumph over the primeval sea-monster it says: 'Tiamat he conquered, he took her sovereignty . . . and at the Gate of the Deep he stationed . . . that the deeds of Tiamat should not be forgotten.'[25]

What exactly was the 'Gate of the Deep', where some kind of sentinel, or watchman, was apparently stationed? From what can be ascertained, it would seem to have been a region of the night sky, but where exactly?

We find that 'the Deep' was an alternative name for Tiamat herself. With this knowledge, L.W. King, the nineteenth-century translator of and commentator on the creation tablets, proposed that a starry 'guardian was stationed by Marduk in order to restrain the waters of the Deep',[26] this being a reference to the deluge Tiamat had threatened to unleash on the world in revenge for the killing of Apsû and his minister Mummu. It would therefore appear as if Marduk's guardian was to ensure that the ocean of the celestial waters, 'viewed under the form of a river',[27] did not penetrate beyond the Gate of the Deep and flood the terrestrial world. Since the celestial River of the Night was synonymous with the Eridanus, then the Gate of the Deep was therefore the south to south-western sky that included both the constellation of Eridanus and that of the sea-monster Cetus, or Tiamat.

Where might such ideas have originated? Could they have developed among the priest-shamans of early neolithic communities such as Nevali Çori, which seems to have been the most sophisti-cated, and perhaps even the most important, cult centre in the whole of eastern Anatolia? Its cult building is silent on such matters, although what we do know is that there is good evidence to suggest that the earliest neolithic inhabitants of the Upper Euphrates would appear to have been aware of certain traditions surrounding the figure of Tiamat. This is evidenced from a flat bone disc found at Çayönü, the bead-producing centre 100 kilometres (60 miles) north-east of Nevali Çori. It has large, round, owl-like eyes with pecked-out indentations as pupils. From the bottom of the eyes come short, deeply gouged lines that seem to represent flowing tears.[28] Another, similar owl-face impression was found alongside the proto-writing on the 10,000-year-old flat, oval-shaped stones unearthed at Jerf el Ahmar on the Upper Euphrates of northern Syria.[29] Were these owl-faced images an early form of Tiamat, whose tears were seen as the sources of the Tigris and Euphrates, which both rise in the snow-capped mountains close to Lake Van in eastern Anatolia? If so, then what else did the neolithic peoples know about this primeval sea-monster, and how, if at all, might this link back to the appearance in the region of Egypt's Elder gods shortly after 9500 BC?

Tiamat derives her name from the Babylonian word *tāmtu*, or *tiamtum*, meaning 'sea' or 'ocean',[30] a reference to the watery abyss, the chaotic darkness that existed before the creation of the world. It is the same root source behind the reference to *Tehôm*, 'the deep', found in the book of Genesis,[31] which states that on the dark face of this watery chaos the 'spirit of God' moved before the creation of the first day.[32] Tiamat was also Leviathan, the 'swift serpent' and 'crooked serpent', or 'the dragon that is in the sea', mentioned elsewhere in the Old Testament.[33] More significantly, Tiamat can be equated directly with the Egyptian primeval serpent Kematef, the guardian of the *bnnt*-embryo and the 'soul' of the primeval hill located in the waters of Nun, which existed in a state of perpetual darkness before the beginning of time.[34]

The strange religious writings of the third-century Peratae gnostics spoke of Kematef (the Chnoubis, Chnoumis or Kneph of Hermetic tradition) as the 'Typhonic [i.e. 'monster serpent'] daughter', who is the 'guard of all sorts of waters'.[35] To them she was also Chorzar, the 'power to whom Thalassa is entrusted'.[36] Thalassa, Thalatth or Omoroca, as she was also known, is described as the 'woman of the sea' and 'the Mother of the Deep',[37] and is simply a

Greek rendering of the sea-monster Tiamat.[38] To the Peratae, Chorzar was the celestial offspring of Tiamat, just as Kematef was seen by the Egyptians as the soul within the primeval waters of Nun.

Could it be possible that behind the creation myths that feature Kematef in Egypt and Tiamat in Mesopotamia, there was some kind of common origin, assimilated at the time of the earliest neolithic settlements of the Upper Euphrates, say between 9500 and 9000 BC? If this is correct, then did the priest-shamans of Nevali Çori align the cult building, with its monumental stone gateway, towards both the stars of Cetus-Tiamat and the celestial ocean, or River of the Night, in celebration of the emergence of the physical world out of the primeval watery chaos, personified by the sea-monster Kematef or Tiamat? Was this the sole reason for the south-westerly orientation of the cult building at Nevali Çori, or was there another, more powerful, and perhaps even more archaic reason for aligning its starry portal towards the Gate of the Deep?

TURNING TO HOME

Places of worship of the Jewish and Muslim faiths are orientated towards their greatest religious centres – synagogues face Jerusalem, while mosques face Mecca. Every care is taken to ensure that exactly the right angle is achieved, necessitating the use of theodolites and accurate calculations. The purpose of such alignments is so that, wherever the worshipper might be in the world, he or she will always remember the significance of their faith's most sacred place.

I wondered whether it was possible that the designers of Nevali Çori's cult building orientated it towards not only the direction most associated with their own myths and legends but also the homeland of their earliest ancestors. This was certainly an exciting prospect, and so I calculated quickly the bearing between Nevali Çori and Giza in Egypt. Having obtained an initial, and potentially revelatory, result using a standard map of Egypt and the Near East, I consulted my

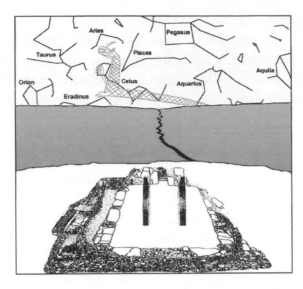

A computer-generated impression of Nevali Çori's cult building, showing
its conceptualised south-westerly relationship to the river Euphrates and
the constellations of Cetus-Tiamat and Eridanus, the starry stream, as
they would have appeared in the pre-dawn sky prior to the spring
equinox, *c.* 8000 BC.

friend and colleague Rodney Hale on this matter. He made various
mathematical calculations, using the coordinates of each location,
which must, of course, take into account the curvature of the earth.
He established that the so-called 'Great Circle' bearing of Giza from
the position of Nevali Çori is 222.08 degrees,[39] a full 1.52 degrees
out from the 223.6-degree orientation of the standing monolith and
a massive 2.82 degrees if we take into consideration the orientation
of the cult building itself.

Such inaccuracies might seem small, but when transferred on to a
large-scale map, they represent the difference between hitting the
Great Pyramid and veering several kilometres off into the Libyan
desert. On the other hand such assumptions are made on the basis
that the founders of Nevali Çori would have been able to calculate,
with almost laser precision, the exact bearing from their cult building
to their suspected homeland over 1080 kilometres (670 miles) away.
Perhaps the whole process involved much less precision, making the

south-western orientation more of a symbolic act of faith.

If the alignment linking Nevali Çori with Egypt is at all valid, then it suggests that its priest-shamans really did see the south-west as the direction most associated with the creation of their world. The fact that the imaginary line stretches across the waters of the eastern Mediterranean Sea is also perhaps significant. With Egypt as their ancestral homeland, this sea journey might have been compared with the emergence of cosmic order out of the chaotic waters of *apsû* at the beginning of time. Having conquered the face of the Deep, in other words the Mediterranean Sea, to arrive in the Levant, the surviving Elders, as the first gods of Mesopotamia, would have been seen as initiating a new world order. In this mythical epoch, mortal kind were seen to have lived alongside their immortal teachers – utopic memories that led to the much later legends concerning the paradisical realm, known in Hebrew as Eden and in Akkadian and Sumerian as Dilmun.

These were once again startling revelations that really did point towards a direct connection between the high culture of Egypt and the emergence of the neolithic world. The ancestral worship found at Nevali Çori, and apparently embodied in the orientation of its cult building, clearly implied a racial memory of its community's Egyptian roots. The clear connections with a deluge or flood would also seem to imply that its neolithic priest-shamans preserved an abstract memory of the geological and climatic upheavals, personified in the myth of Tiamat, that their first ancestors had endured before they reached the new land – ideas strangely reminiscent of the stories of the Great Flood preserved in both biblical and Mesopotamian tradition.

THE END OF AN AGE

From what we have seen, it would seem as if Tiamat came to represent the fading memories of the dark, cyclopean world left behind in Egypt by the last Elder gods. In the minds of the priest-shamans at places such as Nevali Çori, this bygone age would appear to have been viewed in terms of the darkness and chaos that ruled before their divine forebears had crossed the watery abyss to enter their world, at what was seen as the *beginning* of time. The south-western Gate of the Deep defined by the orientation of the cult building and the stars of Cetus and Eridanus was, in effect, the exit from that primordial world, abstractly characterised by the cataclysmic destruction that had apparently eclipsed this earlier epoch. In Mesopotamian myth and ritual a sentinel was posted to guard this south-western portal in the belief that this chaos and disorder could spill out into their own age, causing darkness to once again engulf the world. It would seem likely they believed that only by constantly reaffirming this guardianship through magical spells could it be prevented from happening.

In much later times this proto-memory of humanity's former existence in another world was somehow transformed into the myths and stories surrounding the sea-monster Tiamat, and how she was vanquished by Marduk, the bringer of light and supposed progenitor of the human race. It must have been at around this time that the true significance of the Gate of the Deep was distorted beyond all recognition. Yet despite the perhaps deliberate severing with past traditions, one blatant link does remain which directly connects Nevali Çori's south-westerly orientation with its ruling elite's proposed ancestral homeland.

In an important work on ancient Euphratean star-lore written by Aratus, a noted Greek astronomer and poet who lived around 270 BC, the sea-monster Cetus is referred to as 'the dusky Monster'[40] – a name that was said to express 'the blue-black of the nocturnal sky'.[41] To the Assyrians and Babylonians, Cetus was known by the name *Kumaru*, 'the Dusky',[42] or *Mul Kumar*, 'the Dusky Constellation'.[43] Both names are borrowed from the much earlier Sumero-Akkadian word *kumar*, meaning 'dusky' or 'dark'.[44] In Aramaic Hebrew, which is a Semitic language linked closely to Akkadian, this same word becomes *akem*, 'to be black' and 'sunburned'.[45] In the Egyptian language this word becomes *kem*, 'black', or Kemet (from *kmt*), meaning 'black land' – the name given to Ancient Egypt by its own inhabitants. Mythological legend asserts that this name refers to the black silt left covering the first land, i.e. Egypt, after the waters of Nun had receded from the primeval mound at the beginning of time, reflected in the very real alluvial deposits left covering the Nile valley after the yearly inundation.

More curiously, we find that the word *kem* was also used in the Ancient Egyptian language to denote 'the end, end of a period, completion, a finish',[46] while *kemet* can also mean 'to end, to bring to an end, end years, the end of a moment'.[47] All these definitions imply a *completion* to a period or cycle of time, expressions reminiscent of the serpent Kematef, who is described in the Theban creation myth as 'he whose moment of living had ended or was thought buried'[48] or 'he who [has] completed his time'.[49] Is it possible that Kemet was the name originally given to Egypt as the primeval homeland by the descendants of the Elder gods who entered the Near East in around 9500 BC? Was the name an abstract memory of the alluvial deposits that must have covered large parts of the Nile valley after the constant series of high floods that occurred during the eleventh to tenth millennia BC? Did it also preserve a memory of the culmination, or conclusion, of this period of chaos and destruction, brought about by the events that accompanied the end of the last Ice Age, *c.* 10,500–9500 BC?

If these thoughts are correct, then it is likely that these memories were carried into the Upper Euphrates region by the last Elder gods and kept alive by the priest-shamans of the neolithic communities. As a result, they began using variations of the word *kem*, *kemet*, Kematef and later *kumar* and *kumaru* to refer to the cluster of stars that formed the Draconian influence thought to lie beyond the Gate of the Deep. Should this be so, then it suggests that Kematef, like Tiamat and Cetus, was simply an expression of *kemet* – the embodiment of the events that had surrounded the departure of the Elder gods from Egypt after it was seen to have been engulfed not only in darkness and chaos but also in a universal deluge. It was in this manner that the inhabitants of neolithic sites such as Nevali Çori kept alive abstract memories of all that had happened in the ancestral homeland – seeing these events not in terms of historical fact but as mythological stories involving a primeval sea-monster and a universal flood that ended a previous world age.

This, then, was the starry legacy preserved in stone within the cult building at Nevali Çori. Yet if this were the case, then how might we explain the presence here of clear aquatic imagery in the form of the flipper-like hands on the anthropomorphic monoliths and stone roof supports? How might this fit into the emerging mythological picture? To answer these questions we will have to make a journey that will ultimately culminate in the rise of one of the greatest civilisations of the ancient world.

CHAPTER NINETEEN

THE STARRY WISDOM

Many thousands of years ago the peoples of Kurdistan, from the mountains of Armenia through to the fertile valleys of Turkey and Syria, were united under the leadership of a ruling elite known as the Hurrians. These Indo-European-speaking warlords appeared almost out of nowhere during the third millennium BC and quickly drew together the many different tribal factions, who built beautiful cities and towns, and established a kingdom that lasted over 1000 years. In spite of the fact that history has recorded very little about their sophisticated culture, we do know that they were the forerunners of both the Hittite empire of Turkey and the kings of Mitanni, or Naharin, who became Egypt's allies during its Eighteenth Dynasty.

The Hurrians possessed their own unique religion which, although truly indigenous to Kurdistan, had a profound influence on the development of mythology down on the plains of Ancient Iraq. Many of their myths seemed to focus on the beliefs of the people who lived between the Upper Euphrates and Tigris rivers, where their great religious centre was ancient Harran, home of the Sabian star-worshippers. From ancient inscriptions we learn that one of the Hurrians' greatest deities was Kumarbi, a dark water-god, comparable with Neptune in the Roman pantheon. His animal form was the pond turtle, and creation myths speak of him raising himself out of the primeval waters at the beginning of time. His hard, knobbly shell became the mountains, while the tears that fell from his eyes became the sources of the Euphrates and Tigris.[1]

THE CREATURE OF CANCER

The name Kumarbi derives from the Sumero-Akkadian root *kumar*, 'dusky', which, as previously stated, is the root behind the name given to the star constellation Cetus by the various Mesopotamian cultures. It is therefore safe to presume that Kumarbi, the dark water-god of the Hurrians, was linked directly with the Euphratean sea-monster.

So in addition to being a whale and a sea-monster, Cetus would also appear to have been equated by the peoples of the Upper Euphrates with the pond turtle – a symbol that even today features prominently in Kurdish folklore. It is emblazoned in abstract form on locally made *kilim* rugs, which are based on traditional designs that are known to date back several thousand years.[2] The Kurds also see the pond turtle as the symbol of Khidir, a powerful spirit whose omnipotent influence is felt both on land and in water.[3] In many ways he is the Kurdish equivalent of the Green Man, the living spirit of the wildwood, whose vine-sprouting stone face still gazes down from the Gothic masonry of hundreds of churches and cathedrals all over Europe. Khidir means 'green' or 'crawler', and it is said that he 'dwells primarily in deep, still ponds'.[4] More significantly, the turtle was likened to the Euphrates, since its waters were seen as slow-moving, in contrast to the Tigris, the fast-moving waters of which were compared with the swift movement of the hare.[5]

This age-old connection between turtles and Kurdistan might help explain a very curious limestone water-bowl found by Harald Hauptmann at Nevali Çori. In an almost naive manner, its unknown artist has chiselled in low relief an upright-standing turtle, each side of which is a naked figure, one male and the other female. Their hands are raised high in the air as if in an ecstatic state – Hauptmann suggests they are in fact dancers.[6] The strange imagery on this unique water-vessel may well provide evidence to suggest that the indigenous peoples of Kurdistan have revered the sanctity of the pond turtle for at least 10,000 years, an astonishing realisation in itself. Yet the presence of the turtle at Nevali Çori has even greater implications for our understanding of its geomythic relationship to the celestial horizon.

In the pre-dawn light of the spring equinox of 8000 BC, the stars of Cetus, the dusky constellation that dwells within the Gate of the Deep, would have been seen low on the south-western horizon. Strung between the 'paws' of this sea-monster – equated with both Tiamat and Kumarbi – and Rigel, the left foot of Orion, would have been seen the stars of Eridanus, the River of the Night and the celestial counterpart of the mighty Euphrates. This much we know. Yet if we were then to turn our heads towards the east, where the sun was about to rise in all its splendour, we would see that immediately above the horizon was the constellation of Cancer – the zodiacal sign that defined the precessional age after the final setting of Leo on the equinoctial horizon some time around 9220 BC.

Since classical times the star constellation of Cancer has been symbolised by the crab. Yet thousands of years before it gained this association, Cancer was looked on by the peoples of Mesopotamia as the turtle.[7] Giorgio Santillana and Hertha von Dechend, the authors of *Hamlet's Mill*, have argued that many primitive societies before the rise of civilisation were somehow aware of both the 12-fold division of the zodiac and the phenomenon of precession. If this is so, then it seems likely that the neolithic priest-shamans of the Upper Euphrates would have been aware of the astrological influences that governed the destiny of their own precessional age. I therefore find it curious that, similar to the mythology behind the constellation of Cetus, the Cancerian turtle is an amphibian linked not just with the pre-dawn equinoctial sky of the ninth millennium BC but also with

The Mesopotamian turtle, symbol of the god Enki, or Ea, the constellation of Cancer and the river Euphrates.

Nevali Çori *and* the nearby river Euphrates. Could it be possible that the mythological traditions surrounding the stars of Cetus were so strong that they became closely interwoven with the star-lore attached to the constellation that defined the astrological influence of the age in question? Could the proto-memories of the ancestral homeland and the primordial watery chaos that existed before the beginning of time have influenced the *very nature* of the Cancerian age?

REALMS OF THE RIVER-GOD

To answer these questions we must look further at the myths and legends surrounding the god Enki. He was seen in Euphratean myth as presiding over the subterranean waters of the *apsû*, and in this capacity he was considered to bring forth the two great rivers, the Euphrates and Tigris, confirming his close association with this region, seen by Mehrdad Izady as the land of Dilmun, Enki's paradisical realm. In representations of Enki, these two rivers were shown as twin streams flowing either from the god's shoulders or from a vase held in one hand. Fish swim in the midst of the streams, like salmon attempting to ride the current to reach the source of a river.

Strangely enough, in a star-map that accompanies Aratus' famous third-century BC discourse on Euphratean star-lore, the constellation of Eridanus is shown as a recumbent river-god, with a short beard and flowing locks, who holds in one hand a stalk of 'some aquatic plant', while his other hand rests on an urn, 'whence flow right and left two streams of water'.[8] Depictions of Eridanus found in other classical sources also show variations on this river-god theme, even though the figure is depicted occasionally as a reclining river nymph.[9] Since we know that Eridanus was the celestial form of the Euphrates river, then it seems quite certain that Aratus' river-god was simply a

The god Enki, or Ea, showing the waters of the Euphrates and Tigris rivers flowing from his shoulders. His two-faced minister stands behind him, while upon his hand rests the vulture – an abstract symbol of the neolithic cult of the dead.

classical memory of Enki's guardianship of the two great rivers.

In the light of Enki's connection with the Euphrates in particular, it is perhaps not surprising to find that his main symbol was the turtle.[10] This association obviously reflected the god's affiliation with the subterranean waters of the *apsû*, which were believed to rise up into the terrestrial world through bottomless springs and ponds – domains of the pond turtle. Yet as the *apsû* also had a celestial counterpart, it made sense that the turtle was also seen as a constellation in its own right. This, of course, was Cancer, which became the spirit of the astrological epoch in which these traditions would appear to have first been laid down at neolithic temple sites such as Nevali Çori.

Confirmation that both Enki and the turtle were linked with the equinoctial horizon during the Age of Cancer comes from the knowledge that the god's other main animal form was the mythological goat-fish.[11] In Mesopotamian tradition it was said that the turtle and the goat-fish struggled constantly to become Enki's favourite animal; indeed, sometimes the turtle is placed on the back of the goat-fish as if to show its ultimate superiority in this long-standing battle for supremacy.[12]

The turtle can be associated with the constellation of Cancer, the equinoctial marker during the three building phases of Nevali Çori's cult building, but what about the goat-fish? Did this creature also have a starry counterpart? The answer, of course, is yes. The goat-fish is the earliest known representation of Capricorn,[13] the zodiacal constellation that lies in direct opposition to Cancer. In other words, as Cancer rose with the sun on the spring equinox, Capricorn would have been seen on the western horizon. At the autumn equinox, the roles would have been reversed, with Capricorn rising with the sun, while Cancer was on the western horizon. This opposing relationship between the two zodiacal constellations would have created a visual effect something akin to a celestial seesaw in the skies above Nevali Çori on the equinoxes during the Age of Cancer.

This, then, was the eternal struggle for supremacy between these two aquatic creatures, both familiars of the god Enki. The god

The Mesopotamian goat-fish, symbol of the god Enki and the
constellation of Capricorn.

himself played a prominent role in the wars that waged between the
demon-brood of Tiamat and the Anunnaki, the name given to the
gods of heaven and earth in Mesopotamian myth. Enki was thus
connected not just with the sources of the Euphrates and Tigris
rivers, which rose in the mythical land of Dilmun, but also with the
key components of the starry sky as it would have appeared before
sunrise on the spring equinox during the astrological Age of Cancer,
estimated to have occurred *c.* 9220–7060 BC.[14]

THE REPULSIVE ONES

Ancient cuneiform texts tell us that, following the creation of the
physical world, Enki, having departed from Dilmun, provided mankind with the divine arts and crafts that enabled him to achieve a
state of civilisation:[15] this is a statement that makes complete sense of
archaeological discoveries made on the plains of Mesopotamia. The
oldest known place of worship in pre-Sumerian Iraq is Eridu, a city
located by the mouth of the Lower Euphrates on the edge of the
Persian Gulf. Here, a temple was first established in around 5500 BC,
and at the very earliest occupational levels excavations have revealed
the presence of countless numbers of fish bones.[16] This can be seen
as evidence of supplication to some proto-form of Enki, who later
became the patron god of Eridu. What *exactly* was worshipped here,

2000 years before the rise of the Sumerian civilisation, remains uncertain. However, we do know that the worship of Enki was linked very much with the fecundity of the irrigated lands fed by the Euphrates. This integral link with the river eventually led to Enki being represented in reliefs, particularly at Eridu, as a man adorned in the garb of a fish.[17]

The memory of the knowledge and wisdom imparted by Enki to the first inhabitants of ancient Iraq, some time around 5500 BC, was recorded by Berossus, a celebrated priest and scribe of Babylon's temple of Bel (or Bel-Marduk), who lived during the third century BC. He composed a three-volume discourse on the legendary history of his race, including their forebears the Sumerians, entitled *Babyloniaka*. Sadly, our only knowledge of this now lost work comes from quotations or commentaries found in the writings of other authors, such as Alexander Polyhistor, Apollodorus, Abydenus and Flavius Josephus, which were themselves saved by being preserved in the works of much later Christian writers, such as Eusebius of Caesarea (AD 264–340) and George Syncellus (*fl.* ninth century). These passages include curious accounts of the visits made to Babylon by a strange fish-man named Oannes, who was said to have appeared out of the 'Erythraean Sea' in the 'first year' and spent his days among mankind, providing them with:

> . . . an insight into letters and sciences, and arts of every kind. He taught them to construct cities, to found temples, to compile laws, and explained to them the principles of geometrical knowledge. He made them distinguish the seeds of the earth, and shewed them how to collect the fruits: in short, he instructed them in every thing which could tend to soften manners and humanize their lives. From that time, nothing material has been added by way of improvement to his instructions.[18]

So wrote Berossus concerning the foundations of the Babylonian (i.e.

the preceding Sumerian) race. Of Oannes himself, it was said that he was an Annedotus, a 'repulsive one', and that his 'whole body was that of a fish'. Furthermore, 'that under the fish's head he had another head, with feet also below, similar to those of a man, subjoined to the fish's tail. His voice too, and language, was articulate and human; and a representation of him is preserved even to this day.'[19] Berossus also recorded that after Oannes had conversed with mortal kind, he would return to the sea where he 'passed the night in the deep; for he was amphibious'.[20]

Berossus goes on to state that following the appearance of Oannes, 10 great kings reigned over Babylon (i.e. Sumer), the last of whom was Xisuthrus, during whose reign occurred the 'great deluge', a subject I have examined in great detail elsewhere.[21] Before this time a total of five (one version says seven)[22] Annedoti, the first of whom being Oannes himself, were said to have appeared in the land of Babylon.[23]

It is impossible now to know exactly what Berossus was attempting to convey by preserving the strange legends surrounding the appearance of these wisdom-bringing fish-men. It is, however, quite clear that Oannes himself is simply a Greek rendering of Enki, based on his Akkadian name *Ea*. The five Annedoti, on the other hand, correspond very well with the five 'ministers' said to have served the monster serpent Chorzar, the daughter of Thalassa – the Greek name for Tiamat – in the curious writings of the Peratae gnostics.[24]

The fact that Berossus cites Oannes as having appeared out of the Erythraean Sea – the ancient name for the Arabian Sea,[25] connected via a channel to the Persian Gulf – would seem at first to contradict the knowledge that Enki was linked with the sources of the Euphrates and Tigris. This conclusion is also suggested by the presence close to the mouth of the Euphrates river of the principal temple of Enki at Eridu. However, in view of Dilmun's association with Enki and the sources of the great rivers, it seems clear that something is wrong here, and the confusion almost certainly derives from the Sumerian belief that the 'mouth', or estuary, of a river was its source, out of which the waters flowed.[26] Admittedly, this same argument has been

Kulullu or fish-man – a form of the god Enki, Ea, A'a or Oannes, the
bringer of civilisation in ancient Hurrian and Mesopotamian mythology.

used by Mesopotamian scholars to prove exactly the opposite – that
the Sumerians saw the source of a river as its 'mouth', or estuary –
but to me this seems entirely wrong.[27]

Great confusion has arisen in this respect, and it seems certain
that it existed even in Berossus' day, when he spoke of Oannes and
the rest of the Annedoti coming out of the Erythraean Sea. If, as
seems more likely, he was working from original Akkadian or
Sumerian sources, which spoke of them coming out of the 'mouths'
of the rivers, then he would have presumed this meant the open sea.
In my opinion, there is every reason to believe that in the story of
Oannes, Berossus was recording an age-old memory concerning the
descent from the land of Dilmun of individuals, personified as the
five Annedoti, who were seen as having brought the art of civilisation
to the earliest peoples of the Fertile Crescent.

That the leader of these amphibious wisdom-bringers was a form
of the god Enki, or Ea, seems to link them directly with the ruling

elite, the astronomer-priests of the earliest neolithic communities of eastern Anatolia. Their starry wisdom, apparently established during the astrological Age of Cancer, would appear to have become embroiled in much later Mesopotamian myth. This astronomical mythology would seem to have included an assortment of clearly aquatic themes and symbols such as the sea-monster Tiamat as the personification of the Gate of the Deep; the starry stream Eridanus as the celestial Euphrates; the turtle as the creature of Cancer; the goat-fish as the earliest form of the constellation of Capricorn; and, of course, Enki himself, who was declared a *kulullu*, a fish-man.

Yet who, or what, exactly was Enki? Was he simply a mythical being, or had he been an actual person – a living god who once inhabited the land of Dilmun as the legends imply?

As previously noted, the Akkadians of northern Iraq revered Enki under the name of Ea, from which we derive the name Oannes. I was therefore intrigued to discover that in the Indo-European language of the Hurrians he was known as A'a.[28] This strange sounding name is composed of two letter As broken by a missing consonant denoted by a character known as an *aleph*. Although this has no direct English translation, it is generally interpreted as a guttural A.

Scholars of Mesopotamian studies would consider that the Hurrians borrowed the myths surrounding Ea from the Akkadians, some time during the third millennium BC. If, however, he was of Upper Euphratean origin, as now seems clear, it is far more plausible that he began his life as a Hurrian god. Regardless of where exactly his myths might have originated, in the name A'a we are now presented with an Indo-European form of Mesopotamia's great civiliser. This is important, for as we know from the Edfu Building Texts, the names given to the leaders of the Shebtiu who 'sailed' away to another primordial world after completing the second period of creation at Wetjeset-Neter are Wa and 'Aa. This second name, which is composed of two letter As prefixed by an *aleph*, is phonetically the same as the Hurrian A'a. Both are pronounced something like *ah-ah*.

Since we have already identified the Shebtiu as one of the primary names of the Elder gods who departed Egypt for the Near East in around 9500 BC, I find it beyond coincidence that one of their two leaders bears exactly the same name as the great wisdom-bringer of Hurrian tradition. Is it possible that their neolithic forebears somehow preserved the name of one of the original Elder gods who arrived in the mythical land of Dilmun following the age of darkness and chaos personified by Tiamat, the dragon of the deep? Do A'a, Ea and Enki derive their root from one of the two leaders of the Shebtiu? Can it be possible that the great deeds of this living god were preserved across millennia? Were they then transformed into the story of how the knowledge of civilisation was passed on to humanity by the amphibious being spoken of so poignantly in the writings of Berossus under the name of Oannes?

This *kulullu*, or fish-man, would appear to have become a symbol of the starry wisdom mastered at astronomically aligned observatories such as the cult building at Nevali Çori on the Upper Euphrates, where the descendants of Egypt's Elder gods would seem to have established their first settlements during the epoch which we define today as the Age of Cancer. Yet A'a, Ea, Enki or Oannes would seem to have been far more than simply a later Mesopotamian memory of the Elders' influence in the Near East, for in my opinion his image is embodied in the minimalistic anthropomorphic form carved on the enormous rectilinear monoliths at Nevali Çori. As I have previously noted, the figure's hands end not in four fingers and a thumb (as is present on other reliefs found at the site, such as the 'dancers' on the limestone water-bowl) but in five fingers of equal length which are, in my opinion, meant to signify the flippers of an amphibious creature.

Just as the five Annedoti appear to be synonymous with the five 'ministers' of Chorzar, the cosmic serpent entrusted with the power of Thalassa, or Tiamat, so the neolithic ruling elite of the Upper Euphrates became the first 'ministers' of the cosmological doctrine that emerged from the dark primeval world that lay beyond the Gate of the Deep, the starry doorway through to the Black Land of Egypt.

It was from these strange beginnings that civilised life arose in the fertile valleys of eastern Anatolia, northern Syria.

THE BIRTH OF SUMER

In the opinion of archaeologists and historians alike, the city-states of Sumer constitute the earliest known civilisation of the Old World. From their very first foundations in the sixth millennium BC, they grew over a period of 3000 years to become the most sophisticated society on earth. As was ably demonstrated by Samuel Noah Kramer in his classic work *History Begins at Sumer*, the number of 'firsts' attributed to the Sumerians is virtually endless. They designed the first coloured pottery. They conducted the first medical operations. They made the first musical instruments. They introduced the first veterinary skills and developed the first written language. They also became highly accomplished engineers, mathematicians, librarians, authors, archivists, judges and priests. Yet despite all this no one is quite sure who the Sumerians were or why they would appear to have evolved so much faster than any other race.

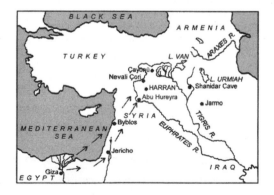

Suggested migrational route of the Egyptian Elder culture, the proposed gods of Eden, following their dispersion into the Near East, *c.* 9500–9000 BC.

There is ample evidence to show that the innovative capabilities of the Sumerians derived from what they inherited from their mountain forebears, such as the ruling elite of the Halaf and Ubaid cultures. It was from these priest-shamans, the descendants perhaps of Egypt's Elder gods, that they gained their knowledge of civilisation.

Completing the cycle is the knowledge that the earliest Sumerians, as well as the pre-Phoenician mariners of Byblos in Lebanon, entered Egypt during predynastic times and helped initiate the Pharaonic age, which began with the institution of the First Dynasty in around 3100 BC.[29] In many respects, this migration to Egypt was like returning to the source – returning to their ancestral homeland. This idea is expressed no better than in the pilgrimages made to the Great Sphinx by the star-worshipping Sabians of Harran during the early second millennium BC, or in the firm belief of the Mandaeans that their most ancient ancestors came originally from Egypt.

The influence of the peoples of Mesopotamia on the first three dynasties of Egyptian history initiated the pyramid age. Here, all the ideas of those who had preserved the seed of the Elder culture, such as the Divine Souls of Heliopolis and the Companions of Re, were finally realised and put into effect. Although they might have been the inheritors of the Elder gods' Egyptian legacy, which seems to have included the art of sonic technology, these individuals were probably only small religious groups who kept alive archaic traditions at cult centres such as Heliopolis in the north and Abydos in the south. Alone they could do very little. They had no real influence over the ruling tribal dynasties and were not in a position to reignite the splendour of their divine ancestors. Yet with the aid of incoming architects, craftsmen, designers, religious leaders, as well as a new ruling elite, they were able to begin the process of continuing the glories of the Elder culture, which had dispersed to various parts of the globe several thousand years beforehand.

Imhotep was the architect of the first ever stone pyramid, built at Saqqara during the Third Dynasty for his king, the mighty Djoser. Its stepped design is very reminiscent of the seven-tiered ziggurat structures of Mesopotamia, while the façades of the temenos walls that surround the pyramid complex are strikingly similar to the design of the exterior walls of cult buildings in Ancient Iraq – the temple of Enki at Eridu being a prime example.

Such comparisons between Mesopotamia and Egypt have long been known to Egyptologists. Yet the greatest significance of this external influence on the architecture of Ancient Egypt is the sheer fact that within just 150 years of Djoser's reign, it had led to the Elder culture's surviving technological capability being combined with local building skills to produce what is arguably the world's greatest architectural achievement, the Great Pyramid. This monument – built to a design based on archaic knowledge preserved by the astronomer-priests of Heliopolis – was the crowning glory, not only of Egypt, but of everything that had been secretly kept alive since the age of the *netjeru*-gods, the epoch of the First Time. The precision science, geometry, orientation, stone cutting, hole drilling and architectural planning of the Great Pyramid was the result of a legacy preserved not simply by the wise old priests of Egypt, but by a number of diverse cultures across the Near East. Their most distant ancestors were the neolithic gods of Eden, whose own forebears had left Egypt for the fertile valleys of eastern Anatolia during the geological and climatic upheavals that had accompanied the end of the last Ice Age. It is to these unique individuals, the living descendants of a divine race with a lifestyle that would seem almost alien today, that we owe the genesis of civilisation.

CHAPTER TWENTY

MILLENNIAL MIDNIGHT

It is now seven o'clock in the morning and the Giza plateau is already hot enough to warm the body and soul, following a chilly morning watching the redness of the sun blotting out the array of stars scattered across the equinoctial horizon. The first tourists are beginning to arrive, marvelling at the sheer immensity of the three great pyramids, many having read and digested popular books that speak openly of the epoch of the First Time, the age of the Elder gods. Our own quest to reveal their ultimate secrets is almost over, yet before we can move on it is important to understand the impact that the knowledge of their existence is having on the world as it enters the next millennium.

When the world's TV cameras are focused on the *mardi gras-*style celebrations in Rio de Janeiro, or joining the great countdown inside the millennial dome at Greenwich, the unofficial focus of attention during the final hours of 1999 will be the Great Pyramid. Tens, perhaps even hundreds of thousands of people will flock to the Giza plateau from all over the globe. Nearly every flight to Cairo is already fully booked, while leading promoters are vying for the opportunity to stage an almighty rock concert next to the Great Pyramid. For some reason this immense wonder of a bygone age has come to express what the world expects as it readies itself for the next 1000 years. But why should this be so? What is so special about the

Great Pyramid, which, as we have seen, so perfectly embodies the power and glory of the ancient world?

It might be argued that ever since the heady hippie era of the 1960s the alternative new-age movement has adopted the Great Pyramid, and the Ancient Egyptian world in general, as a utopic sign of the re emergence of spirituality among a younger generation. It could equally be said that this growing popularity with all things Egyptian comes from reading Bible stories at school that feature the likes of Abraham, Joseph and Moses, or from conjured visions of such romantic figures as Cleopatra, Nefertiti and Tutankhamun. I concur with these suppositions, yet there seems to be something much deeper involved here. No other monument or civilisation anywhere in the ancient world prompts the same kind of emotional response. It is as if the Great Pyramid, and the Giza plateau as a whole, is drawing us instinctively towards it for some kind of grand finale in the greatest show on earth.

Is this grand finale linked in some way with that which stirs *beneath* the Giza plateau? As outlined in Chapter One, very soon the starry canopy will become an exact mirror image of how it would have looked to the Elder gods of Egypt during the time of the Age of Leo, *c.* 10,500 BC – the first time this has happened since that distant epoch. This is perhaps significant, for as we move closer to millennial midnight, and the Age of Aquarius, the veils that conceal our past heritage are being lifted at an ever-increasing rate. Let me give you an example. In medieval times Stonehenge was looked on as a memorial erected by Merlin the Magician in memory of the 480 British leaders and 'men of high rank' treacherously slain by invading Saxons, *c.* AD 450.[1] In the sixteenth and seventeenth centuries this same monument was thought to have been constructed by Druid priests during Roman times, *c.* AD 50.[2] In the mid-nineteenth century it was seen to have been built by one of the lost tribes of Israel, *c.* 1200 BC.[3] Now we know that, like most other megalithic structures scattered across the landscape of Western Europe, it was erected by neolithic peoples, *c.* 2800–2600 BC.[4] This means that in just 800 years we have gradually pushed back the construction date of Stonehenge by more than 3000 years. Carbon-14 testing, thermoluminescence (a method of dating substances exposed to high temperature) and the sequence dating of pottery have all helped us better to define the correct age of archaeological sites and prehistoric monuments such as Stonehenge. Our picture of history is gradually becoming clearer, but it is still only half complete, and further progress is being hampered by the stubborn, and often bombastic, attitude of the academic community.

Take, for instance, the Great Sphinx. It was always thought to date to the reign of the Pharaoh Khafre, *c.* 2550–2525 BC, and yet through a better understanding of its geological erosion and a more open-minded approach to the astronomical and solar alignments connected with the Giza plateau, we can now date it to nearer 9500 BC, and possibly even as early as 10,500 BC.

The only people against the new dating of the Sphinx are old-school Egyptologists and the Egyptian authorities, who refuse simply to even contemplate such far-reaching notions. Their only official response has been to dismiss these revolutionary findings as 'new-age archaeology'.[5] This is itself a strange irony, for I can reveal that several more open-minded Egyptologists are now beginning to accept – in private at least – the well-argued theories of individuals such as Dr Robert Schoch, John Anthony West, Robert Bauval and Graham Hancock.

Adding to the problem are double standards on the part of the Egyptian authorities. The Supreme Council of Antiquities has spoken out vehemently against any notion of an Elder culture having existed in Egypt, and it is strictly opposed to the idea that any kind of 'Hall of Records' is located beneath the Giza plateau. Over the past five years the organisation has effectively put a stop to Schoch's geological survey of the Great Sphinx and the Valley Temple, Thomas Dobecki's and Joseph Schor's seismic soundings within the Sphinx enclosure and Rudolf Gantenbrink's incredible robotics work inside the Queen's Chamber of the Great Pyramid. Licences have been revoked without adequate explanation, and active members of the parties concerned have been told they are no longer welcome on the Giza plateau.

This is a very sad situation indeed. In their defence, the Egyptians are sick and tired of foreigners coming into their country and making major discoveries. They simply do not wish to be upstaged in the same manner as they were in 1922 when Howard Carter, under the patronage of Lord Carnarvon, discovered the greatest treasure ever in modern Egyptian history – the undisturbed tomb of Tutankhamun. There is, however, another good reason for their hatred of 'new-age archaeology'. It is the constant claims, made particularly by followers of Edgar Cayce, that Egypt's most ancient monuments were built not by native Egyptians but by survivors from the lost continent of Atlantis. The authorities' firm stance on unorthodox forms of research and exploration is thus explained in terms of national pride. Giving ground to the 'new-age' archaeologists will, in their opinion, undermine their own academic standing in the Egyptological field. I both respect and understand these sentiments.

STRANGE THINGS AFOOT

It is therefore curious that we should find a high level of apparently unofficial activity taking place on the Giza plateau, which totally contradicts their firm stance on supposed 'new-age archaeology'. For instance, there seems to be something strange afoot inside the Great Pyramid. In mid-1997 explorations began in what is known as Davison's Chamber, a small room situated above the narrow corridor between the Grand Gallery and the King's Chamber. Out of its small hole-like entrance, high above head height, a rope dangled while laid horizontally against the side wall of the passageway was a long ladder. Directly below the opening were stacked burlap bags full of limestone chips, the waste material from some kind of drilling operation. This conclusion was strengthened both by the amount of stone dust that coated the nearby floor and walls and by the presence of a heavy electric cable that climbed the Grand Gallery and was seen to enter the chamber.

The Supreme Council of Antiquities has spoken of these clandestine activities as 'restoration work', even though local guards and Egyptian guides questioned on the subject by my colleague Simon Cox and myself during October 1997 stated that this work was being carried out in complete secrecy during the early hours of the morning.

So what exactly is going on?

We have no satisfactory answers, although very strong rumours abound. New chambers have been found inside the Great Pyramid bearing clear inscriptions, and announcements are to be made soon by the Egyptian authorities. A remote fibre-optic camera has penetrated the concealed chamber discovered by Rudolf Gantenbrink at the end of the southern shaft of the Queen's Chamber. It is now known what it contains, and attempts have been made to reach this concealed room via Davidson's Chamber. These same sources claim that a team has been boring downwards from the base of the subterranean pit deep beneath the Great Pyramid. It is looking for the 'tomb of Imhotep', Ancient Egypt's greatest architect. Why exactly these individuals should believe his last resting-place is below the Great Pyramid seems unclear.

In addition to the clandestine activities inside the Great Pyramid, the bedrock in the vicinity of the Sphinx's right paw has once again been the focus of deep-scan seismic soundings, conducted on this occasion by faceless individuals. The only official explanation given by the Egyptian authorities is that this well-equipped team is – similar to 1996 – monitoring the enclosure floor for safety reasons. Rumours also abound as to who exactly is behind these continued explorations.

It can be no coincidence that the right paw of the Sphinx was singled out by American psychic Edgar Cayce as the most likely location of the entrance tunnel leading down to the hidden Hall of Records. It takes little imagination to realise that these individuals are searching for that elusive entrance. At the same time they are attempting to validate the earlier findings of Joseph Schor and his colleagues from the Schor Foundation and the University of Florida, who in 1996 used similar ground-scan equipment to locate nine previously unknown chambers beneath the Sphinx enclosure.

The gradual build-up of activity on the Giza plateau is not without good reason, for Edgar Cayce also predicted that the Hall of Records would be found specifically in 1998.[6] Many scholars of Egyptology are justifiably sceptical of his much-celebrated prophecies; however, whether or not his so-called 'psychic' readings are real in the true sense of the word is now irrelevant. The sheer fact that they were meticulously recorded and preserved by his followers has meant that they stand today as predictions with the same potency as any prophecy left to the world by the likes of Nostradamus, the Brahan Seer or Old Mother Shipton, as may be seen from the following account.

ENTER OPERATION HERMES

On 10 August 1997 *The Sunday Times* carried a remarkable story concerning the intended explorations in Egypt of a scientific team going under the name of Operation Hermes. In a very serious and sober manner, the article claimed that project director Nigel Appleby, by profession an engineering designer and art publisher, along with his colleague Adam Child, had discovered the exact whereabouts of what they believed was the 'Hall of Records'. This they had achieved by using a combination of clues gleaned both from examining ancient religious texts, such as the Egyptian Book of the Dead, and by defining the position of the dog-star Sirius, or Sothis, as it would have appeared in relation to the stars of Orion when superimposed on the landscape around Giza. These calculations had apparently brought to light a location 'eight miles [thirteen kilometres] north of the Sphinx'.[7] The article claimed that Appleby was now to head a party of 18 people, including geophysicists, who would survey the site and then submit a report to the Egyptian authorities, pending a full excavation at some later date.

On first learning of these incredible claims, I was inevitably sceptical, especially when, after having spoken to my colleague Graham Hancock, he confirmed that neither he nor his writing partner Robert Bauval had any knowledge whatsoever of Nigel Appleby or his extraordinary revelations. This appeared strange as Appleby seemed to be employing certain themes familiar from Bauval's 1994 book *The Orion Mystery*. They included the idea that the pyramids of Giza reflected the positions of the three stars of Orion's belt as they would have appeared in the skies above Egypt in around 10,500 BC.

Having just completed an in-depth study of various Egyptian religious texts, including the Book of the Dead, I had detected nothing whatsoever which might have suggested that the Under-world of the Soul was located thirteen kilometres (eight miles) away from the pyramid field. Indeed, there was every reason to suggest that it lay at the end of a long passageway or corridor accessed via a concealed stairwell and antechamber, located somewhere to the east of the Sphinx monument and Valley Temple.

The matter-of-fact tone of the *Sunday Times* article was almost unbelievable. The half-page piece spoke of a hidden chamber shaped like a pyramid which lay some nine metres beneath the shifting desert sands. It was apparently 'made of granite and sheathed in gold'.[8] Inside it would be found an ark-like box containing 'documents on the history of mankind which "will herald a new dawn for civilisa-tion" '.[9]

Accompanying the story was a three-dimensional illustration produced by computer graphics. It showed a cutaway section of the underground complex, which consisted of a central 'hall' surrounded by what seemed to be a ring of 12 circular-shaped outer chambers. This was, of course, the exact conclusion I had drawn in respect to the Underworld of the Soul referred to in the Edfu Building Texts. I was therefore intrigued to learn more of Appleby's claimed discover-ies, as well as his plans for the future.

I was fortunate enough to be able to speak at length with Nigel Appleby inside a week of the story's appearance, and at a time when he was still being inundated by a barrage of telephone calls from virtually every major newspaper in the world. My research assistant Simon Cox, who had spoken to Appleby in advance of myself, was suitably impressed by his genuine sincerity and urged me to speak to him. When I finally did so, we shared our own respective theories regarding the nature of what might popularly be referred to as the Hall of Records (although I find this title truly inappropriate).

It transpires that Nigel Appleby and his colleagues, who come across as respectable businessmen, have been working on the Operation Hermes project since 1983. Appleby was first drawn into this arena through studying the science of sacred geometry – the design and arrangement of ancient places and religious structures in accordance with the principles of divine or cosmic order. He believed that the source of this sacred canon of numbers – which is derived from precessional information and the recurring theme of 12 circles around a thirteenth one – had originated in Ancient Egypt. Thereafter he became convinced that somewhere in the vicinity of Giza was an underground complex that reflected these hidden mathematical principles, and so he set about finding it. It was this determination and drive that had eventually led him to the site he intends to survey in July 1998.

Appleby has been able to gain so much support for his theories because he is a no-nonsense, level-headed individual who believes very strongly in his findings. Operation Hermes' carefully worded web-site on the Internet has attracted not only a number of interested parties but also enough money to finance the activities of its 18-strong team. Through the influence of one colleague, Appleby has even been able to obtain the support of the British army. The barracks in his home town of Colchester have allowed the project's four-wheel-drive vehicles to be housed on the premises, while seven 'off-duty' members of Her Majesty's Armed Forces will accompany the team out to Egypt.

I questioned Appleby about his belief that the hidden chambers would be found not, as most people seemed to believe, beneath the Giza plateau but thirteen kilometres (eight miles) north of here. According to his reckoning the *true* entrance into the underground complex is in the vicinity of the Great Sphinx. Yet in his opinion it is now totally inaccessible. To reach the Hall of Records today, he believes that we must trace the direction of its long passageway and then enter the chambers from directly above; there may even be a second entrance. Incredibly, he has concluded that they are located thirteen kilometres away, at his proposed site of excavation.

How exactly he came to these conclusions will be revealed in due course, but what seems immediately more important is that he is attempting to fulfil Cayce's well-known prophecy. When America's so-called 'sleeping prophet' casually stated that 1998 would mark the year when the Hall of Records would be entered by three chosen 'keepers',[10] he created an important nexus point that now absorbs almost all of the time, money and effort being ploughed into excavations on the Giza plateau.

Against all the odds, Nigel Appleby and his Operation Hermes have managed to convince the Egyptian authorities that something that previously existed only in myth and legend is now awaiting discovery beneath the Sahara sands. He must be applauded and wished every success in this venture. Whether or not his findings really will reveal the true location of the Hall of Records remains to be seen. Yet whatever the outcome, Operation Hermes has set a precedent for an entirely new field of exploration in Egypt.

THE ANTEDILUVIAN WORLD

Nigel Appleby is not just after the *Egyptian* Hall of Records; he is convinced that others await discovery elsewhere in the world. Cayce believed that, in addition to the one in Egypt, two others would be found – one in Tibet,[11] or possibly Poseidia (i.e. Bimini or the Bahamas; see below),[12] and the other 'in the Aryan or Yucatán land',[13] a reference to the country of the Maya in Mexico. In contrast, Appleby feels that, whereas there *is* one in Tibet, the other is located on the border between Bolivia and Brazil. Here we find ourselves in the uneasy realms of personal opinion and complete speculation. Yet as I have attempted to demonstrate in respect to Cayce's prophecy concerning the discovery of the Egyptian Hall of Records, the power of prediction goes beyond what might be seen as basic logic.

The idea is gaining momentum that, in the wake of its demise in around 9500 BC, the remnants of Egypt's Elder culture moved into new territories and forged links with other high cultures that existed at this time. We have already spoken about the probable incursions by these people into the Near East, where they were almost certainly responsible for the initiation of the neolithic age. There is, however, much more, for one modern-day British psychic named Bernard G., who has consistently made accurate predictions in respect to the Elder culture,[14] tells us that just prior to the climatic changes that overtook Egypt towards the end of the last Ice Age, many of the remaining Elders entered the Chambers of First Creation and removed the 12 hand-held crystals (i.e. the *iht*-relics of the Edfu documents). All but one of these were then taken to suitable locations in foreign lands where they would be safe from the impending cataclysms. We are told that one site was situated near Mount Athos in Greece, another was close to Erciyas Dağ, a snow-capped mountain in eastern Turkey, while a third was secreted inside an isolated cave on a tributary of the Amazon river in the Marañón region of northern Peru. As early as 1986 this same psychic also predicted that evidence of the Elder culture would be found in such far-flung places as Australia, China, Chile, Mexico, India, Japan, Tanzania, France and the United Kingdom.

At this stage it would be madness even to pass comment on individual predictions and claims, although I feel it is necessary to keep an open mind in respect to such matters. What seems much more important is the implication that what was happening in Egypt and the Near East during the eleventh and tenth millennia

BC was not isolated, and that other, similar high cultures also existed at this time. Like their counterparts in Egypt, they too may have been forced to abandon their homeland and move to pastures new at the onset of the catastrophic events that ended the last Ice Age. Sceptics would say that there is simply no evidence for any such cultures, but if we look hard enough it can be found all around the world. We have already referred to the mysterious city of Tiahuanaco on the Bolivian Altiplano. In 1911 Professor Arthur Posnansky of La Paz University dated the eastern entrance gateway of the Kalasasaya temple palace to 15,000 BC.[15] These calculations, which were based on minor alterations in the positions that the sun rises and falls in accordance with the slow rocking motion of the earth,[16] have recently been confirmed by archaeologist Neil Steede, who estimated, however, that the date is more likely to be around 10,000 BC.[17] In spite of this alteration based on more modern forms of calculation, this still makes Tiahuanaco the oldest city in the world.

RISING FROM THE DEEP

As we race towards millennial midnight the earth appears to be giving up even more of its age-old secrets. In 1968 an underwater archaeologist and zoologist at the University of Miami named J. Manson Valentine felt he had identified a man-made structure in shallow waters off the north-western coast of Bimini, a tiny Bahaman island located some 95 kilometres (60 miles) east of Miami, Florida. It consisted of two parallel rows of enormous close-fitting stones that ran for a distance of 579 metres before making an abrupt U-turn and finally disappearing beneath the sand. Some of the blocks were found to rest on tiny cornerstones, or plugs (a number composed of granite),[18] very much like the megalithic dolmens of Western Europe and New England. Others would appear to have been drilled, or bored, through their widths, like something out of the Egyptian pyramid age.[19] One example examined and brought to the surface by geologist Richard Wingate bore a deep hole that was not circular but clearly *star-shaped* – a feat that begs the question of how exactly this was achieved using conventional drilling methods.[20]

The J-shaped site, which was christened the Bimini Road, was investigated for several consecutive years during the 1970s by a research team headed by ancient mysteries writer David Zink.[21] Although both Valentine and Zink became convinced that the stone road was man made, and even discovered other, similar structures in the waters off Bimini, oceanographic archaeologists and geologists have repeatedly dismissed all such claims as simply natural formations of beach-rock.[22]

Since the 1970s many more examples of inexplicable large stones, as well as wall-like structures and even underwater 'mounds', have been detected in the shallow waters of the Bahamas Great Bank, which stretches between Bimini and the islands of the Bahamas.[23] Never has the archaeological community taken even the slightest interest in these strange underwater anomalies. Their reason is plain: because such structures do not fit into the accepted chronology of American prehistory they cannot be man-made. Other, more blatant human artefacts, such as column stems or jointed stones, are explained away either as the cargo of shipwrecks or as objects lost, thrown or dropped overboard by passing seagoing vessels over the past 500 years.

Such was the situation on 21 June 1997, when a curious e-mail began to circulate among press agencies in the United States. It claimed that irrefutable evidence of antediluvian 'temples' had been discovered off the coast of Bimini. All would be revealed at a press conference to be organised by one Aaron Duval, the president of a local 'Egyptological Society' and the author of the e-mail, at the Miami Museum of Science on 25 July.

In subsequent 'releases' to the same sources dispatched between 6 and 15 July, tantalising details of the alleged discoveries were outlined by Duval. The 'Ancient Bimini Temples' were said to be constructed of huge blocks of stone, each around 1.8 metres in thickness and ranging in length from 2.7 to 3.6 metres[24] – 'cyclopean' by any standards. These came in three different colours – red, white and black – bringing to mind the multicoloured walls that Plato, the Greek philosopher of the fourth century BC, spoke of in his classic account of the lost city of Atlantis.[25] Even further linking the Bimini 'temples' with Atlantis was Duval's statement that the 'walls' were coated in three different types of metal – later revealed as brass, copper and iron.[26] Plato had also claimed that the walls of the lost city were coated in three different metals – brass, tin and an unknown substance called orichalcum, which was said to have 'flashed' with a 'red light'.[27]

More peculiarly, Duval linked the alleged site with Ancient Egypt. He claimed, for instance, that 'casing stones', like those that originally covered the Great Pyramid, had been found at the site.[28] Furthermore, he spoke of the presence of 'bore-holes', similar to examples present in the bedrock beside some of the unfinished obelisks and stone blocks to be seen in the famous granite quarries at Aswan.

Duval called off his press conference at the last minute. Despite this, Simon Cox and I still travelled to Miami and were able to meet him in our hotel foyer. After some polite conversation we got down to business, and yet in the three hours we spent in his company he revealed next to nothing about the so-called Scott Stones, named after the site's alleged discoverer. This was despite our clear enthusiasm for his apparent discoveries.

Instead, Duval spoke much about Edgar Cayce. In 1940 the American 'sleeping prophet' predicted that part of 'Poseidia will be among the first portions of Atlantis to rise again. Expect it in '68 or '69.'[29] Incredibly, he had gone on to state that: 'A portion of the [Atlantean] temple may yet be discovered under the slime of ages of seawater – near what is known as Bimini, off the coast of Florida.'[30] J. Manson Valentine had been completely unaware of this prophecy when he first discovered the Bimini Road in 1968,[31] a fact that had placed Cayce in high esteem among Atlantologists even before his Egyptian predictions started to take a grip on reality. It has also ensured that the Edgar Cayce Foundation has continued to take an active interest in the shallow waters off Bimini and the Bahamas right down to the present day.[32]

Once it became clear that Duval had no intention whatsoever of giving anything away, the meeting was finally closed. We had shown him pictures and ground-plans of Nevali Çori in eastern Anatolia, and yet he had given us nothing in return. We later learned that the most probable reason behind Duval's reticence to reveal any information was that he had been urged to call off the press conference by a British publicist and literary agent, who had already offered him a seven-figure advance for a book contract with a major international publisher.

Unfortunately, no one is going to know the real truth behind Duval's wild claims for some time to come, for the book contract depends entirely on total exclusivity. Only after the supposed discovery of the Scott Stones has been serialised in major newspapers around the world, immediately prior to the publication of the first of two books to be written by Duval, will the world learn any more about this matter. We feel it is a tragedy that big money has been so easily able to silence Duval, and in doing so has effectively halted the progress of knowledge.

Even if it is found that Duval has nothing new to offer the archaeological community, there are still major discoveries to be made beneath the shallow waters of the Bahamas Great Bank. After his death in 1994, it was found that J. Manson Valentine had left for posterity a detailed catalogue of no fewer than *sixty-five* proposed archaeological sites, all of them in the vicinity of either Bimini or the more northerly Bahaman islands.[33] Should these prove to be as ancient as many now believe, then it is clear that Egypt's high culture of *c.* 10,500–9500 BC was not alone in the world and is simply one small piece of a much larger jigsaw.

Tiahuanaco, Bimini and a number of other world-wide sites have all produced positive evidence of cyclopean building structures. In my opinion, this hints strongly at the fact that there are pages missing from our understanding of what exactly was going on during the primordial age. Yet only when we truly know what we are looking for will these pages be restored to their rightful place. I am convinced that the cult building and carvings found at Nevali Çori show clear similarities with both the art and architecture of Tiahuanaco because both cultures were somehow influenced by a common source with clear maritime capabilities.

Is it really possible that South America, Bimini, Egypt, Peru, the Near East and, presumably, other areas as well were all touched by an even greater culture of global proportions that thrived at the same time as these disparate colonies? Were they all somehow linked through trade and mutual cooperation? Only by bringing into perspective the various strands of evidence can we determine exactly what was happening around the world during this distant epoch. Let this be the cornerstone of our quest for knowledge as humanity steps boldly into the new millennium here on the Giza plateau, with the Great Sphinx to our right, and the Great Pyramid standing proudly before us, not as a symbol of our past glories but as a vision of our future destiny.

POSTSCRIPT

Research continues into the origins and lost history of the Egyptian Elder culture and their effects on the genesis of civilisation. Many talented writers, researchers and specialists in their own particular fields of expertise are now coming together in an attempt to take on the orthodox academic community and demonstrate the existence of advanced high culture in prehistoric and primordial times.

Gods of Eden is one of the new genre of scholarly books that are now challenging our accepted views of the past. If, through reading the book, it has inspired you to begin your own investigations into this area of study, or if it simply makes you question our current understanding of human evolution and world history, then it has achieved its aims.

If you wish to take these matters further, then I suggest you review the list of books, articles and papers given in the Bibliography. Almost all of the titles are available through the library Interloan service. Ask your local librarian for details.

Should you feel that you can add to our understanding regarding any of the topics dealt with in this book, and/or you wish to be kept informed of future publications, conferences and developments, both in this field and in the author's own ongoing research, then please write to me, Andrew Collins, at PO Box 189, Leigh-on-Sea, Essex SS9 1NF.

NOTES AND REFERENCES

Chapter One
ECHOES OF ELDER GODS

1. All dynastic dates cited in this book have been taken from the king-list given in 'Manetho, the King-lists, and the Monuments', included as an appendix in Gardiner, *Egypt of the Pharaohs*, pp. 419–53.
2. West, *Serpent in the Sky*, p. 207.
3. Dr Robert Schoch holds a PhD in geology and geophysics, attained at Yale University, and is a specialist in the effects of weather erosion on rocks.
4. Schoch; West (on behalf of Schoch), 'John West has his say on the Sphinx-age Controversy'.
5. Modern astronomers have been able to ascertain that the true period of the present precessional cycle is in fact 25,773 years, meaning that it takes each sign 2148 years to cross the equinoctial line and 71.6 years to move one degree of a cycle. However, to save confusion I have decided to remain with the ancient calculations.
6. All calculations are based on the Skyglobe 3.6 computer program.
7. West, *The Traveller's Key to Ancient Egypt*, p. 70.
8. Hartner; Santillana and von Dechend, pp. 124–5.
9. Sellers, pp. 194–215, 224; Bauval and Hancock, *Keeper of Genesis*, pp. 154–5, 194–5.
10. Schwaller de Lubicz, p. 86.
11. Fix, p. 108.
12. Infinitely more curious, however, is Herodotus' note to the effect that: 'during this time they affirm that the sun has twice risen in parts different from what is his customary place, that is to say, has twice risen where he now sets, and has also twice set where he now rises'. See Herodotus, 'Canon of the Kings of Egypt', in Cory, p. 171.

    The implications of these words, if true, are quite staggering, for the statement about the sun twice rising where it now sets, and twice setting where it now rises, can only be a reference to the transit of the stellar background as it makes a 360-degree revolution of the firmament during the precessional cycle of 25,920 years. Herodotus was therefore implying that one and a half precessional cycles, in other words *38,880 years*, had elapsed since the foundation of Ancient Egypt.

    Pomponius Mela, a Spanish cartographer of the first century AD, quotes a period of 13,000 years during which time 330 kings ruled Egypt. See ibid., p. 177. He repeats Herodutus' curious claim about the sun twice setting where it now rises, adding that 'the Egyptians, according to their own accounts, are the most ancient of men', and that 'since the commencement of the Egyptian race, the stars have completed four revolutions'. This last statement is truly bizarre, as it implies the completion of no fewer than *four* precessional cycles – a period of 103,680 years! See ibid.

13. Rundle Clark, pp. 263–4.
14. See Bauval and Hancock, *Keeper of Genesis.*
15. Chadwick, p. 76.
16. Ibid., pp. 76–7.
17. For instance, at four sites supporting late palaeolithic communities along the Upper Nile, clear evidence has been unearthed to suggest that between 12,500 and 9500 BC selected groups grew their own cereal crops. Stone sickle blades were used to reap, while grinding stones were employed to extract the maximum amount of grain. Not only did these so-called Isnan and Qadan communities possess a primitive form of agriculture, but they would also appear to have mastered animal husbandry and possessed a highly advanced microblade industry. See Hoffman, pp. 85–90; Butzer, p. 7. See also Chapter Fifteen.
18. Bar-Yosef, p. 157.
19. Hawass, 'The Pyramids and Temples of Egypt: An Update', pp. 122–4, in Petrie, *The Pyramids and Temples of Gizeh*, 1990.
20. Ibid., p. 126.
21. Mariette said that the Temple of the Sphinx, i.e. the Valley Temple, was 'the most ancient known sepulchre in the world'. See Bonwick, p. 109.
22. Fix, p. 40.
23. Naville, *The Times*, cf. Hancock, p. 406.
24. Naville, 'Excavations at Abydos', cf. Corliss, p. 325.
25. Hancock, pp. 404–5
26. Tompkins, p. 1; weight of the Great Pyramid: Fix, p. 12.
27. Tompkins, p. 1.
28. Based on the measurements of the Great Pyramid as given in Cole.
29. See Stecchini, in Tompkins, pp. 287–382.
30. Fix, p. 24. Pythagoras believed that the measures of antiquity were derived from Egyptian standards. It therefore seemed logical to assume that the Great Pyramid embodied the dimensions of the earth. See Tompkins, p. 22.
31. See Stecchini, in Tompkins, pp. 287–382.
32. Fix calculated that from the base of the Great Pyramid's 21½-inch-thick foundation platform to the tip of its apex is 482.75751 feet (147.14479 metres). This figure multiplied by 43,200 is 3949.834 miles, or

6356.6549 kilometres, just 0.0741 miles or 0.1191 kilometres short of the polar radius of the earth, or the distance from the centre of the earth to the North Pole. See *Pyramid Odyssey*, pp. 30–1.

33. Based on calculations made by Rodney Hale and his son Robert, using the dimensions and tolerances quoted by Cole, and Petrie in *The Pyramids and Temples of Gizeh*, and applying the Monte Carlo statistical system. According to a report prepared by Rodney Hale dated 26 February 1997: 'This involves repeatedly calculating the value of perimeter/2 × height, each time using a random selection of possible measurements, all of which, of course, do not exceed the extreme limits pertaining to each measurement.' In his final opinion, 'therefore we can again say from the measurements provided, an accurate value of *pi could* have been used by the Great Pyramid builders. There is no case to say that the builders knew only of the approximation of *pi*, namely 22/7.' See Hale, 'Notes on the Dimensions of the Great Pyramid, Giza', and Hale, 'Further Notes on the Dimensions of the Great Pyramid, Giza'. Copies available from the author on request.

34. Tompkins, p. xiv.

35. Smyth, pl. II and pp. 66–7.

36. Tompkins, pp. 101, 103.

37. Ibid., p. 48.

38. Stecchini, in Tompkins, p. 324.

39. The Greek historian Herodotus cited the builder of the Great Pyramid as Cheops, the Greek name for Khufu, who took the throne in around 2596 BC and ruled for 23 years, according to the Palermo list. There was no evidence of this attribution until 1837–8 when Col. R.W. Howard Vyse (1784–1853) and J.S. Perring (1813–69) broke through into the pyramid's uppermost relieving chamber and apparently discovered crudely painted masons' marks which included variations of the royal name Khufu. Due to clear errors in the use of hieroglyphs featured in these inscriptions, many pyramid researchers have questioned their authenticity. In my opinion, the meticulous recording of the work undertaken by these men, particularly Perring, and found in Vyse's three-volume work makes this theory a complete non-starter. For a full account of this controversy, see Jochmans, pp. 194–5.

40. Rutherford, Vol. 1, p. 35; Mas'ūdi, quoted as an appendix in Vyse, Vol. 2, pp. 324–5. Extracted with thanks from the British Library copy by Gareth Medway.

41. Haigh. See also 'Mysteries of the Sphinx', NBC-TV; Bauval and Hancock, *Hieroglyph – the Bauval & Hancock Newsletter*.

42. Ammianus Marcellinus, xxii, 15, 30.

43. I refer to the sun's yearly course through the constellations as viewed at the time of the equinoxes and solstices.

Chapter Two
APING THE ANCIENTS

1. Lehner, 'The Pyramid', in *Secrets of Lost Empires*, p. 62.
2. Ibid., p. 93.
3. For weights of blocks used in the construction of the Valley Temple, see Fix, p. 40; Murray, p. 20; 'Mysteries of the Sphinx', NBC-TV.
4. For sizes of blocks used in the Valley Temple, see Hancock, p. 341; West, *Serpent in the Sky*, p. 223, 'Mysteries of the Sphinx', NBC TV.
5. Emery, pp. 176–7.
6. Details of current crane loads were supplied by Liebherr of Welham Green, Hertfordshire.
7. Three blocks used in the construction of the Roman temple complex at Baalbek in Lebanon, and known collectively as the Trilithon, each weigh an estimated 1000 tonnes apiece, while a fourth block still remaining in a nearby quarry is thought to be as much as 1200 tonnes in weight. See Ragette, pp. 33, 114. In India, the roof of the famous Black Pagoda was said to have been carved out of a single piece of rock weighing approximately 1000 tonnes.
8. Lehner, 'The Pyramid', in *Secrets of Lost Empires*, pp. 74–6.
9. See Page, 'Stonehenge', in *Secrets of Lost Empires*, pp. 38–40.
10. Lehner, 'The Pyramid', in *Secrets of Lost Empires*, p. 77.
11. During the 1950s Professor Richard Atkinson, a leading authority on Stonehenge, made similar calculations in respect to the transport of its famous sarsen stones to their present site on Salisbury Plain. He concluded that it would have required a workforce of 1100 men to haul a 50-tonne block over flat land. See Atkinson, pp. 120–1. Using Atkinson's calculations, it would therefore have required 4400 people to haul a 200-tonne block over level ground – just 400 more than the figure I suggested using Lehner's estimates for moving a 1-tonne stone block up a gradual incline.
12. Ragette, pp. 118–19.

Chapter Three
THE OLD COPT'S TALE

1. Watterson, p. ix.
2. Ibid., p. 22.
3. Ibid., p. 24.
4. Ibid., p. 123.
5. Nicholson, p. 352.
6. Ibid.

7. Mas'ūdi, Vol. 2, sections 787–803, pp. 372–98.
8. Mas'ūdi, quoted as an appendix in Vyse, Vol. 2, p. 322.
9. Ibid.
10. Ibid., p. 323.
11. Ibid., p. 232 n. 9.
12. Ibid., p. 324.
13. Ibid., pp. 324–5.
14. Ibid., pp. 321–2; Bonwick, pp. 117–19.
15. See Chapter 23 of Collins, *From the Ashes of Angels*.
16. Vyse, Vol. 2, p. 332.
17. A 20-minute period prior to sunrise was used for the purpose of predicting the heliacal rising of Regulus at the time of the vernal equinox in the tenth millennium BC.
18. For information on the great pavements that once surrounded the Giza pyramids, as well as their probable role in the pyramids' use as an almanac, see Tompkins, pp. 121–6, and West, *The Traveller's Guide to Ancient Egypt*, pp. 92–4, both cf. the work of Moses B. Cotsworth (1859–1943).
19. Mas'ūdi, quoted as an appendix in Vyse, Vol. 2, p. 325.
20. Tompkins, pp. 47, 106, cf. the work of seventeenth-century scientist Isaac Newton.
21. Nicholson, p. 353.
22. Ibid., p. 353 n. 3.
23. Besant, pp. 111–12.
24. Sinnett, p. 16.
25. Ibid., p. 23.
26. Owen, pp. 66–7.
27. Leslie and Adamski, p. 174.
28. Often these writers, or their translators, have introduced even further confusion in respect to Walter Owen's fictitious 'priests of On' quotation. For instance, Louis Pauwels and Jacques Bergier in the first English edition of their best-selling work *The Morning of the Magicians*, published in 1963, refer to the 'priests of On' raising stones 'by means of sound' instead of 'by means of magical words'. See p. 123.

Worse still was Andrew Tomas in his highly entertaining book *We Are Not the First*, first published in the UK during 1971. By somehow misreading 'On' for 'Babylon', he transforms Owen's original quotation into: 'by means of sounds the priests of *ancient Babylon* were able to raise into the air heavy rocks which a thousand men could not have lifted [author's italics]'! See p. 128. This fundamental error by Tomas was inadvertently picked up and copied by later authors such as Robert Scrutton in his 1978 book *Secrets of Lost Atland* – see pp. 111–12 – and by Roy Norvill in his 1979 work *Giants – The Vanished Race of*

Mighty Men. In this last instance the author manages to elevate Tomas' own distortion of the facts into: 'Babylonian clay tablets exist which tell of stones being lifted by sound.' See p. 143.

Lastly, in Warren Smith's *The Secret Forces of the Pyramids*, first published in 1977, the author not only manages to twist Walter Owen's original 'priests of On' quotation by altering 'by means of magic words' to 'by means of magic wands', but goes on to blindly copy Tomas' corruption by stating that 'Records from ancient Babylon also tell of sound being used to lift stones', thus supposing that the two quotations support each other! See pp. 149–50.

All this goes to show the extreme caution that must be taken when scanning through modern-day books about ancient mysteries looking for new lines of enquiry or confirmation of personal theories. I feel there is a lesson to be learned here somewhere.

I would like to thank London researcher Gareth Medway for his invaluable help in tracking down the original source behind the infamous 'priests of On' quotation. I would also like to thank Amber McCauley for reading the original 1874 French edition of François Lenormant's *La Magie Chez les Chaldeens* in search of that non-existent reference.

Chapter Four
PRECISION IMPOSSIBLE

1. Deuel, p. 54.
2. Petrie, *Ten Years' Digging in Egypt, 1881–1891*, p. 15.
3. Ibid., p. 19.
4. Tompkins, p. 101.
5. Ibid., p. 22.
6. Deuel, p. 56.
7. Petrie, *Ten Years' Digging in Egypt, 1881–1891*, p. 22.
8. Petrie, *The Pyramids and Temples of Gizeh*, p. 93.
9. Tompkins, p. 101.
10. Wilson, Colin, p. 36.
11. Petrie, *Ten Years' Digging in Egypt, 1881–1891*, p. 19.
12. Ibid.
13. Ibid., pp. 20–1.
14. Ibid., p. 21.
15. Emery, p. 39.
16. Ibid., p. 40.
17. Schwaller de Lubicz, p. 86.
18. Emery goes on to say: 'The racial origin of these invaders is not known

and the route they took in their penetration of Egypt is equally obscure.' See *Archaic Egypt*, p. 40. He then compares the unique architecture of this culture with that of ancient Mesopotamia, hinting at a common origin for both civilisations. He refers to this hypothetical link culture as the 'third party', although I prefer the term 'Third Force'.

Emery, I feel, confuses two separate influences, firstly a race indigenous to Egypt since the fragmentation of the Sphinx-building Elder culture, *c.* 9500 BC, and, secondly, an apparent Third Force which would appear to have entered Egypt *c.* 3500 BC and revitalised its ancient culture and religion and reaffirmed certain dynastic alliances. Who exactly this Third Force might have been is undecided, although in my opinion it seems likely to have been the pre-Phoenician Byblos culture of Lebanon, which reached its height between *c.* 4000 and 3000 BC and undoubtedly influenced the foundations of Ancient Sumer, *c.* 3000 BC. See Collins, 'Baalbek: Lebanon's Sacred Fortress'.

There is also new evidence to suggest that the 'Eastern invaders' could have been Akkadians and Sumerians entering Egypt via the Red Sea. Thousands of examples of graffiti found in the eastern desert show seagoing vessels with high prows, like those discovered in boat burials at Giza and Abydos, containing literally dozens of oarsmen. Most of this graffiti is considered to be predynastic in origin, and may well record the arrival of a foreign culture with maritime capabilities. Researcher and orientalist Simon Cox, who has made an extensive study of the whole question of 'Eastern invaders', believes they show incoming Mesopotamian vessels, some even being towed by their oarsmen through the desert wadis, which would have been much wetter in past ages. See Cox and Pegg.

19. Petrie, *The Pyramids and Temples of Egypt*, p. 13.
20. Ibid.
21. Ibid.
22. Ibid., p. 76.
23. Ibid., p. 29.
24. Ibid., p. 74.
25. Ibid., p. 75.
26. Ibid., p. 76.
27. Ibid., p. 77.
28. Petrie, *Ten Years' Digging in Egypt, 1881–1891*, p. 28.
29. Ibid.
30. Petrie, *The Pyramids and Temples of Gizeh*, p. 76.
31. Ibid.
32. Ibid., p. 77.
33. Wilson, Colin, p. 36.

34. Ibid.
35. Adams, Barbara, p. 33.
36. Lehner, 'The Pyramid', in *Secrets of Lost Empires*, p. 73.
37. See Petrie, *The Pyramids and Temples of Gizeh*, p. 74, for his views on the use of abrasive slurries in association with sawing, and p. 75, where he states: 'That the blades of the saws were of bronze, we know from the green staining on the sides of saw cuts, and on grains of sand left in a saw cut.'
38. Stocks, p. 698.
39. Petrie, *The Pyramids and Temples of Gizeh*, p. 78.
40. Dunn, 'Advanced Machining in Ancient Egypt'.
41. Dunn, 'Hi-Tech Pharaohs?'.
42. Petrie, *The Pyramids and Temples of Gizeh*, p. 76.
43. Ibid., p. 75.
44. Ibid.
45. Ibid.
46. Ibid., p. 78. The facsimile of the 1885 edition used in this current work actually reads: 'On the granite core, No. 7, the spiral of the cut sinks *1 inch* [instead of .100 inch] in the circumference of 6 inches, or 1 in 60, a rate of ploughing out of the quartz and felspar which is astonishing.' This alteration to the measurement seems to have been merely a typographical error on the part of the publishers and has been corrected in the text so as not to confuse readers.
47. Dunn, 'Hi-Tech Pharaohs?', December 1995, p. 42. This gives the figures in imperial units.
48. Ibid.
49. Ibid.
50. Dunn, 'Hi-Tech Pharaohs?', January 1996, p. 38.
51. Ibid.

Chapter Five
TO THE SOUND OF A TRUMPET

1. Bellamy, pp. 72–4.
2. Delair and Oppé.
3. Posnansky, Vol. 2, pp. 87–92. See also Bellamy.
4. These scholars were Dr Hans Ludendorff, the director of the Astronomical Observatory of Potsdam, and three astronomers: Professor Dr Arnold Kohlschütter of the University of Bonn, Dr Rolf Müller of the Astrophysical Institute of Potsdam and Dr Friedrich Becker of the Specula Vaticana. See Posnansky, Vol. 2, p. 47.
5. *The Times, Past Worlds: Atlas of Archaeology*, p. 212.

6. Spence, pp. 306–7.
7. Osborne, *Indians of the Andes: Aymaras and Quechuas*, p. 64; Time-Life Books, *Feats and Wisdom of the Ancients*, p. 55.
8. Hancock, p. 47, quoting Francisco de Avila, 'A Narrative of the Errors, False Gods, and Other Superstitions and Diabolical Rites in Which the Indians of the Province of Huarochiri Lived in Ancient Times', in *Narratives of the Rites and Laws of the Yncas* (trans. and ed. Clemens R. Markhem), Hakluyt Society, London, 1873, Vol. XLVIII, p. 124.
9. Osborne, *South American Mythology*, pp. 68–9, 72, 74, 78, 87; Hemming, p. 97.
10. Osborne, *South American Mythology*, pp. 74, 87.
11. Ibid., p. 76.
12. Coe, p. 275.
13. Fisher, p. 503.
14. Bierhorst, p. 8.
15. Thompson, *Maya History and Religion*, p. 340.
16. Ibid., pp. 340–1.
17. Lemprière, s.v. 'Cadmus', p. 114.
18. Horace, *Odes and Epodes*, iii, ode xi, ll. 1–4; Horace, *The Ars Poetica*, ll. 394–6; Statius, *Thebaid*, i, ll. 9–11; Propertius, *Elegies*, ix, ll. 9–10; Apollodorus, *The Library*, iii, verse 5.
19. Pausanias, *Description of Greece: Boeotia*, v. 7–8.
20. Apollonius Rhodius, *The Argonautica*, i. 735–41.
21. Lemprière, s.v. 'Cadmus', p. 114.
22. Sanchoniatho wrote in his native language, taking his information mostly from city archives and temple records. In all, he compiled nine books, which were translated into Greek by Philo, a native of Byblos on the Levant coast, who lived during the reign of the emperor Hadrian, who reigned AD 117–38. Fragments of his translation were fortunately preserved by an early Christian writer named Eusebius (AD 264–340). See Cory, p. viii.
23. Sanchoniatho, in Cory, pp. 8–14.
24. Ibid., p. 14; Ward, p. 20.
25. Ibid., p. 10.
26. Firm evidence of the pre-Phoenician Byblos culture's maritime capabilities is supported by the recent discovery by divers off Hayling Island, near Portsmouth in Hampshire, of a large boat made of cedar. Carbon-14 testing on wood samples has suggested a date of 6431 BP (before present), which, if proved accurate, implies that by 4431 BC Britain was receiving visits from seagoing vessels from the Levant coast, where the cedar almost certainly originated. See *The Independent*, 7 May 1997, and *Yorkshire Post*, 7 May 1997. It would therefore seem likely that this unknown Mediterranean culture influenced the

development of Europe's megalithic culture which began *c.* 4500 BC in places such as Malta, Iberia, Ireland and mainland Britain. E.M. Whishaw, in her important work *Atlantis in Andalucia,* first published in 1930, uses excavated evidence of neolithic and possibly even palaeolithic seaports, sea walls, cyclopean ruins and hydraulic works around the towns of Niebla and Huelva in southern Spain to show the existence of an advanced seafaring culture in prehistoric times. See, for example, pp. 21–31, 58–95.

27. Ward, p. 18.
28. Ibid., pp. 18–19.
29. Ibid., pp. 19–20.
30. Flask-like vessels in common use during the Archaic period of Egypt's history, *c.* 3100–2700 BC, have also been found in corresponding strata at Byblos, suggesting that Lebanon was their original place of manufacture, or vice versa. See Emery, p. 204. It is a similar story with Egypt's stone vessels that have been found at Mediterranean seaports, including Byblos (see ibid., p. 205), prompting the question of whether or not the Byblos culture helped influence the development of Egypt's stoneware industry.
31. There is no English translation of Kjellson's 1961 book *Försvunnen teknik.* The account featured in this work has been taken from the Danish translation, published in 1974 by Nihil, Copenhagen, under the title *Forsvunden Teknik.* I am indebted to Iben Lund Jørgensen for her invaluable translation of this text.
32. Kjellson, *Forsvunden Teknik,* p. 49.
33. Ibid., p. 52.
34. Ibid.
35. Ibid., p. 53.
36. Ibid., p. 56.
37. The small drum was 20 centimetres in diameter and 30 centimetres long. See ibid., p. 54.
38. The medium-sized drums were 0.7 metres in diameter and 1 metre long. See ibid.
39. The *ragdon*-trumpets were 3.12 metres long, with 30-centimetre openings. They consisted of five separate sections that could be withdrawn one into another, like a telescope. The largest drums were 1 metre in diameter, 1.5 metres long and weighed an estimated 150 kilograms. See ibid.
40. Ibid., p. 53.
41. Ibid., p. 54.
42. Ibid.
43. Ibid., p. 56.
44. Ibid.

45. Ibid., p. 54.
46. Ibid., p. 56.
47. Ibid., p. 53.
48. Ibid.
49. For instance, see Namdak, p. 102, which states in connection with a meditational practice known as Tögel: 'At that time you can focus on rocks and move them if you want to' (i.e. after reaching this particular stage in spiritual evolution).
50. Kjellson, *Forsvunden Teknik*, p. 40.
51. Ibid.
52. Ibid.
53. Ibid.
54. Ibid.
55. Ibid.
56. Ibid.
57. Ibid., p. 40.

Chapter Six
CREATING SONIC PLATFORMS

1. Devereux and Jahn.
2. See, for example, Bord, pp. 101, 104, 106, 172–3.
3. Tompkins, p. 103.
4. West, *The Traveller's Key to Ancient Egypt*, p. 250.
5. Ibid., p. 251.
6. Ibid., p. 252.
7. Discovered by accident on a visit in 1981, and see also ibid., p. 252, and Hancock, *The Sign and the Seal*, p. 307. Sadly, the obelisk has now (September 1997) been concreted on to support pillars, so is unable to sustain its resonant note for any more than a few brief seconds.
8. See Van Kirk.
9. Ibid., p. 1.
10. Ibid.
11. Ibid., p. 3, cf. Brunhouse, *Sylvanus G. Morley*, 1971.
12. Ibid., p. 2.
13. Ibid., p. 5.
14. Ibid., p. 1.
15. Ibid., p. 4, cf. Frank Hodgson, 'Parametric Amplification of Sound – Ancient Mayan Wall Provides Example for Design of Modern Acoustical Surfaces', *Wall Journal*, May/June 1994.
16. Ibid., p. 3, cf. Manuel Cirerol Sansores, *Chi Cheen Itza*, 1947.

Chapter Seven
THE GENIUS OF SOUND

1. Bloomfield-Moore, in Pond, *Universal Laws never before Revealed: Keely's Secrets*, p. 24.
2. Hall, 'John Keely – A Personal Interview', in Pond, ibid., p. 239.
3. Ibid.
4 Plum, in Pond, ibid., pp. 54–60.
5. Hudson, 'Mr Keely's Researches – Sound Shown to be a Substantial Force', in Pond, ibid., p. 244.
6. Plum, in Pond, ibid., p. 56.
7. Ibid., pp. 56–7.
8. Ibid., p. 57.
9. Ibid.
10. Ibid., p. 58.
11. Ibid.
12. Ibid.
13. Ibid.
14. Ibid., p. 59.
15. Hall, 'A Second Visit to Mr Keely', in Pond, ibid., p. 241.
16. Hudson, 'The Keely Motor Illustrated', in Pond, ibid., p. 252.
17. Pond, ibid., p. 100.
18. Scrutton, *Secrets of Lost Atland*, p. 125.
19. Ibid.
20. Pond, *Universal Laws never before Revealed: Keely's Secrets*, p. 113.
21. Hall, 'John Keely – A Personal Interview', in Pond, ibid., p. 238.
22. Pond, 'Keely's Trexar a Superconductive Wire', in Pond, ibid., pp. 232–3.
23. Blavatsky, *The Secret Doctrine*, Vol. i, p. 613.
24. Harte, in Pond, *Universal Laws never before Revealed: Keely's Secrets*, p. 10.
25. Hall, 'John Keely – A Personal Interview', in Pond, ibid., p. 238.
26. Ibid.
27. Harte, in Pond, ibid., p. 9.
28. Ibid., p. 12.
29. Anyone wishing to learn more about Keely's work into sympathetic vibratory physics should begin by purchasing a copy of Pond, *Universal Laws never before Revealed: Keely's Secrets* (see Bibliography for further details). See also *The Journal of Sympathetic Vibratory Physics*, edited by Dale Pond and published by Delta Spectrum Research, PO Box 316, Valentine, Nebraska 69201, USA.

Chapter Eight
WALLS COME TUMBLING DOWN

1. Josh. iv, 13, 19; v, 9–10.
2. Josh. v, 13.
3. Josh. v, 14.
4. Josh. v, 14.
5. Josh. v, 15.
6. Josh. vi, 2.
7. Josh. vi, 3–5.
8. Josh. vi, 10.
9. Josh. vi, 15, 20.
10. Easton, *The Illustrated Bible Dictionary*, s.v. 'Jericho', pp. 369–70.
11. Bucaille, p. 136.
12. Kenyon, p. 73; Wilson, Ian, p. 35.
13. Kenyon, p. 74.
14. Ibid., pp. 74–5.
15. Ibid., p. 75.

Chapter Nine
THE HERETIC KING

1. Wright, *The Illustrated Bible Treasury*, p. 173.
2. Ex. xii, 40.
3. Wilson, Ian, p. 65, cf. the work of Dr John Bimson of Trinity Theological College, Bristol.
4. This form of numerological exaggeration is evidenced, for instance, in the book of Joshua which tells us that the people of Israel were instructed to keep a distance of 2000 cubits between themselves and the Ark of the Covenant, lest they be afflicted by its powers (Josh. iii, 4). This figure amounts to nearly a kilometre, which seems to make nonsense of the whole story. Another, similar example is the 600,000 Israelites *and* their families who are said to have departed Egypt at the time of the Exodus. Such a number would have eclipsed the entire population of Egypt at the time!

   Periods of time such as the 40 days Moses twice spent communing with God on Mount Sinai; the 40 years between his birth and his flight out of Egypt; the 40 years he spent in the Sinai; and the 40 years Israel is said to have wandered in the wilderness, are all to be seen more as symbolic than actual time. The number 40 in this context almost certainly held some special significance relating to both purity and divinity.
5. Ex. i, 9–11.

6. Ex. i, 8.
7. Wilson, Ian, p. 30.
8. See Bietak.
9. Wilson, Ian, p. 25.
10. Ibid., p. 25.
11. Bietak, p. 237.
12. Aldred, *Akhenaten – King of Egypt*, pp. 149, 283, 293.
13. Ibid., p. 180.
14. Harris, p. 97.
15. Osman, pp. 67, 93.
16. Ibid., p. 5.
17. Freud, pp. 97–8.
18. Ibid., p. 42.
19. Ex. xii, 12.
20. Freud, pp. 44–6.
21. Osman, pp. 7–8.
22. Deut. xxxiv, 7.
23. Manetho, *Aegyptiaca*, quoted in Josephus, 'Flavius Josephus Against Apion', i, 26–31.
24. Ibid., i, 26.
25. Ibid.
26. Ibid.
27. Ibid.
28. Ibid.
29. Ibid.
30. Ibid., i, 27.
31. Ibid., i, 31.
32. See Gardiner, p. 444, cf. Manetho's king-list, for the name 'Hor', or 'Oros' as Horemheb. See Redford, *Pharaonic King-Lists, Annals and Day-Books*, for various references for and against Manetho's 'Amenophis', 'Hor' or 'Oros' being a memory of Horemheb, particularly pp. 248–51. In respect to Amenophis being one and the same as 'Hor', or 'Oros', Donald Redford states on p. 250 of ibid.: 'In the post-Manethonian transmission of the text the two names "Hor" and "Amenophis" were falsely understood as two different kings, and with the passing from memory of Manetho's simple format, its position in the *Aegyptiaca* was construed as its correct historical placement. That is to say, it belonged to a king called "Amenophis" who had followed Ramesses the Great.'
33. Manetho, *Aegyptiaca*, quoted in Josephus, 'Flavius Josephus Against Apion', i, 26.
34. See, for example, Osman, pp. 30–2, 57–8, 97.
35. Redford, *Pharaonic King-Lists, Annals and Day-books*, p. 293.

36. Ibid., p. 293.
37. Osman, pp. 88–9.
38. Ibid., p. 185.
39. The answer is very likely to be yes, especially in the light of the publication of *Act of God*, an essential work on the Amarna kings and their relationship to the foundation of Mosaic Judaism by historical writer Graham Phillips. It cites new evidence to show that the volcanic eruption known to have destroyed the Mediterranean island of Thera (Santorini) in antiquity actually took place *c.* 1370–1365 BC and not around 1450 BC as has generally been believed. This dramatic revision puts the time-frame for this event at the beginning of Akhenaten's reign (almost certainly during the co-regency with his father, Amenhotep III). It must therefore have had an immense impact on the whole of the Amarna period.

    The greatest significance in revising the date of Thera's destruction is the knowledge that it throws new light on the plagues of Egypt recorded in the book of Exodus. In a book entitled *The Exodus Enigma*, first published in 1985, writer Ian Wilson (after the work of Dr Hans Goedicke) compared the descriptions of these apocalyptic events with the known effects of massive volcanic eruptions. He concluded that Thera's final disintegration, in around 1500 BC, showed that the events surrounding the Exodus occurred during the reign of Queen Hatshepsut, *c.* 1490–1468 BC. See, for example, Wilson, Ian, chart on p. 180. Bringing forward the date of the Mediterranean's greatest known volcanic eruption to *c.* 1370–1365 BC creates a whole new ball-game realised and explored for the first time by Phillips in his ground-breaking work.
40. Manetho, *Aegyptiaca*, quoted in Josephus, 'Flavius Josephus Against Apion', i, 26.
41. Personal communication with the Egyptian Antiquities Department of the British Museum.
42. Osman, pp. 184, 228.
43. Ibid., p. 167.
44. Petrie, *Researches in Sinai*, p. 127.
45. Ibid., p. 127; Kitchen, *Ramesside Inscriptions*, Pt. 1, p. 1.
46. Petrie, *Researches in Sinai*, p. 127.
47. Kitchen, *Pharaoh Triumphant*, p. 19.
48. Osman, p. 42.

Chapter Ten
FIRST CREATION

1. Apion, *Aegyptiaca*, quoted in Josephus, 'Flavius Josephus Against Apion', ii, 2.

2. Redford, *Pharaonic King-Lists, Annals and Day-books*, pp. 288–9.
3. Ibid.
4. As found in Gen. xlii, 45, 50.
5. Few scholars would deny that Akhenaten based *his* entire religion on certain preferred aspects of the Heliopolitan cult of Re, especially the sun-god's role as Re-harakhty, Re as Horus of the Horizon. See, for instance, Budge, Vol. 2, p. 71. Many early inscriptions from his reign speak of the god Re as the hidden light of the Aten, while on the walls of the Aten temple at Karnak, Thebes' religious centre, Re-harakhty was shown openly in his traditional form as a male god with the head of a falcon, surmounted by a sun disc encircled with the *uraeus*-serpent. See, for instance, Aldred, *Akhenaten – King of Egypt*, pl. 27 opp. p. 96, for a sandstone low relief of Re-harakhty taken to Berlin from Karnak in 1845. Furthermore, one of the chief priestly positions at Heliopolis was 'Greatest of Seers', a title held by Mery-re II, Akhenaten's personal vizier, as a high priest of the Aten at Amarna. His own name also honours the Heliopolitan sun-god. See Redford, *Akhenaten the Heretic King*, p. 152.
6. Saleh, p. 33.
7. Herodotus, *History*, ii, 3.
8. Saleh, pp. 22, 37.
9. Herodotus, *History*, ii, 4.
10. Ibid.
11. Ibid.
12. Weigall, pp. 155–6, cf. Mariette, *Abydos*, II, 28.
13. Saleh, p. 37.
14. Ibid.
15. Antoniadi, pp. 3-4.
16. Budge, *The Gods of the Egyptians*, Vol. 1, p. 331.
17. Edwards, p. 286.
18. Al-Makrizi, quoted in Ivimy, pp. 23–4.
19. Breasted, Vol. 2, pp. 320–4.
20. Ibid., pp. 322–4.
21. Ibid., pp. 321–2.
22. Budge, *The Gods of the Egyptians*, Vol. 1, p. 471; Vol. 2, p. 361.
23. Aldred, *Akhenaten – King of Egypt*, p. 142; Redford, *Akhenaten the Heretic King*, p. 74.
24. Aldred, *Akhenaten – King of Egypt*, p. 142.
25. Ibid., pp. 261, 273.
26. Ibid., pp. 147, 239.
27. Ibid., p. 175.
28. Budge, *The Gods of the Egyptians*, Vol. 1, p. 26; Vol. 2, pp. 351–2.

29. Aldred, *Akhenaten – King of Egypt*, pp. 43, 260; Redford, *Akhenaten the Heretic King*, p. 149.

30. Relief scenes found in one of the tombs located in the limestone cliffs beyond Tell el-Amarna show what is considered to be a blind orchestra with accompanying singers, standing before a round-topped stela positioned on a dais. Egyptologists can tell from the background imagery that this pillar was situated somewhere within Akhetaten's Mansion of the Benben. When excavators searched the spot indicated in the tomb-scene they found a number of loose fragments of quartzite. This was the same stone that had been used to fashion a round-topped stela, erected at Heliopolis during Akhenaten's reign and showing the king and his family prostrating themselves before the sun-disc. This discovery not only showed Akhenaten's personal venera-tion of the sun-disc at Heliopolis, where he is known to have built a royal palace governed by a Heliopolitan priest, but it also confirmed that the quartzite fragments found in the sun temple at Amarna were very probably the remnants of its stylised *benben*-stone. See Redford, *Akhenaten the Heretic King*, pp. 146–7.

31. Aldred, *Akhenaten – King of Egypt*, pp. 87, 273.

32. Redford, *Akhenaten the Heretic King*, p. 147.

33. Aldred, *Akhenaten – King of Egypt*, p. 265.

34. Apion, *Aegyptiaca*, quoted in Josephus, 'Flavius Josephus Against Apion', ii, 2.

35. Redford, *Akhenaten the Heretic King*, pp. 73–4.

36. See, for instance, Faulkner, trans., *The Ancient Egyptian Pyramid Texts*, utterance 600, section 1652.

37. Rundle Clark, p. 37.

38. See, for instance, Faulkner, *The Ancient Egyptian Pyramid Texts*, utterance 303, section 460; utterance 325, section 531; utterance 468, section 904; utterance 505, section 1090; utterance 532, section 1261–2; utterance 535, section 1289; utterance 539, sections 1305 and 1315.

39. Saleh, p. 33.

40. Ibid.

41. Ibid.

Chapter Eleven
SPIRIT OF THE AGE

1. Leiden Papyrus I. 350 includes a quote that refers to Thebes as 'a mound when the earth came into being'. It goes on to say that 'mankind also came into being within her [i.e. Thebes], with the

purpose of founding every city in her proper name. For all are called "City" after the example of Thebes.' See Kemp, p. 201, which confirms that this is a reference to the mound of creation that emerged out of the primeval waters and on which the first act of creation was performed.

2. For more information on *omphali* see Wainwright; Tompkins, p. 182, showing an illustration of the *omphalos*-stone found by Reisner 'in the great temple of Amon'; Stecchini, in Tompkins, ibid., p. 302: 'the god [i.e. Amun] and the geodetic point most probably was indicated by the same object, the *omphalos*, "navel" '. See also ibid., p. 338.

3. Hastings, s.v. 'Omphalos', Vol. 9, p. 492.

4. Ibid.

5. Stecchini, in Tompkins, p. 302.

6. Weigall, Vol. 2, p. 39.

7. Blackman and Fairman, p. 32.

8. Aldred, *Akhenaten – King of Egypt*, p. 118.

9. Gardiner, p. 443.

10. See Aldred, *Akhenaten – King of Egypt*, p. 142.

11. Ibid., p. 269.

12. Ibid., p. 45.

13. Ibid., p. 49.

14. Ibid., pp. 45, 50.

15. Ibid., p. 111.

16. Saleh, notes relating to pp. 5–12.

17. Budge, *The Gods of the Egyptians*, Vol. 1, p. 416.

18. Ibid., p. 417.

19. Ibid.

20. Aldred, *Akhenaten – King of Egypt*, p. 111.

21. Ibid., p. 268.

22. Ibid., p. 89; Lichtheim, pp. 26–7.

23. Stecchini, in Tompkins, p. 338.

24. Ibid., pp. 287–322, especially pp. 295, 297.

25. Ibid., p. 340.

26. This value is calculated by Stecchini as 47,233.1 metres. See ibid., p. 342. For reference purposes, an *atur* has a value of 15,000 royal cubits (7862.2 metres) or 17,000 geographical cubits (7848.8 metres), while the *khe* has a value of 350 royal cubits (183.45 metres) or 400 geographical cubits (184.68 metres). Since ¾ *khe* fits in perfectly with the geographical cubit, Stecchini concluded that it was these that had been used in the geographical placement of the boundary stelae.

27. Ibid., pp. 342–3.

28. Ibid., p. 343.

29. Ibid.

30. Budge, *The Gods of the Egyptians*, Vol. 2, p. 72.
31. See Faulkner, trans., *The Ancient Egyptian Pyramid Texts*, utterance 305, sections 472, 474; Phillips, Ellen, p. 74; Massey, *A Book of the Beginnings*, Vol. 1, pp. 330–2.
32. Adams, W. Marsham, p. 71.
33. Rundle Clark, p. 247.
34. Herodotus, *History*, ii, 73.
35. Rundle Clark, p. 246.
36. Adams, W. Marsham, p. 71. See also Massey, *A Book of Beginnings*, Vol. 1, p. 107.
37. Bauval and Hancock, *Keeper of Genesis*, pp. 154. 194.
38. Schwaller de Lubicz, p. 86.
39. Breasted, Vol. 2, p. 323.
40. Ibid.
41. Hurry, p. 21, cf. B. Gunn, *Annales du Service des Antiquités de l'Egypte*, No. XXVI, 1926.
42. Rundle Clark, p. 37.
43. Breasted, Vol. 2, p. 323.

Chapter Twelve
THE SECRET OF ROSTAU

1. Budge, *The Egyptian Heaven and Hell*, Vol. 1, p. viii.
2. Ibid., p. 13.
3. Faulkner, trans., *The Ancient Egyptian Pyramid Texts*, pp. vii–viii, after the work of Kurt Sethe, *Komm.* i, 49ff.
4. Ibid.
5. There are three main ancient texts outlining the passage of the sun-god through the *duat*-underworld: a) *Per-em-hru* – The Book of the Coming Forth by Day, otherwise known as the Egyptian, or 'Theban recension of' the Book of the Dead; b) *Shat-ent-am-tuat* – The Book of that which is in the Duat; c) The Book of Gates. This listing is taken from Budge, *The Egyptian Heaven and Hell*, Vol. 1, p. ix.
6. Rundle Clark, p. 153.
7. Budge, *The Gods of the Egyptians*, Vol. 2, p. 98.
8. Bauval and Hancock, *Keeper of Genesis*, p. 138.
9. Ibid.
10. Ibid., pp. 170–5.
11. Barton, p. 20.
12. Ibid.
13. Allen, p. 20.
14. See, for instance, Hassan, Selim, p. 265; Lehner, *The Egyptian*

Heritage, p. 119; Bauval and Hancock, *Keeper of Genesis*, pp. 147–9.

15. Budge, *The Gods of the Egyptians*, Vol. 1, p. 207.

16. Budge, *The Egyptian Heaven and Hell*, Vol. 1, p. 62.

17. Breasted, Vol. 2, p. 322.

18. Faulkner, trans., *The Ancient Egyptian Pyramid Texts*, utterance 364, section 620.

19. See, for example, Tompkins, pp. 258–9, and Bauval and Hancock, *Keeper of Genesis*, pp. 146 fig. 38, 147. Such thoughts have, on the other hand, led various authors such as W. Marsham Adams in his thought-provoking work *The Book of the Master of the Hidden Places*, published in 1933, to conclude that, in addition to its function as a royal tomb, the interior of the Great Pyramid was once the setting for initiatory rituals where the chosen candidate was able to journey into the afterlife on a spiritual level.

20. Budge, *The Egyptian Heaven and Hell*, Vol. 1, p. 62.

21. Ibid., p. 65.

22. Hassan, Selim, p. 265.

23. Budge, *The Egyptian Heaven and Hell*, Vol. 1, p. 89.

24. Ibid., p. 106.

25. Stecchini, in Tompkins, pp. 297–8.

26. Budge, *The Egyptian Heaven and Hell*, Vol. 1, p. 94.

27. Ibid., p. 93.

28. Ibid.

29. Ibid., p. 94.

30. Saleh, pp. 20–1.

31. Ibid., p. 22.

32. Kamil, p. 91.

33. Hassan, Selim, p. 287.

34. Ibid.

35. Lehner, *The Egyptian Heritage*, pp. 93–100.

36. Randall-Stevens, pp. 95–113.

37. Ammianus Marcellinus, xxii, 15, 30.

38. Haigh. See also 'Mysteries of the Sphinx', NBC-TV.

39. Haigh; Bauval and Hancock, *Hieroglyph – The Bauval & Hancock Newsletter*.

40. Personal conversation with psychic Anne Walker in 1995, who has had direct contact with members of the presidential family. See also Bauval and Hancock, *Hieroglyph – The Bauval & Hancock Newsletter*.

41. Bauval and Hancock, *Hieroglyph – The Bauval & Hancock Newsletter*.

42. Lehner, *The Egyptian Heritage*, p. 101, reading 378–14.

43. Ibid., p. 99, reading 378–16.

44. Ibid., pp. 95–8.

Chapter Thirteen
ISLAND OF THE GODS

1. Hurry, p. 17.
2. Ibid. See also Reymond, p. 317.
3. Budge, *The Gods of the Egyptians*, Vol. 1, p. 85.
4. Ibid., pp. 84–5.
5. Reymond, pp. 8–10.
6. See, for example, ibid., pp. 6–7.
7. Ibid., pp. 134, 142.
8. Ibid., p. 123.
9. Ibid., p. 34.
10. Ibid., pp. 77, 103.
11. Ibid., p. 76.
12. Ibid., pp. 107–9.
13. Ibid., pp. 35, 113.
14. Ibid., p. 114.
15. Ibid., p. 103.
16. Ibid., p. 109.
17. Ibid., p. 107.
18. Ibid., pp. 87–8, 114, 126.
19. Ibid., pp. 12–13, 55, 106–7.
20. *dw3t n b3*. See ibid., pp. 15, 110.
21. Ibid., pp. 108, 118.
22. Ibid., p. 116.
23. Ibid., p. 119; Jelinkova, p. 51.
24. Jelinkova, p. 41, cf. E. VI. 358.13.
25. Ibid., p. 51, cf. E. IV. 359, 4–6.
26. Ibid., p. 52, c. E. IV. 358.10.
27. Reymond, pp. 116, 123–4, 131.
28. Ibid., pp. 177, 179.
29. Jelinkova, p. 42, cf. Wb. I, 328 (14); 329 (1); p. 43., cf. E. IV. 358, 11–12.
30. Reymond, p. 120.
31. Ibid., pp. 142–3.
32. Ibid., p. 28.
33. Ibid., p. 208.
34. Ibid., p. 29.
35. Ibid.
36. Ibid.
37. Ibid., p. 27.
38. Ibid., pp. 31, 162.
39. Ibid., p. 154.
40. Ibid., p. 27.

41. Ibid., p. 180.
42. Ibid., pp. 208, 250.
43. Ibid., p. 28.
44. Ibid., pp. 104, 318–19.
45. Ibid., pp. 45, 101.
46. Ibid., p. 103.
47. Ibid., p. 229.
48. Ibid., p. 263.
49. Jelínková, p. 51.
50. Reymond, p. 110.
51. Budge, *The Gods of the Egyptians*, Vol. 1, p. 184.
52. Breasted, Vol. 1, p. 85.
53. Hancock, pp. 344–5.
54. Personal communication with David Jeffreys, lecturer at University College, London, Egypt Exploration Society archaeologist currently digging at Memphis.
55. Lehner, 'Giza', *Archiv früh Orientforschung*, p. 153.
56. Hoffman, pp. 90, 98, quoting the work of Fekri Hassan.
57. Bonwick, p. 105, cf. the work of Thevenot and De Breves.
58. Ibid., p. 117.
59. Standard English Dictionary, s.v. 'cistern', p. 59.
60. Herodotus, *History*, ii, 124.
61. Ibid., ii, 127.
62. Bonwick, p. 7.
63. Sethe, pp. 49–50.
64. Budge, *The Egyptian Heaven and Hell*, Vol. 1, pp. 93–4, 97, 99.
65. Ibid., p. 93.
66. Ibid., p. 101.
67. Ibid., p. 105.
68. Reymond, p. 266.
69. Ibid., p. 74.
70. Aldred, *Egypt to the End of the Old Kingdom*, pp. 46, 48 pl. 37; Gardiner, p. 402.
71. Clayton, p. 20.
72. Reymond, p. 170.
73. Ibid., p. 103.
74. Ibid., pp. 95–6.
75. Aldred, *Akhenaten – King of Egypt*, p. 162.
76. Ibid.
77. Reymond, p. 103.
78. Ibid., p. 104.
79. Curtis, p. 26.
80. Ibid., cf. Yasht 19, 36–7.

Chapter Fourteen
UNDERWORLD OF THE SOUL

1. Reymond, pp. 55, 111, 132, 153–4.
2. Ibid., p. 114.
3. Ibid., pp. 152, 155.
4. Ibid., p. 19.
5. Ibid., pp. 181, 200.
6. Jochmans, p. 248.
7. Reymond, pp. 155–6.
8. Ibid., p. 154.
9. Ibid., pp. 64, 68, 77.
10. Ibid., p. 68
11. Sethe, p. 118.
12. Reymond, p. 72.
13. Ibid., pp. 69–70, 84–5.
14. Ibid., p. 70.
15. Ibid., p. 108.
16. Ibid.
17. Budge, *An Egyptian Hieroglyphyic Dictionary*, s.v. 'benn', Vol. 2, p. 217.
18. Baines, p. 399. The author in fact notes that *bnbn* derives from the same root as *bnnt*, which he interprets as 'primeval hill', *bnnwt*, 'virility' and 'erectness', and *bnnu*-bird. See ibid., pp. 390–2, 397, 399–400.
19. Indeed, the word *bnbn* is twice associated with the House of Sokar, as it can be used to denote either a fire offering or a light-god inside this mythical domain. See Budge, *An Egyptian Hieroglyphic Dictionary*, s.v. 'benben', Vol. 1, p. 217.
20. Zimmer, p. 127.
21. Ibid., p. 128 fn.
22. Faulkner, *The Ancient Egyptian Coffin Texts*, spell 1080, p. 147.
23. Budge, *The Egyptian Heaven and Hell*, Vol. 1, p. 106.
24. 1 En. xiv. All quotes from 1 Enoch taken from Charles.
25. 1 En. xiv, 10–12.
26. 1 En. xiv, 15–16, 18.
27. 1 En. xiv, 18–20.
28. Reymond, pp. 67, 153–4.
29. Personal communication with *dzogchen* master Ven Lama Chime Rinpoche of the Kham Centre, Saffron Walden, Essex, in 1987. See also Norbu.
30. Allen, p. 2, quoting from William Henry Smyth (1788–1865). Origin of statement unknown.

31. Hall, Manly P., p. 173.
32. Horne, p. 233.
33. Hall, Manly P., p. 173.
34. Budge, *The Gods of the Eygptians*, Vol. 1, p. 205.
35. Ibid., p. 339.
36. Reymond, pp. 26–7, 160–2, 164.
37. Similar inscriptions are also found at a temple in Medinet Habu. See Sethe, p. 55.
38. Ibid., p. 118.
39. *Km3t.f.* See, for example, ibid., p. 58.
40. Ibid., p. 118.
41. Ibid., p. 55. This is a direct translation of the German original, with thanks to Catherine Hale.
42. Ibid.
43. Ibid.
44. Ibid.
45. Hart, pp. 15–16.
46. Reymond, p. 64 n. 2, a re-translation of the German translation in Sethe, p. 118.
47. Hart, p. 15.
48. Hastings, s.v. 'Omphalos', Vol. 9, p. 493.
49. Lindsay, pp. 304–5.
50. Ibid., pp. 303–4, 308–9; Hart, p. 15.
51. Lindsay, pp. 303–13.
52. Ibid., p. 312.
53. Ibid., p. 306.
54. After Typhon, the Greek name for Set, the Egyptian god of violence and chaos, who was 'a monster serpent'. See Budge, *The Gods of the Egyptians*, Vol. 2, p. 245.
55. Hippolytus, *Philosophumena*, Bk. 5, 14.
56. Budge, *The Gods of the Egyptians*, Vol. 1, pp. 330–1. Nut was the feminine form of Nu.
57. Legge, Vol. 2, p. 151 n. 1, after Cruice, who points out that in Hebrew the word for 'eyes' and 'wells', *ain*, is exactly the same.
58. Hippolytus, *Philosophumena*, Bk. 5, 14.
59. Since Christmas was originally celebrated on 6 January, there is every reason to link the concept of the birth of Christ with the myth and ritual surrounding the Egyptian cult of Kore in the first century BC. See Gilbert, pp. 171–2, 229.
60. Cayce, p. 148, reading 378-16.

Chapter Fifteen
THE CRADLE OF CIVILISATION

1. Reymond, p. 187.
2. Ibid., p. 180.
3. Jelinkova, p. 51.
4. Reymond, pp. 177, 179.
5. Sanchoniatho, quoted in Cory, p. 9.
6. Ibid.
7. Hapgood, *Maps of the Ancient Sea Kings*, p. 221.
8. Wendorf and Schild, 'The Paleolithic of the Lower Nile Valley', pp. 127–69; Butzer, p. 7; Hoffman, p. 89.
9. Wendorf and Schild, *Prehistory of the Nile Valley*, p. 291; Hoffman, p. 87.
10. Hoffman, pp. 86–7.
11. Butzer, pp. 6–7.
12. Ibid.
13. Hoffman, pp. 90, 98; Hassan, Fekri; Butzer, p. 9 n. 11.
14. Hoffman, pp. 90, 98; Hassan, Fekri; Butzer, p. 7 n 11.
15. See Hapgood, *The Path of the Pole*, pp. 275–6, citing F.C. Hibben, *The Lost Americans*, pp. 90–2. See also the author's *From the Ashes of Angels*, Chapter 20, for a full account of these violent cataclysms.
16. Moore, pp. 50–4.
17. Ibid., pp. 50, 53–4.
18. Izady, p. 24.
19. Knauth, p. 33.
20. Ibid.
21. Ibid.
22. Time-Life Books, *Anatolia: Cauldron of Cultures*, p. 35.
23. Braidwood, 'Miscellaneous Analyses of Materials from Jarmo', ed. Braidwood, *Prehistoric Archaeology Along the Zagros Flanks*, pp. 538, 542.
24. Izady, p. 24.
25. I use the term 'Old World' as there is mounting evidence to show that individuals comparable in advancement with the inhabitants of early neolithic communities in the Near East existed in North America as early as 8000 BC. See, for instance, the discovery of a mummified corpse discovered in the so-called Spirit Cave of Nevada in 1940 and recently carbon-14 dated to 10,000 BP. See *The Observer*, 27 April 1997. Anatomically it is 'different from modern Indians in the narrow, relatively small face, long and narrow cranium and simple cranial features'. It is likely to be the oldest mummified human remains yet discovered and was found to be wearing well-preserved textile cloth and leather moccasins. Wrapped around

the body were burial mats and a blanket made of what appeared to be rabbit skin. The presence of this piece of textile rivals the linen fabric dated to 9000 BP found wrapped around an antler handle at Çayönü in eastern Anatolia.

26. Time-Life Books, *Anatolia: Cauldron of Cultures*, p. 35.
27. Roux, p. 59.
28. Izady, p. 24.
29. Moore, pp. 57–8.
30. Report in *Nature*, 6 June 1996.
31. Crabb.
32. Izady, p. 25.
33. Roux, p. 59.
34. Izady, p. 23.
35. Personal communication with Mehrdad Izady.
36. Moore, pp. 55, 57.
37. Time-Life Books, *Anatolia: Cauldron of Cultures*, p. 33.
38. Moore, pp. 55–6; Esin, pp. 125–6, after Todd, 1966.
39. Gorelick and Gwinnett, p. 25.
40. Kenoyer and Vidale, p. 495.
41. Gorelick and Gwinnett, p. 27; Kenoyer and Vidale, p. 498.
42. Gorelick and Gwinnett, p. 30; Kenoyer and Vidale, p. 506.
43. Kenoyer and Vidale, pp. 504–5.
44. Ibid., pp. 506–7, 512–13.
45. Ibid., pp. 514–15.
46. Ibid., p. 514.
47. Gorelick and Gwinnett, pp. 25, 32.
48. Kenoyer and Vidale, p. 513.
49. Meyers, s.v. 'Çayönü', Vol. 4, p. 446.
50. Time-Life Books, *Anatolia: Cauldron of Cultures*, p. 158.
51. Indeed, the Mountain of the Madai was also known as 'Inner Harran'. See Drower, pp. 6, 8–9, which states: 'That this [the Tura d Madai] was a mountainous country and stretched to Harran is clearly indicated.'
52. Cottrell, pp. 82, 84 n. 1.
53. Drower, p. 10: 'Still more inexplicable is the assertion that the Egyptians were co-religionists, and that the original ancestors of the Mandaean race went from Egypt to the Tura d Madai.'
54. Ibid., p. 6, quoting an unnamed Mandaean text.
55. Ibid., p. 197.
56. Sitchin, p. 77.
57. Drower, pp. xvi-xviii.
58. Hassan, Selim, p. 45.
59. Ibid., pp. 34–5, 45.

60. Found in the Geographical Dictionary *Mo'gam-et-Buldan*, VIII, p. 457 (Cairo edition), quoted in ibid., p. 45.
61. Ibid., p. 45.
62. Ibid.
63. Gen. xii, 4–10.
64. Lindsay, p. 315.
65. Ibid., p. 314.
66. Ibid.

Chapter Sixteen
GATEWAY TO EDEN

1. Gen. ii, 8–10.
2. Ez. xxvii, 23.
3. Ez. xxvii, 24.
4. Warren, pp. 126–7, 126 n. 2, cf. Smith, *Assyrian Discoveries*, pp. 392–3; Massey, *The Natural Genesis*, Vol. 2, p. 21.
5. Walker. I am indebted to Brent Russ for enclosing a copy of this article along with a covering letter dated 25 August 1996.
6. Ibid.
7. Ibid.
8. Wigram and Wigram, p. 264.
9. Massey, *The Natural Genesis*, Vol. 2, p. 231.
10. Heinberg, p. 42; Roux, p. 106.
11. Gen. iii, 22.
12. Kramer, *Sumerian Mythology*, p. 81.
13. Kramer, 'Dilmun, the Land of the Living', p. 21.
14. Izady, p. 19.
15. Ibid., p. 44.
16. Ibid.
17. Ibid.
18. See, for example, *The Daily Telegraph*, 15 May 1997, and *The Times*, 15 May 1997.
19. Meyers, s.v. 'Nevali Çori', Vol. 4, p. 131.
20. See Time-Life Books, *Anatolia: Cauldron of Cultures*, pp. 30–1, which, aside from the unique colour picture of Nevali Çori's cult building, is highly recommended as an introduction to the prehistory of eastern Turkey.
21. Meyers, s.v. 'Nevali Çori', Vol. 4, p. 131.
22. Ibid.
23. Ibid.
24. Hauptmann, p. 39.

25. Bienert, pp. 16–17.
26. See Hauptmann, p. 41.
27. Ibid., p. 42.
28. Ibid., p. 43.
29. Ibid., p. 47.
30. Ibid., p. 45.
31. Ibid., p. 66.
32. Ibid., p. 48.
33. Ibid., p. 50.
34. Ibid., pp. 52–3.
35. Ibid., p. 55.
36. Ibid., p. 57.
37. Ibid., p. 55.
38. Meyers, s.v. 'Nevali Çori', Vol. 4, p. 133.
39. Hauptmann, p. 66.
40. Ibid., p. 57.
41. Meyers, s.v. 'Çayönü', Vol. 4, p. 445.
42. Ibid.
43. Ibid.
44. Time-Life Books, *Anatolia: Cauldron of Cultures*, p. 35.
45. Hauptmann, p. 38. Thanks go to Simon Cox for tracking down this obscure monograph and to Catherine Hale for her English translation of the German original.
46. Posnansky, Vol. 2, p. 91.
47. Ibid., p. 181.
48. Ibid., p. 182.
49. Ibid.
50. Ibid., pp. 181, 181 n. 166.
51. Ibid., p. 183.

Chapter Seventeen
FEATHERED SERPENTS

1. Hauptmann, p. 66.
2. Reply by fax dated 16 July 1997 from Harald Hauptmann to my research assistant Simon Cox on the subject of vulture imagery.
3. See Bienert.
4. Ibid., p. 16.
5. The evidence of skull, long bone and secondary burials at Nevali Çori dates to the late neolithic period of the seventh and sixth millennia BC.
6. Herodotus, *History*, i, 140.
7. Drower, p. 200 n. 6.

8. Mellaart, pp. 19, 207.
9. Carbon-14 tests produced a date of 10,870 years BP (+/−300 years). See Solecki.
10. Ibid., p. 42, cf. Reed, 1959.
11. Ibid.
12. Ibid., p. 44.
13. Ibid.
14. Ibid., p. 47.
15. Ibid.
16. See Mellaart; Bacon, pp. 110–26.
17. Gimbutas, p. 238 fig. 7–26:2.
18. Cameron, p. 28, cf. *Anatolian Studies*, Vol. 14, 1964, p. 64; Mellaart, p. 168.
19. Mellaart, p. 167; Bacon, pp. 121–2.
20. Mellaart, p. 20.
21. Ibid., p. 84; Bacon, p. 124.
22. Reply by fax dated 16 July 1997 from Harald Hauptmann to my research assistant Simon Cox on the subject of vulture imagery.
23. Hauptmann, p. 60.
24. Cameron, p. 27.
25. Roux, p. 67.
26. Ibid., p. 69; Braidwood, 'Miscellaneous Analyses of Materials', ed. Braidwood, *Prehistoric Archaeology Along the Zagros Flanks*, p. 543.
27. Roux, p. 72.
28. Ibid.
29. Mundkur, p. 187, cf. Sir L. Woolley, *Ur Excavations*, Vol. 4, 'The Early Periods', 1955, pp. 12–13.
30. Morales, in Braidwood, pp. 369–83.
31. See the author's *From the Ashes of Angels*, Chapters 13 and 14, for a full rundown on the Kurdish association with the cult of the snake.
32. Personal communication with Paula O'Keefe, an American correspondent, during 1996. See also Partridge, p. 757.
33. Molleson and Campbell, in Campbell and Green, p. 45.
34. Molleson and Campbell, in Campbell and Green pp. 45–55.
35. Ibid., p. 47.
36. Ibid., p. 49.
37. Ibid., p. 47, quoting Mallowan, 1969, p. 52.
38. This conclusion revolves around the presence of extra-large ossicles (small bones in the inner ear), large teeth, as well as observations on the hypodontia (absence or incomplete formation of teeth) and extra-sutural bones (located in the joints of certain cranial bones). See ibid., pp. 49–50.
39. Ibid.

40. Ibid., p. 50.
41. Ibid.
42. Ibid., p. 51.
43. Ibid., p. 50.
44. For example, a late Halaf skull found at Kurban Höyük, eastern Anatolia, was found to be deformed. See Alpagut, pp. 151–3.
45. Molleson and Campbell, in Campbell and Green, p. 50.
46. Ibid.
47. Ibid., pp. 51–2.
48. Ibid., p. 52.
49. Ibid.
50. Ibid., p. 52 fig. 9.4.1.
51. Ibid., p. 52.
52. Ibid.
53. Gilbert and Cotterell, pp. 118–25, quoting the work of José Diaz Bolio.
54. Ibid.
55. Mackenzie, p. 257.
56. Wendorf and Schild, p. 146: 'As a group the population is characterised by long, heavy craniums, with short, broad faces and well-developed supraorbital ridges. They closely resemble the "Mechta" variety of Cro-Magnon *Homo sapiens* which occur in several seemingly contemporary graveyards in the Maghreb (Anderson, 1968).'
57. Reymond, p. 103.
58. Jelinkova, p. 51, cf. E. IV. 359, 4–6.

Chapter Eighteen
THE BLACK LAND

1. Hauptmann.
2. Allen, pp. 160–1.
3. Lemprière, s.v. 'Eridanus', p. 226.
4. Allen, p. 161.
5. See, for instance, Brown Jnr, *Eridanus: River and Constellation*, pp. 44–5, 51–2; Brown Jnr, *Researches into the Origin of the Primitive Constellations of the Greeks, Phoenicians and Babylonians*, Vol. 1, pp. 93–6.
6. See, for instance, Brown Jnr, *Eridanus: River and Constellation*, pp. 44–5, 51–2.
7. Allen, pp. 216–17, summarising the researches of Robert Brown Jnr in his book *Eridanus: River and Constellation*.

8. The *us* in Eridanus is a singularisation of Eridan, while the *n* is simply a Latinised place-name ending as in Baby*lon*, from the original *Babel*. Left with Erida, the *a* is transposed easily with the Assyrian *u*, as in the biblical *A*rarat from the Akkadian *U*rartu.

9. Allen, p. 217.

10. Brown Jnr, *Eridanus: River and Constellation*, p. 60.

11. Ibid.

12. Lenormant, p. 153.

13. Brown Jnr, *Eridanus: River and Constellation*, p. 43.

14. Ibid., p. 72; King, Vol. 1, p. xciv n. 3.

15. King, Vol. 1, pp. xciv n. 2, 128 n. 1.

16. Allen, pp. 216–17.

17. Brown Jnr, *Researches into the Origin of the Primitive Constellations of the Greeks, Phoenicians and Babylonians*, Vol. 1, pp. 89, 108; Brown Jnr, *Eridanus: River and Constellation*, p. 16.

18. King, Vol. 1, pp. xciv n. 2–3, lxxxiii n. 2.

19. Ibid., Tablet 1, ll. 117–18, p. 17.

20. Black and Green, *Gods, Demons and Symbols of Ancient Mesopotamia*, s.v. 'Tiamat's creatures', pp. 177–8.

21. See, for example, King, Vol. 1, pp. xx-xxi, 204–18.

22. Black and Green, *Gods, Demons and Symbols of Ancient Mesopotamia*, s.v. 'Tiamat', p. 177.

23. Brown Jnr, *Eridanus: River and Constellation*, p. 82.

24. Ibid., p. 81.

25. King, Vol. 1, Tablet 55, 466, ll. 3, 5, p. 209.

26. Ibid., p. 210.

27. Lenormant, p. 153.

28. Time-Life Books, *Anatolia: Cauldron of Cultures*, p. 35.

29. Crabb.

30. King, Vol. 1, p. xlv, cf. Robertson Smith, *Zeits. für Assyr.*, vi, p. 339; Black and Green, *Gods, Demons and Symbols of Ancient Mesopotamia*, s.v. 'Tiamat', p. 177.

31. Brown Jnr, *Eridanus: River and Constellation*, p. 16.

32. Gen. i, 2.

33. See, for example, Isa. xxvii, 1.

34. Sethe, pp. 55, 118–19.

35. Hippolytus, *Philosophumena*, Bk 5, 14.

36. Ibid.

37. '*Om 'orqa*, 'the Mother of the Deep', King, Vol. 1, p. xlv n. 1.

38. She appears under all three of these names in surviving fragments of a three-volume work on the history and culture of the Babylonians entitled *Babyloniaka*, written in Greek by a third-century BC priest of the temple of Bel-Marduk at Babylon named Berossus. See Cory,

p. 21. Since she is cited as the creator of all sorts of hideous monsters that are slain by the god 'Belus', there seems little doubt that Thalassa, Thalatth or Omoroca were all simply late Babylonian or Greek forms of Tiamat. See Legge, Vol. 1, col. 1, p. 151 n. 2, cf. Rogers, *Religion of Babylonia and Assyrians*, p. 107.

39. Great Circle bearing calculated by Rodney Hale in July 1997 based on the coordinates of 29° 58.84′ N, 31° 08′ E for Giza and 37.58° N, 38.65° E for Nevali Çori. The Great Circle bearing of Nevali Çori from Giza calculates at 37.8° east of north. The two readings are not reciprocal due to the convergence of lines of longitude. The method employed to make these calculations was taken from Bannister and Stephenson, pp. 73–275.

40. Brown Jnr, *Researches into the Origin of the Primitive Constellations of the Greeks, Phoenicians and Babylonians*, Vol. 1, pp. 90–1, cf. Phainom, 398.

41. Ibid., p. 90.

42. Ibid.

43. Ibid., p. 91.

44. Ibid., p. 90.

45. Ibid.

46. Budge, *An Egyptian Hieroglyphic Dictionary*, s.v. 'kam', Vol. 2, p. 787. See also Faulkner, *A Concise Dictionary of Middle Egypt*, s.v. 'Km', p. 286.

47. Ibid., s.v. 'kam-t', p. 787. See also Faulkner, *A Concise Dictionary of Middle Egypt*, s.v. 'Kmt', p. 286.

48. Sethe, p. 55.

49. Rundle Clark, p. 50.

Chapter Nineteen
THE STARRY WISDOM

1. Personal communication with Mehrdad Izady.

2. Izady, pp. 253, 254 fig. 3; Mellaart, pp. 152–4.

3. Izady, pp. 239–40.

4. Ibid., p. 240.

5. Personal communication with Mehrdad Izady.

6. Hauptmann, p. 68.

7. Allen, p. 109; Brown Jnr, *Researches into the Origin of the Primitive Constellations of the Greeks, Phoenicians and Babylonians*, Vol. 1, pp. 209–11; Gleadow, p. 192.

8. Brown Jnr, *Eridanus: River and Constellation*, p. 81, cf. 'Harleian Collection (British Museum) MS No. 647, described as the "ancient

manuscript of Cicero's translation of Aratus" (Ottley, in *Archaeologia*, XXVI, 101)'.

9. See ibid. for other examples of Eridanus as a river-god.
10. Black and Green, *Gods, Demons and Symbols of Ancient Mesopotamia*, s.v. 'turtle', p. 179.
11. Ibid.
12. Ibid.
13. Brown Jnr, *Researches into the Origin of the Primitive Constellations of the Greeks, Phoenicians and Babylonians*, Vol. 1, pp. 79–82; Gleadow, p. 163 table 17.
14. The dates for the Age of Cancer were calculated using the Skyglobe 3.6 computer program, based on the final setting of the star Regulus, the royal star of Leo, as an equinoctial marker in around 9220 BC.
15. Black and Green, *Gods, Demons and Symbols of Ancient Mesopotamia*, s.v. 'Enki (Ea)', p. 75.
16. Roux, p. 71.
17. Gleadow, p. 165.
18. Berossus, cf. Alexander Polyhistor, in Cory, p. 19.
19. Ibid.
20. Ibid.
21. See the author's *From the Ashes of Angels*, pp. 238–40.
22. Berossus, cf. Abydenus, in Cory, pp. 28–9.
23. Berossus, cf. Apollodorus, in Cory, pp. 26–7.
24. These are given as the first 'Ou, 2nd Aoai, 3rd Ouô, 4th Ouöab, (and) 5th (name now lost) . . .'. See Hippolytus, *Philosophumena*, Bk. 5, 14.
25. Lemprière, s.v. 'Erythraeum mare', p. 227.
26. Kramer, 'Dilmun, the Land of the Living', p. 27 n. 41 (on p. 28).
27. Ibid.
28. Wilhelm, pp. 54–5.
29. See Rohl, and Cox and Pegg, for the latest theories on the idea of 'Eastern invaders' having influenced the foundations of Egyptian civilisation.

Chapter Twenty
MILLENNIAL MIDNIGHT

1. Geoffrey of Monmouth, pp. 142–3, 167, 172–4.
2. See, for example, the works of antiquarians such as John Aubrey (1626–97) and William Stukeley (1687–1765).
3. See, for example, *The Popular Biblical Educator*, Vol. 1, pp. 103–7, which speaks of Stonehenge as an altar in the style of the one set up by Jacob at Bethel. See also various tracts published during the mid- to late nineteenth century by the British Israelite Society.

4. See, for example, Keys, cf. the work of archaeologist Aubrey Burl.
5. Quoting American Egyptologist Mark Lehner on the TV documentary 'Mysteries of the Sphinx', NBC-TV.
6. Lehner, *The Egyptian Heritage*, p. 101, reading 378-14.
7. Norton.
8. Ibid.
9. Ibid.
10. Edgar Cayce Prophecies, ARE CD-ROM, reading 378-14, life M-56, 26 September 1933.
11. Edgar Cayce Prophecies, ARE CD-ROM, reading 5750-001, 12 November 1933.
12. Ibid., reading 2012-1.
13. Cayce, p. 146, reading 2012-1.
14. I speak here of Bernard G., the Essex psychic, who features in a number of the author's books.
15. Posnansky, Vol. 1, p. 39; Vol. 2, pp. 90–1.
16. This is known as the obliquity of the ecliptic, which alters the northerly and southerly positions of the sun's rising and setting across a cycle of 41,000 years.
17. See Neil Steede's contribution to the Discovery TV documentary 'Myths of Mankind', narrated by Colin Wilson and first broadcast across Europe in August 1997.
18. Zink, p. 50, and personal communication with retired archaeologist Oren Patrick Purcell regarding the work of geologist Richard Wingate, who used pressurised water to blast out the sand from beneath the stone blocks to reveal the presence of the stone plugs.
19. E-mail from Oren Patrick Purcell, 19 September 1997.
20. Personal communication with Oren Patrick Purcell on 21 September 1997, reviewing the fascinating work of Richard Wingate during the late 1970s and early 1980s.
21. See Zink, pp. 16–64, 140–61.
22. Gifford.
23. E-mail communication with Oren Patrick Purcell, 17 September 1997, outlining a whole series of discoveries on the Bahamas Great Bank since the 1960s.
24. Personal communication with Aaron Duval, 17 July 1997.
25. Donnelly, pp. 15–16, cf. Plato.
26. Personal communication with Aaron Duval, August 1997.
27. Donnelly, p.16, cf. Plato.
28. Duval, e-mail to US press agencies, 6 July 1997.
29. Berlitz, p. 99.
30. Ibid.
31. Ibid., p. 96.

32. Personal communication with Oren Patrick Purcell, 19 September 1997.
33. E-mail communication with Oren Patrick Purcell, 17 September 1997.

BIBLIOGRAPHY

Notes: If two dates are shown, the first denotes the first edition of the book or publication; nd. = no date, *circa* given.
Abbreviations: *JEA* = *Journal of Egyptology*, OUP = Oxford University Press, *ZAS* = *Zeitschrift für Agyptische Sprache*, Leipzig

Adams, Barbara, *Predynastic Egypt*, Shire Egyptology, London, 1988

Adams, W. Marsham, *The Book of the Master of the Hidden Places*, Search Publishing, London, 1933

Aldred, Cyril, *Akhenaten – King of Egypt*, 1988, Thames and Hudson, London, 1991

Aldred, Cyril, *Egypt to the End of the Old Kingdom*, 1965, Book Club Associates, London, 1974

Allen, Richard Hinckley, *Star Names – Their Lore and Meaning*, 1899, Dover Publications, New York, 1963

Alpagut, Berna, 'The Human Skeletal Remains from Kurban Höyük, *Anatolica*, No. XIII, 1986, pp. 149–74

Ammianus Marcellinus, trans. John C. Rolfe, Loeb edition, 3 vols., Heinemann, London, 1956

Antoniadi, E.M., *L'Astronomie Egyptienne*, Imprimerie Gauthier-Villars, Paris, 1934

Apion, *Aegpytiaca*, quoted in Josephus, 'Flavius Josephus Against Apion'

Apollodorus, *The Library*, English trans. Sir James G. Frazer, 2 vols., Wm. Heinemann, London, 1921

Apollonius Rhodius, *The Argonautica*, English trans. R.C. Seaton, 1912, Wm. Heinemann, London, 1919

Atkinson, R.J.C., *Stonehenge*, 1956, Penguin, London, 1979

Bacon, Edward, *Archaeology Discoveries in the 1960s*, Cassell, London, 1971

Baines, John, '*Bnbn* – Mythological and Linguistic Notes', *Orientalia*, No. 39/2, 1970, pp. 389–404, Pontificum Institutum Biblicum, Rome

Bannister, A., and H.W. Stephenson, *Solutions of Problems in Surveying and Field Astronomy*, 1955, Sir Isaac Pitman, London, 1974

Bar-Yosef, O., 'The Walls of Jericho: An Alternative Interpretation', *Current Anthropology*, Vol. 27, No. 2, April 1986, pp. 157–62

Barton, Tamsyn, *Ancient Astrology*, Routledge, London, 1994

Bauval, Robert, and Graham Hancock, *Hieroglyph – The Bauval & Hancock Newsletter*, No. 1, January 1997

Bauval, Robert, and Graham Hancock, *Keeper of Genesis*, Wm. Heinemann, London, 1996

Bellamy, H.S., *Built Before the Flood: The Problem of the Tiahuanaco Ruins*, Faber & Faber, London, 1943

Bellamy, H.S., and P. Allan, *The Calendar of Tiahuanaco*, Faber & Faber, London, 1956

Berlitz, Charles, *Atlantis – The Lost Continent Revealed*, Macmillan, London, 1984

Berossus, *Babyloniaka*, in Cory

Besant, Annie, *The Pedigree of Man*, Theosophical Publishing Society, Adyar, Madras, 1908

Bienert, Hans-Dieter, 'Skull Cult in the Prehistoric Near East', *Journal of Prehistoric Religion*, Vol. 5, Paul Åströms Förlag Jonsered, Copenhagen, 1991, pp. 9–23

Bierhorst, John, *The Mythology of Mexico and Central America*, Wm. Morrow & Co., New York, 1990

Bietak, Manfred, *Avaris and Piramesse: Archaeological Exploration in the Eastern Nile Delta*, Proceedings of the British Academy, London, 1981

Black, Jeremy, and Anthony Green, *Gods, Demons and Symbols of Ancient Mesopotamia – An Illustrated Dictionary*, British Muesum Press, London, 1992

Blackman, A.M., and H.W. Fairman, 'The Myth of Horus at Edfu – II', *JEA*, Vol. 28, 1942, pp. 32–8

Blavatsky, Helena Petrova, *The Secret Doctrine*, 1893, 4 vols., Theosophical Publishing House, Madras, 1918

Bloomfield-Moore, Mrs Clara Jessup, 'Etheric Force Identified as Dynaspheric Force', in Pond, *Universal Laws never before Revealed: Keely's Secrets*

Bonwick, James, *Pyramid Facts and Fancies*, C. Kegan Paul & Co., London, 1877

Bord, Janet and Colin, *The Secret Country*, 1976, Paladin, London, 1979

Braidwood, Robert J., ed., *Prehistoric Archaeology Along the Zagros Flanks*, The Oriental Institute of the University of Chicago, 1983

Breasted, James, *Ancient Records of Egypt*, 5 vols., University of Chicago, 1906

Brown Jnr, Robert, *Eridanus, River and Constellation*, Longman, Green, London, 1883

Brown Jnr, Robert, *Researches into the Origin of the Primitive Constellations of the Greeks, Phoenicians and Babylonians*, 2 vols., Williams & Norgate, London, 1899

Bucaille, Dr Maurice, *Moses and Pharaoh: The Hebrews in Egypt*, NTT Mediascope, Tokyo, 1994

Budge, E.A. Wallis, *The Egyptian Heaven and Hell*, 1905, 3 vols. in 1, Martin Hopkinson, London, 1925

Budge, E.A. Wallis, *An Egyptian Hieroglyphic Dictionary*, 1920, 2 vols., Dover Publications, New York, 1978

Budge, E.A. Wallis, *The Gods of the Egyptians*, 1904, 2 vols., Dover Publications, New York, 1969

Butzer, Karl W., *Early Hydraulic Civilisation in Egypt: A Study in Cultural Ecology*, The University of Chicago Press, Chicago and London, 1976

Cameron, D.O., *Symbols of Birth and of Death in the Neolithic Era*, Kenyon-Deane, London, 1981

Cayce, Edgar, *Edgar Cayce on Atlantis*, ed. Hugh Lynn Cayce, 1968, Howard Baker, London, 1969

Cayce, Edgar Evans, *Edgar Cayce Prophecies*, CD-ROM, ARE, Virginia Beach, Va., 1993

Chadwick, Robert, 'The So-called "Orion Mystery" – A Rebuttal to New Age Notions about Ancient Egyptian Astronomy & Funerary Architecture', *KMT: A Modern Journal of Ancient Egypt*, Vol. 7, No. 3, Fall 1996, pp. 74–83

Charles, R.H., *The Book of Enoch or 1 Enoch*, OUP, 1912

Charles-Picard, Gilbert, ed., *Larousse Encyclopaedia of Archaeology*, 1969, Hamlyn, London, 1974

Clayton, Peter A., *Chronicle of the Pharaohs*, Thames and Hudson, London, 1994

Coe, Michael D., *Breaking the Maya Code*, Thames and Hudson, London, 1992

Cole, J.H., *The Determination of the Exact Size and Orientation of the Great Pyramid of Giza*, Government Press, Cairo, 1925

Collins, Andrew, 'Baalbek – Lebanon's Sacred Fortress', *Amateur Astronomy and Earth Sciences*, Vol. 2, No. 2–3, 1997; *Quest for Knowledge*, Vol. 1, No. 3, 1997

Collins, Andrew, *From the Ashes of Angels*, Michael Joseph, London, 1996

Corliss, William, *Ancient Man: A Handbook of Puzzling Artifacts*, 1978, The Sourcebook Project, Glen Arm, Maryland 21057, 1980

Cory, I.C., *Ancient Fragments*, 1832, Wizards Bookshelf, Minneapolis, Minn., 1975

Cottrell, Leonard, *The Land of Shinar*, Souvenir Press, London, 1965

Cox, Simon, and Jacqueline Pegg, *Egyptian Genesis*, unpublished manuscript

Crabb, Charlene, ' "Missing Link" is written in stone', *New Scientist*, 14 December 1996, p. 9

Curtis, Vesta Sarkhosh, *Persian Myths*, British Museum Press, London, 1993

Delair, J.B., and E.F. Oppé, 'The Evidence of Violent Extinction in South America', in Hapgood, *The Path of the Pole*, pp. 280–6

Deuel, Leo, ed., *The Treasures of Time*, Pan, Souvenir Press, London, 1961

Devereux, Paul, and R.G. Jahn, 'Preliminary investigations and cognitive considerations of the acoustical resonances of selected archaeological sites', *Antiquity*, Vol. 70, No. 269, September 1996, pp. 665–6

Donnelly, Ignatius, *Atlantis – The Antediluvian World*, 1882, Harper & Brothers, New York and London, 1902

Drower, E.S., *The Mandaeans of Iraq and Iran*, OUP, 1937

Dunn, Christopher, 'Advanced Machining in Ancient Egypt', privately published, 1983, available @ http://www.lauralee.com/chrisdunn/index.htm

Dunn, Christopher, 'Hi-Tech Pharaohs?', *Amateur Astronomy and Earth Sciences*, December 1995, pp. 38–42; January 1996, pp. 38–40; February 1996, pp. 40–41

Edwards, I.E.S., *Pyramids of Egypt*, Penguin, London, 1993

Emery, Walter B., *Archaic Egypt*, Penguin, Harmondsworth, Middlesex, 1961

Esin, Ufuk, 'Salvage Excavations at the Pre-pottery Site of Ashikli Höyük in Central Anatolia', *Anatolica*, No. XVII, 1991, pp. 123–74

Faulkner, R.O., trans., *The Ancient Egyptian Coffin Texts*, Vol. 3, Spells 788–1185, Aris & Phillips, Warminster, Wiltshire, 1978

Faulkner, R.O., trans., *The Ancient Egyptian Pyramid Texts*, OUP, 1969

Faulkner, R.O., *A Concise Dictionary of Middle Egypt*, Griffith Institute, Oxford, 1962

Fisher, John, *Mexico: Rough Guide*, 1985, The Rough Guides, London, 1995

Fix, William R., *Pyramid Odyssey*, Jonathan-James Books, Toronto, 1978

Freud, Sigmund, *Moses and Monotheism*, Hogarth Press and the Institute of Psychoanalysis, London, 1940

Gardiner, Sir Alan, *Egypt of the Pharaohs*, 1961, OUP, 1964

Geoffrey of Monmouth, *The History of the Kings of Britain*, trans. Lewis Thorpe, 1966, The Folio Society, London, 1969

Gifford, John, 'The Bimini "Cyclopean" Complex', *International Journal of Nautical Archaeology and Underwater Exploration*, Vol. 2, 1973, p. 1

Gilbert, Adrian, *Magi – The Quest for a Secret Tradition*, Bloomsbury, London, 1996

Gilbert, Adrian, and Maurice M. Cotterell, *The Mayan Prophecies*, Element, Shaftesbury, Dorset, 1995

Gimbutas, Marija, *The Civilization of the Goddess*, Harper, San Francisco, 1991

Gleadow, Rupert, *The Origin of the Zodiac*, Jonathan Cape, London, 1968

Gorelick, Leonard, and John Gwinnett, 'Innovative Lapidary Craft Techniques in Neolithic Jarmo', *Archeomaterials 4*, 1990, pp. 25–32

Haigh, T., *Psychic News*, No. 3245, 20 August 1994, pp. 1, 3

Hale, R.B., 'Further Notes on the Dimensions of the Great Pyramid, Giza', privately published, 26 February 1997

Hale, R.B., 'Notes on the Dimensions of the Great Pyramid, Giza', privately published, 16 January 1997

Hall, Dr., 'John Keely – A Personal Interview', *Scientific Arena*, January 1887, in Pond, *Universal Laws never before Revealed: Keely's Secrets*

Hall, Dr., 'A Second Visit to Mr Keely', *Scientific Arena*, nd., *c.* 1888, in Pond, *Universal Laws never before Revealed: Keely's Secrets*

Hall, Manly P., *An Encyclopedic Outline of Masonic, Hermetic, Qabbalistic & Rosicrucian Symbolic Philosophy*, 1901, Philosophical Research Society, Los Angeles, 1977

Hancock, Graham, *Fingerprints of the Gods*, Wm. Heinemann, London, 1995

Hapgood, Professor Charles, *The Path of the Pole*, Chilton, New York, 1970

Hapgood, Professor Charles, *Maps of the Ancient Sea Kings*, 1966, Turnstone Books, London, 1979

Harris, J.R., 'How long was the Reign of Horemheb?', *JEA*, Vol. 54, 1968, pp. 95–9

Hart, George, *A Dictionary of Egyptian Gods and Goddesses*, Routledge & Kegan Paul, London, 1978

Harte, R., 'Disintegration of Stone', in Pond, *Universal Laws never before Revealed: Keely's Secrets*

Hartner, Willy, 'The Earliest History of the Constellations in the Near East and the Motif of the Lion-Bull Combat', *Journal of Near Eastern Studies*, January–April 1965, Vol. XXIV, Nos. 1 and 2, pp. 1–15

Hassan, Fekri, 'Note on Sebilian Sites from Dishna Plain', *Chronique d'Egypte*, No. XLVII, 1972, pp. 11–16

Hassan, Selim, *Excavations at Giza, 1934–5*, Vol. 6, Pt. 1, Service des Antiquités de l'Egypte, Government Press, Cairo, 1946

Hastings, James, ed., *Encyclopaedia of Religion and Ethics*, 13 vols., 1915, T. & T. Clark, Edinburgh, 1930

Hauptmann, Harald, 'Ein Kultgebäude in Nevali Çori,' *Between the Rivers and over the Mountains: Archaeologica Anatolica et Mesopotamica, Alba Palmieri Dedicata*, ed. Marcella Frangipane *et al.*, Rome, 1993, pp. 37–69

Heinberg, Richard, *Memories & Visions of Paradise*, 1989, Aquarian Press, Wellingborough, Northants, 1990

Hemming, John, *The Conquest of the Incas*, Macmillan, London, 1993

Herodotus, *History*, trans. George Rawlinson, 2 vols., (1858), J.M. Dent, London, 1940

Hippolytus, *Philosophumena or the Refutation of All Heresies etc.*, *c.* third century AD. See Legge

Hoffmann, Michael A., *Egypt Before the Pharaohs*, 1980, Ark, London, 1984

Horace, *The Ars Poetica*, ed. Augustus S. Wilkins, Macmillan, London, 1971

Horace, *Odes and Epodes*, English trans. C.E. Bennett, 1914, Wm. Heinemann, London, 1964

Horne, Alex, *King Solomon's Temple in the Masonic Tradition*, 1972, Aquarian Press, Wellingborough, Northants, 1975

Hudson, Henry B., 'Mr Keely's Researches – Sound Shown to be a Substantial Force', *Scientific Arena*, December 1886, in Pond, *Universal Laws never before Revealed: Keely's Secrets*

Hudson, Henry B., 'The Keely Motor Illustrated', *Scientific Arena*, January 1887, in Pond, *Universal Laws never before Revealed: Keely's Secrets*

Hurry, Jamieson B., *Imhotep – The Vizier and Physician of King Zoser etc.*, nd., OUP, 1928

Ivimy, John, *The Sphinx and the Megaliths*, Turnstone, London, 1974

Izady, Mehrdad R., *The Kurds – A Concise Handbook*, Crane Russak, London, 1992

Jelinkova, E.A.E., 'The Shebtiw in the temple of Edfu', *ZAS*, No. 87, 1962, pp. 41–54

Jochmans, Joseph, *Hall of Records: Part One, Revelations of the Great Pyramid and Sphinx, Chapter II, A Glimmer at Giza – The Lost Hall and its Secret Brotherhood*, privately published, 1985

Josephus, Flavius, 'The Antiquities of the Jews', and 'Flavius Josephus Against Apion' in *The Works of Flavius Josephus*, trans. Wm. Whiston, Wm. P. Nimmo, Edinburgh, nd., *c*. 1870

Kamil, Jill, *Coptic Eygpt: History and Guide*, 1987, American University in Cairo Press, Cairo, 1988

Kemp, Barry, *Ancient Egypt – Anatomy of a Civilisation*, Routledge, London, 1989

Kenoyer, J. Mark, and Massimo Vidale, 'A new look at stone drills of the Indus Valley Tradition', *Material Resources Symposium Proceeds*, Vol. 267, 1992, pp. 495–518

Kenyon, Kathleen M., *The Bible and Recent Archaeology*, 1978, British Museum Publications, London, 1987

Keys, David, 'Stonehenge is French imposter', *Independent*, 1 March 1997

King, Leonard William, *Enuma Elish: The Seven Tablets of Creation*, 2 vols., 1902, Library of Bryn Mawr College, New York, 1976

King James Bible, Revision of the Authorised Version, OUP, 1905

Kitchen, Kenneth, *Ramesside Inscriptions*, B.H. Blackwell, Oxford, 1975

Kitchen, Kenneth, *Pharaoh Triumphant*, Aris and Phillips, Warminster, Wiltshire, 1982

Kjellson, Henry, *Forsvunden Teknik*, 1961, Nihil, Copenhagen, 1974

Knauth, Percy, *The Metalsmiths*, 1974, Time-Life Books, Amsterdam, 1976

Kramer, Samuel Noah, 'Dilmun, the Land of the Living', *Bulletin of the*

American Schools of Oriental Research, No. 96, December 1944, pp. 18–28

Kramer, Samuel Noah, *History Begins at Sumer*, 1956, Thames and Hudson, London, 1958

Kramer, Samuel Noah, *Sumerian Mythology*, Philadelphia, 1944

Legge, F., trans. and comm., *Philosophumena or the Refutation of All Heresies*, 2 vols., Society for Promoting Christian Knowledge, London, 1921

Lehner, Mark, *The Egyptian Heritage – Based on the Edgar Cayce Readings*, Edgar Cayce Foundation, Virginia Beach, Va., 1974

Lehner, Mark, 'Giza', *Archiv früh Orientforschung*, No. 32, 1985, pp. 136–58

Lehner, Mark, 'The Pyramid', in *Secrets of Lost Empires*, BBC Books, London, 1996

Lemprière, J., *A Classical Dictionary*, Geo. Routledge, London, 1919

Lenormant, François, *Chaldean Magic: Its Origin and Development*, 1874, Samuel Bagster, London, 1877

Leslie, Desmond, and George Adamski, *Flying Saucers Have Landed*, 1953, Futura, London, 1977

Lichtheim, Miriam, *Ancient Egyptian Literature*, University of California Press, Berkeley and Los Angeles, 1976

Lindsay, Jack, *The Origins of Alchemy in Graeco-Roman Egypt*, Fredk. Muller, London, 1970

Mackenzie, Donald A., *Myths of Pre-Columbian America*, Gresham Publishing Co., London, nd., *c.* 1910

Maçoudi, *Les Prairies d'Or*, ed. C. Barbier de Meynard and Pavet de Courteille, C. Benjamin Duprat, 5 vols., A l'Imprimerie Impériale, Paris, 1863

Massey, Gerald, *A Book of the Beginnings*, 2 vols., Williams & Norgate, London, 1881

Massey, Gerald, *The Natural Genesis*, 2 vols., Williams & Norgate, London, 1883

Mas'ūdi, *Kitāb Murūj al-Dhahab wa Ma'ādin al-Jawhar (Les Prairies d'Or)* [The Meadows of Gold and Mines of Gems], ed. C. Barbier de Meynard and Pavet de Courteille, revised and corrected by Charles Pellat, 5 vols., Publications de l'Université Libanaise, Section des Etudes Historiques, Vol. 2, 1966–74

Mellaart, James, *Çatal Hüyük – A Neolithic Town in Anatolia*, Thames and Hudson, London, 1967

Meyers, Eric M., ed., *Oxford Encyclopaedia of Archaeology in the Near East*, 4 vols., OUP, 1997

Molleson, Theya, and Stuart Campbell, 'Deformed Skulls at Tell Arpachiyah: The Social Context', in S. Campbell and A. Green, eds., *The*

Archaeology of Death in the Ancient Near East, Oxbow Monograph No. 51, 1995, pp. 45–55

Moore, Andrew M.T., 'A Pre-Neolithic Farmers' Village on the Euphrates', *Scientific American*, No. 241, August 1979, pp. 50–8

Morales, V.B., 'Jarmo Figurines and Other Clay Objects', in Braidwood, pp. 369–83

Mundkur, Balaji, *The Cult of the Serpent – an Interdisciplinary Survey of its Manifestations and Origins*, State University of New York Press, Albany, NY, 1983

Murray, Margaret A., *Egyptian Temples*, Sampson Low, Marston, London, nd., *c.* 1930

Namdak, Lopon Tenzin, *Heart Drops of Dharmakaya: Dzogchen Practice of the Bön Tradition*, Snow Lion Publications, Ithaca, NY, 1993

Naville, Edouard, 'Excavations at Abydos', Smithsonian Institution Annual Report, 1914, pp. 579–85, cf. Corliss, p. 325

Naville, Edouard, *The Times*, London, 17 March 1914, cf. Hancock, p. 404

Nicholson, Reynold A., *A Literary History of the Arabs*, Cambridge University Press, 1956

Norbu, Namkhai, *The Crystal and the Way of Light: Sutra, Tantra and Dzogchen*, Routledge & Kegan Paul, London, 1986

Norton, Cherry, 'Raiders of the lost archives "find pharaohs' records" ', *The Sunday Times*, 10 August 1997

Norvill, Roy, *Giants: The Vanished Race of Mighty Men*, Aquarian Press, Wellingborough, Northants, 1979

Osborne, Harold, *Indians of the Andes: Aymaras and Quechuas*, Routledge & Kegan Paul, London, 1952

Osborne, Harold, *South American Mythology*, Paul Hamlyn, London, 1968

Osman, Ahmed, *Moses Pharaoh of Egypt*, Grafton Books, London, 1990

Owen, Walter, *More Things in Heaven*, Andrew Dakers, London, 1947

Page, Cynthia, 'Stonehenge', in *Secrets of Lost Empires*, BBC Books, London, 1996

Partridge, Eric, *Dictionary of the Underworld*, Routledge and Kegan Paul, London, 1950

Pauwels, Louis, and Jacques Bergier, *The Morning of the Magicians*, 1960, Mayflower, Frogmore, St Albans, Herts, 1975

Pausanias, *Description of Greece*, English trans. W.H.S. Jones, 5 vols., Wm. Heinemann, London, 1935

Petrie, W.M. Flinders, *The Pyramids and Temples of Gizeh*, 1883, with update by Zahi Hawass, Histories & Mysteries of Man, London, 1990

Petrie, W.M. Flinders, *Researches in Sinai*, John Murray, London, 1906

Petrie, W.M. Flinders, *Ten Years' Digging in Egypt, 1881–1891*, The Religious Tract Society, London, 1893

Phillips, Ellen, ed., *The Age of the God-Kings 3000–1500 BC*, Time-Life Books, Amsterdam, 1987

Phillips, Graham, *Act of God*, Macmillan, London, 1998

Plum, Mr, 'Mr Plum's Visit to Keely's Laboratory', in *Dashed Against the Rock*, 1893, in Pond, *Universal Laws never before Revealed: Keely's Secrets*

Pond, Dale, *Universal Laws never before Revealed: Keely's Secrets*, 1990, The Message Company, 4 Camino Azul, Santa Fe, NM 87505, 1996

Pond, Dale, 'Keely's Trexar a Superconductive Wire', in Pond, *Universal Laws never before Revealed. Keely's Secrets*

The Popular Biblical Educator, Vol. 1, John Cassell, London, 1854

Posnansky, Prof. Ing. Arthur, *Tihuanacu: The Cradle of American Man*, Vols. 1–2, J. Augustin, New York, 1945; Vols. 3–4, Ministerio de Educación, La Paz, Bolivia, 1957

Propertius, *Elegies*, ed. and English trans. G.P. Goold, Harvard University Press, Cambridge, Mass., 1990

Ragette, Friedrich, *Baalbek*, Chatto & Windus, London, 1980

Randall-Stevens, Hugh C., *A Voice Out of Egypt*, Francis Mott, London, 1935

Redford, Donald B., *Akhenaten the Heretic King*, 1984, Princeton University Press, Princeton, NJ, 1987

Redford, Donald B., *Pharaonic King-Lists, Annals and Day-books: A Contribution to the Study of the Egyptian Sense of History*, Benben Publications, Mississauga, Ontario, 1986

Reymond, E.A.E., *The Mythical Origin of the Egyptian Temple*, Manchester University Press, 1969

Rohl, David, *Legend*, Century, London, 1998

Roux, Georges, *Ancient Iraq*, 1966, Penguin Books, London, 1980

Rundle Clark, R.T., *Myths and Symbols in Ancient Egypt*, 1958, Thames and Hudson, London, 1978

Rutherford, Adam, *Pyramidology*, 3 vols., The Institute of Pyramidology, Dunstable, Beds., Vol. 1, first ed. 1957, second ed. 1961; Vol. 2, 1962; Vol. 3, 1966

Saleh, Abdel-Aziz, *Excavations at Heliopolis*, Vol. 1, Faculty of Archaeology, Cairo University, 1981

Santillana, Giorgio, and Hertha von Dechend, *Hamlet's Mill*, 1969, Macmillan, London, 1970

Schoch, Robert M., 'Redating the Great Sphinx of Giza', *KMT*, 3:2, Summer 1992, pp. 52–9, 66–70

Schwaller de Lubicz, R.A., *Sacred Science*, Inner Traditions Inc., Rochester, Vt., 1961

Scrutton, Robert, *Secrets of Lost Atland*, 1978, Sphere, London, 1979

Sellers, Jane B., *The Death of Gods in Ancient Egypt*, Penguin Books, London, 1992

Sethe, Kurt, 'Amun und die Acht Urgötter von Hermopolis', 1930, *Leipziger und Berliner Akademieschriften (1902–1934)*, Zentralantiquariat, Leipzig, 1976

Sinnett, A.P., *The Pyramids and Stonehenge*, 1893, Theosophical Publishing House, London, 1958

Sitchin, Zecharia, *The Stairway to Heaven*, 1980, Avon Books, New York, 1983

Smith, Warren, *The Secret Forces of the Pyramids*, Sphere, London, 1977

Smyth, C. Piazzi, *Our Inheritance in the Great Pyramid*, 1864, Charles Burnet, London, 1890

Solecki, Rose L., 'Predatory Bird Rituals at Zawi Chemi Shanidar', *Sumer*, No. XXXIII, Pt. 1, 1977, pp. 42–7

Spence, Lewis, *Myths of Mexico and Peru*, 1913, Harrap, London, 1920

Statius, *Thebaid*, English trans. J.H. Mozley, 2 vols., 1928, Wm. Heinemann, London, 1982

Stecchini, Livio Catullo, 'Notes on the Relation of Ancient Measures to the Great Pyramid', in Tompkins, pp. 287–382

Stocks, D.A., 'Making Stone Vessels in Ancient Mesopotamia and Egypt', *Antiquity*, Vol. 67, No. 256, September 1993, pp. 596–603

Thompson, J. Eric, *The Rise and Fall of Maya Civilisation*, 1954, Pimlico, London, 1993

Thompson, J. Eric S., *Maya History and Religion*, University of Oklahoma, Norman, Okla. 1970

Time-Life Books, *Anatolia: Cauldron of Cultures*, Richmond, Va., 1995

Time-Life Books, *Feats and Wisdom of the Ancients*, Alexandria, Va., 1990

The Times, Past Worlds: Atlas of Archaeology, 1989, BCA, London, 1993

Tomas, Andrew, *We Are Not the First*, 1971, Sphere, London, 1972

Tompkins, Peter, *Secrets of the Great Pyramid*, Allen Lane, London, 1971

Van Kirk, Wayne, 'Mayan Ruins and Unexplained Acoustics,' 1996, available from the web-page of the World Forum for Acoustic Ecology at e-mail: LQYM67A@Prodigy.Com

Vyse, Colonel R.W. Howard, *Operations Carried on at the Pyramids of Gizeh in 1837*, 3 vols., James Fraser, London, 1840

Wainwright, G.A., 'Amun's Meteorite & Omphali,' *ZAS*, 1935, pp. 41–4

Walker, R.A., 'The Real Land of Eden', *Newsletter of the Ancient and Medieval History Book Club*, No. 11, nd., *c.* 1986

Ward, William A., 'Ancient Lebanon', in *Cultural Resources in Lebanon*, Beirut College for Women, 1969

Warren, William F., *Paradise Found – The Cradle of the Human Race at the North Pole*, Sampson Low, Marston, Searle & Rivington, London, 1885

Watterson, Barbara, *Coptic Egypt*, Scottish Academic Press, Edinburgh, 1988

Weigall, Arthur, *A History of the Pharaohs*, Vol. 2, Thornton Butterworth, London, 1927

Wendorf, Fred, and Romauld Schild, *Prehistory of the Nile Valley*, Academic Press, New York, 1976

Wendorf, Fred, and Romauld Schild, 'The Paleolithic of the Lower Nile Valley', in *Problems in Prehistory: North Africa and the Levant*, ed. Wendorf and Marks, SMU Press, Dallas, Texas, 1975, pp. 127–69

West, John A., 'John West has his say on the Sphinx-age Controversy', *KMT*, 7:1, Spring 1996, pp. 3–6

West, John Anthony, *Serpent in the Sky – The High Wisdom of Ancient Egypt*, Wildwood House, London, 1979

West, John Anthony, *The Traveller's Key to Ancient Egypt*, Harrap Columbus, London, 1987

Wigram, the Rev. W.A., and Edgar T.A. Wigram, *The Cradle of Mankind – Life in Eastern Kurdistan*, Adam and Charles Black, London, 1914

Wilhelm, Gernot, *The Hurrians*, Aris and Phillips, Warminster, Wiltshire, 1989

Wilson, Colin, *From Atlantis to the Sphinx*, Virgin, London, 1996

Wilson, Ian, *The Exodus Enigma*, 1985, Guild Publishing, London, 1986

Wishaw, E.M., *Atlantis in Andalucia: A Study of Folk Memory*, Rider, London, 1930

Wright, William, *The Illustrated Bible Treasury*, Thomas Nelson, London, 1897

Zimmer, Heinrich, *Myths and Symbols in Indian Art and Civilisation*, 1946, Princeton-Bollingen, Princeton, NJ, 1972

Zink, Dr David, *The Stones of Atlantis*, Prentice-Hall, Ontario, 1978

Documentaries

'Mysteries of the Sphinx', NBC American edit, 1994

'Myths of Mankind', narrated by Colin Wilson and first broadcast across Europe by Discovery Channel, August 1997

INDEX

Note: Page numbers in **bold** refer to illustrations